The Non-Jewish Origins of the Sephardic Jews

SUNY Series in Anthropology and Judaic Studies
Walter P. Zenner, editor

The Non-Jewish Origins of the Sephardic Jews

Paul Wexler

State University of New York Press

Published by
State University of New York Press, Albany

Printed in the United States of America

For information, address State University of New York Press,
State University Plaza, Albany, NY 12246

Production by Cynthia Tenace Lassonde
Marketing by Bernadette LaManna

Library of Congress Cataloging-in-Publication Data

Wexler, Paul.
The non-Jewish origins of the Sephardic Jews / Paul Wexler.
p. cm. — (SUNY series in anthropology and Judaic studies)
Includes bibliographical references and index.
ISBN 0-7914-2795-1 (alk. paper). — ISBN 0-7914-2796-X (pbk. : alk. paper)
1. Sephardim—Origin. 2. Jews—Spain—Origin. 3. Jews—Africa, North—Origin. 4. Spain—Ethnic relations. 5. Ladino language—Foreign elements—Arabic. 6. Berbers—Social life and customs. 7. Africa, North—Social life and customs. 8. Proselytes and proselyting, Jewish—History. I. Title. II. Series.
DS134.W48 1996
946'.004924—dc20 95-22275
CIP

10 9 8 7 6 5 4 3 2 1

To the memory of Robert Austerlitz (1923–1994)
teacher, friend, and rare cosmopolitan.

Contents

Abbreviations and Citations

The following abbreviated language names are used with examples:

Afr—African
Alcaz—Alcazarquivir
Alg—Algerian, Algiers (before Judeo-Arabic)
And—Andalusian
Ar—Arabic
Arag—Aragonese
Aram—Aramaic
Bal—Balkan
Ber—Berber
Bg—Bulgarian
Bib—Biblical
Bit—Bitolj
Bos—Bosnian
Cat—Catalan
Cl—Classical
Cr—Crimean
E—Eastern
Eg—Egyptian
Eng—English
G—German
Gk—Greek
Go—Gothic
He—Hebrew
Ib—Iberian
Ir—Iraqi
Ist—Istanbul
It—Italian
J—Judeo-
Kar—Karaite
Lad—Ladino
Lar—Larache
Lat—Latin
M—Muslim
Mac—Macedonian
Malt—Maltese
Mod—Modern
Mor—Moroccan
Moz—Mozarabic
N—North(ern)
O—Old
Per—Persian
Pr—Provençal
Pt—Portuguese
Pun—Punic
R—Russian
Rom—Romance
Rum—Rumanian
S—Southern
Sal—Saloniki
Sar—Sarajevo
Sard—Sardinian
Ser—Serbian
Sl—Slavic
Sor—Upper Sorbian
Sp—Spanish
St—Standard
Tet—Tetuan
Tu—Turkish
Tun—Tunisian
Val—Valencian
W—Western
Y—Yiddish
Yem—Yemenite

A Note on Citations and Linguistic Terminology

I have relied on the *DCECH* for the earliest attestation of Ibero-Romance examples. Iberian Jewish names are cited in either their Hebrew or Arabic form. Hebrew examples are given in transliteration with vowels added; Hebrew bibliographical references are cited in modern Israeli pronunciation. Judeo-Spanish examples are cited in a broad phonetic transcription, including examples taken from the dictionaries of Benoliel 1926–52 and Nehama 1977, which use a Castilianized orthography. I use *j* to denote the voiced alveopalatal affricate (~ the *j* of English *jar*), δ for the voiced interdental fricative (~ the *th* of English *that*), and θ for the voiceless interdental fricative (~ the *th* of English *thing*). Long vowels are not indicated in Arabic and Hebrew names, but are given in Arabic examples, titles, and toponyms. North African Judeo-Arabic examples are cited in the source transcriptions.

I refer to the Hebrew and Judeo-Aramaic literature composed by native speakers of Judeo-Arabic and Judeo-Spanish as "Hebrew/Judeo-Aramaic." The quotation marks are intended to emphasize that the so-called "Hebrew" and "Judeo-Aramaic" texts, composed by non-native speakers of these languages, by definition utilize the grammar of the scribe's spoken language and, hence, are written in that language, and not in Old Semitic Hebrew or Judeo-Aramaic; only the lexicon of these texts is derived from Semitic Hebrew and Judeo-Aramaic. Thus, the "Ashkenazic Hebrew" written by Yiddish-speaking Jews is Yiddish with a Semitic Old Hebrew vocabulary, and the "Hebrew" written by Sephardic Jews is, in fact, Judeo-Arabic or Judeo-Spanish with a genuine Old Hebrew vocabulary. By the same token, "Modern Hebrew" is also not genetically a Semitic language, by virtue of the fact that it is descended from a non-spoken form of "Ashkenazic Hebrew," which acquired new spoken functions in the late 19th century. For further discussion, see chapter 4 of the present volume, as well as Wexler 1990b, 1991, 1993c, and Horvath and Wexler 1994. Similarly, "Medieval Latin" is not genetically related to native spoken or written Latin, but rather utilizes the grammar of the scribe (English, German, Polish, Swedish, etc.), with only its vocabulary taken from native Latin.

The Judeo-Spanish lexicon that was used in the creation of literal renditions of the Hebrew Bible is traditionally called Ladino; because Biblical Hebrew syntax was preserved in these texts, I regard Ladino "translations" of the Bible as genetically Hebrew, with a uniquely Castilian vocabulary. While no scholars distinguish between Ladino texts composed by Judeo-Spanish and Judeo-Portuguese speakers (Lazar 1972 exemplifies the reigning imprecision), I believe that a terminological distinction is obligatory, since the lexicons of the two unspoken Ladino recensions are not always identical; I will call Ladino written by Judeo-Spanish speakers "Ladino" (see the Istanbul Pentateuch of 1547 in

Hebrew characters), and the Ladino written by Judeo-Portuguese speakers "Portuguese Ladino" (see the Ferrara Bible of 1553 in Latin characters). For further discussion, see Wexler 1987a.

Preface

Many people think that the sailing of Columbus to the Americas, and the expulsion of the Jews from the Kingdom of Spain in late 1492, inaugurated the "colonial" history of Castilian: while Columbus is said to have brought Castilian to the New World, the expulsion of the Jews brought the language to North Africa and the eastern Mediterranean.

The events of 1492 indeed made possible the birth of non-Iberian varieties of Castilian, but did not inaugurate the colonial period of the language. The colonial period of Castilian actually began in the Iberian Peninsula in the 11th century when Castilian spread to new areas that were formerly home to Berber, Arabic, and non-Castilian Ibero-Romance speech. The history of the Jews in Spain encapsulates the very spread of Castilian in the peninsula at the expense of other languages, and thus can shed considerable light on how non-Castilian speakers must have acquired the new state language.

The present book attempts to break fresh ground in a number of areas:

(a) Linguistic, ethnographic and, to a lesser extent, historical data are at the basis of my innovative claim that Sephardic Jews are primarily descended from Arabs, Berbers, and Europeans who converted to Judaism between the creation of the first Jewish diaspora communities in western Asia, North Africa, and southern Europe, and approximately the 12th century; the Palestinian Jewish component in the early Sephardic ethnic component makeup was minimal.

The premise that linguistic data can be drawn upon as a source for historical reconstruction is not widely appreciated, in particular among historians. Yet, language data tend to be more reliable than the fragmentary documentation that historians usually have to work with. It is generally accepted that language can provide clues to past history (in particular, migrational history) and culture, but I am also assuming that language, taken together with ethnographic data, may also offer invaluable clues to ethnic origins. This premise is less generally accepted than the first one, except when racial evidence can corroborate assumptions based on linguistic or ethnographic data (the presence of African vocabulary in American English might establish an African origin for the black speakers, but not necessarily for whites). In the case of the Sephardic Jews, the volume of Berber and Arab customs is so great, and the absence of a Hebrew terminology for many of the practices is so striking, that it is hard to believe that the Sephardic Jews were heirs to Old Palestinian Jews and Jewish culture. The evidence of widespread conversion to Judaism up to about 1200, and the gradual "Judaization" of Sephardic customs that took place after this date, see point (d), reinforce my assumption of a non-Jewish origin of the Sephardic Jews.

To be sure, the use of language to identify ethnic and cultural roots is always problematic, since we need to establish historical contacts between communities that are not always recoverable. Also, the ease with which a community can substitute a new foreign language for its own, adds to the complications of reconstruction. For example, the French, in large part of Celtic stock, speak a Romance language derived from Latin, yet they call their national group and language by a Germanic tribal name; the Byzantine Greeks called themselves "Romans," due to Roman conquests (see also Ar *rūm* in this meaning), but they remained loyal to their native language. The Baltic Prussians no longer exist as an ethnic group, but their name lives on as an administrative unit in the German-speaking lands (Treimer 1922:21).

(b) A motley population of converts and descendants of ethnic Palestinian Jews first created Sephardic culture in North Africa in the late 7th century, prior to the invasion of Spain. This community brought Berber, Arabic, and possibly North African Romance and an essentially non-Jewish Arabized North African culture to the Iberian Peninsula.

(c) Despite the use today of a form of Spanish that still remains largely intelligible to Spanish Christians, and the retention of elements of Iberian Christian folklore, I believe that the Sephardic Jews became speakers of Spanish, and relatively superficial bearers of Ibero-Romance Christian culture, as a result of a shift from Judeo-Arabic, and possibly Judeo-Berber, that began in the 11th century and terminated in the early 1400s. Specifically, I suspect that for several generations after the "shift" from Judeo-Arabic, many Arab Jews in the peninsula first acquired only a Spanish lexicon, while retaining their native Arabic grammar and phonology, i.e., they spoke a "relexified"

Arabic (a language with an Arabic grammar and sound system and a predominantly Ibero-Romance vocabulary). By 1492, most Iberian Jews were native speakers of some form of Romance. In contrast to language, the original Berbero-Arab cultural and religious patrimony of the Sephardic Jews has remained surprisingly resistant to change or replacement up to our very days.

(d) By the end of the first millennium, or the beginning of the second millennium, Old Palestinian literature such as the Bible and the Talmud became available in North Africa and Spain for the first time. In the second millennium, acts of conversion to Judaism tapered off due to the institutionalization of Islam and Christianity. In response to growing social segregation and discrimination, the Iberian Jews began a process of Judaization that reflected itself mainly in the search for biblical and talmudic precedents for non-Jewish customs that could not be readily extirpated, and in the retention of non-Jewish customs that had by then become obsolete among non-Jews.

(e) Finally, again in the domain of language, I submit that Ladino and the *Šarḥ*, regarded traditionally as the unwritten Judaized "Ibero-Romance" and "Arabic calque translations" of the Hebrew Bible, are in reality instances of a Hebrew grammar and derivational system with an Ibero-Romance and Arabic lexicon, respectively; as such, Ladino and the *Šarḥ* should be defined as bizarre forms of Biblical Hebrew—relexified to Castilian and Arabic, respectively. Conversely, the original Hebrew and Judeo-Aramaic texts written by Medieval Iberian Jews are best defined as bizarre variants of the native Judeo-Arabic and Spanish of the scribes, and not as "continuations" of Old Palestinian Hebrew and Judeo-Aramaic, since these texts utilized the grammars of the native languages of the scribes.

I have made every attempt to substantiate these theses with a heterogeneous body of evidence, both new and old, but it is inevitable that the new research agenda in Jewish history and linguistics that I am calling for necessitates leaving many topics for deeper study in the future; some suggestions are difficult to substantiate satisfactorily at present. I hope that ethnographers and historians will join with linguists to fill in the remaining lacunae, as well as to suggest ways of repairing infelicitous ideas and formulations that appear in the present study.

The chief evidence for my innovative thesis is linguistic. However, I would like to make the present book accessible to a broad audience that includes historians, social scientists, and the educated reading public, as well as linguists; hence, the linguistic data, that to non-specialists may often appear dry or unintelligible, will be set off from the text by smaller typeface. In that way the reader disinterested in the linguistic details can more easily keep track of the main argumentation.

It is my pleasant duty to thank Iacob Hassán for providing the opportunity to work in the Sephardic library of the Consejo Superior de Investigaciones Científicas in Madrid in early 1986, the two anonymous reviewers for offering constructive suggestions and corrections, Mary Jack and Ana María López Álvarez for supplying xeroxed materials from America and Spain, which were unavailable to me in Israel at the time of writing, and finally Walter P. Zenner for accepting this work in his monograph series.

Paul Wexler
Tel-Aviv
Summer 1994

1

Approaches to the Study of Jewish Ethnicity and Ethnic Myths

Ethnicity and nationalism have always played a central role in the shaping of society. A people's conception of itself and its relationship to coterritorial, contiguous, and geographically distant peoples influences the interpretation and transmission of ethnic myths, as well as the shape of society and its aspirations for the future. Recently, the phenomenon of ethnic and national self-definition has been enjoying mounting attention among scholars and laymen alike. Within an ethnic group, as well as among outside observers, the topic often generates impassioned debates. The internecine fighting and "ethnic cleansing" that have followed in the wake of the recent dismantlement and reshaping of the former Yugoslavia and Soviet Union are two extreme cases in point. Even in the absence of violence, few Greeks are likely to react with equanimity to the proposition that their ancestors might have been in the main descended from non-Hellenic ethnic stock, say Slavs, Illyrians, and Turks. The recent objections of the Greek government to the use of the name "Macedonia," the name of a Greek province, by a neighboring sovereign Slavic state (there was no problem as long as the territory was a part of the Yugoslav federation), is yet another example of the volatility that attends discussions of ethnicity.

Beliefs in historical origins often necessitate largescale rewriting of historical facts (Lowenthal 1985). This means that the student of ethnic and historical origins has to reconstruct two related, but independent, phenomena: the historical facts surrounding the ethnic origins of the group, and the factors determining how the group chooses to fashion its myths of origin. Exploring ethnic origins is a fascinating exercise in historical and linguistic reconstruction and in group identification, and requires the combined efforts of a number of disciplines. The present study will attempt to shed light on both questions—the ethnic origins of the Sephardic Jews, as well as the origins of their myths of origin and self-definition. Finally, this study will indirectly cast light on the question of how and when the notion of a single "Jewish people" may have been contrived. The origins of the "Jews"—taken either in their totality or in individual groups—is a particularly intriguing conundrum due to the centuries-long "dispersal" of the Jews across Africa, Asia, and Europe, and their heterogeneous racial and cultural makeup. The role of Judaism in the creation and dissemination of Christianity and Islam has always assured a considerable interest in the history of the Jews, and has lead many observers to accept post-Christian and post-Islamic Judaism and Jewish culture as direct continuations of Old Palestinian Judaism and Jewish culture.

In this volume, I will argue that early diaspora Judaism and Jewish culture, from their formation up to approximately the 10th century of our era, were syncretistic constructs of pagan, Christian, and Muslim elements and some Palestinian Jewish elements in varying degrees of authenticity. Following the 12th century, widespread conversion to Judaism ceased and Judaism and Jewish culture in a number of Christian and Arab lands underwent a process of "Judaization" (usually accompanied by some degree of Hebraization of the vernacular languages and religious terminology); this enhanced the links of diaspora Jewish cultures and religion to their alleged Old Palestinian forebears. Hence, all contemporary forms of Judaism and Jewish culture are relatively recently "Judaized" non-Jewish constructs rather than direct evolutions of Old Palestinian Judaism and Jewish culture.

According to the *opinio communalis*, Jewish diaspora groups developed when Palestinian Jews began to emigrate in large numbers to Egypt and Asia Minor, and in smaller numbers to southern Europe as early as the 3rd century B.C.; after the Romans destroyed the Second Temple in Jerusalem in 70 A.D., Palestinian Jews emigrated to southern Europe in ever growing numbers. I do not see how Palestinian Jews could have provided the nucleus of the newly forming European Jewish communities, since most of the Jews abroad, as well as in Palestine, early espoused non-Jewish cultures or the form of Judaism known as Christianity, which was ultimately to distance itself sharply from those few Jewish groups that retained some sort of Jewish identity. Linguistically, most of the diaspora Jews appear to have switched to Greek as their native or dominant language, continuing a development that had already been in progress in Palestine itself for several centuries.

Hence, in my view, the Jewish diaspora communities must have comprised from the outset a majority non-Palestinian, non-Jewish population that became attached to the Jewish communities (either informally or through an official act of conversion), and a minority Palestinian Jewish component. This is the main reason why both Palestinian Jewish languages—Hebrew and Judeo-Aramaic—were abandoned abroad in such a short period of time. The loss of distinctiveness of the Jews in Europe was accelerated when Jewish cultural and religious patterns were adopted by large numbers of non-Jews and migration of Jews from Palestine tapered off. Despite the radical change in definition that I have proposed, I will continue to use the ethnonym "Jew" in the following discussions, in order to avoid terminological complications. The reader should note that in reference to Palestine, up to about the 3rd century A.D., I will use the term "Jew" as the designation of a Semitic people in Palestine speaking one or more Semitic languages, Hebrew and Judeo-Aramaic, or Judeo-Greek; in the diasporas that first developed in the early Christian era in North Africa and Europe, I use the term "Jew" to denote rather a member of a religious community, whose ethnic origins were more often than not non-Palestinian, and whose native language was usually a Judaized version of a coterritorial non-Jewish language—but never Hebrew or Judeo-Aramaic.

Not all the claims of Jewish groups to be descended from the Old Palestinian Jews have been readily accepted. This is because many scholars who have sought to identify historical venues of conversion to Judaism on the basis of racial criteria have operated with two assumptions: that it is possible in principle to distinguish between "more" and "less" genuine Jewish roots among the contemporary Jews, and since the majority of the contemporary Jews are members of the Caucasian race, "genuine" Jews should look like Europeans. By this reasoning, small non-European Jewish communities in India, Ethiopia, and China would be classified as the descendants of converts to Judaism.

There are three further reasons for stigmatizing non-European Jews as descendants of converts. They are usually relatively small in number; they have lived for centuries in isolation from other Jewish groups, and as a result do not share all innovations that characterize many less isolated and larger Jewish communities; and when they have had contact with larger Jewish groups, such as the Ashkenazim and Sephardim, they tend to be dependent on the latter for religious instruction and literature. This creates the impression that their knowledge of Judaism and Jewish practices was historically superficial or derivative.

Among the non-European Jews, only some of the Arab Jews (Yemenites and Iraqis) have ever been granted an authentic Jewish pedigree by some observers—on the assumption that the contemporary communities were the uninterrupted descendants of the Jews attested in those areas over two thousand years ago. Gerson-Kiwi (1981:157) and Johnson (1987:182) are impressed with the "Palestinian pedigree" of the Yemenite Jews, but the 19th-century German sociologist, Andree, characterized non-European Jews, such as the western Libyan Jews (from Ġaryān), Kurdish Jews, Indian Jews (from Cochin), and Chinese Jews, as all of non-Jewish origin since they were similar in racial and cultural traits to the coterritorial non-Jews (1881:205, 219, 242, 245, 247). Curiously, the latter condition does not seem to have disqualified the European Jews for Andree! The Yemenites themselves were dubious about the Jewish roots of the European Jews with whom they came in contact in the late 19th and early 20th century. (For further discussion, see Landberg 1906: 273, cited by Godbey 1930:186 and fn 20, and the discussion by Goitein 1931, and Ben-Zvi 1961 in chapter 3 this volume.) The contemporary Iranian-speaking Jews in Iran, northern Iraq, southeast Turkey, Afghanistan, Daghestan (the Caucasus), and Uzbekistan, though first attested in the Iranian cultural and linguistic area from the first millennium B.C., have never been named as certain descendants of the Old Palestinian Jews (perhaps because they are speakers of non-Semitic languages). For a discussion of the origins of the Iranian Jewish communities, see Weissenberg 1911, 1913a, 1913b, and Efron 1994:116–17; the latter provides a detailed analysis of the late 19th- and early 20th-century views of Jews on the possible existence of a Palestinian Jewish prototype among contemporary diaspora Jews.

Obviously, the sheer numbers of Jews with a "European" countenance cannot render the Ashkenazim and Sephardim the obvious heirs to the "Jewish people." The predominantly Palestinian Jewish ethnic origins of the two major constituent members of the Jewish people have to be demonstrated with more rigorous arguments than statistics.

The student who seeks to uncover the ethnic origins of the Jews (or of any people for that matter) faces three complications:

(a) The content of a native ethnonym may have shifted through time and space; for example, *Ashkenazic* originally designated an

Iranian non-Jewish people, then the Slavs, and finally the Germans along with the coterritorial Germano-West Slavic Jews; for the last several centuries, only the descendants of the latter, most of whom had migrated since the 13th century to monolingual Slavic-speaking lands, are designated Ashkenazim. Such extreme denotational shifts through time and space are not at all unusual. The name *Rus'* originally designated a Slavic state in what is now the southeastern Ukraine, whereas subsequently the name became attached to the ancestors of the Russians, thus precipitating a change in the naming of the Ukrainians. For example, R *malorossy*, literally "little Russians," or R *ukraincy*, Ukrainian *ukrajinci*, literally, "the people living in the border lands (of southern Russia)." In addition, the Ukrainians have a number of regional ethnic names, especially in the western-most reaches of their historical territory, but no widely accepted native all-inclusive ethnic name.

(b) Ethnic groups often believe they are descended from another contemporary or extinct group, for example, many Berbers believe they are descended from the Philistines (see chapter 2); coterritorial Arabs and Jews often share this belief. Sometimes natives and non-natives espouse different views of descent, for example, until recently many Russians believed that the Belorussian language broke off from "Old Russian" stock due to the differential impact of foreign (Lithuanian and Polish) influences on the former. For further discussion, see Wexler 1977a, chapter 3 regarding the impact of these views on the development of Slavic historical linguistics. The idea that Belorussian resulted from a relatively recent splitting off from an "Old Russian" trunk was rejected by most Belorussians who were in a position to express their views free of Czarist or Soviet censorship; a balanced analysis would ascribe roughly equal antiquity to the formation of each of the present three Eastern Slavic languages—Belorussian, Russian, and Ukrainian.

(c) As a result of mass migrations, the homeland of a people may shift, for example, the Albanians are now located in the southwestern corner of the Balkan Peninsula, but linguistic facts show that they were once neighbors of the Rumanians in the east. A cursory comparison of the ethnic map of the European continent now and 1,500 years ago would show the extent of such migrations. If the contemporary Jews were indeed descended from the Old Palestinian Jews, then they would constitute the most dramatic case of homeland abandonment, since the overwhelming majority of the Jews became dispersed across Africa, Asia, and Europe, while, until recently, only tiny remnants were historically resident at any one time in the alleged ancestral homeland, Palestine.

For several years I have been examining a variety of linguistic and non-linguistic data with the hope of finding a plausible origin for the Ashkenazic, or north European, historically Yiddish-speaking, Jews. In a recent book entitled *The Ashkenazic Jews: a Slavo-Turkic people in search of a Jewish identity* (1993), I concluded that it is unlikely that the Ashkenazic Jews, who constitute the overwhelming majority of the Jews in the world today, could be descended in significant numbers from Eastern Mediterranean Palestinian Jewish ethnic stock. All the indices—genetic, ethnographic, religious, and linguistic—reveal little evidence of an uninterrupted link between the contemporary Jews and the Old Palestinian Jews. At best, I can reveal attempts by a scattered so-called "Jewish" population in parts of Europe, Asia, and Africa less than a millennium ago to *establish* a Jewish identity by imitating genuine Old Palestinian Jewish practices (as recorded in the Bible and talmudic literature), and by borrowing heavily upon Biblical Hebrew terminology to denote their religious practices (of Jewish and non-Jewish origins both). Indeed, the linguistic and ethnographic data of the Ashkenazic Jews lead me inexorably to the conclusion that the Ashkenazic Jews very likely descended from a population mix whose primary components were Slavo-Turkic proselytes, and a considerably intermarried Palestinian Jewish minority.

I maintain that ethnic Palestinian Jews in Hellenized Asia Minor, and to a lesser extent in Italy, practicing various forms of Judaism, succeeded in attracting to their communities sizeable numbers of non-Jews, both pagans and Christians. In the early Christian period, when largescale immigration of Jews out of Palestine had virtually ceased, all the Jewish communities that took root in Europe, North Africa, and Asia Minor consisted of a majority proselyte population and a minority of Palestinian ethnic Jews. Greek (in a slightly Judaized form) was probably the native language of most European diaspora Jews in an enormous territory spanning Asia Minor and the Black Sea region in the east, and North Africa and Spain in the west (Wexler 1985).

The crystalization of the Ashkenazic Jews, resulting from a mix of mainly Slavic and Turkic proselytes to Judaism and Palestinian Jewish ethnic stock, took place in three major venues. These are, in chronological order: the Balkans, where Slavs, Turkic Avars, and Jews of various geographical and ethnic origins could have met for the first time in the 6th century; Kievan Rus' and the neighboring Ponto-Caspian steppes—the modern Ukraine, where the Turkic ruling class of the Khazar empire converted to Judaism in the 8th century, an act which also probably resulted in the conversion to Judaism of some Eastern Slavs and Iranians who were subject to Khazar domination as well; and the mixed Germano-Slavic lands—present-day eastern Germany which, I suspect, provided numerous Sorbian and some German proselytes to Judaism, approximately between the 9th and 12th centuries. Elements of Balkan and Germano-Slavic folklore and religious practices are still very prominent among the Ashkenazim (Wexler 1991, 1992, and 1993c).

In my book on the ethnic origins of the Ashkenazic Jews, I also presented the fruits of recent linguistic research that prompted me to formulate two new hypotheses regarding the origins of the languages spoken and written traditionally by the Ashkenazic Jews:

(a) In my view, the traditional language of the Ashkenazic Jews, Yiddish, developed when Jewish speakers of Sorbian, a Western Slavic language (spoken today by a dwindling group of at most 70,000 Sorbs in Germany who are almost all bilingual in German), relexified their language, i.e., made a partial language shift, to High German vocabulary, between the 9th and 12th centuries. Since the original Sorbian syntactic and phonological systems were retained, and only the Slavic lexicon was replaced by German, Yiddish must be classified as a member of the Slavic family of languages. It is the preponderance of German lexicon in Yiddish that has created the nearly universally accepted illusion that Yiddish is a form of High German. The Ashkenazic Jews also carried out relexification of their unspoken language of literature and liturgy, when they replaced the lexicon of Old Hebrew texts by German vocabulary to produce a "Yiddish" calque language, which was actually Hebrew grammar and derivational strategies combined with German vocabulary.

(b) It is clear that Modern Israeli Hebrew cannot be a "revived" form of Old Semitic Hebrew, because "linguistic revival" is totally impossible. In fact, Modern Hebrew utilizes the syntactic and phonological systems of Yiddish (the native language of the first Hebrew language planners), with only the vocabulary being of Semitic (mainly

Biblical) Hebrew stock. Hence, Modern Hebrew, like its genetic parent Yiddish, must also be defined as a Western Slavic language. The Old Semitic Hebrew morphological processes that Modern Hebrew exhibits were received through the medium of the borrowed Hebrew vocabulary and cannot constitute an argument against my claim (Horvath and Wexler 1994). For the last century or so, Modern Hebrew has been cultivating additional cognate Polish and Eastern Slavic patterns of discourse and derivation; hence, Modern Hebrew is unique among the Slavic languages in manifesting such a diversified Slavic impact (Wexler 1990b and 1995).

The Slavo-Turkic proselytic origins that I postulated for the Ashkenazic Jews and the relexification processes that produced spoken and written Yiddish and the unspoken "Yiddish" translation language of Biblical Hebrew are relevant for four reasons to understanding the ethnic makeup of the non-Ashkenazic Jewish groups and their linguistic profile:

(a) Like the Ashkenazic Jews, the Sephardic Jews also descend from a proselyte majority and an Old Palestinian Jewish minority. There is no basis to the claim that the Sephardic Jews are "more Semitic" in racial type than the Ashkenazic Jews (Weissenberg 1909: 235, Efron 1994:114–17).

(b) Almost everywhere in the world, the Slavo-Turkic Ashkenazim, as the overwhelming majority group among the Jews, have been exercising a strong influence on other Jewish groups. As I will show, Sephardic culture first became exposed to Ashkenazic influences in the early 14th century *in Spain* (by which time the Jews in the Germano-Slavic lands had fully relexified their Western Slavic language, Sorbian, to High German vocabulary); the expulsion of the Jews from Spain in 1492 catapulted the Sephardic Jews into even more extensive contact with Ashkenazic (and other) Jews in the Ottoman Empire, North Africa, and elsewhere. Thus, the rapid on-going Ashkenazicizing of the non-Ashkenazic Jews in Israel has roots reaching back some seven centuries.

(c) Significant numbers of Slavs, mainly, but not exclusively from the Germano-Slavic lands, were sold into slavery in the Iberian Peninsula and North Africa between the 10th and 15th centuries; as I will discuss in chapter 2, this population could have included Slavs who were already Jews or Judaizers in their previous homelands or who became such in the employ of Jewish owners in their new homelands.

(d) The Sephardic Jews, both in Muslim and Christian Spain, replaced the native lexicon of unspoken Old Hebrew texts by Arabic and Spanish to produce their own calque "translations" of Old Hebrew; it is also quite likely that when the Iberian Jews began switching from colloquial Judeo-Arabic to Spanish after the 11th century, many of them also carried out a partial language shift, by relexifying Judeo-Arabic to Spanish, rather than adopt standard Spanish outright.

This book applies the methodology developed in my *Ashkenazic Jews: A Slavo-Turkic people in search of a Jewish identity*, whereby linguistic and ethnographic data are taken as the primary tools for the reconstruction of the geographic and ethnic origins of a Jewish group, with historical documentation serving as corroborating evidence. As I have just indicated, while there are considerable parallels between the formation and evolution of the Ashkenazic and Sephardic Jews (see also chapter 6 this volume), the lack of parallels in historical development and in the availability of the data, requires from time to time adjustments in the common methodology to deal with the unique research challenges that arise in the Sephardic context.

In the absence of unequivocal genetic or historical documentation, I had to base my claims for the origins of the Ashkenazic Jews almost exclusively on linguistic and ethnographic data. In many instances, the nonhistorical data helped me to formulate fresh interpretations of documented facts whose significance has long been debated. This is tantamount to claiming that historical data can only have a secondary, corroborating role to play in historical linguistic and ethnographic research. This point has been made before; consider the remarks of Ewald Wagner regarding the reconstruction of a Yemenite substratum in Iberian Arabic (a topic I shall have occasion to return to in chapter 4):

> . . .historical facts do not contradict the possibility today of a transplanting of Ethiopian linguistic material from Yemen to North Africa. On the contrary, linguistics might perhaps in this case assist history somewhat in the face of sparse information about the tribal composition of the North African Arabs (1966:278–79).

A student of Jewish history cannot help but notice the extent to which Jewish communities around the world display numerous cultural, religious, and linguistic similarities with the surrounding non-Jewish majorities; often the similarities descend to the level of very minute details. There are four explanations for these similarities:

(a) Cultural and religious patterns shared by Jews and non-Jews could be chance independent developments in each community that did not arise through contact.

(b) Non-Jews borrowed cultural and religious patterns from Jews.

(c) Jews borrowed cultural and religious patterns from non-Jews.

(d) Jews received cultural and religious patterns from non-Jews when the latter joined Jewish communities, and eventually formed the majority components of the latter. If all "Jewish" diaspora communities comprised far more members of non-Jewish proselyte origin than ethnic Palestinian Jews, then it would be more appropriate to speak of the originally non-Jewish cultural and religious practices as inherited from the non-Jews.

The first explanation is unlikely given the extent of the similarities involved; while the second and third explanations are valid at different historical periods, the varied evidence suggests that the fourth explanation best accounts for the rise of the Jewish diaspora communities before and after the collapse of independent Judea at the hands of the Romans in the late 1st century A.D. A major implication of the fourth model is that the so-called Jewish languages may turn out to have been developed by non-Jewish proselytes to Judaism and not by the descendants of Old Palestinian Jews. In such a case, the term "Jewish languages" is misleading (chapter 6 this volume).

I reconstruct a major proselyte contribution to the ethnic origins of the Iberian Jews for two reasons:

(a) The volume of linguistic and ethnographic features that link the Iberian Jews with Berbers and Arabs argues against mere diffusion of non-Jewish patterns of speech and cultural behavior to the coterritorial Jews.

(b) A major proselyte component has already been identified, at least to my satisfaction, in the formation of the Ashkenazic Jews—who today constitute some 80 percent of the Jewish population in the world.

The results of my study of the Ashkenazic Jews aroused my curiosity about the ethnic roots of other Jewish communities. In particular, I was interested in determining whether there were any Jewish communities that might be able to lay claim to a more significant Palestinian Jewish component in their ethnogenesis than the Ashkenazim.

The very preoccupation with this question is somewhat of a novelty in recent times; most scholars do not regard the topic of Sephardic (or of any other Jewish) ethnic origins to be a burning issue. Most students of the Jews, as well as the Sephardic Jews themselves, assume that the Iberian Jews are overwhelmingly of Palestinian Jewish origin who have historically always been closely identified with the Ibero-Romance language and culture area since the dawn of their diaspora. The clearly demonstrable Berbero-Arab impact on the Iberian Jews has usually been envisaged as transitory, though it was profound at different historical periods. The disinterest in exploring the ethnic roots of the Sephardic (as well as other) Jews stems, first and foremost, from the paucity of available historical documentation of Jewish settlement in Europe, Asia, and North Africa during the first millennium A.D. In more recent times, the disinterest in Jewish ethnic origins is also fueled by ideological agendas, such as political Zionism, that is predicated on the belief that the contemporary Jews were in the main the direct descendants of the Old Palestinian Jews. Once we recognize that the necessarily fragmentary historical documentation of events that took place so far back in the past (the interpretation of which is fraught with difficulties in the best of cases) should not be the primary evidence upon which to base our claims, new, more promising research agendas can be formulated. The key to progress in the reconstruction of ethnicity lies in the study of Jewish languages and ethnography.

One of the distinctive properties of language is that it retains traces of linguistic and cultural developments dating from periods that long predate the historical records of the speech communities. As far as the Jews of the Iberian Peninsula are concerned, we have fragmentary Latin and Greek inscriptions written by Jews from approximately the second half of the first millennium, with Arabic, Hebrew, and Ibero-Romance documentation beginning with the 10th century. As I will show in chapter 4, the absence of unequivocal historical documentation does not preclude utilizing linguistic data to reconstruct, at least *grosso modo*, the origins of these early Jewish settlers to the Iberian Peninsula, and to recommend a reconstruction of Sephardic history that so far has never been proposed by historians. The nonspecialist in linguistics may be surprised to learn that even contemporary Judeo-Spanish and Judeo-Arabic data can offer invaluable clues to the geographical and ethnic origins of the Sephardic

Jews; we are fortunate in possessing rich documentation of these two languages for the last several centuries, as well as an important secondary linguistic literature.

The Spanish-speaking Jews are a particularly inviting field of study for four reasons:

(a) They are the third largest Jewish group after the Ashkenazic and Arab Jews. (In speaking of "groups," I am aware that no Jewish community is completely monolithic in culture or in ethnic origin. Still most groups had, at least historically, a common Jewish or Judaized language and often a belief in a common historical past that justifies positing separate groups of "Ashkenazic," "Sephardic," and even "Arab" Jews; though the latter, to be sure, do not always share common origins, even though they speak variants of a common language.)

(b) The Sephardim have had a strong cultural impact on coterritorial Arab and Balkan Jews, and on non-coterritorial Ashkenazim, via their religious literature.

(c) The history of the Iberian Jews has been intertwined with that of Arabic- and Berber-speaking Jews for almost as long as Jews have been attested on Iberian soil. Hence, revealing the origin of the Iberian Jews has immediate implications for the reconstruction of the historical origins of the North African Berber- and Arabic-speaking Jews as well.

(d) A sizeable body of primary and secondary literature has accumulated on the history, language, and folklore of the Iberian and North African Jews, which makes innovative research possible. For further discussion, see the bibliographies compiled by Singerman 1975, 1993, Bunis 1981, and Wexler 1989a.

I will argue in the following chapters that Sephardic Jewry was created when significant numbers of Romance-, Berber-, and Arabic-speaking proselytes to Judaism intermarried with a handful of descendants of Palestinian Jews in North Africa and on the Iberian Peninsula. This demographic and cultural merger took place cyclically—at three different historical periods in two venues:

(a) First, in North Africa in the 7th and early 8th century (pursuant to the Arab settlement of North Africa).

(b) Then, in the Iberian Peninsula between 711 and 1492 (the respective dates of the Muslim invasion, and the expulsion of the Jews from the Kingdom of Spain by the Christian monarchs).

(c) Finally, again in North Africa after 1391 (where Iberian Jews began to settle in large numbers as a result of the nation-wide pogroms against the Jews in the Iberian Peninsula). The bulk of Sephardic culture—Berber and Arab in origin—owes its formation to the early centuries of settlement of the Jews in the Iberian Peninsula, but subsequent mergers were not without significance. In the first act of merger, *non-Jews*, along with a minority Palestinian Jewish nucleus, played a dominant role in the formation of the Sephardic people; in the last two cases, it was the "Judaized" descendants of Arab, Berber, and Iberian converts to Judaism who merged into a homogeneous Jewish community. As I will discuss later, subsequent historical events have not supplanted all of the original North African Berbero-Arab cultural and linguistic patrimony of the Sephardic Jews, much of which dates back to the 8th century, even though the bulk of the Iberian Jews, by the time of their expulsion from Spain in 1492, were already monolingual speakers of Spanish, and imbued to varying degrees with Iberian Christian culture.

In order to ascertain the origins of the Iberian Jews, we first have to determine, beginning with the 8th century, the makeup of the North African populations that entered Spain and Portugal. Jewish migratory patterns rarely differ from those of the coterritorial non-Jews, except in cases where the Jews alone are subject to banishment. Linguists and historians have identified Berber and Yemenite (the latter includes South Arabian) substrata in Iberian Arabic. For further discussion, see especially E. Wagner 1966 and Corriente 1977, 1989 for linguistic examples. In chapter 2, I will show that the identical linguistic and ethnic components appear to have attended the formation of the Iberian Jews.

In North Africa, Arabic dialects, which were similar to those initially introduced into Spain after 711, would probably have long since become radically altered, if not entirely replaced, by the new forms of Arabic brought to North Africa in the wake of the Bedouin invasions of the 11th and 12th centuries. Hence, forms of the original North African Judeo-Arabic that were brought back from Spain by emigrés especially after 1391, are likely to shed light on colloquial Iberian and Old North African Arabic; most of the descendants of the Iberian Muslims, who were "repatriating" to Morocco, Algeria, and Tunisia up to the early 17th century, assimilated long ago to newer North African variants of Arabic, and are thus less useful than the Iberian Jews for reconstructing older forms of North African or Iberian Arabic.

A systematic comparison of North African Judeo-Arabic with the Spanish Arabic spoken and written by all religious groups would reveal which North African Judeo-Arabic dialects were possibly of immediate Iberian origin, and which Jewish dialects (along with all the coterritorial North African Muslim dialects) of Arabic developed *in situ* after the settlement of Spain. I suspect that the Judeo-Arabic of Algiers that was studied in detail by Marcel Cohen in 1912 may be of immediate Iberian origin. For similar suggestions, see Blanc 1964:110, 182, fn 2, 185, fn 20 and Niehoff-Panagiotidis 1994:533.

Up until now, our information about spoken Iberian Arabic has been gleaned almost entirely from contemporary grammars written by Christians and the enormous Arabic component embedded in Ibero-Romance. Written Arabic texts, being composed in Classical Arabic, tend to mask spoken reality. As far as I know, no Arabists have ever entertained the possibility that some dialects of North African Judeo-Arabic might provide valuable data for the reconstruction of the colloquial Arabic that was brought to Spain in the early 8th century.

An important future research goal should be the comparison of the Iberian linguistic and ethnographic patrimony of the Jews and Andalusian Muslims who settled in North Africa—the Jews between the late 14th and late 15th centuries, the Muslims between the 15th and 17th centuries (the last Spanish Muslim settlers to arrive in North Africa were speakers of Spanish). For example, the Arabic of the Iberian Muslims who settled on the Tunisian coast between Tunis and Bizerte became mixed with local dialectal features to produce a new regional dialect. Today there are only two locales near Bizerte which preserve an Andalusian form of Arabic. For further discussion, see Boughanmi et al., 1979:23, Zavadovskij 1979:18–19. The awareness of an Iberian origin among contemporary North African Muslims should also be mapped across North Africa. The first Iberian Jews to settle in North Africa after the pogroms of 1391 might still have included Arabic speakers, while those who came in 1492 were probably exclusively Spanish-speaking; for example, the *taqqanot* (regulations) of the Iberian Jewish community in Morocco, published in Fès in 1494, were composed in Hebrew and Judeo-Spanish (Anqawa 1871). This suggests, at least, that the intelligentsia were Spanish-speaking. Corcos has suggested that Ḥakitía (the native glottonym for Moroccan Judeo-Spanish) was preserved in Tetuan because coterritorial Muslims also spoke Spanish up to the 18th century (1972:xxix); this would still not explain why Ḥakitía was preserved in other areas where Muslims did *not* speak Spanish. While North African Muslims of Iberian origin have generally lost awareness of their Iberian roots (Andalusian Muslim immigrants to North Africa who could speak only Spanish were not highly regarded in North Africa), the Jews have broadly preserved and cultivated their Iberian roots (Guershon 1993:19).

A major challenge for Jewish historical scholarship is to uncover the ethnographic and religious profile of Iberian Jewish society prior to its official dissolution in 1492. This is difficult to do in light of the sparse documentation, both Jewish and non-Jewish. A direct source of information is the rabbinical decisions that survive from Muslim and Christian Spain and North Africa between the 12th and 15th centuries. An indirect source is the Inquisition descriptions of the vestigial Jewish culture and religious practice among the Marranos—the body of Jews who converted to Catholicism, either by volition or under duress between the late 14th and late 15th centuries. Many Marranos developed clandestine syncretistic cultural and religious patterns that were derived from an idiosyncratic mix of Jewish and non-Jewish elements. Some of these unique cultural and religious patterns, still discernible among the contemporary descendants of Marranos in central and northern Portugal, Mallorca, the southwest of the United States, and possibly Latin America and the Caribbean, provide a means of evaluating the authenticity of the Spanish and Portuguese Inquisition pronouncements. For examples, as well as a discussion of the origin of the Spanish term *marrano*, see chapter 2 this volume. Also, Christian ecclesiastical literature of the 16th century occasionally rebukes "Old Christians" (i.e., Christians of non-Jewish or non-Muslim origins) for following allegedly "Jewish" and "Muslim" practices and superstitions (de Guevara 1541); scholars should study these materials systematically for the information they may provide on Iberian Jewish (and Muslim) practices. Finally, illuminations in Iberian Jewish books occasionally provide insights into Iberian Jewish society not readily available from written sources themselves.

The extant linguistic and ethnographic evidence from the two Iberian diasporas after 1492 is more voluminous and detailed than that of the pre-1492 period, yet serious problems of interpretation still remain. In

North Africa, the difficulty is how to differentiate Berbero-Arab linguistic and ethnographic features among the descendants of the Sephardim which are of Iberian origin, from subsequent influences acquired from the indigenous Arabic- and Berber-speaking Jews and Muslims after 1391—the date of the first mass resettlement of Iberian Jews in North Africa. In the Ottoman Empire, there is the difficulty of separating Iberian Islamic features in Sephardic culture and language from those which were borrowed, after 1492, from the coterritorial (Arabized) Turks.

Fortunately, the Iberian Jewish and Marrano exiles (the Jews were expelled en masse from Spain and Portugal between 1492 and 1498, while the Marranos left voluntarily as individuals throughout the 16th and early 17th centuries) initially settled in two geographically distinct areas that enjoyed minimal contact with one another: North Africa (modern-day Morocco, Algeria, and marginally Tunisia), and the Eastern Mediterranean successor states of the Ottoman Empire (the Balkans, Turkey, Arab Western Asia and, marginally, Egypt). The bifurcated settlement history permits us to claim that cultural features shared by North African and Balkan Sephardim are most likely of Iberian provenience. Linguistic and non-linguistic features found in only one of the Iberian Jewish diasporas (North Africa or the Balkans) might also be considered Iberian in origin and not post-1492 borrowings from the contiguous (non-)Jews, provided there are precedents in Iberian Jewish society as well. Fortunately, most later North African and Turkish linguistic and ethnographic features can be easily identified. Of course, not all pan-Sephardic features need have an Iberian source. For example, it is conceivable that pan-Arabic and Islamic influences were all acquired independently in Spain, North Africa, and the Balkans, or that a feature shared by both Sephardic diasporas could be of Iberian origin in one locale, but a local post-1492 borrowing in the other.

Many folk practices shared by Balkan and North African Sephardim have unmistakable North African Berber and/or Arab parallels; the Iberian origin of the former can be posited with some certainty whenever North African Jews, Berbers, and Arabs differ in the chronological or spatial details, or whenever Berber features surface in the Balkans, where there are no Berbers in the immediate environment. Since the Spanish Jews who settled in North Africa initially looked down upon the indigenous Jews, even to the point of accusing them of idolatry and religious fanaticism (Abbou 1953:380), and for a long time shunned intermarriage (this is the opposite of the low ranking that Andalusian Muslims enjoyed in North Africa—discussed earlier), it is unikely that they would have imitated North African Jewish customs that differed radically from their own in the early periods of settlement. Hence, I assume that North African Sephardic customs with parallels in the (Judeo-)Berber communities (of non-Iberian origin) need not necessarily have all been acquired from the latter in Africa after 1391. Ultimately, due to the sweeping migrational history of the Arabs and Arab Jews, it will be useful to compare the putative Arab and Berber imprint in the folk practices of the Sephardic Jews with cultural patterns throughout the entire North African area, and even beyond in Arabia and the Near East (Corso 1935:35); unfortunately, such an ambitious task will, for the most part, have to be left for the future.

An historical event that facilitates the interpretation of Sephardic ethnographic and linguistic evidence (both in Judeo-Spanish and Judeo-Arabic) is the invasion of North Africa by the banu Hilal and Ma'qil Bedouins in the mid-11th and 12th centuries. These invasions brought new linguistic and cultural patterns to North Africa that supplanted many of the earlier features that had been deposited by the first Arab invasion in the late 7th century or in Spain in the early 8th century. Not all the newer features succeeded in spreading to Islamic Spain. Hence, Spanish Arabic and Spanish Muslim culture may be more archaic than the North African counterparts. Linguistic and ethnographic differences among the Iberian and North African Jews will allow us to reconstruct to some extent the various waves of North African Jewish settlement in Spain, and later, Iberian Jewish settlement in North Africa. I would expect Iberian Jewish data to cast valuable light on the historical development of the Jewish communities in the Near East and the Arabian Peninsula as well. As far as I know, no scholar has ever proposed such a research agenda.

For example, there are some Arabic terms found among the Iberian Jews and their descendants outside the peninsula that are presently unknown in parts of North Africa. JSp *adefina* "sabbath food" < Ar *ad-dfina* "the burial," is presently unattested in Morocco, but is found in the territory between Algeria and Libya; (J)Ar *šnūġa* "synagogue" < Arabized Lat *synagōga*, known now only in a handful of points in Algeria and northeastern Morocco, is probably a loan from Judeo-Spanish. Conversely, North African Jews have Arabisms not attested among Iberian Jews. For example, JAr *ṣlā* "synagogue" < "prayer," that is a pan-Afro-Asian semantic development among the Jews (and encompasses numerous Judaized languages other than Arabic), is unknown in Spanish Arabic. I would tentatively ascribe *adefina* and *šnūġa* to the first Berbero-Arab invasions of Spain anytime between the early 8th and the early 10th centuries, and *ṣlā* to the later Bedouin invasions of North Africa in the 11th and 12th centuries (see chapter 4 this volume).

All too often the history of the Jews is treated as an independent, self-contained topic, as if the Jews were a migrant Palestinian people that occasionally absorbed a number of linguistic and cultural influences from the coterritorial peoples—i.e., the Palestinian Jews became "Arabized," "Berberized," and "Iberianized/Christianized"—while managing to maintain their original identity throughout history. For further discussion, see, most recently, Johnson's characterization of the Jews in this vein in 1987.

The relatively late transmission of written Hebrew and Judeo-Aramaic, as well as the Jewish liturgical literature (for example, the Hebrew Bible and Judeo-Aramaic Talmud) from Palestine and the Near East to Europe, convince me that many of the genuinely Old Palestinian Jewish traditions and religious lore of the contemporary Sephardic and Ashkenazic Jews must be the result of more recent processes of "Judaization," rather than uninterrupted inheritance from Palestine. By Judaization, I mean the process by means of which contemporary non-Jewish customs came to acquire Old Palestinian Jewish pedigrees by being linked to "precedents" in the Bible and Talmud (see chapter 5 this volume). Differences between the Sephardic pronunciation of Hebrew in Spain, and the diasporas, also point to serious breaks in the transmission of Iberian Jewish practices to the Balkan and North African diasporas after 1492. The successful implementation of Judaization means that only the end points of the time line of Jewish history share common patterns of behavior, for example, contemporary Jewish culture can resemble Old Palestinian Jewish culture more closely than it does the culture of the intervening periods. Such a picture suggests that the latest stage is unlikely to be a direct evolution from the first Palestinian stage.

If I am right that the Sephardic Jews are descended mainly from Berbers and Arabs, and only marginally from Old Palestinian Jews, then the Sephardim (and to some extent the North African Jews of Arab and Berber language and culture whose ancestors never sojourned in the Iberian Peninsula) may be priceless repositories of Old Berber and Arab cultural and linguistic patterns. In that case, the Sephardic Jews could offer a parallel to the Ashkenazim who retain Old Sorbian pre-Christian and Christian ethnographic and religious patterns that have become obsolete among the few remaining Sorbs themselves (Wexler 1993c).

The reason that Sephardic Jews succeeded in retaining so much of their original Berbero-Arab ethnographic patrimony, even after separation from living Arab and Berber cultures, is that the latter could provide the Jews with a unique religious, cultural, and linguistic profile, which was, after all, one of the goals of the Judaization process. This first happened in Muslim Spain, when non-Jewish customs became obsolete in the coterritorial Berber culture due to the acceleration of Arabization, but not among the Jews; it occurred again in Christian Spain when the Jews began to seek a distinctly "Jewish" profile that could set them apart from all the surrounding non-Jews. In the Balkan and North African diasporas, the cultivation of the Berbero-Arab patrimony and the Spanish language could enable the Sephardic emigrés to continue to preserve a separate profile in proximity to indigenous non-Iberian Jewish and non-Jewish (including Berber) communities. In fact, since Spanish was not spoken by non-Jews at all in the Balkans, and only to a limited extent in the North African diaspora, the Sephardic Jews outside of Spain became less prone to cultivating specifically Judaized variants of Spanish. In North Africa, the Jews eventually replaced Judeo-Spanish (Ḥakitía) with standard Spanish in the early 20th century; even in the Balkans where there was no immediate Spanish stimulus, Judeo-Spanish periodically underwent transformations leading to convergence with standard Spanish (Bunis 1993a).

Whether we regard the Sephardic Jews as "Judaized" Arabs, Berbers, and Iberians, or as "Arabized, Berberized, and Iberianized" Palestinian Jews and their descendants, it is imperative that the history of the Sephardic Jews be studied in a cross-disciplinary framework that exploits the expertise of historians, linguists, and ethnographers, and takes care to study the Jews in a broad context that includes the coterritorial and contiguous non-Jewish groups. Collaboration of historians, archaeologists, and linguists is imperative since it is unlikely that much new historical or archaeological data of the Iberian Jewish presence in the first millennium will come to light that could radically alter our present views; moreover, linguistic data without corroborative historical and archaeologicial data usually offer insufficient underpinning for innovative theories.

2

Conversion to Judaism in the Asian, African, and Iberian Lands up to c.1200 A.D.

The Role of Conversion in the Formation of the Sephardic Jews

Most historians have either ignored the role that conversion played in the creation of diaspora Jewish communities or have assumed that proselytism was at best limited to a few locales, such as Adiabene (Parthia, now Iraq) or the Khazar kingdom (Ponto-Caspian steppelands). Two reasons are frequently cited to motivate the claim that widespread conversion to Judaism in Europe and North Africa was unlikely:

(a) Conversion to Judaism would have had to proceed according to orthodox Jewish religious law, He *halaxah* (M. A. Cohen 1992:10). In this spirit, Bachrach criticizes the medieval church preoccupation with intermarriage, and alleged Jewish proselytizing, on the grounds that Jews would not have married non-Jews without a conversion ceremony (1973:15, fn 13). This is an anachronistic argument. I believe that both Cohen and Bachrach err in assuming that Iberian Jews uniformly practiced forms of Judaism that were consonant with Old Palestinian Talmudic law. Heterogeneity characterized Sephardic Judaism just as it did Hellenized Judaism in the first millennium. The reciprocal influences between religious groups, which led to the rise of syncretistic beliefs, encouraged conversion from one religion to another; a particularly striking example is the phenomenon of Marranism, whereby large numbers of Jews in Spain and Portugal in the late 14th through 16th centuries converted voluntarily to official Catholicism, but often practiced highly idiosyncratic forms of Catholicism (discussed later in this chapter). It is perfectly plausible that some

Jews married non-Jews without the formal conversion of the non-Jewish spouse (as is the practice in Islam).

It is instructive to note the comment by Lancelot Addison, an English Christian visitor to Morocco in the late 17th century, that the Jews did not rigorously require circumcision of non-Jews lest the candidates be put off (1676:65); according to him, the Jews had a special practice of drawing some blood from the convert on the eighth day after conversion, which is not found in the law of Moses (ibid.:67). This suggests that some Jews had a nonorthodox procedure for receiving converts, while the very existence of a procedure suggests that conversion was not altogether a rarity. Conversely, Addison may have been witnessing the practice of *haṭafat dam*, the symbolic drawing of blood from a male who was already circumcised in some fashion (as was the case with some Muslims) or born without a foreskin. Addison adds that the Jews believed that a *ṭallit* (Hebrew for "prayer shawl"—he actually wrote He *cicit* "fringes on the prayer shawl," but the entire garment is understood from his remarks) not only delivers the Jews from sin, but also attracts proselytes.

(b) Non-Jewish clerical and religious authorities in Muslim and Christian Spain both opposed conversion to any religion, except the majority state religion: "entry into [the Jewish community] was impossible for a Muslim and difficult for a Christian" (Wasserstein 1985:190, commenting on Islamic Spain in the 11th century). Hiršberg also expresses the popular view that with the advent and institutionalization of Islam, it became impossible for Jews to proselytize in North Africa or in Spain (2:1965:26). This argument is not convincing. It is important to remember that the institutionalization of Islam and Christianity in North Africa and Spain were gradual processes that repeatedly experienced setbacks. Competition between various sects of Christianity, Islam, and the indigenous religions continued for many centuries. The prohibitions against Muslims and Christians becoming Jews notwithstanding, numerous cases of conversion to Judaism are, in fact, recorded in the literature of all religious groups.

The unsubstantiated assertion that proselytism could only have played a minor role in the creation of diaspora Jewish communities in turn fosters the myth that the contemporary Jews must be largely the direct decendants of Palestinian Jews. The hypothesis of proselyte origins of a Jewish community should be raised wherever the indigenous Jewish population became, historically, quite numerous. For example, while Rome was a major gateway to Europe for Palestinian Jewish emigrés in the early years of the Christian era, and the site of one of the oldest Jewish communities in Europe, neither Rome nor the successor Italian states ever acquired a significant Jewish population. There is also evidence that conversion to Judaism was less widespread in pagan or early Christian Rome than in contemporaneous Hellenized Asia Minor. Conversely, Hellenized Asia Minor and more distant realms, such as the Germano-Slavic or Iberian lands, like Iraq and Yemen, became home to substantial Jewish populations. Given the racial variety of the Jewish communities, it is impossible to accept the claim that since Jews who married non-Jews did not as a rule raise their offspring as Jews, intermarriage had little impact on Jewish racial purity (Auerbach 1907:334, cited by Efron 1994:129). The Jews had a rich literature in Judeo-Greek, such as the Septuagint translation of the Hebrew Bible that was begun in the 3rd century B.C. and the New Testament. However, there is no literature in a Judaized Latin, so that many scholars even doubt that such a language was ever created.

The enormous Jewry that developed in Poland by the 18th century, in spite of repeated pogroms and banishments, can hardly be ascribed solely, or even primarily, to natural increases among the descendants of a small group of ethnic Jews. Assuming immigration from the monolingual German lands would mean positing a very large Jewish population there, an assumption for which there is absolutely no evidence. It should not come as a surprise, then, that in both the Iberian and mixed Germano-Slavic realms there is considerable evidence of conversion to Judaism (discussed later in this chapter, and Wexler 1993c, respectively).

By conversion to Judaism, I have in mind both a formal act in accordance with a Jewish ritual, as well as informal association of non-Jews with Jewish communities, for example as reflected in participation in selected Jewish rituals. An example of informal association of non-Jews with the Jewish community in the early Christian period is the so-called "God-fearers," attested primarily in Asia Minor and Greece; these were non-Jews who associated themselves with synagogues either as observers of Jewish religious services and/or as contributors to synagogue construction projects, but who did not convert formally to Judaism. To the best of my knowledge, the most detailed original description of the God-fearers comes from a Judeo-Greek inscription thought to date from the 3rd century A.D. that was found in the 1970s at Aphrodisias (in modern-day Anatolia). For references and discussion, see Wexler 1993c and chapter 6 this volume. The ritual of conversion must have varied with each diaspora community, since not all forms of diaspora Judaism in North Africa, Egypt, Asia Minor, or southern Europe adhered to the talmudic Judaism practiced in Palestine at the time. Unfortunately, conversion to Judaism is hardly ever described in detail in the contemporary literature, whether Jewish or non-Jewish (except for the occasional mention in Jewish reports of benedictions that had to be recited during the act of conversion).

The most frequent motivation for individual conversion to Judaism was religious and cultural identification with the Jews, but in other cases, especially involving a large proselyte population, conversion was apparently prompted by the desire to enhance the political independence of the group in the face of contiguous or coterritorial threats. This was presumably the reason for widescale conversion in Adiabene, Yemen, and in the Khazar Kingdom in the Ponto-Caspian steppelands (discussed later in this chapter). For the Khazars, conversion to Judaism was a means of assuring neutrality in the competition then raging between Byzantine Christianity and Islam.

The very variety of Jewish expression that characterized Jewish life, especially outside of Palestine, made it possible for large numbers of non-Jews to identify themselves with the Jewish community. It is important to remember that Judaism in the diasporas was not simply an extension of rabbinic Judaism. It was also a religion of the Roman Empire, that both influenced and was influenced by Roman religions and Christianity (Kraabel 1979:502–503).

Nowadays, the Jewish clerical hierarchy is sympathetic to conversion almost only in cases of mixed marriage, and even then the requirements of the non-Jewish partner to receive religious instruction are extremely rigorous, especially among the so-called orthodox Jews. The fact that formal conversion to Judaism is not now encouraged may be a reaction to the many centuries when conversion in Muslim and Christian lands was illegal and carried with it a sizeable punishment, leveled both on the converter, as well as on the candidate for conversion; for several centuries, many Christians who converted to Judaism in Europe moved to Arab lands, especially Egypt, where they were not subject to prosecution. Egypt may have become a haven for European converts since here historically the competition between Islam and Christianity could have provided fertile ground for Jewish proselytizing activities. The Christians in Egypt first became a minority in the 10th century, the very period when the mass conversion of Coptic Christians to Islam seems to have ended in Egypt (Wasserstein 1985:225).

The Migration of Western Asian Jews to the Western Mediterranean

The Islamic population that settled in the Iberian Peninsula beginning with the early 8th century was primarily of North African Berber origin; only a minority of the invaders were ethnic Arabs from the Arabian Peninsula, Syria, and Iraq. Most of the Berber settlers were Muslims, while some espoused Christianity, Judaism, or an indigenous religion. The Berbers spoke Arabic, Berber, and possibly North African Romance, but their sole written language appears to have been Arabic. While the available historical documentation indicates that the Arab minority in the Iberian Peninsula and North Africa traces its origins to Arabs and Arabized peoples from Syria, Iraq, Yemen, and other parts of the Arabian Peninsula (Hitti 1951:578), a linguistic analysis of Spanish and North African Arabic dialects reveals, in addition, a South Arabian (Ḥimyarite) and Berber substratal element (Kampfmeyer 1899, 1900:624–29, Colin 1930b:101–102, 112–13, Dubler 1942, de las Cagigas 1946a, E. Wagner 1966, Corriente 1969, passim, 1977:41, fn 45, 46, fn 58, 50, 53, fn 73, 55, 76, 81, fn 119, 98, fn 141, 103, fn 159, 104, fn 162, 123, fn 211, 1989, and Kontzi 1985:544–45). Ḥimyarite was spoken in the Arabian Peninsula until the 10th century (E. Wagner 1966: 274–75).

The linguistic and historical evidence also allows us to delineate two chronologically distinct waves of Arab migration from east to west, culminating in settlements in North Africa and the Iberian Peninsula. The first wave came in the late 7th and early 8th century, and resulted in the Arabization of North Africa and the invasion of the Iberian Peninsula. The second wave involved the invasion of the banu Hilal and Maʿqil Bedouins from northern Arabia in the mid-11th century, which resulted in the accelerated displacement of the Berber language in North Africa (ibid.:276–79).

The Sephardic Jewish population had the same constellation of geographical origins as the Arabs and Berbers. Historical, ethnographic, and onomastic evidence shows that, in addition to a North African component in the Iberian Jewish community, Jews from Syria, Iraq, and the Arabian Peninsula also accompanied the Arabs to North Africa and

Spain (on the westward march of Jews and Bedouins, see Saada 1982). There seems to have been one significant difference in the Jewish and non-Jewish migrations: whereas Muslim migrations from North Africa to Spain continued through the 12th and 13th centuries with varying intensities, the Jews seem to have participated primarily in only an early wave of migration to Spain between the 8th and 10th centuries.

The Eastern Arabic or South Arabian features that can be identified in North African or Spanish Judeo-Arabic in themselves would not establish a unique Eastern Arabic and South Arabian (i.e., Ḥimyarite) or Yemenite component in the creation of the Sephardic Jews, since these linguistic features could just as easily have been acquired from coterritorial Arabic dialects. Some Yemeni features surface in Algiers Judeo-Arabic, but not in the immediately coterritorial Muslim dialects. An example is the use of *di* as a genitive particle (M. Cohen 1912:363 and E. Wagner 1966:266; Zavadovskij 1962:109 entertains the possibility that the morpheme is from Berber); however, since this feature is also attested in a number of Moroccan Muslim dialects, it cannot point to a specifically Judeo-Yemenite strain (Kampfmeyer 1900:624–29). The example of *di* is valuable evidence that some Iberian Jews came back to North Africa as speakers of "Yemenized" Iberian Arabic, but there is no way to determine whether they arrived in Africa after the nationwide Spanish pogroms in 1391 or in the wake of the definitive expulsion of the Jews from the Kingdom of Spain in 1492. Hence, Slouschz's assertion that a Judaized Berber tribe may have been of "Judeo-Ḥimyarite" origin is plausible (1908:390, fn 1, 395; on Ḥimyarite-Jewish relations, see Newby 1988), though not necessarily his specific example of *Behloula*, which appears to be < Ber "simple, foolish." For example, a certain Yona ibn Bahlul was a native of Molina, Murcia in the mid-13th century (Laredo 1978:397–98, who states that the Berber tribe by this name practiced Judaism up until the 8th century, and Zafrani 1986:168). Curiously, the Zaragozan Hebrew grammarian, Yicxak ben Yosef ibn Barun (c.1100) referred to Ḥimyarite and Ḥijāzī Arabic cognates of Biblical Hebrew words in his *Kitāb al-muwāzana bayn al-luġa al-ʿibrāniyya wa'l-ʿarabiyya* (Eppenstein 1900:245 and fn 6).

In the absence of significant linguistic data, I have to rely on historical documentation to establish that there were contacts between Iraqi Jewish scholars and their counterparts in North Africa and Spain between the 8th and 10th centuries: Iraqi Jews settled in Spain and North Africa, while Spanish Jews enrolled in Jewish academies in Iraq (on links between

Sijilmāsah, Morocco, and Iraq, see Ashtor 1972 and Tobi 1982:407; on the settlement of Iraqi Jews in Cairo in the 9th century, see Goitein 2:1971:284). A particularly intriguing early instance of East-West networking among farflung Jewish communities is the correspondence between the Turkic Khazar king Yosef and the celebrated 10th-century Arab Jewish diplomat Ḥasday ibn Šapruṭ, who was born in Jaén (c.910–970; on a possible Khazar migration to Spain, see the following discussion).

Iraqi and Yemenite Jews might have transmitted some terms to Spain—in addition to the Talmud and the Hebrew-Judeo-Aramaic Bible. Note that He *micvah* "commandment" has assumed the secondary meaning of funeral or coffin only in Judeo-Spanish and Iraqi Judeo-Arabic (chapter 4 this volume); the appearance of Ar *al-minbar* "the pulpit in the mosque" in Judeo-French of the 11th century, and in all dialects of Yiddish (in stark contrast to its absence in Sephardic sources) also raises the possibility of an Iraqi source for this Arabism (after Iraqi Jews migrated to northern Europe; note previous discussion in this chapter).

In looking to the east for models of scholarship and religion, the Jews followed Andalusian Muslim practice; only after 1000 did the cultural and religious institutions of the Iberian Jews and Muslims become independent of foreign models and institutions (Ashtor 1972, Stillman 1979b:54, 56, 77, fn 20 and Levtzion 1982:259 and fn 26). The Iberian receptivity to innovations from the Near East and Egypt may account for the spread of the Arabic administrative title *muqaddam* "community leader, judge, appointed executive" from Egypt to Spain, since it appears in the former in the late 11th century, but in Spain only by the 13th and 14th centuries (Stillman 1979b:69; also SpAr *muquedèm* "prince," *muquéddem* "majordomo, overseer" appears in de Alcalá 1505, cited by Corriente 1977:85, 103, fn 159); this term also appears in translation as Sp *adelantado* both among Jews and Christians (van Wijk 1951 and chapter 4 this volume).

The Role of Western Asian Converts in the Formation of the Sephardic Jews

The acts of widespread conversion to Judaism that might have influenced the formation of the Iberian Jewish communities must be sought in the peninsula and in North Africa, Arabia (Arab and Ḥimyarite territories both), and in Iraq, before and after the institutionalization of Christianity and Islam. The latter two areas are germane to the formation of the Sephardim, since both had Jewish populations whose substantial size was in large part due to accretions of converts to Judaism, and "Jews" from these areas are known to have migrated in significant numbers to North Africa and Spain.

Historically recorded acts of widespread conversion in the territories of interest to us are only three in number: in Adiabene (Parthia, now Iraq) in the early 1st century A.D. (Bickermann 1928 and Gutmann 1929:892–93, 904), Yemen during the reign of the Ḥimyarite king, Yusuf Dhu Nuwas in the 6th century, and in the Khazar Kingdom, when the ruling, predominantly Turkic, tribes converted to Judaism in the 8th century (Golb and Pritsak 1982 and Wexler 1993c, chapter 6). In addition, ancient traditions preserved in Jewish, Christian, and Islamic literature relate that large numbers of Berbers in the pre-Islamic period professed Judaism, but there is no independent evidence for these claims (see details following).

The first event of conversion in Adiabene was noted both in the Talmud and by the Jewish historian Flavius Josephus (c.38–c.100). The existence of special Jewish rites for preparing non-Jewish women for marriage suggests that conversion was widespread (Newby 1988:75). The reciprocal influences between the Jewish communities of Iraq and Yemen, before the rise of Islam, provide a basis for the belief that the two proselyte communities mingled. The heterogeneity of Jewish culture in many parts of the Arab world before the institutionalization of Islam suggests that there may have been other early acts of conversion to Judaism, in addition to that of Dhu Nuwas. On the memorializing of the conversion to Judaism of the Ḥimyarite king Abu Karib Asʿad Kamil (c.385–420) in Arab balladry, see Hitti 1951:60; Newby discusses conversion to Judaism in Taymā and Madīna in the 5th and 6th centuries (1988:41, 53).

It would be especially useful to know the geographical parameters and relative chronologies of conversion in Yemen, since the contemporary Yemenite Jewish population is racially heterogeneous. For example, recent studies suggest that the Jews living until the 1950s in the southern regions of Yemen had a higher frequency of African marker genes than those living in the north of the country (Mourant et al., 1978:31, Patai and Patai-Wing 1989:331, Livshits et al., 1991). Goitein provides a linguistic parallel in his observation that Jews in Ṣanʿā', the capital of Yemen located in the central part of the country, essentially spoke the Arabic of the coterritorial Muslims, while the speech of Jews in the south of the country differed from that of their neighbors (1931:357, 361, fn 2, 1960:359). Hence, I see no reason to accept Ahroni's claim, based on the absence of references in Jewish sources, that the Ḥimyarite conversion to Judaism was superficial (1986:47).

In any case, the dismantlement of the Jewish kingdoms does not absolve Ahroni from the requirement of exploring the fate of the Jewish inhabitants. Political collapse would have been a good reason for the indigenous Jews, of whatever origin, to emigrate (say to Ethiopia, and beyond to North Africa). The Arabian Peninsula was a major area for Christian missionizing in the pre-Islamic period. The territory lay in the center of struggles between Egyptian and Ethiopian Monophysites, Syrian Jacobites, Nestorians, Greek Orthodox Christians, and Persians (Newby 1988:9). An area that witnessed so much competition among religious groups might also be expected to have been receptive to proselytizing efforts, including those by Jews. As M. J. Kister points out (1989: 340), the reciprocal penetration of Judaism and Islam was so intense that it is difficult to separate Islamic beliefs from Judaism and Christianity. In Yemen, Jews who converted to Islam also preserved a number of Jewish practices, for example, the observance of the Sabbath (Kister and Kister 1979:243, fn 55; see also M. J. Kister 1989:350); these residual Jewish practices could have spread to the non-Jewish community at large, thus generating a common culture among Jews and non-Jews in Arabia. M. J. Kister also points out that Muslims were warned not to adopt ideas and customs from the Jews and Christians (ibid.:329).

The nature of Yemenite Jewish culture in the early Islamic era may be reconstructed in part by Ethiopian Jewish practices, many of which are very likely of Yemenite origin. Leslau believes that Yemenite Jews probably brought Judaism to Ethiopia around the 3rd and 5th centuries A.D. (1957:1). The linguistic evidence is instructive.

For example, Ar *masjid* "mosque" < Aramaic is used in a number of Ethiopian languages to denote the synagogue, for example *mäsgid* in Amharic, Čaha, Eža, Gogot, and Gyeto, and *mäsgīd* in Harari (Leslau 1979). This term, in the unvocalized form *msgdn*, is also found in an Aramaic inscription from Ṣanʿāʾ (Müller 1973:151 and Biella 1982:327). On the use of the term by Arabic-speaking Jews to designate the synagogue prior to the rise of Islam, see Hiršberg 1975:156. A number of Arabic dialects also used a single term to denote both the mosque and the synagogue, including Sicilian Arabic, for example *mesit, misit, misida, misita* (Colin 1931:17, fn 4; on this term and Ar *knīs[a]*, see also chapter 4 this volume). This naming practice may have begun among the Jews. An unusual form of the Arabism is JSp *almagid* "mosque" in Arragel 1422–33 (Morreale 1961:149).

Leslau assumes that the Ethiopian Jews acquired this Arabism directly from South Arabian, while the Ethiopian Christians got the surface cognate from Arabic (1979:427, but no evidence for this claim is forthcoming). Note also his citation of Gogot, Masqan, and Soddo *dəfun*, and Wolane, Zway *dufun* "inferior quality of bread" < Ar *d-f-n* "conceal" (ibid.:201)—the same root as in JSp *adefina* "food prepared on Friday and left to simmer in a pot for consumption on the Sabbath." The Arabic root is rarely attested in the meaning of food among Muslims; the specific Jewish meaning is found only in Judeo-Spanish and Judeo-Arabic (Spanish Christian writers also used the term in the Jewish meaning; see discussion of JSp *adefina* in chapters 4 and 5 this volume). Aškoli also cites Geez *tährat* "purification among the Jews" (1936:284) that may also be of Arabic origin (see Ar *ṭ-h-r* "purify," but the cognate Hebrew root might also be the source).

There is one piece of evidence that Yemenite Jews (some, all?) may have been originally foreigners to Yemen. From Arabic sources, we learn that the Jews of Madīna at the time of Muḥammad spoke differently from other inhabitants, for example, *kāna yarṭanū bi-l-yahūdiyya* "they speak in an incomprehensible Jewish language" (Fück 1955:88 and fn 1). There are five conceivable interpretations of what the root Ar *r-ṭ-n* "speak in an incomprehensible way" meant in this passage:

(a) The reference is to a Judaized dialect of Arabic. This explanation is unappealing since Judeo-Arabic dialects, though sometimes quite distinct from coterritorial or contiguous non-Jewish Arabic dialects, are largely comprehensible to speakers of the latter (see also discussion in chapter 6 this volume; on Judeo-Arabic, see Blau 1959, 1964, 1965, 1978, 1984, 1992 and Newby 1971).

(b) A dialect of Aramaic was implied. If so, the Jews could have come to Arabia from either Palestine or Iraq where Aramaic was spoken, or they could have been descended from Judaized Aramaeans who settled in Yemen (Hitti 1951:61, 104). That means that they would have comprised ethnic Jews and indigenous converts to Judaism, probably with the emphasis on the latter. An Aramaic identification is attractive since Goitein has observed that there are many Arabic proverbs used by Yemenite Jews today which appear to be of talmudic origin, but are in reality Old Aramaic proverbs that entered both Old Hebrew and Arabic literature (1931:373; also Avisur 1993). Other scholars, such as Idelsohn, doubt that Yemenite Jews came from an Aramaic-speaking territory (1913:529). There is no appreciable Judeo-Aramaic substratum in Judeo-Arabic, as there is in Palestinian Christian Arabic (Blau 1964:136–37).

(c) The alleged linguistic separateness of the Yemeni Jews might find an explanation in a South Arabian, Ḥimyarite origin. Ḥimyarite was still spoken at this time in the Arabian Peninsula.

(d) Gil thinks *r-ṭ-n* may have referred to Persian, but he gives no evidence (1984:205–206).

(e) Ar *r-ṭ-n* may have referred to a secret lexicon used by Jews in Arabic for magical purposes or in order not to be understood by non-Jews. This assumption is based on the fact that cognate JAram *rṭan* means to murmur magical formulas (Greenfield 1974).

Aramaic could link Yemenite Jews specifically to either a Palestinian or Iraqi homeland. In any event, Jews from Iraq and Yemen migrated westward to North Africa and eventually to Spain, along with Muslims, beginning with the 9th century, and possibly earlier (Levtzion 1982:259). The Iraqi Jewish immigrants could have consisted not only of Palestinian Jewish emigrés and indigenous converts, but also of refugees from the former Khazar Kingdom (who were themselves primarily of ethnic Jewish and non-Jewish origin), after the latter was destroyed by the Kingdom of Rus' (the ancestors of the Ukrainians) in the late 10th century. The Khazar Kingdom at its heyday extended from Kiev in the west, up to Khwārizm in the east, and from Bulġar on the Volga in the north, to the Crimea and Caucasus in the south. The Khazar king, Yosef, was in correspondence with the Arab Jewish statesman, Ḥasday ibn Šapruṭ, in the employ of the caliph ʿAbd ar-Raḥman of Córdoba in the mid-10th century (Golb and Pritsak 1982, chapter 9). This correspondence is the basis for my hypothesis that the contacts between Spain and Khazar Jews were not merely a function of correspondence from a distance, but that Khazar Jewish immigrants might have found their way to the Iberian Peninsula. Given the presence in Spain of Iraqi Jews and Karaites (a Judaizing sect that originated in the 8th century in Iraq, and that rejects the authority of the Talmud), a Khazar Jewish presence is hardly far-fetched. Either the Iraqi Jews, or the Yemenite Jews who received the Babylonian Talmud from the latter (Morag 1988:35–59), or both groups, could have brought the texts of the Talmud (in both the Palestinian and Iraqi variants?), and the Bible to Spain (and other parts of Europe).

Until the 10th century, there is no indication that either the Talmud or the Bible (at least in the original languages) were available to Iberian and North African Jews. Among the first Iberian Jewish talmudic, biblical and Hebrew language scholars were Menaxem ben Ya'akov ben Saruq (Tortosa 910–970), Moše ben Xanox (Córdoba d. 965), Dunaš ben Labraṭ ha-Levi (c.920–c.980, born in North Africa or Iraq), Yosef ben Sutanas ibn Ali Tur (Mérida mid-10th century), Yehuda ibn Da'ud al-Fasi Xayuž (Fès c.940–Córdoba c.1000), Xanox ben Moše (Córdoba d. 1014), Yona ibn Janaḥ (Córdoba? b.985/990), Šmuel ben Yosef ibn Nagrella ha-Nagid (Córdoba, 993–1056), Ḥasan ben Mar Ḥasan (10th century, born in southern Italy), Yicxak ben Ya'akov al-Fasi (Fès 1013–Lucena 1103), Abun (Granada 11th and 12th centuries), Yicxak ben Barux ibn al-Baliah (Córdoba 1035–1094), Yicxak ben Yehuda ibn Gayyat (Lucena 1038–1089), Yicxak ben Re'uven al-Barceloni (b. c.1043), Yosef ha-Levi ben Me'ir ha-Levi ibn Migaš (Seville 1077–1114—on this surname, see following discussion) and Barux ben Yicxak al-Baliah (Seville 1077–1126). The earliest translations of (Judeo-)Arabic literature into Hebrew were not done until the 12th century; translators included Yosef ben Yicxak Qimxi (Andalusia c.1105–Narbonne, Provence c.1170), Yehuda ben Ša'ul ibn Tibbon (Granada c.1120–Lunel, Provence 1190?), and Yehuda ben Šlomo al-Ḥarizi (c.1170–1230).

The suggestion that non-Jews in the Near East who converted to Judaism found their way to Spain and North Africa might be supported by the family name *Migaš*, borne by three Iberian Jewish scholars, all members of a single family, Yosef ha-Levi ben Me'ir ha-Levi ibn Migaš (1077–1114), his son Me'ir Abu Yusuf Migaš, a native of Granada in the 11th century, and the latter's grandson Me'ir ben Yosef ibn Migaš (12th century).

Goitein suggested, without any argumentation whatsoever, that the name was < Gk *megas* "large" (1974:332; chapter 4 this volume). I argue that, while such a Greek etymon is acceptable from the point of view of phonological developments (see following discussion), it is unconvincing given the paucity of Greek names used by the Iberian Jews at this time, and the nonexistence of direct Grecisms received by Iberian Judeo-Arabic or Judeo-Spanish. The name is not attested among North African Jews or Muslims, or among Iberian non-Jews; hence, a Berber or Arabic origin is unlikely.

In addition to a possible Greek etymon, I would prefer to derive *Migaš* < OPer *maguš* "sorcerer," that surfaces in Greek as *magos*, and in Arabic as *majūš*. Ar *al-majūš*—as the designation for Vikings—is first attested in 795 (in the writings of ibn al-Athir, 1160–1234; Melvinger 1955:9); other meanings associated with the term are Vandals (ar-Razi, 865–925, recorded in a 14th-century text; ibid.:47, 85), and pagan Berbers (including those in Spain) (in ibn Xaldun, 1332–1406, quoting al-Idrisi, also cited by ibid.:76, 78). The term was also applied to Slavic pagans (ibid.:49, 78). If JAr *Migaš* is indeed < Ar *majūš*, then we have an important indication that non-Jewish populations in North Africa or Europe converted to Judaism. The name would then also be unusual for calling attention to the bearer's non-Jewish past.

The following hypothetical set of (chronologically unordered) sound changes motivates my derivation of *Migaš* from OPer *maguš*:
OPer *maguš* > JAr **máguš* > **míguš* > *mígaš*:

(a) OPer *maguš* > JAr **máguš*: penultimate stress is characteristic of Spanish Arabic (Steiger 1932:76). The asterisk denoting reconstruction may be unnecessary, if the name *bn M'ʿš* /ben Mágiš(?)/, cited by Baer in a Mozarabic text from Toledo 1161 (1934:230), is related; Ar -ʿ- occasionally > Sp *-g-* (Ar *al-nāʿūra* "*water wheel*" > OSp *alnagora*, cited by Steiger 1932:287), but the absence of /u/ in the second syllable makes me hesitate to connect the two forms.

(b) JAr **máguš* > **míguš*: the raising of a > *i* in the initial syllable, known as *imāla*, is especially characteristic of Granada Arabic (ibid.:62; Corriente 1977:25). The phenomenon of *imāla* (consisting of two stages, *a* > *e*, and then *e* > *i*), is usually dated in the 13th century for Spanish Arabic, but Corriente regards it as much earlier (ibid.:24).

(c) JAr **míguš* > *mígaš*: after a velar, /u/ could sometimes > /a/ in Spanish Arabic, for example, Ar *al-qunnabī* > SpAr *alcanavy* "made out of hemp" (ibid.:28); there are also sporadic cases of Ar *u* > *a* not following a velar, as in SpAr *maʿallam* "teacher" for ClAr *muʿallam* (ibid.:79); see ClAr *muṣḥaf* ~ *mi-* ~ AlgJAr *məṣḥ̆af* "book" (M. Cohen 1912:304), and the discussion of this term in chapter 5 this volume.

I assume that the voiced velar stop of the Persian original remained intact in Judeo-Arabic. Corriente claims that /g/ for Semitic *g was brought to Spain by Yemenis (1977:50; on the recency of *g* in Egyptian Arabic, see Blanc 1969 and Hopkins 1984:35-6; for details on the geography of *g* ~ *j* ~ *ž* in early and contemporary Arabic dialects, see Cantineau 1960:56–62). However, Spanish Arabic generally lacked *g*, and cases of Ar *j* > Sp *g* are rare and very often doubtful (Steiger 1932:185–86, *DCECH*, under *almogama*). The change of *ž* (< *g^y) > *g* is attested in Moroccan and Western Algerian (Oran) dialects of Arabic before a syllable with *s* or *z*, and sometimes *š*, for example, AlgAr *gäzzār* "butcher" (~ ClAr *jazzār*), MorAr *gīš* "sultan's guard on a trip" (~ ClAr *jayš* "army"; Cantineau 1960:61).

If the Iberian Jews had inherited the name from Greek, then the chain of events could be reconstructed as follows:

Gk *magos* > Ar **máguš* > *migaš*:

(aa) Gk *magos* > JAr **mágus* in accordance with the stress rule cited in (a);

(bb) JAr **mágus* > **máguš*; Lat (and Gk) *s* > Ar *š* (see discussion of Lat *synagōga* "synagogue" > Ar *šnūġa* in chapter 4);

(cc) JAr **máguš* > *migaš* as in rules (b-c) above.

There is some additional evidence for the proselyte origins of the indigenous Jewish communities of Arabia that is of more limited value, given the relative lateness of documentation:

(a) The north Italian Jewish traveler, Ovadia ben Avraham of Bertinoro (c.1450–c.1510), noted c.1488 that fierce Jewish tribes in Arabia were called "giants" (Newby 1988:101–102). This suggests that Jews had political independence or at least participated in military campaigns; if so, it is not unreasonable to posit a non-Jewish origin for these Jews.

There was also an identification of Jews and giants in those parts of Europe that were periodically subject to Turkic Avar military raids and control between the 5th and 7th centuries; I interpreted this association as a reflection of the fact that Avars had converted to Judaism (1993c:196–98). Historians of the Jews have yet to comment on the spectacular discovery by (ex-)Yugoslav archaeologists in 1976 of an Avar necropolis at Čelarevo, Vojvodina (Serbia), thought to date from the 8th century, that contained numerous brick fragments with Jewish motifs and one Hebrew inscription (ibid.:30 and Bunardžić 1980).

(b) In an enormous sweep of territory, encompassing Europe, North Africa, Yemen, Buxara, the Caucasus, Iran, China, Cochin, and the Crimea, local Jews have a tradition that the Jewish settlements in these areas are extremely old, often predating the birth of Christ. The historian Bernard Weinryb dismissed these traditions as devoid of factual basis on the grounds that these Jewish communities all preserved post-70 A.D. forms of Judaism and talmudic traditions (1962: 449, 451). Weinryb's scepticism is unjustified, since these traditions may reflect the attempts by proselytes to Judaism, or their descendants, to defend their historically justified claims to a local origin. Also the argument of post-exilic forms of Judaism and talmudism is not convincing since these could have been adopted by the Jewish diaspora communities at a later date; note that the Talmud was brought to

Europe and North Africa only by the close of the first millennium (see following discussion and Wexler 1993c:217–18).

Aside from the recorded acts of conversion cited earlier, there is evidence for conversion, as well as the rise of syncretistic Judeo-Muslim beliefs and practices among Jewish communities in the Eastern Arab countries. In a book written in Baghdad, c.980, Abu Bakr al-Baqillani described the Jews as consisting of Rabbanites (the majority sect which accepted the authority of the Talmud), Karaites (who rejected the authority of the Talmud), Samaritans, and Issawites (ʿĪsawiyya). The latter was a sect founded by an Iranian Jew who regarded Christ and Muḥammad as prophets whose teachings did not annul the teachings of Judaism (Brunschvig 1954:226); the Issawites were ultimately absorbed by the Karaites in the 10th century. ʿAli ibn Ḥazm, the grandson of a Spanish Christian convert to Islam, who lived from 994 to 1064, encountered some Jews who espoused views close to those of the Issawites (Perlmann 1948–49:280). On the existence of a Jewish sect with Christian overtones in pre-Islamic Egypt, see Golb 1965:260. According to Nemoy, the Karaites (unfortunately, he does not specify where or when) also regarded Christianity as a Jewish sect, though one which had gone much further afield than others (1974:698). In some cases, syncretistic beliefs may have resulted from ignorance of other religions, for example Abu ʿUthman ʿAmr ibn-Baḥr al-Jaḥiz (d. 868–69) of Iraq apparently thought, along with many other Muslims, that the Jews "believed" in Christ (N. Roth 1983b:186).

Turning to North Africa, there is considerable discussion of the Jewish origins or Judaizing practices of many indigenous Berber tribes (Monceaux 1902a, 1902b, le Bohec 1981a, 1981b, and the detailed discussion in Hiršberg 1963, 1965; the absence of relevant Berber topics in Attal's bibliography from 1973 is astonishing; see also chapter 3 this volume). Significantly, those scholars who downplay the proselyte component in the North African Jewish communities are unable to explain how and when ethnic Palestinian Jews might have reached North Africa. For example, the Jews are said variously to have come to North Africa from the Eastern Mediterranean together with the Phoenicians, the documented Jewish settlements in Egypt and Cyrenaica (present-day eastern Libya) during the Ptolemy (or Lagide) dynasty (between 330–23 B.C.), Arabia during the reign of King David to Ethiopia, and from there to the Sahara, or Palestine after the Roman conquest in 70 A.D. (Camps

1982:59). The inability of historians to substantiate any of these hypothetical paths of emigration could reflect the ravages of time on the historical records or the fact that Palestinian Jewish migration to North Africa (as distinct from "Jewish" migration from other locales such as Yemen, Ethiopia or Egypt) actually never took place.

Conversion to Judaism in North Africa and Spain

A central topic that has long been debated by scholars, but that has generated little in the way of innovative scholarship in the last few years, is the extent to which non-Jewish converts to Judaism might have contributed to the *Iberian* Jewish community (see previous discussion this chapter). For a number of scholars, massive conversion to Judaism in North Africa is a foregone conclusion (Voinot 1948:103, Poliakov 1961:13, Chouraqui 1968:xvi, 21, 23, 38, Mourant, Kopeć and Domaniewska-Sobczak 1978:30). Mourant et al., also claim to identify a North African, Iraqi, and Egyptian origin for some of the genetic features of the Sephardic Jews (ibid.:43–44).

The first reference to Jewish Berbers appears in the writings of the 12th-century Moroccan Muslim geographer-cartographer al-Idrisi (Levtzion 1982:254); later Muslim, Christian, and Jewish writers confirmed and often amplified this claim. For example, the Tunisian Muslim historian, ʽAbd ar-Raḥman ibn Xaldun (1332–1406) provided a list of Berber Jewish tribes (1:[1852]:208–209). The Spanish Christian Luis del Mármol Carvajal proposed that the Moroccan Muslims were originally Jews (2:1573:fol 11r, cited by Ángel de Bunes Ibarra 1989:132). The Muslim writer al-Maqqari from Tlemcen, Algeria wrote in the 17th century that the Islamic invaders of Spain included Jewish Berbers (S. Katz 1937:116). The tradition that the North African Jews descended from Berbers did not surface in Jewish writings until the 16th century (Simon 1946, Pérès 1953:268–69, Hiršberg 1:1965:106, Didier 1981:94, Camps 1982 and de Felipe 1990). In addition, there is an oft quoted tradition that the Berbers are of Eastern Mediterranean, specifically Philistine, origin. An early Jewish reference for this claim is Avraham ben David ha-Levi ibn Da'ud (c.1110–80; in his *Sefer hakabala* 1160–61; Krauss 1935:406). Of course, how reliable are these "transported" or "recalibrated" ethnonyms? Note that in the Balkans, the Sephardim used the term "Philistines" to denote the Armenians (M. Weinreich 3:1973:129), and Punic speakers also had a tradition of calling themselves Canaanites, according to the Berber St. Augustine (d.430) (ibid.:298). See also the discussion of redefined Jewish ethnonyms (due usually to emigration) in chapter 1 this volume.

Other scholars cast doubts on the importance of conversion in the ethnogenesis of the North African and Iberian Jews. For example, Hiršberg, while admitting a strong Berber influence on the customs and superstitions of the North African Jews, denies a significant Berber component in their ethnic makeup (in part, apparently, because of his erroneous belief that the Jews never wrote in Berber: 1:1965:108–109; see also Galand-Pernet and Zafrani 1970). Instances of conversion are difficult to ascertain due to our ignorance of what conversion processes entailed. Since the only African site mentioned in the Talmud is Carthage (in reference to rabbis), we may assume that talmudic Judaism was only (or predominantly) strong there, while in the Roman provinces of Numidia and Mauretania, Jewish customs may have become merged with pagan customs (le Bohec 1981a:169–70).

In the recent quincentennial literature commemorating the expulsion of the Jews from the Kingdom of Spain in 1492, the belief in widespread conversion to Judaism in the African arena has again surfaced:

> By 1492, the Jews, like the rest of the Iberian population, comprised a racially mixed but distinctively Iberian community. Their small numbers in the Roman days had continuously swelled with people of indigenous stock and periodically with immigrants from Africa and Asia (M. A. Cohen 1992:3).

While this statement is in part a repetition of an earlier unsubstantiated claim that the Jewish population spawned by the original Roman Jewish settlers in the pre-Islamic period was the immediate source of the post-Islamic Jewish population (Olagüe 1969:129), M. A. Cohen's remarks further on about the ethnic makeup of the Iberian Jewish community following the Muslim invasion of the Peninsula in 711 are innovative. According to him, the Jewish community comprised indigenous Visigothic Jews (including returning exiles, presumably from North Africa), immigrants from other Muslim lands (I suppose he means North Africa, Egypt, Iraq, and Yemen), and undetermined masses of non-Jews who adopted Judaism in numbers that:

> in all likelihood, [were] comparable to the massive non-Muslim adoption of Islam, particularly in the tenth and eleventh centuries (1992:17).

This is an improvement over the noncomittal statement by Stillman, that:

> Islamic Spain at the dawn of the ninth century must have had a very large Jewish population whose ranks were continually swelled by immigration from the Levant and North Africa (1979a:56).

The overwhelming majority of Spanish Muslims were converted indigenous pagans, Christians, and Jews; the Arab and Berber invaders (especially the former) constituted only a fraction of the total Iberian Muslim population. Hence, Cohen's suggestion that the *overwhelming majority* of the Iberian Jews were of non-Jewish stock is dramatic, and echoes the claims that Voinot and others had made earlier about the Moroccan Jews:

> The overwhelming majority of Moroccan Jews do not have Israelite blood. The indigenous predominate... Moreover, there undoubtedly exist among the elements that come from Europe, a rather large number of converted Slavs, Vandals, Goths, Visigoths, and Iberians (1948:103).

The innovative flavor of Cohen's pronouncements can best be appreciated by comparison with Stillman who does not have a single entry on the topic of conversion to Judaism in his survey of the Jews in Arab lands (1979b).

Unfortunately, Cohen makes no attempt to document his innovative claims with fresh evidence, or to specify whether non-Jews joined the Jewish communities in North Africa, Spain, or in both territories (ibid.:8, 10, 24, 29). In no case does he enumerate the language(s) of each group, information that could ultimately have been of great use to him. It is unclear if Cohen's noncitation of evidence reflects his reluctance to trust the historical documentation or contemporary testimonies of alleged Jewish ancestry from Berber and Arab groups in North Africa. This evidence should, however, be taken into account.

For example, Abitbol mentions the existence of south Tunisian Arabs who are called by the Muslims *yahūd al-ʿarab* "Jewish Arabs" (or "the Jews of the Arabs?") and by the Jews *baḥucim*, an innovative Hebraism meaning literally "outside" plus the Hebrew plural suffix (1982:243, fn 43, Camps 1982:58 and chapter 3 this volume). It is difficult to interpret the significance of these facts. The repeated debates over the interpretation of sparse, and often fragmentary, historical documentation can probably never be resolved, so long as historians restrict themselves to the extant historical materials alone. The best evidence to support Cohen's dramatic claim is linguistic and, to a lesser extent, ethnographic, since only such evidence can be subjected to an examination within a system of interlocking oppositions; this property allows us to guarantee that the data are likely to be old and facilitates reconstruction of those stages for which there is no written attestation.

Conversion to Judaism might not have been restricted to Berber communities. Punic (i.e., North African Phoenician) speakers may also have espoused Judaism, given the facility with which Aramaic-speaking Jews could have intermarried with speakers of closely related Punic; in addition, Jews and Phoenicians (both in North Africa and in their eastern Mediterranean homeland, now Lebanon) would have shared a common culture and mythology. The Punic language apparently survived in parts of North Africa up to the 4th and even early 5th century A.D., for example, in Tripolitania (what is now eastern Algeria and western Libya; Millar 1968:133). Christian (Donatist) opponents of Orthodox Christianity in North Africa during the Vandal domination (429–534) even wrote in Punic (Voinot 1948:100, Brown 1968 and Röllig 1980:297).

Prior to the arrival of the Muslims, there is evidence of Christian opposition to Jewish proselyte activity in North Africa, for example, the Church Council of Carthage (near modern-day Tunis) in 336 prohibited intermarriage between Christians and Jews and the circumcision of slaves held by Jews (Laredo 1954:170), and St. Augustine complained in the 5th century that the bishop of Tozeur (Thusurus) Judaized (Monceaux 1902b:217). A rare reflection of nonorthodox forms of Judaism is the existence of mixed Jewish-Christian cemeteries in North Africa (Blondheim 1925:xxi, fn 8). Biritual burial is also found in Rome at the beginning of the Christian era, and in Roman Pannonia (now southern Hungary and neighboring areas of ex-Yugoslavia), as the mixed Avar-Jewish graves at Čelarevo, Vojvodina show (see previous discussion).

The arrival of the Arabs in North Africa in the late 7th century only led to the superficial Islamization of many Berbers, which meant that in principle the latter could have still continued to be receptive to some Jewish practices, including those which did not find immediate parallels in Islam (Nahon 1909:259). For example, Berbers remained pagan for several centuries after their official conversion to Islam, in Kairouan c. 850, and around Igli, the capital of the southern Moroccan province of Sūs, in the late 11th century; according to the Tunisian historian ibn Xaldun (1332–1406), the Berber tribes living between Tripoli and Tangiers accepted and rejected Islam no less than twelve times (Lewicki 1967:143–44). On syncretistic Christian-Muslim beliefs among Moroccan Berber groups closely related to the Barġawaṭa as late as the mid-16th century, see Marcy 1936:48, fn 1. The Lamtuna tribe of Berbers that migrated to Spain in the late 11th century was also only nominally Muslim. The institutionalization of Christianity in Spain was also an extremely slow process, extending through several centuries (for rich bibliographical references, see Baldinger 1972:220–21, fn 278).

In the 8th and 9th centuries, doctrinal deviations and heresies proliferated both within Spanish Christianity and Moroccan Islam (Harnack 5:1903:281–83, Castro 1984:114, fn 23, Guichard 1985:19). For example, some of the Barġawaṭa Berbers who settled on the Atlantic coast of Morocco between Salé and Safi created a syncretistic Christian-Muslim religion at the end of the 8th century (Oliver Asín 1973:368). All of the extant Berber and Arab ethnographic practices should be painstakingly combed for references to conversion (in any direction). There is a Moroccan Berber (Tamazight) festival, during which one of the characters is dressed up as a Jew. According to practitioners of this festival, the Aïth Ndhir, if such a person dies within forty days, he dies as a Jew (Laoust 1921:294). Could this mirror the ease and frequency with which conversion to Judaism was once carried out?

Close Berber-Jewish links in Spain also provide an environment which might have been conducive to Berber conversion to Judaism. It is interesting that the "Golden Age" of Iberian Jewish literature, composed in Arabic and "Hebrew" (there are no extant Berber texts, whether Jewish or otherwise, produced in Spain), encompasses the period of the 10th to the late 12th century. This period overlaps with the reign of the Zirid state of Granada (1012–90), which for a time encompassed other regions, for example, Málaga. Furthermore, Granada was the only Muslim city in which a Jew, Šmuel ibn Nagrella ha-Nagid (d. 1055), exercised the powerful position of vizir. The Berbers also exercised political power for a time in northern Spanish regions where Jewish culture is known to have flourished. For example, Toledo was occupied by the Berber family, the banu Dhu an-Nun (1032–85), until the city was captured by Alfonso VI of León and Castile. In Zaragoza, Aragón, the banu Hud Berbers held control from 1039 until they were overpowered by the Christians in 1141 (for a description of the spread of Berber princedoms in Spain, see Pérès 1962 and Wasserstein 1985). It is noteworthy that there were political alliances between Berbers and Jews in the 11th century

(Glick 1979:184). In Spain, Abu Bakr ibn ʿAmmar (1031–83) wrote a poem to the king of Seville in which he identified the Jews and Berbers as the same people (N. Roth 1983b:199).

The first indication of Jewish proselyte activity in Christian Spain dates from the Elvira Church Council of 306, that inveighed against intermarriage between Jews and Christians and against the participation of pagans and Christians in Jewish religious rituals (S. Katz 1937:124). This is not the only sign of Jewish proselytizing activity from before the Muslim invasion; a Jewish proselyte group of unknown age and origin was noted in Granada in the 4th century (Thouvenot 1943:211), and there are mentions of attempts to Judaize Christians in the 6th and 8th centuries (Ayuso Marazuela 1944 and Vega 1941, respectively). The late 8th century witnessed a rash of Christian heresies in northern Spain, some with Judaizing tendencies (Ashtor 1:1960:52, 274, fn 18). Bachrach suggests that Visigothic Arians in the late 6th century in Spain might have found it more desirable to become Jews than Christians (1973:13), but he provides no evidence for this claim. If M. A. Cohen is correct that at the time of the Muslim invasion only about 15 percent of the Iberian population actually professed Christianity (1992:6–7), then the weakness of the official church would have provided ample room for proselytizing activities of all sorts, including Jewish; furthermore, the small size of the Christian population would have required the latter to intermarry with pagans and Jews (Hefele 1907:231).

The Christian evidence, together with some Jewish epigraphic data (see the *IHE*), establishes a Jewish presence in the Iberian Peninsula before the arrival of Afro-Asian Jews in 711. The pre-Islamic Roman or Greek Jews in Spain were descendants of Palestinian Jewish emigrants to Europe and their European non-Jewish spouses, and European converts to Judaism. An open question is whether the pre-711 Jewish communities still existed at the time of the Muslim invasions, given the periodic Visigothic persecutions of the Jews that generated the migration of the latter to North Africa. If any Iberian Jews survived the Visigothic period to witness the Muslim invasion of the Peninsula in 711, then I can include a minor European component in the Iberian Jewish "rebirth" after 711.

There is some important non-linguistic evidence to suggest that European Jews could have participated in the Iberian Jewish communities after 711. The historian Cecil Roth noted (1953) that an archaic Jewish artistic tradition that had roots in the synagogue wall paintings from Dura-Europos (northeast Syria), including human representation, surfaced not only in Christian art, but in Jewish art from Spain, especially from 14th-century Catalunya. Roth attempted to explain how such a tradition might have survived in the iconoclastic Islamic environment in which most Iberian Jews resided after 711. The smoothest explanation is that an ancient Jewish (nontalmudic) artistic tradition of Near Eastern (Syrian) origin was retained in the north of Spain. Roth noted that there were illuminated manuscripts of the Hebrew Bible in the early centuries of the Christian era in the Near East (ibid.:44). The conventional subject matter comprised a representation of the interior of the sanctuary or the synagogue, centering around the tabernacle or the Torah shrine. The subject matter of the Jewish bible illustrations (none of which has survived) was taken over by the Christians and appears in early Christian book art. It is probable that a human figure was sometimes incorporated in the conventional picture in the Hebrew manuscripts. Though there are no extant copies of illuminated Hebrew Bibles accompanied by a full cycle of representational illustrations, there is an example in the frescoes from the synagogue at Dura-Europos, northeast Syria, that date from the 3rd century A.D. (they are now housed in the National Museum, Damascus). This artistic tradition was in vogue among Near Eastern Jews between the 3rd century up to the rise of Islam in the 7th century.

However, even if it could be shown that a pre-Islamic Jewish iconographic tradition was transplanted from the Near East to Spain in the pre-Islamic period and survived the Islamic invasion of 711, there is no evidence that it had much impact on the new Iberian Jewish culture that was developing primarily on a North African basis. Note the remark of Ṣa'id al-Andalusi, who lived in the 11th century, that:

> previously, [the Spanish Jews] had recourse to Jews of Baghdad in order to learn the law of their faith and in order to adjust the calendar and determine the dates of their holidays (quoted by Stillmann 1979b:60).

Al-Andalusi's remark is an important indication that if some of the Romance-speaking Jews who resided in the Peninsula during the Visigoth persecutions indeed were still there in 711, they would not have been in a position to provide the masses of North African Jewish emigrés with instruction in Judaism or communal leadership. There is no evidence whatsoever that the European Jews in pre-Islamic Spain had access to the Hebrew-Judeo-Aramaic texts of the Bible or Talmud (see also discussion in chapter 4 this volume).

It is precisely the migration of Judeo-Aramaic-speaking Babylonian (Iraqi), Arabian, and possibly even Palestinian Jews to Europe during the 9th and 10th centuries, if not earlier, that was to provide the impetus and sources for "Judaization" among the European Jews and Judaizers in the early second millennium (chapter 5 this volume). I presume that it was these Near Eastern immigrants who brought the text of the Talmud (both the Palestinian and the more important Babylonian version?), first to southern Italy and the Iberian Peninsula, and subsequently, to the Germano-Slavic lands (J. Mann 1916–17:477–87, Clemen 1931:42, M. Weinreich 1:1973:352, 3:377–79, Wexler 1993c, chapter 7). This is not to suggest that the new Iraqi, Palestinian, and Arabian Jewish emigrés necessarily comprised a larger percentage of ethnic Jews than the Jewish population of North Africa, Spain, or northern Europe, but rather that only the Near Eastern Jewish scholarly élite seems to have achieved proficiency in Jewish scholarship. This is perhaps because the colloquial Aramaic language of Jews throughout the Near East was very similar to the Aramaic language in which much of the Jewish liturgical literature was composed. Furthermore, by virtue of being Aramaic speakers, the Iraqi (and possibly Yemenite and Palestinian) Jews would also have been in a position to understand the Hebrew Bible much more readily than Jews who did not speak a Semitic language. The rise of a vast Arabic-speaking Jewry—between Arabia and Iraq in the east and Spain and North Africa in the west—may have encouraged the study of the Old Semitic liturgical literature of the Jews, given the closeness of Biblical Hebrew and Judeo-Aramaic to Arabic.

It is difficult to determine the extent to which the Sephardic Jews might have included Palestinian Jewish ethnic forbears, and the significance of the Palestinian Jewish component (as opposed to Near Eastern and European proselytes) in diffusing Judaism outside of Palestine in the early centuries of the Christian era, since there is no reliable way to plot the emigration of Palestinian Jews to Spain either directly or via Rome and other European locales or North Africa.

In principle, there are three ways in which a Palestinian Jewish ethnic element in the Sephardic ethnogenesis might be established:

(a) We can collect information on the acts of conversion to Judaism by individuals and groups in Spain, as well as in the Asian and African lands from which prospective immigrants to Spain might have come.

(b) We can examine the Jewish and non-Jewish elements in the Sephardic linguistic and ethnographic baggage.

The significant non-Jewish component in early Sephardic ethnography and religious practice stands in sharp contrast with the growing use of Hebrew terminology in the late medieval period; while the former is an indication of widespread acts of conversion to Judaism that I believe took place in the first millennium and shortly thereafter, the Hebrew terminology reflects a subsequent desire to "Judaize" established non-Jewish practices that could not be readily uprooted, in the face of community opposition. Despite the process of Judaization (and concomitant Hebraization), that may have begun in Spain as early as the 15th century, and which gathered momentum in the Sephardic diasporas, there are still many non-Hebrew terms designating aspects of the Jewish religion in broad use among the Sephardic Jews that allow us to reconstruct the manner in which the Sephardic Jewish community was constituted in North Africa.

(c) We could try to identify colloquial Old Hebrew elements in each Jewish language that might allow us to reconstruct possible paths and relative chronologies of migration from Palestine to southern Europe and North Africa, as well as historical links between various Jewish diaspora communities (Wexler 1990a). However, this avenue of research is problematic, since a reliable corpus of common colloquial Old Hebrew elements in Jewish languages is small.

The plethora of ecclesiastical bulls in Spain and most other parts of Christian Europe denouncing Christian participation in Jewish religious rituals and intermarriage between the 4th and 13th centuries suggests that neither formal conversion nor informal association with the Jewish community was an uncommon occurrence (S. Katz 1937:16, 21, 49, 53, 98 and Wexler 1993c, chapter 6 give non-Iberian parallels). The *Siete partidas* of Alfonso the Wise (1252–84) not only declared that intermarriage was forbidden, but also that Jews were forbidden to read anti-Jewish literature (Carpenter 1986:95). The church council of Tarragona, Catalunya of 1234 decreed that Muslims and Jews could only convert to Christianity, but not to one another's religion (Grayzel 1933, xxvii, Baer 1/2:1936:46, Didier 1981:103). A particularly curious example of "reciprocal conversion" is illustrated by Bodo, a deacon at the court of Louis the Pious of the Holy Roman Empire in Mainz who converted to Judaism at Zaragoza in 838; there he engaged in polemics with the Christian nationalist, Álvaro, who was himself of Jewish extraction (Lévi-Provençal 1:1950:234, Pérès 1962:726)!

Paradoxically, the Christian insistence on public religious disputes with Jews and Muslims, such as the famous dispute between Moše Cohen de Tordesillas and Catholic authorities in 1375 (Loeb 1889:228–29, Castro 1914 and Cardaillac 1977:156), though intended to induce the Jews to convert to Christianity, may also have encouraged Christian conversion to Judaism by spreading knowledge of Judaic practices and beliefs among Christians. Jewish converts to Islam or Christianity, either by force or volition, might also have introduced non-Jewish practices to Judaism on the occasion of their return to their ancestral religion, for example, in Granada, Jews were converted by force to Islam in the late 11th century, but subsequently were allowed to revert to Judaism (Didier 1981:99, 101). On cyclical conversion, from Judaism to Christianity and back to Judaism, see the documents assembled by Baer (1:1929:201, 207, 264, 610, and 653 that present examples from Játiva 1311, Tarragona 1313, Valencia 1331, Monzon 1389, and Barcelona 1391, respectively).

In North Africa and Spain, a major source of converts to Judaism would have been the large slave population—Muslim slaves in areas dominated by the Christians, Christian slaves in areas dominated by the Muslims. Despite the existence of laws in both domains against conversion except to the dominant state religion, Islam and Christianity, respectively, there is ample documentation in both Jewish and non-Jewish sources that the slaves of Jews often assumed the religion of their owners. A graphic illustration of the conversion of household slaves of Jews comes from the "Sarajevo Haggadah," believed to have been written in Aragón around 1350; the manuscript (named after its present location in the National Museum of Sarajevo, Bosnia-Hercegovina) contains an illustration of a black woman seated at the foot of the Passover table together with a Jewish family. Verber assumes she was an African who had converted to Judaism, and as such, would have been allowed to participate in the home ritual (1983:35). Given the presence of proselytizing Jews in the western Sudan in the 12th century, according to the Muslim traveler, al-Idrisi (Ceuta, Morocco 1100–d. 1166), I would not rule out the possibility that some Africans might have been brought to Spain as Jews (Williams 1930 and Monteil 1951). The skeletal remains of blacks are also found in three graves in the Barcelona Jewish necropolis at Montjuich that was used between the years 1091 and 1391 (Prevosti 1951:82). On black slaves in the service of Jews in Marrakesh, Morocco, see Voinot

1948:52. The Mexican Inquisition proceedings between 1646 and 1738 mention several people accused of Judaizing who were described as mulattos (Liebman 1971:392, 399, 1974:40, 57, 127, 134); it is significant that crypto-Judaism spread to the offspring of marriages between Jews and African or Indian slaves.

The participation of Jews in the international slave trade between northern Europe and Spain and North Africa, up until the end of the first millennium, may have facilitated the conversion of slaves to Judaism; the slave trade continued longer, but it appears that the Jewish role in the trade declined after this date. (For further discussion on the role of Jews in the transshipment of European slaves to Spain and North Africa, see Verlinden 1955–77, 1958, 1974a, 1974b, 1977, 1979, 1983, Lewicki 1958:67–88, 1964a, 1964b, and Swoboda 1975). Verlinden specifically notes that the Iberian Christian clergy feared that Slavic slaves would convert to Judaism or Islam (1983:123). It is difficult to identify Slavs in Iberian Arabic documents since they always appear in the records bearing Arabic names (Canard 1958:131, fn 269), and the term "Slav" in Arabic was often given to slaves of any European extraction. In fact, all ethnic groups in Islamic Spain tend to have Arabic names—at least in Arabic documents (on a descendant of Goths who bore an Arabic name, see Melvinger 1955:28). It would be useful to collect the names of Jews who converted to Islam; for 15th-century examples from Fès, Morocco, see García-Arenal 1987:141.

Many of the European slaves sent to Spain were pagan Slavs of Baltic and East German origin (Wexler 1993c, chapter 6); such slaves were being transshipped to Catalunya as late as the early 15th century. Verlinden (1967) discusses the case of Bosnian Christian sectarians or Bogomils who became slaves, Camós Cabruja (1946) discusses Tatar, Greek, Bulgarian, and Bosnian slaves in Barcelona in 1382, while Canard (1958) describes Slavic slaves in the service of the Fatimids in the late 10th century. Binyamin ben Yona de Tudela, a Navarran Jew (c.1130–c.1175) who traveled widely in Europe and the Near East, has two words in his Hebrew travelogue that Wasserstein identified as Slavic (1983, disagreeing with Wolf [1977] who had rejected a Slavic identification of the two words in question); in view of the fact that de Tudela did not personally visit any Slavic lands, I wonder if Slavicisms could not have been acquired in Spain from Slavic slaves (Wasserstein did not raise this possibility). One of the forms in question, *w'ywrgys* "squirrel" bears a strong similarity to Sor *wjewjerčo* "small squirrel," *wjewjerčka* "squirrel" or possibly Czech *veveřice* (the pagan Sorbs were one of the main Slavic groups to be sold into slavery and the group most receptive to Judaism, in my view; Wexler 1993c); the other alleged Slavism, *zblyn'c* "sable," due to the *z-* and *-n-*, may, in fact, be of immediate Italian origin (It *zibellino* vs. Sor *sobot*).

Documented contacts between Spanish Jews and the Slavic lands date from the end of the first millennium. The only Jewish slaver known to us by name—the Catalan diplomat-traveller Ibrahim ibn Ya'qub from Tortosa—traveled to Slavic areas c.965. According to accounts of the Persian geographer ibn Xordadhbeh (d. c.912; 1889:114, 153), the peripetetic Jewish merchants, known as the Radhanites (of Iraqi origin, if we accept Gil [1974]), spoke a variety of languages (including Arabic and Slavic) and traveled back and forth between Spain and Asia in the 9th century; these merchants also dealt in slaves, *inter alia*, possibly of Slavic origin too (Lewicki 1969:21, 29, 79–80, citing ibn al-Faqih, early 10th century).

I know of only two possible references to Slavic slaves in the possession of Iberian Jews in the Hebrew writings of Šlomo ben Adret, the well-known rabbi from Barcelona (c.1230–c.1310): "Re'uven who had a Canaanite or Ishmaelite [Arab] slave" (cited by Assaf 1943:238, fn 114). The meaning of the Hebrew term "Canaanite" is problematic: in North European (Ashkenazic) "Hebrew" writing, *kna'an* referred invariably to Slavs (which might be the meaning here since the Canaanites were reduced to slavery, according to the biblical accounts), but in Yemen (and other Arabic-speaking areas?), it denoted African blacks (Goitein 1931:365); in view of the tradition that the Carthaginians who settled in modern-day Tunisia descended from Canaanites—discussed earlier—the reference might even have been to Tunisian slaves. Bunis observes that the Serbian Sephardi Papo (1862) used He *kna'ani* in the meaning of (Southern) Slav, but in the non-Slavicized Judeo-Spanish spoken in Izmir at the turn of this century the term only denoted the biblical Canaanites (1993:264). The non-colloquial status and relative newness of the term is suggested by the fact that the letter *'ayin* is not pronounced as /x/ in Judeo-Spanish, but as zero in this Hebrew word (chapter 4 this volume discusses variant pronunciations of this letter).

The same ben Adret also alludes to the hypersensitivity of some Jews about the slave origins of their ancestors; according to him, two Jews accused of being descendants of slaves tried to clear their names at Austerlitz (= Slavkov, Moravia). The venue suggests they might have been of Slavic origin. For discussion of slaves (though not necessarily of Slavic origin) in the writings of Maimonides (1135–1204), ben Adret and Ašer ben Yexiel (1250–1327/8), see Neuman 2:1942: 188, 202, 209, 278, fn 22, 287, fn 47 (where Muslim slaves are mentioned), 329, fn 179, and Finkel 1990. On Maimonides' favorable attitude to proselytism, especially of Christian converts, see Goitein 2:1971:304; on slave girls who became Jews, see ibid.:1:1967:139, 1962, and 5:1988:143, 147–50. On references to conversion in the Cairo Genizah manuscripts, see ibid.: 2:1971:79, 129, 153, 299–311, 416, fn 18; for references in the Genizah manuscripts to slaves, see ibid.:189, 257, 305, 311, 349, and 402. On the possession of slaves by Jews noted in Christian documents, see Baer 1:1929:144 (for Figueras 1285), ibid.:202 (Játiva 1311), 569 (Valencia 1369—where the Barcelona Jewish community was obliged to sell its "Tatar and Turkish" slaves) and 919 (Navarra 1115; on Tatar and other slaves, see the earlier reference to Camós Cabruja 1946).

Ben Adret describes the order of blessings to be recited upon the initiation of proselytes (Neuman 2:1942:325, fn 93); a Jewish ritual concerned with proselytes could only exist if the need arose repeatedly. In mentioning an old custom of putting gold and silver crowns from the Torah scrolls on the heads of children and those called up to read from the Torah in the synagogue service, ben Adret records his opposition to the placing of the crowns on the heads of non-Jewish slaves (I. Epstein 1925:59).

A future study should explore the changing attitudes of Jews toward conversion through time and space. Attitudes of the Sephardic Jews to conversion may offer a clue to incipient Judaization processes (chapter 5 this volume). For example, the decision of the poet-physician, Yehuda (Abu l-Ḥasan) ben Šmuel ha-Levi (Tudela, c.1070–1141) to rank converts to Judaism as inferior to born Jews suggests that this practicing Jew (who eventually emigrated to Palestine after being disappointed that the Messiah did not arrive in 1130) may have doubted that conversions were always carried out strictly according to the *halaxah*. This attitude might also be in part a consequence of his theory of Jewish chosenness and of his selective, particularistic reading of rabbinic sources (this is the view of Lasker 1990), or, alternatively, it was a reaction to Christian and Muslim prohibitions against Jewish proselytizing activities, and fear that the Jewish community was being (or had already been) exposed to too many non-Jewish practices.

By the 13th century, overt widescale Jewish missionizing was virtually over in the Christian areas, but the church continued to voice concern through the 15th century that Jews would convert their non-Christian slaves (Carpenter 1986:95). Such pronouncements suggest that the practice of Jews holding non-Jewish slaves existed almost up to the expulsion. Jews who circumcised Muslim slaves were being admonished by Juan I of Castile as late as 1380 (Neuman 2:1942:212, Baron 1962:43, fn 1). A contemporaneous mention of Jews holding non-Jewish slaves (in this case, Muslims) comes also from Mallorca in 1381, some 150 years after the island was reoccupied by the Christians (Gais 1970:29). The Ordinance of Fernando I in Barcelona in 1413 specifically inveighed against proselytism. On the prosecution of proselytes to Judaism in Calatayud in 1327, see Neuman 2:1942:196 and also ibid.:102–105, 325, fn 89. As late as 1465, the church was declaring that Jews could not hold slaves in Medina del Campo and Christians could not convert to Judaism (Baer 1/2:1936:330, Neuman 2:1942:212). For a general discussion of church pronouncements, encompassing Spain and other parts of Europe, see Grayzel 1933.

In some areas, Jews could hold slaves provided they were not Christians. For further discussion, see the remarks of the Catalan Franciscan friar Francesc Eiximenis, 1325–1409 in Viera 1985:207. Once Muslim lands were reconquered by the Christian forces, conversion of slaves to Judaism would have virtually ceased, since by Christian law, a Muslim slave could gain his freedom by converting to Christianity; under these circumstances, there would be less motivation for a Muslim to stay in the employ of Jewish owners or convert to Judaism—unless the Muslim felt more cultural and religious affinity with Jews. Discussed in detail later in this volume are the Inquisition protocols that Muslims practiced Jewish customs, and the report by the Spanish traveller de Haedo in 1612 (1927:112) that North African Jews held Christian slaves.

It may be possible to put an approximate terminal date on Jewish proselytizing in Iberian Muslim areas. Conversion of Christians and Jews to Islam seems to have been slow up until the 10th century, assuming massive proportions by around 1100 (Glick 1979:34); if these dates are accurate, that would mean the Jewish communities very likely received most of their non-Jewish converts before 1100, the date when many Arabic-speaking Jews began to resettle in the Christian north.

By and large, the Iberian Jewish records make little mention of conversion to Judaism, since acceptance of converts by the organized

Jewish community often resulted in severe punishment by the Christian authorities of both the Jewish converters and their Christian or Muslim converts; punishment was also meted out in the case of Jewish converts to Catholicism, and their descendants, who sought to revert to their ancestral religion. Consider the case of Juan de Ciudad, a Castilian Jewish convert to Catholicism who reentered the Jewish community at Huesca in 1465 through the auspices of rabbi Avraham ben Šem Tov Bibago (or Bivach); the Marrano in question was said to have been circumcised at that date (which suggests that he had not been circumcised as a Jew at birth?), after which time he emigrated to Jerusalem. Twenty-four years later, in 1489, the Inquisition sentenced several members of the Huesca Jewish community to the pyre for assisting in the defection of the convert (Sáenz-Badillos and Targarona Borrás 1988:6, 54).

Despite the knowledge in Spain that the Turkic Khazars had converted to Judaism, as discribed in the correspondence between the Khazars and Ḥasday ibn Šapruṭ, this dramatic act of mass conversion is barely noted in Jewish literature—either in Spain or elsewhere. There could have been three reasons for this silence: fear of arousing the wrath of the Christian and Muslim ecclesiastical and political authorities; suspicion that the conversion of the Khazars to Judaism might not have been sincere or according to orthodox practice; embarrassment over the fact that the Khazar kingdom was destroyed in the 10th century and its population dispersed. (Scholars are still unable to determine with certainty the fate of the Judaized Khazar population after the collapse of the kingdom; some of the Khazar Jews are believed to have joined the newly forming Ashkenazic Jewish communities in Eastern Europe and the existing Jewish communities in Iraq. For a bibliography of Khazar studies, see Wexler 1993c.)

At the same time, the dramatic conversion of the Khazars to Judaism in the 8th century (two centuries prior to the collapse of the Khazar Kingdom) may have inspired European Jews to engage in proselytism (Löwe 1988:168), an act that in turn might have provoked strong Christian ecclesiastical opposition. Perhaps Khazars migrated to Spain? After all, it was following the Khazar conversion that Archbishop Agobard of Lyon (816–40) expressed concern over Jewish preachers appearing in front of Christian audiences (ibid.:162–63, Battenberg 1990:54–55). It is well documented that fear of persecution in their countries of origin forced many European Christian converts to Judaism between the 11th and 14th centuries to take up residence in the Jewish communities in Muslim countries, primarily in Egypt; aside from the case of Bodo the Frank who converted to Judaism in Muslim Zaragoza in the 9th century, discussed earlier, I know of no other documented cases of Christian converts to Judaism (either known by name or anonymous) who sought refuge in Muslim Spain, but this may be because the converts were not famous or former Christian clergymen, like Bodo.

The Contribution of Women Converts to the Formation of the Sephardic Jews

There is varied linguistic evidence that non-Jewish females converted more readily to Judaism than males. For example, Jewish women tend to employ a higher percentage of non-Jewish names than Jewish men; this is true for Arabic-speaking areas such as contemporary Morocco (Abbou 1953:396–98) and Jerba, Tunisia (Udovitch and Valensi 1984:29), as well as for pre-expulsion Spain (see the names assembled in Baer 1929–36), and Moroccan Berber areas (Zafrani 1986:168). The reason why females might have been more inclined to join the Jewish community (either in a formal act of conversion or informally) is that orthodox Jewish conversion ritual does not require circumcision of women as it does of men. Moreover, traditional Jewish law posits transmission of Judaism to the offspring through the mother; hence, there is no need for the non-Jewish husband of a woman proselyte to undergo conversion (involving circumcision).

Another reason has been advanced to explain the higher frequency of non-Jewish names among women, i.e., that the latter do not participate in the synagogue ritual, and hence, do not need to have a Hebrew name; with very few exceptions, men require Hebrew names in the synagogue service, for example, when they are called up to read from the Torah (Zunz 1837:70–71). This argument need not obviate my claim that a higher percentage of non-Jewish names among women points to a higher conversion rate among women than among men. Jewish males often had two names—a Hebrew name for religious functions and for use in inner-Jewish situations and a non-Jewish name for use in the non-Jewish community (the latter might eventually become "Jewish" by default if they came to be used exclusively by Jews). In fact, in Arab Jewish communities, it was the custom to be called to the Torah by an Arab name as well; also in Ashkenazic circles two non-Jewish names acquired a liturgical function, for example (J)Gk *Aleksander* and the uniquely JGk

Kalonimos (the model for the later "He" *Šem-ṭov*, literally "good name"). Moreover, we cannot be sure that additional non-Hebrew names were not permitted in the synagogue ritual in earlier times. Hence, while I can agree with Goldberg that the use of Berber names by contemporary Libyan Jews does not indicate conclusively that the ancestors of the name-bearers had converted to Judaism (1972:247), I cannot accept Goldberg's reasoning that if Berbers had converted to Judaism they would have adopted Jewish names, as a symbolic breaking with their earlier identity (chapter 4 this volume).

The argument that women performed few religious roles in general, and none in the synagogue that would have required the use of a Hebrew name, loses its force when we examine the role of women in diaspora Jewish societies in the first millennium A.D. There is ample evidence from this period that women in many regions indeed enjoyed equality with men in the maintenance and construction of the synagogue and in the performance of the cult. The status of women in this early period stands in sharp contrast to their diminished role in European Jewish societies since the early 13th and 14th centuries. Though in some parts of Europe, the practice of giving intensive religious instruction to women may have persisted into the early 15th century. For example, an illustration in the "Darmstadt Haggadah" of Upper Rhine origin (dated c.1430) portrays teachers instructing a group of mainly female students (Wexler 1993c:102). The suppressed condition of women in contemporary orthodox Jewish circles should not influence our appreciation of the position women enjoyed in early diaspora Judaism. While we are relatively well informed about the status of women in Jewish society in Hellenistic and Roman Jewish society, much more research is needed on the role of women in later European and Afro-Asian Jewish communities. The linguistic evidence should prove instructive.

Contemporary MorJSp *rebísa* and SalJSp *rubísa* denote the wife of a rabbi or religious school teacher < *rebí, rubí* "rabbi" plus *-isa* feminine agentive suffix (~ Lat *-essa* or Gk *-issa*) (G. Pimienta 1991:138 and Nehama 1977, respectively). I wonder if an earlier additional meaning of this word might not have been "woman rabbi," since the Yiddish surface cognate, *rébecn*, means either rabbi's wife or erudite woman (for a discussion of this unique double Yiddish feminine suffix *-ecn* < Slavicized Gk *-issa*/Sl *-ica* plus G *-n*, see Wexler 1993c:100–101). Christian Latin texts from the early 14th century from Zaragoza and Huesca have references to a *sinoga de las mujeres* "synagogue of the women," which was apparently led by a *rabisse*. Alternatively, might the phrase refer to the women's section of the synagogue (discussed further below)? Nirenberg's interpretation of *rabisse* as "woman rabbi" is perfectly plausible (1991:181, fn 6), especially since the Inquisition protocols make frequent reference to women within the Marrano (or converso) community who were accused of performing religious functions. For further discussion, see also *profetissas* "Marrano prophetesses" (Rivkin 1957:202, fn 19, citing Lea 1906:194), as well as Sp *rabinista* in a 17th-century Christian document and *rabina* "woman rabbi" (Mexico 1649, discussed by Caro Baroja 2:1978:243 and Liebman 1964:105, #1150 [who glosses it as "wife of a rabbi"], 1971:98, 235, respectively). Note also the innovative "Hebraism" *cohena* "priestess" that appears in the *Cancionero de Baena* (1445–53, possibly written by a Jewish convert to Christianity; Schmid 1951:39) < He *kohen* "priest" (though in the first Ladino Bible "translation," from Istanbul 1547, the latter denoted "pagan priest"; "priestess" in Hebrew would ordinarily be *kohenet*). JAr *kanīsat al-muʿallima* "synagogue of the woman teacher" offers an Arabic parallel (cited by Goitein 3:1978:355, unfortunately, without indication of source and date).

Loupias is of the opinion that the role of women in transmitting crypto-Jewish religious beliefs to their children was more significant than in the transmission of beliefs among crypto-Muslims. He bases this judgement on the number of women hauled before the Inquisition courts on charges of Judaizing and Islamizing (1965:124, 126, fn 37). The details of Jewish ritual that appear in the Inquisition protocols make it unlikely that the church authorities were misinformed about the role of women in the allegedly crypto-Jewish communities. For further details on the role of women in Marrano communities, see Levine Melamed 1992.

The forebear of the term JSp *rebísa, rubísa* may be a Judeo-Greek or Judeo-Latin term, while the profession of woman rabbi may have its roots in either pagan Greek or Latin societies. In a number of Judeo-Greek inscriptions from Greece, Italy, and Malta spanning the period from the 2nd century B.C. to the 6th century A.D., we find repeated use of feminine nouns connected with important community roles performed by Jewish women, for example, Gk *arxēgissa* "(synagogue) founder," *presbetérēssa, arxisynagōgissa* "synagogue elder," Lat *pateressa* "synagogue functionary, board member" (curiously < Lat *pater* "father" and not from *māter* "mother": Brooten 1982, Trebilco 1991, chapter 5). These forms attest to the equality that women enjoyed with men in the performance of functions associated with the synagogue and the Jewish community at large.

An important desideratum of Jewish historical research is to establish the chronology and geography of the deterioration in the status of women in Jewish diaspora society. There is evidence that in Christian Spain, major changes may have taken place in the status of women not long before the expulsion of 1492. Two of the three surviving synagogue buildings in Spain, "El Tránsito" in Toledo and the one in Córdoba that were both constructed in the 14th century (i.e., when both cities were long in Christian hands), have a separate upper section for women worshippers which suggests that the latter played a purely passive role in the synagogue service. However, I. Epstein has noted that Iberian Jewish women could own and dispose of men's seats in the synagogue that they bought and sold (1925:63). Conversely, two illuminated manuscripts from 14th-century Aragón display men and women side by side in the synagogue, which implies the absence of segregated public worship (Metzger and Metzger 1982:61—citing the "Sarajevo" and "Kaufmann Haggadahs"; see also Kedourie 1979:76). Might there have been a difference in the status of women in Aragonese vs. Castilian and Andalusian society? The paucity of evidence makes any generalization difficult.

A comparison of Iberian and Germano-Slavic synagogue architecture is instructive. In Ashkenazic Northern Europe, a separate women's section is first attested in the 13th century as an appendage to southwest German synagogues that had been constructed earlier, for example those at Köln, Speyer, Worms. Yet, there are exceptions; the Regensburg synagogue that was constructed in the 14th century (and destroyed in 1519) shows no sign of ever having had a separate section for women (Krautheimer 1927 and Künzl 1988a:62–63, 65–66, 85, 1988b:89–90). In Poland, only synagogues constructed in the 16th century were provided with a women's section from the very outset. These data suggest that in northern Europe the custom of segregating women in the synagogue service may have begun in southwestern Germany, gradually spreading from there to Bavaria and the West Slavic lands.

An open question is whether the women's section in the synagogue could have spread from the Ashkenazic to the Sephardic Jews. We know that German Jewish scholars began to arrive in Spain (Toledo) in the early 14th century (chapters 3 and 5 this volume). The relative newness of the women's section is suggested by the very term used to designate the latter in the Balkans, for example, contemporary SalJSp *eznoga*, which, as recently as the mid-16th century, still denoted the entire synagogue building (its original meaning), SalJSp *'yšnwg'* /e$\overset{(\check{})}{s}$noga/ (Karo 1568:10b, cited by Bunis 1993a:21). This term has an Ibero-Romance phonetic shape (vs. [J]Ar *šnūġa*). I propose to derive both of these syncopated forms of Gk *synagōgē* from North African Romance; see chapter 4 this volume.

If the change in the meaning of *eznoga* had originated in Spain, then it might have developed in areas where another term for synagogue was in use; such an area could have been Catalunya or Valencia before 1492, where the building was ordinarily denoted by reflexes of Lat *schola* "school," or in the Balkans after 1492 where He *qahal* "Jewish community" assumed the meaning synagogue in Judeo-Spanish, now in the form *kal* (in Catalunya before 1492 *cal[l]* denoted the Jewish community, corresponding in Iberian non-Catalan areas to the Arabism *aljama*; chapter 5 this volume). The fusion of Catalan and non-Catalan Jewries began in earnest in Castile after the plagues of 1366–70 and 1378–85 had decimated the general Catalan population (Baron 10:1965:366, fn 33), and the nation-wide pogroms of 1391 had destroyed the Catalan Jewish communities. Valencian data are difficult to evaluate since this area was colonized from other parts of the country during the Reconquista.

Continuing with the assumption that the institution of a separate women's section in the synagogue may have developed in the Iberian Peninsula before 1492, it is tempting to hypothesize, however tentatively, that the institution had its roots either in Catalunya, perhaps less than a century before the expulsion of 1492, and possibly under the influence of neighboring Provençal Jewish practice, or in Castile/Andalusia under the influence of Ashkenazic Jews who hailed from the southwest German lands (exactly where we first encountered separate women's sections in German synagogues).

There might be, however, a problem in postulating an Ashkenazic influence on Iberian synagogue architecture in the 14th century, if the terminology of the Iberian synagogue can be shown to have influenced that of the Ashkenazic Jews in the 12th century. I am thinking of the appearance of Ar *al-minbar* "the pulpit (in the mosque)" in Yiddish to denote the reading desk in the synagogue, for example, WY *almemer* (in the German-speaking lands) and (the subsequently restructured) EY *balemer* (in the Slavic-speaking lands). For further details, see Wexler 1993c:42–43, 110–11. An Iberian origin for the Yiddish Arabism is tempting, since the surface cognates in Judeo-French of the 12th century have the Arabic definite article, *al-*, a typical feature of Spanish Arabisms, discussed further in chapter 4, but this hypothesis is not problem-free for four reasons.

(a) There is no trace of this Arabism in Judeo-Spanish, though de Alcalá cites it in his Spanish Arabic grammar of 1505 in the form *mínbar* (the *DCECH*, under *alminbar*).

(b) Few Iberian Jewish linguistic influences are known in Judeo-French (Levy 1942).

(c) There is no factual basis to the widely held hypothesis that Ashkenazic Jewish culture and the Yiddish language were created when French and Italian Jews migrated to the southwestern German lands in the 9th and 10th centuries (M. Weinreich 1956, 1973). As I demonstrated in some detail earlier (Wexler 1992), the small unique Romance component in Yiddish can be more smoothly derived from north Italian and Balkan Romance; the only sure Judeo-French component in Yiddish is a handful of male and female anthroponyms, for example, *bunem* < French *bon homme*, literally "good man" (though an Italian etymon cannot be ruled out entirely). An alternative source for the Yiddish Arabism might be a European Turkic language; from Yiddish, the Arabism, along with many words of German stock, could have diffused to Judeo-French (Wexler 1993c).

(d) Both the term and the artifact in the architecture of the mosque appear to have diffused from the Near East to Egypt and North Africa (C. H. Becker 1906).

The status of women in the Iberian synagogue could still have been disadvantaged even in the absence of a women's section. All three religions minimalized the role of women in the religious service, though there was no such enclosure in the church or the mosque. A mid-11th-century Christian document mentions that the debauchery of priests led to the removal of women from the church services in Seville except during official functions (Kassis 1990:89).

Syncretistic Religious Expression in Spain (with special attention to the Marranos)

The nature of syncretistic religious beliefs in pre-15th-century Spain is difficult to reconstruct due to the paucity of data. Yet, we can point out abundant cases where Jews, Christians, and Muslims were familiar with, and participated in one another's rituals and holidays; familiarity with one another's rituals would have set the stage both for the diffusion of religious practices from one group to another, as well as for mutual polemics (on the anti-Christian and anti-Marrano writings of Yehuda ha-Levi, written between 1130–40, Ḥasday Kreskas 1340–1412, and Yicxak ben Moše ha-Levi [Profiaṭ Duran], d. c.1414, see Gonzalo Maeso 1960:491). Syncretistic religious expression implies that:

> Christians and Jews may not have seen themselves as distinct peoples, despite the efforts of. . .religious leaders to create boundaries among people whose relationships may have been marked by great fluidity (Gampel 1992:12).

Receptivity to syncretistic religious expression would also be expected, particularly when Spanish Judaism was organizationally fragmented and a supra-communal authority was either weak or lacking altogether. On the growing communality of Christian and Jewish religious doctrine in Spain after the 14th century, see M. A. Cohen 1992:28.

The Marrano community of Jewish and Muslim origin provides a particularly important reflection of the syncretistic religious practices and beliefs that were circulating in both the Muslim and Christian regions of the peninsula before the expulsion of the Jews from the Kingdom of Spain in 1492. The Spanish term *marrano* was given by the Christians to Catholics of Jewish (or Muslim) origin and their descendants; the term is first attested in Christian literature as an epithet for Jews and Muslims in the 13th century, though in its original meaning of pig, it appeared as early as 965 (*DCECH*; further discussion of the etymology this chapter). A major Marrano Jewish population came into existence in Christian Spain at the close of the 14th century; its ranks continued to swell up until the expulsion of the Jews in 1492. If the term is of Arabic origin, and the phenomenon of unorthodox conversion was attested in Islamic Spain, then the use of *marrano* to denote Jewish converts to Islam (or Christianity) may have begun in Muslim Spain centuries before the Catholic Inquisition was established in the late 15th century to extirpate allegedly lapsed Catholics, such as the Marranos.

I do not accept the common view that Marranos were Jews who were compelled to adopt Catholicism against their will, a fact that forced large numbers of them to practice elements of Judaism clandestinely in Spain, and to emigrate abroad in the 16th and 17th centuries in order to practice Judaism openly. While the Marrano population certainly included such a class of people, it is conceivable that the majority of Jews (and Muslims) who converted to Catholicism did so out of conviction, in large part inspired by their espousal of syncretistic religions that encompassed elements from two or more of the peninsula's faiths. I also regard as untenable the thesis that the charge of crypto-Judaism was fabricated by the enemies of the New Christians (Greenleaf 1969:111; Liebman 1974:28). In the following discussions, I will accept the established practice of using the term *marrano* only in the meaning of Jewish converts to Christianity, and their descendants. Yerushalmi (1971:xv, 12) has drawn a distinction between "Marranos" (converts to Catholicism with proven Judaizing propensities) and "New Christians" (Catholics of Jewish origin not known to have been Judaizers), but this distinction would prove to be unwieldly in practice, and furthermore, was alien to Christians in the 15th and 16th centuries.

Scholars are divided as to the reasons why so many Jews (reliable statistics are lacking) converted to Catholicism. The standard view is that Jews converted to Catholicism mainly under duress, often with the hope of bettering their economic status. However, since the late 1950s, a growing number of historians have begun to depict the Marranos as a heterogeneous group in terms of the motivation for conversion, with religious conviction being the primary reason. For further discussion, see Rivkin 1957 and n.d., Netanyahu 1963, 1966, and n.d., M. A. Cohen 1992:52. I am inclined to concur with these authors. Especially welcome is Faur's recent proposal to distinguish four types of Marranos: converted Jews who regarded themselves as Christians; converted Jews who remained crypto-Jews; converted Jews who preferred to practice both Judaism and Christianity; and converted Jews who wanted to be neither Jews nor Christians (1990:114; 1992, chapter 3). As for the motivation behind the establishment of the Inquisition in Spain and Portugal, we must cite both economic considerations (i.e., a desire to eliminate the competition of a dynamic Marrano middle class), as well as the Christian doctrinal desire to extirpate bi- and triritualism (Didier 1981:109).

Netanyahu, in the first comprehensive reevalution of the Marrano phenomenon (1966), was concerned with the attitudes of practicing Spanish Jews towards the Marranos; hence, he declined to explore the historical origins of the syncretistic nature of their beliefs. The intriguing question is whether the syncretistic religious practices of many Marranos was the reason for their decision to convert, or rather the result of their forced conversion and clandestine retention of selected elements of

Judaism and/or their eventual persecution as "lapsed Jews" by the Inquisition. It would be paradoxical if the decision to espouse Judaic beliefs and practices clandestinely was stimulated by the Inquisition's persecution of the Marranos, ostensibly on charges of Judaizing. In other words, the Inquisition, unintentionally, may have actually created a new class of Judaizers. It appears that most of the Jews who converted to Catholicism in the wake of the nation-wide pogroms of 1391 did so under duress, whereas those who converted in the early 15th century were in the main voluntary converts (ibid.:95). The magnitude of conversion to Catholicism is unprecedented in the annals of Jewish history and cannot be smoothly explained solely by forced conversion—especially since many of the converts reached positions of influence in the Catholic church hierarchy. It therefore is reasonable to suppose that an indeterminable number of Marranos, *prior* to their formal conversion, had already begun to subscribe to a syncretistic religion that included Christian, Jewish, and Muslim beliefs; this syncretistic religion facilitated formal conversion to the official faith, Catholicism.

A telling piece of evidence that supports the view of Rivkin, Netanyahu, and M. A. Cohen is that when Marranos began to depart the peninsula in ever larger numbers in the 16th century, they more often settled in other Christian countries where the practice of Judaism was also fettered than in Muslims lands where they would have been free to practice Judaism openly (Netanyahu 1966:216). This point was also appreciated by Yosef Karo (Toledo? 1488–Palestine 1575), the renowned author of the legal code, *Šulxan arux* (1565), who experienced the expulsion personally:

> [with respect to] Marranos who are able to flee to a place where they can serve God and do not do so, it is a sin to accept their ritual slaughter and to drink the wine that they touch (1568:100a, cited by Bunis 1993a:20, fn 6).

There is other evidence in the contemporary Jewish literature that supports the revisionist view of the Marrano phenomenon. For example, many contemporary Jewish writers blamed the voluntary conversions of Jews to Catholicism on the detrimental impact of "secular philosophy" and "religious confusion" (Netanyahu 1966:97, 102–103), while Yicxak ben Yehuda Abravanel (Lisbon 1437–1508), the illustrious Jewish statesman in the service of the Spanish crown, said that the Marranos were believers of neither Judaism nor Christianity (ibid.:194ff).

Some early Balkan Sephardim express a strong suspicion of the Jewish observances of the Marranos, not so much because of their alleged syncretistic practices, but rather because of their unavoidably close contacts with Christians. Again, it is instructive to quote Karo:

> Marranos, even the good ones among them, cannot be careful about preventing a Gentile from touching [Jewish ritual wine] and since they are suspect with regard to wine, they cannot be believed as to [the fitness of] their wine, even if they take an oath (1568:Y.D.124, cited by Bunis 1993a:20, fn 6).

The Catholic Inquisition believed that the Catholicism of many Marranos was not always orthodox; hence, in 15th-century Spanish Christian literature the Marranos were occasionally called contemptuously by the Arabic term *Alboraique*, a reference to the Quranic legend of Muḥammad ascending to heaven from the Dome of the Rock in Jerusalem on a creature that was half horse, half bird—known as *al-burāq* (see Loeb 1889:238, 242, Gitlitz 1990–93 and discussion of the Christian practice of denoting Muslim and Jewish concepts by Arabic words in chapter 5 this volume). In Spanish and Portuguese parlance of the 16th and 17th centuries, Jews who converted to Catholicism, regardless of whether they were suspected of retaining clandestine Jewish practices, were also called "New Christians," Sp *cristiano nuevo*, Pt *cristão novo, ñáfete* < *neofito* "neophyte" (M. L. Wagner 1953:381), in contrast to the "Old Christians" who were not of Jewish or Muslim origin; curiously, in 1687 we first encounter the Spanish term *judío nuevo* "New Jew" to refer to Christians (of any origin) who lapsed into Jewish practices (Kaplan 1992:230). See also Popkin's use of the term "Jewish(-) Christian" and "Christian(-)Jew" (1992). This terminology is an accurate reflection of the widespread vacillations in faith that characterized many segments of the entire Iberian population before and after the expulsion of the Jews.

The adoption of a syncretistic religion by Jews probably began among segments of the Jewish population in Muslim-dominated areas of the peninsula. This is important to note since the phenomenon of Marranism has become synonymous with the Catholic Inquisition (active in Spain between 1478 and 1826 with a brief interruption in 1808, and in Portugal between 1540 and 1821). Support for my assumption of an Arabic (either Jewish or Muslim) origin for Marranism comes from the word *marrano* itself. While an Aramaic etymology has been proposed by a minority of scholars (for example, by Kahane and Kahane 1964, but see also the critique of this and other etyma in Malkiel 1948:176–77), most researchers now prefer an Arabic source, though there is no total agreement on which Arabic etymon.

The *DCECH* proposed Ar *maḥram* "crime" < *ḥ-r-m* "forbid" as the etymon, in reference to the Jewish (and Muslim) prohibition of consuming pig meat. On the assimilation of *ḥ* > *r*, see also the case of Ar *(al-)miḥlāj* "the cotton-carding machine" > Sp *almarrá*. The *DCECH* admitted that Ar *maḥram* was not attested in Spanish Arabic sources, though other forms of the root *ḥ-r-m* were. The interspersed Hebrew phrases that appear in the Judeo-Spanish texts known as the "Taqqanot of Valladolid" (1432) have the cognate Hebrew root in the forms *məḥuram* "excommunicated" and *maḥrimim* "excommunicating" (lines 947 and 679, respectively; see Minervini 1:1992:255). The first example is in the derived *pi'el* form, which would be expected in Arabic, while the former follows the *hif'il* form, which is the derived form in which the root is customarily used in Hebrew; hence, I suggest that *məḥuram* may be an imitation of the Arabic verb form, *fa''ala* ~ He *pi'el*.

In contrast, Malkiel has proposed that the Arabic etymon was *barrānī* "outsider, foreigner" that subsequently crossed with a native Ibero-Romance term for pig (1948:182, 184, with reflexes of Lat *verrēs, verris* "male swine, boar-pig"; for another example of a blend, JSp *desmazalado*, involving similar-sounding Hebrew and Ibero-Romance roots, see his 1947). Ar *barrānī* was known in Spain, for example in the form of OCat *alborneç* "cold northern wind" (Steiger 1932:78, 311, fn 1) and Sp *barrano* "outsider, stranger" (Albacete, Murcia 1436, cited by Malkiel 1948:184). The *DCECH* cites a number of other examples of *b-* > *m-* in native Ibero-Romance vocabulary (in the discussion of *maraña* "jungle, plot, snarl") that lends support to Malkiel's proposal (though the *DCECH* does not cite these examples in connection with Sp *marrano* and strongly rejects Malkiel's etymology); for example, *bandurria* "musical instrument resembling a small guitar," *berenjena* "eggplant," etc., all have variants with *m-*; see also Sp *matalahuva* "anise" < OSp **batalhúa* < SpAr *ḥabbat al-ḥulūwa* "sweet grain." (For other ethnonyms based on the term "foreigner, outsider," see JSp *forasteros* and Tun"He" *baḥucim*, discussed in chapter 3 this volume.)

Additional support for the etymon *barrānī* comes from non-Iberian Arabic: YemJAr *barrānī* had a ritual meaning, i.e., food that could be consumed with either dairy or meat products (Piamenta 1:1990, citing Goitein 1931:360 where the term is misspelled *bahānī*). The concept of a neutral food category, incidentally, is unknown among the Sephardic Jews, who can cook vegetables in pots suitable either for milk or meat foods; the neutral category of food is found among the Ashkenazic Jews, who call it in Yiddish by the Sorbian Germanism *pareve* (Wexler 1993c:133–34). The notion of "neutrality" that is associated with YemJAr *barrānī* is retained by the Iberian term Marrano—a person who is "neutral" from the point of view of religious affiliation. The use of a term originally meaning outsider to designate Jewish (and Muslim) converts to Catholicism suggests that the converts did, indeed, not become orthodox practitioners of their newly adopted religion. In contrast, note that genuine converts to Christianity were apparently not called by a demeaning term. For example, Sp *almogataz* "baptized

Muslim" < Ar *muġaṭṭas* "baptized" (cited under *almocatracía* by the *DCECH*, following Dozy and Engelmann 1869:171).

Malkiel suggests that originally *marrano* (~ *barrano*) "Jewish convert" were not opprobrious epithets, but merely marked the gulf between Old Christians and newcomers (1948:181), but that in the 14th century (I suggest perhaps a century or so earlier, when the opprobrious meaning of *marrano* is first attested?), as relations between the two groups began to worsen, the terms became associated with similar-sounding Sp *marrano* "hog, pork"—especially since Jews and Muslims officially refrained from consuming the meat of the pig. Malkiel's views thus support my hypothesis that the term *marrano* denoted converts in Ibero-Romance before 1391—the fateful year of the major nationwide pogrom against the Jews that brought about the enforced conversion of many Jews to Catholicism. The suggestion that *marrano* "pig" and *marrano* "insincere Jewish convert to Christianity" were originally derived from two separate roots, one of them Arabic, was first made by Lokotsch 1927. For further discussion, see his suggestion that *marrano* "Jew" < He *mar'ɛh* "appearance" plus Sp *-ano* (#1412) vs. *marrano* "pig" < Ar *muḥarrami* (*sic!*) "forbidden" (#1499). The Hebrew etymology is not out of the question.

While the phenomenon of creating syncretistic religious beliefs could have begun anywhere at anytime (it was also characteristic of North African society in the Christian and Islamic periods both), the forced conversion of Sephardic Jews to Islam would have been especially prevalent during the intolerant Almoravide invasion of Muslim Spain in 1096, and the Almohade invasion in 1146; shortly thereafter, forcibly converted Jews were able to return to Judaism (now diluted with Islamic practices?) either in the Muslim or Christian areas of the peninsula. Hence, I conclude that the first Marranos may have been Arabic-speaking Jews who gave up elements of the practice of Judaism in the south of Spain; when the latter came north and switched to Spanish, little remained to distinguish them from the surrounding Christian majority. Future research will need to determine whether the rise of the Marrano community in Christian Spain was in any way stimulated by or correlated with the language shift from Judeo-Arabic to Spanish that the Jews were undergoing between the 11th and 14th centuries (this volume, chapter 6).

Syncretistic beliefs attributed to Marranos are frequently described in the Christian literature. According to one report, Marranos baptized their children on Saturday, the Jewish Sabbath, as for example in Ciudad Real in 1510–12, thus observing the sanctity of the Jewish Sabbath at the same time that they publically performed a major Christian ritual (Beinart 2:1977:261, 288, 308, 344, 3:1981:275, and fn 161). Marranos are also known to have continued to eat unleavened bread (required for the Passover celebration) that they acquired from Jews, for example, in

Segorbe, Valencia 1393 (Baer 1:1929:706). On the participation of Jewish converts to Catholicism and Judaizers in Jewish religious rituals in late 15th-century Spain, see Carrete Parrondo 1978:16–18. Fernando de Pulgar, a 16th-century Marrano, described Judaizers in Toledo as displaying ignorance of both Judaism and Christianity and hence selective in the laws they chose to observe (Márquez Villanueva n.d.:64, fn 36; see also Mackay 1992:229 and the remark by Abravanel cited earlier); on syncretistic beliefs among monks of Jewish origin in Guadalupe, who coined the concept and expression *Ley del Padre* "the Torah of the Father," see Márquez Villanueva n.d.:65 and fn 39. Other Marranos were accused of simultaneously practicing Judaism and Christianity (Liebman 1964:107, #1176—a very late reference to Mexico 1795; Haliczer 1990:214–15) or Judaism, paganism and various Christian heretical sects (Liebman 1964:84, #914, Mexico 1718). Marranos also admitted to praising Islam (Ginio 1993:146) and reciting Jewish prayers in church (ibid.:133). On the adaptation of Catholic prayers for use by Jews in 17th-century Mexico, see Liebman 1974:146 (under Isabel Texoso).

For further discussion of innovative Marrano beliefs, see C. Roth 1931, 1932, chapter 7; on Portuguese Marrano prayers, see Andrea da Cunha e Freitas 1954:148 and da Costa Fontes 1990–93, 1991. It is this very synthesis of Jewish and non-Jewish features that has prompted some observers to question the genuine Jewish patrimony of the Portuguese Marranos (Salomon 1976:636; for a less sceptical view, see da Costa Fontes 1991:517, fn 10).

As I suggested earlier, the Marranos may have been responsible for introducing syncretistic views to unconverted Jews, both through their contacts with the latter in the peninsula and in the diaspora when some Marranos joined existing Jewish communities or founded new Jewish communities of their own. This question needs further study. See the case of the converso Juan de Ciudad who rejoined the Jewish community in Huesca in 1465 and eventually emigrated to Jerusalem, mentioned earlier. One piece of evidence is the use by the Sephardic Jews of Catholic terms to denote Jewish religious practices (chapter 5 this volume). In addition, the fact that many Jews who emigrated to North Africa and the Balkans after 1492 were receptive to re-Judaization, i.e., accepted Jewish practices from the relatively more Judaized indigenous Jews with whom they came in contact—the North African Arab and Berber Jews and the Balkan Romaniote (Judeo-Greek-speaking) and Ashkenazic Jews—suggests that they may have absorbed quite a number of Marrano practices prior to the expulsion that were deemed unacceptable in the Sephardic diasporas (on Judaization, chapter 5 this volume). For example, Armistead and Silverman (1990) note the veneration of angels in a Judeo-Spanish text from 18th-century Rhodes, as well as in a recent prayer from Saloniki; this feature seems to be of Christian (or Marrano?) origin.

Most Portuguese Marranos in Amsterdam in the 17th century declared their allegiance to the Jewish religion, but a not insignificant group of "marginal" members who were inactive in community life visited Spain and Portugal frequently for business reasons, some of them even settling again in their former homelands and rejoining the Catholic population (Kaplan 1985:210–11). On rare occasions, the cyclical conversion activities of individual Marranos reached dizzying proportions; consider the case of Duarte de Paz, a Jew who became a Christian in Spain and reverted to Judaism in Turkey, but ended his days by becoming a Muslim (Poliakov 1961:241, Didier 1981:121). For a 16th-century Spanish account of a Portuguese Jew who converted twice to Christianity, and reverted back to Judaism twice, see Caro Baroja 1:1978:245. (On a recent case of a Catholic priest in New Mexico converting to Judaism upon discovering his crypto-Jewish antecedents, and subsequently returning to Catholicism, see Parks 1992:15.)

Scholem describes a Spanish Jewish manuscript on magic from Amsterdam, dated 1700, which comprised elements of Muslim (Arab), Jewish, and Christian demonology, coexisting side by side or showing signs of mutual permeation (1965:6). It would be interesting to know whether the Muslim and Christian demonic elements were inherited by the Dutch ex-Marrano Jews directly from the Iberian peninsula, or were introduced into Holland from a Sephardic North African or Balkan source. In either case, the manuscript is poignant evidence of the sort of syncretistic beliefs that must have been circulating among the Iberian Jews at that time. A Purim story printed in Amsterdam by Portuguese Marranos in 1699 refers to Mordexay as *Santo Mordochay* "Saint Mordexay," which looks like a Christian pattern of discourse (van Praag 1940:13, 22).

The process of creating syncretistic religious beliefs was not limited to the Iberian Jews. The fact that even today Iberian Christians unwittingly retain practices that are probably of Jewish provenience suggests either that the practitioners themselves were of Jewish extraction who preserved some Jewish practices or Old Christians whose ancestors acquired some Jewish practices from Jews or Jewish converts to Christianity. It would be interesting to determine whether the presence of such practices depended on the existence of a significant local Jewish population. I am reminded of the fact that Yiddish terms often surface in contemporary German dialects in areas where there were few Jews before the Nazi period (Althaus 1965). Similarly, the South Rhodopian dialect of Southern Bulgaria has the term *papel'aška* ~ *pe-* "(cigarette) paper, book, cigar" < JSp *papel* "paper," though this area historically had few Jews (Kunchev 1979).

Luis Lacave has cited the example of Christians in Lucena (a town in Andalusia that had a significant Jewish population and famous religious institutions during the Muslim period) who today have a habit of cleaning their houses on Saturday, called in Spanish *sabadear* or *hacer sábado* (this is not likely to be an authentic Jewish custom since all work is proscribed on Saturday, the Jewish Sabbath), and of whitewashing their houses after Holy Week, a holiday that falls approximately at Passover time, when the Jews traditionally clean house (1985:17). Perhaps the cleaning of houses on Saturday was an attempt by Marranos to feign disloyalty to Judaism, or a Christian adaptation of a Jewish practice which called for cleaning on a day other than Saturday. In late 15th-century Inquisition protocols *sabadear* also denotes the Jewish manner of praying (Beinart 1965:203, fn 61, 301, 1:1974:242, 572, 2:1977:196, Wexler 1982:76, and fn 41, Bunis 1993a:19). I have no information on whether *sabadear* was ever used by Jews in any meaning.

De las Cagigas claims that Mozarabic Christians in Zaragoza practiced Jewish superstitions, but no examples are given (1947:167); one must exercise caution here since "Jewish" superstitions could well have been either of Berbero-Arab origin, which were diffused to the Christians by the Jews, or original Christian superstitions, which became obsolete among the latter and survived only among Jews—and hence, became known to the Christians as "Jewish" practices. Ashtor reports that an 8th-century Mozarabic priest in Toledo wrote of Christians in Zaragoza who believed that the blood of cattle was unfit to eat (1:1960:222, quoting Migne n.d.:columns 719–21); orthodox Judaism eschews the consumption of animal blood.

Castilian Christians paid Jewesses to recite funeral dirges at Christian funerals (Baer 1/2:1936:162—describing one such instance in Toledo in 1344; see also Poliakov 1961:117). Christians also went to the synagogue to listen to the sermons delivered by rabbis in Cuellar in the late 15th century (Baer 1/2:1936:520, 523–24). Reports of travelers to

Kairouan, Tunisia in the 19th century also make mention of Jewish customs being practiced by indigenous Muslims (D. Cohen 1:1964:2, who does not give details). Jews also displayed readiness to participate in Christian religious services. For example, Baer reprints a document showing that the Jews carried the Torah in a church procession in Seville in 1449 for the purpose of combatting a plague (1/2:1936:315). Jews are also known to have participated in church vigils in Valladolid in 1322 (ibid.:1:1929:198, paragraph 13).

An extreme example of cultural and linguistic diffusion is the Muslim and Christian use of He *ʿacɛrɛt*, a biblical term for "Feast of the Tabernacles." The term surfaces in Arabic in the form *al-ʿanṣara* and designates the bonfires of midsummer eve (24 June). In Spanish the term takes the form *alhanzara* (Westermarck 2:1926:203–205; see also Dozy and Engelmann 1869:135–36, Steiger 1932:283, Shinar 1982:107). The holiday *al-ʿanṣara* is often personified in Morocco by a Jewess, which could indicate that the Berbers may have acquired the rite from the Jews (Westermarck 2:1926:182). Westermarck notes that *al-ʿanṣara* among the Copts denotes "Whitsunday" (ibid.:205). The Muslim custom of lighting midsummer eve bonfires on 24 June spread to the Christians where it is known as the feast of the birthday of John the Baptist (Kassis 1990:85–86).

The Arabic Hebraism is also valuable for reconstructing Hebrew pronunciation norms since it suggests that the letter *ʿayin* was pronounced by Arabic-speaking Jews as a nasal. This is reminiscent of the pronunciation of the *ʿayin* as /n, ñ, ŋ/ by Italian Jews and the Jewish descendants of the Portuguese Marranos in northern Europe; I assume that it was because of Italian Jewish influences that this practice occasionally became rooted among Bavarian and Polish speakers of Yiddish (Wexler 1988:70–71, 102–103). A difference between the Arabic and Jewish pronunciations of the *ʿayin* is that the former retains the *ʿayin* together with a nasal in the word *al-ʿanṣara*, while the Jewish reading norms of Hebrew have dropped the *ʿayin* altogether or substituted a nasal consonant for it. There is scant evidence for pronouncing the *ʿayin* as a nasal in Spain itself, but the Marrano evidence may allow us to reconstruct a nasal at least for the Portuguese area. I wonder whether the Iberian Jewish pronunciation of *ʿayin* was not ultimately of North African origin (chapter 4 this volume). The Spanish spelling with *h* (spellings without *h* also exist, Steiger 1932:283) suggests that Ar *ʿayin* became devoiced to *ḥ*, which finds a parallel in the occasional pronunciation of He ʿ as *x* (now only in syllable-final positions) in contemporary Judeo-Spanish Hebraisms (the feature is unknown in the reading of monolingual Hebrew texts or in the pronunciation of Arabisms). The choice of /x/ as the reflex for historical *ʿayin* in Hebraisms suggests that in Iberian (Judeo-)Arabic, *ʿayin* underwent devoicing in certain environments, for example, syllable final position where voicing may not always have been fully maintained. This phenomenon is not broadly found in Arabic (Corriente 1977:56). The spelling of *h* in some Spanish Arabisms for historical *ʿayin* may also be a hiatus-breaking device and not a sign of an earlier *ḥ* or *x* (Steiger 1932:274ff).

There is also evidence that Christians in Andalusia adopted Muslim practices, such as circumcision and certain dietary customs, as well as doctrinal heresies, for example, Christ was regarded by some Christians as the adopted son of God (Cheyne 1969:82). Occasionally, Christians even denoted Christian concepts with Muslim terminology, for example, in Toledo between 1174–1221 (the city was recaptured by the Christians in 1085), the Christians issued coins in the Arabic style with Arabic inscriptions of the type *al-'imām al-bī'a al-masīḥiyya bābā* "the Pope is the imam of the Christian faith" (Bates 1992:385). The addition of the Arabic article *al-* to *imām* violates Arabic grammar and may reflect Romance interference.

Conversely, non-Islamic holidays were celebrated by Muslims, for example, the latter celebrated the birthday of Jesus Christ—though this holiday was not sanctioned by Islam (de la Granja 1969:2–3; see also Menéndez Pidal 1929:444, Idris 1974:173, Kassis 1990:85–86). Muslims used the Christian calender for certain purposes, venerated at least one Christian saint at a shrine in southwest Spain and celebrated some feasts together with Christians (de la Granja 1969–70, quoting Torres Balbás 1954 [for a 13th-century example], Idris 1974:178, fn 34, 183, fn 62 [for an 11th-century example], and Wasserstein 1985:243). For an account of a Muslim who went to church in the 12th century, see de la Granja 1970 and Kassis 1990:86.

In addition to their receptivity to Christian practices, Jews were apparently also attracted to Islam in Christian Spain. For example, a rich Jew in Mallorca in the early 14th century was punished by the Christian authorities for praying in the Muslim fashion in the company of his Muslim slaves (Baer 1:1929:646, paragraph 7, Sánchez Albornoz 2:1956:286, Poliakov 1961:120–21, Didier 1981:103—who also notes a tendency among Jews to "Mohammedanize"). An Aragonese Judaizer in the late 15th century was accused of saying Jewish prayers while prostrating on the ground in the Muslim fashion (Cantera Montenegro 1985:72); of course, prostration might have been practiced by Iberian Jews. For further discussion of this practice by Egyptian Jews, see chapters 4 and 5 this volume. The Inquisition at Coimbra, Portugal in 1623 described the Jewish manner of prayer as consisting of holding an open hand over one's head and passing it across the face, while reciting "God of Abraham, God of Isaac and God of Jacob" (Andrea da Cunha e Freitas 1954:148; da Costa Fontes 1991:512). This practice is reminiscent of Muslim prayer habits.

Jews were also alleged to have joined Muslims in the mosque and to have publicly praised Islam. For further details, see the description by the Ashkenazic Jew Yosef ben Šalom Aškenazi in Catalunya in the early 14th century, given by Vajda 1956:135. The Moroccan Berber ibn Tumart (c.1078–c.1130) also tells of a Jew who frequented the mosque in Bougie, Algeria for twenty years (Stillman 1975). A converso in Aragón in 1490 declared himself to be a "turco" when he married an ex-Muslim woman; though he remained in touch with the local Jewish community and ate kosher meat, he was denounced to the Inquisition by two Jews (Cabezudo Astrain 1956:107, 112). Jews in Játiva, Valencia converted to Islam between the years 1280–84 (D. Romano 1976) and Judaizers in Ciudad Real, Castile in 1484, and in Aragón in 1492 admitted to eating meat slaughtered by Muslims for ritual reasons (Beinart 1:1974:340 and Cantera Montenegro 1985:71, respectively); Jewish ritual food requirements are stricter than those of Muslims, hence practicing Jews would not have consumed Muslim *ḥalāl* meat.

The receptivity of Iberian Jews and Marranos to some Muslim practices also finds a reflection in the writings of Jews outside the peninsula. For example, Raš"i, the noted French commentator on the Bible and Talmud who lived in Champagne (1025 or 1040–1104), wrote that it was acceptable for Jews to say the blessing of *havdalah* (marking the conclusion of the Sabbath on Saturday evening) over the candles and spices of Muslims, but not over those of Christians, because the latter were idolators (N. Roth 1983b:211, fn 77). A "bond" between Jews and Muslims was also assumed by Iberian Christians, who referred to Muslim and Jewish practices by a common (Arabic!) terminology (chapter 5 this volume).

There are also a small number of Spanish terms used by the Jews that denote aspects of their ritual and religion (chapter 5 this volume). I suppose that the use of Spanish terms reflects a Christian origin for the practices in question; had these practices been followed in Muslim Spain and transported to Christian Spain, I would have expected the Jews to retain the original Arabic terminology. However, there could be customs acquired by the Jews from Arabs and Berbers that eventually acquired a Spanish name. A parallel Ashkenazic example concerns the festive bread, known in Yiddish as *xale*; the standard view derives *xale* < He *ḥallah* "portion of uncooked dough offered to the priest in the biblical temple in Jerusalem." The traditional braided shape of this festive bread was invented by the Greeks and Romans and could have been brought by Balkan Jews to the Germano-Sorbian lands, but the origin of the word *xale* has to be sought in G *Holle*, the name of a pagan

Germanic goddess to whom braided bread was once given in offering. G *Holle* was replaced at a later date—under the pressure of Judaization—by He *ḥallah*, which bore formal and semantic similarity (Wexler 1993c: 115–78). In Iberian Jewish circles, He *ḥallah* is never used to denote a bread, only the unbaked dough given as a tithe (Bunis 1993a:217 and chapter 5 this volume). The practice of religious Jewish women removing a piece of dough for burning is described in a Sephardic source from approximately 1483 (Loeb 1889:235).

There are also indications that Iberian Muslims were receptive to the creation of syncretistic beliefs and converted both to Judaism and Christianity (Olagüe 1974, chapter 9). For example, Muslim converts to Christianity were accused in the Inquisition protocols of clandestinely practicing Judaism. García-Arenal attributed this charge to the ignorance of the Christian authorities (1978:113), but the existence of syncretistic beliefs in all three religious communities in both the Muslim and Christian regions of the peninsula leads me to believe that by and large the Inquisition reports were probably accurate. Of course, the existence of an Inquisition checklist of authentic Jewish and Muslim practices would not mean that no Inquisition authorities were confused about the differences between Jewish and Muslim practices.

The adoption by Muslims of Jewish practices and the adoption by Jews of Muslim practices may not have been fortuitous. It is quite likely that the development of syncretistic beliefs began in the Muslim south where they were adopted by a sizeable part of the local Jewish population (note the hypothesis, expressed earlier, that the word *marrano* is of Arabic origin and that the phenomenon had its roots in Muslim Spain). It thus would have been relatively easy for Jews, whose religious observance was relatively lax in the first place, to espouse Christianity (especially in its regionally Islamized forms) when they shifted from Arabic to Ibero-Romance in the Christian-dominated areas of the country. Arab Jews who had already given up most of their Judaism in the Muslim south would have differed from their Christian neighbors in the north almost exclusively by virtue of their Arabic speech and Arab-Berber ethnography. It would be interesting to determine whether the chronology of language shift from Judeo-Arabic to Spanish among the Jews parallels the periods of their accelerated conversion to Christianity.

The reason why Muslims might have converted to Judaism was that after the Reconquista they enjoyed a lower social status in Christian society than the Jews (Neuman 2:1942:195, Poliakov 1961:123, Didier

1981:104). The existence of ritual prescriptions shared by Judaism and Islam might have made Judaism more attractive to some Muslims than Christianity (for example, neither Judaism nor Islam permitted the consumption of pork or anthropomorphic representations in art, and both required a ritual slaughtering of animals for food). Among similar practices of crypto-Muslims and crypto-Jews I may note the habit of putting on clean clothes on Friday (García-Arenal 1978:75), or the Muslim use of amulets with Greek and Hebrew inscriptions (ibid.:112); though in the 14th century, North African Muslims were told not to use talismans with Hebrew letters to cure fever, exorcize spirits (*jinns*), stop children from crying and chase away bedbugs (Idris 1974:187). On the conversion of a Muslim to Judaism in Andalusia in the 10th century, see ibid.:176. On Muslim conversion to Judaism in North Africa in the 17th century, see Addison 1676, and chapter 1 this volume.

Furthermore, conversion to Judaism might have been attractive to Muslims if the latter felt a closer affinity to the Arabic-speaking Jews than to the Spanish-speaking Christians. Future research into the geographical parameters of Muslim conversion to Judaism might allow us to determine whether this sort of conversion was most typical of areas that had a substantial Jewish population.

A comprehensive comparison of Iberian crypto-Judaism and crypto-Islam remains to be carried out. So far, it is apparent that most crypto-Muslims and crypto-Jews abandoned the practice of circumcision early on; this is to be expected, since circumcision could easily be identified by the Inquisition as a blatant sign of Judaizing or Islamizing (for a Muslim testimony from 1630, see García-Arenal 1978:59; on the rarity of circumcision among crypto-Jews, see C.Roth 1932:174). Still, circumcision was kept among crypto-Muslims primarily in Valencia, less so in Aragón, and almost not at all in Christian Cuenca, Castile, and Andalusia (García-Arenal 1978:59, 82). The topic of Muslim conversion to Judaism has been sorely neglected in the scholarly literature, and no one has studied the geographical parameters of circumcision by clandestine Jews.

A Muslim poet, in a poem addressed to the Jewish courtesan Šmuel (Abu Ibrahim) ben Yosef ibn Nagrella ha-Nagid (Córdoba 993–1055), wrote that he professed the Jewish religion openly in the company of Jews and in secret with Muslims (Perlmann 1948–49:289 and Pérès 1953:269). In Wasserstein's opinion, the poet was simply flattering the addressee by this comment on Judaism (1985:216). He disagrees with Pérès who thought that the Muslim poet had secretly converted to Judaism.

Wasserstein does not take into consideration the Muslim clerical admonition from the second half of the 13th century to the effect that Muslims should beware of converting "unwittingly" to Judaism or Christianity (de la Granja 1969:41).

Christians and Jews were said to be better off than Muslims (according to Harun ibn Ḥabib of the 9th century; Agnadé 1986:63). In the 15th century in "extreme" Morocco Muslims used the Jewish ram's horn (He *šofar,* Ar *būq*) in the mosque during Ramaḍān nights to announce the end of prayer and to alert Muslims that they could still eat before daybreak; prior to this the ram's horn was used in Andalusia to announce the beginning of the fast from sunrise to sunset as well as the end of the Ramaḍān period (Idris 1974:191). Friday, the Muslim Sabbath, is not a holiday for Muslims, who only require time off for prayer; yet, interestingly, in 16th-century Granada, Friday became a holiday (Gallego y Burín and Gámir Sandoval 1968:75), either under the influence of the Christian Sunday and/or the Jewish Sabbath (prior to 1492).

Curiously, the attraction that Judaism held for some Spanish Muslims (and Christians) continued into the 16th and 17th centuries, some time after the expulsion of the Jews from the Kingdom of Spain. For example, in Málaga in 1569, Muslims are alleged to have professed Christian and Jewish beliefs along with Islam, which Christian sources attributed to the lack of Muslim religious instruction and to the presence of many Portuguese crypto-Jews and Protestant merchants (Garrad 1960:69). Cardaillac relates that the Inquisition accused a Morisco from Berlanga of converting to Judaism in 1568 (1977:73). The Inquisition protocols of 1580 in Palermo, Sicily also report that a Muslim girl, who converted to Christianity, subsequently converted to Judaism and then finally reverted to Islam—but here the motivation in each case was to espouse the religion of her latest paramour (Carrasco and González 1984:58, fn 38, González Raymond 1989:114). Christian converts to Judaism (including monks and friars) are occasionally mentioned in the Inquisition protocols. For the cases of Francisco Ruiz de Luna, Mexico 1590 and José Díaz Pimienta, Caracas 1720, see Liebman 1974.

In 1587, the bishop of Segorbe even suggested that the existence of common ceremonies in Islam and Judaism showed that the Muslims derived from the Jews; he also accused the Muslims of removing a gland from the leg of the mutton, just as the Jews do (Cardaillac and Dedieu 1990:17–18). This practice is not traditionally observed by Muslims; either the bishop erred or else Spanish Muslims actually acquired this custom from the Jews. Muslims could eat meat slaughtered by Jews, but the latter could not eat Muslim meat. The bishop also accused the Muslims of not working on Saturday (ibid.:18). Selke reports the case of a Moor who had originally converted to Christianity converting again to Judaism in Mallorca in 1688 (due to contact with crypto-Jews—some of whose descendants, known as *chuetas*, remain on the island to this day), but this may have been a unique case (1986:177ff). These instances of Muslim conversion to Judaism, no matter how small their numbers, might be an indication that Spain (especially in areas with a vestigial Muslim population) was less *judenrein* after 1492 than is popularly believed.

The Inquisition accused many Muslims of syncretistic behavior (Lagarta and García Arenal 1981:129). A Spanish inquisitorial document from Aragón from 1495 accused a Christian defendant of converting to Islam, at the same time that he accepted some Jewish practices, and of stating that the Law of the Jews was superior to that of the Christians (ibid.:129, 132; for a similar account, see Fernández Nieva 1990:269). At his Inquisition trial in 1499, the Muslim Alonso Días de Bellinchón of Tarancón (Castile) admitted practicing both Judaism and Islam (i.e., features of Judaism and Islam?) and being an atheist (Cirac Estopañán 1965, #523 and Loupias 1965:120). Curiously, the Inquisition protocols of Cartagena (Colombia) in 1681 mention a certain Fernando Rauniez de Arvellano of Oran, Algeria, a Franciscan friar, who was reconciled for being a *judío mahometano* ("Muslim Jew": Adler 1904:37). (The topic of Muslims and Islamizers in the Spanish and Portuguese colonies in the New World calls out for study; see de Granda 1988. A careful search of the ecclesiastical literature on the Judaizers might shed light on this topic.)

A 16th-century crypto-Muslim, Mancebo de Arévalo, had knowledge of Hebrew, that he presumably acquired from a Jewish friend (Narváez 1981:145, 150, 153). In the Inquisition proceedings of 1579, the ex-Muslim wife of Diego de Mora Quintanar de la Orden was accused of performing Jewish ceremonies. For example, she did not let the oil lamp go out on Friday night and the Friday night meal remained on the embers so as to avoid the need to cook on Saturday, the Jewish Sabbath, when all work was prohibited; the woman allegedly spent Saturday spinning and winding threads (García-Arenal 1978:113). On syncretistic Muslim-Christian beliefs in late 16th-century books from Granada, see Cabanelas 1981:344 and fn 19.

Curiously, crypto-Muslims in Granada persecuted by the Catholic Inquisition were advised by a Moroccan Muslim cleric in 1504 that in the event that they were asked to curse Muḥammad, they should mispronounce the name *Muḥammad* as *Mamad*, which the cleric explained was the Christian pronunciation of the name or as *mahamad*, defined as a "Jewish title" (Harvey 1964:169). The similarity of the "Jewish title" with He *ma'amad* "synagogue deputy" comes to mind, but this has no connection with the name Muḥammad; it would be also strange if a Moroccan Muslim cleric were familiar with such a Hebrew term. This advice suggests that in some cases it might have been advantageous for crypto-Muslims to pretend to be Jews. It is also curious that the alleged Christian and Jewish pronunciations of the Prophet's name are very similar to the Medieval Berber pronunciation of Muḥammad—*Mām(e)d* (in Arabic spelled *m'md*), as found, for example, in the Nefūsa dialect of Libya (Lewicki 1974:19). Curiously, in an anti-Muslim holy book of the Barġawaṭa Berbers in the province of Tamesna in western Morocco in the mid-8th century, the name *Muḥammad* appears in the form *Mām(e)t* (ibid.:21). See also the pejorative Hebrew reinterpretation of *Muḥammad* as *maxmiṭ* discussed in chapter 5 this volume.

3

The North African Homeland of the Sephardic Jews and the Origin of the Term "Sephardic"

A central problem in Sephardic studies is the reconstruction of the source and original meanings of the Hebrew toponym-ethnonym *sfarad* "Spain," *sfaradi* "Spaniard, Spanish or Sephardic Jew." The word appears only once as a toponym in the Bible, in Ovadiah 20, where it appears to designate a locale in Asia Minor. The Talmud and Midraš (probably completed in the main by the 5th century A.D. in Palestine and Babylonia/Iraq) have names for Spanish and North African locales, for example, He *'spmy'* /ispamya ~ a-/ "Spain," *m'wryṭ'ny'* /mawretania/ "Mauretania," *'fryqy* /afriki/ "Roman Tunisia" and *lwvy'* /luvia/ "Libya," but lack any mention of a *sfarad*. However, the Aramaic (Syriac) translation of the Bible known as the Pešiṭṭo made in the 2nd century A.D. in Edessa (now Urfa, northern Syria) gives *sfarad* as Spain (Laredo 1944:351, 358). Like the Biblical Hebrew toponym *aškənaz*, that originally denoted a number of non-Jewish groups (Iranians, Slavs, and Germans, in that chronological order), but now denotes exclusively the Yiddish-speaking Jews of Northern Europe, *sfarad* is also applied to Iberian Jews and non-Jews. Since the 14th century, the term Sephardic in Jewish circles has exclusively designated "Judeo-Spanish-speaking" Jews in the Iberian Peninsula and their descendants abroad (regardless of whether they still speak Judeo-Spanish).

A much discussed question is whether He *sfarad* originally denoted all of Spain or only the Christian or the Muslim domain. The answer depends on the age of the term as an Iberian Jewish toponym. If I accept the hypothesis of Bruckus that the Jews assigned the Biblical Hebrew toponym to Spain because of its formal similarity to the Visigothic word for "black," for example, Go *swarts*, a cognate of ModG *schwarz* (Bruckus gives the form *svard*, 1942:11), then *sfarad* might have denoted all of the peninsula—at that time entirely under Visigothic domination. *Sfarad* would then be the earliest known example of altering the form of a non-Hebrew element in a language spoken by the Sephardic Jews to make it resemble a Hebrew term of similar form and function (further discussion in chapter 5 this volume). According to Bruckus, the Visigoths called the indigenous population of Spain "black" since the latter were of darker complexion than the Visigoths. A similar naming change characterizes Sp *moros* "Moors, i.e., the Berbero-Arab population of North Africa and Spain" < Gk *mauros* "black."

Bruckus' Gothic etymology for He *sfarad* is plausible, given the existence of numerous Gothic placenames in the Iberian peninsula. For example, Sp *Andalucía*/Ar *al-'Andalus* appears to be derived from the name of the Germanic Vandal tribe. Spanish apparently received this term from the Berbers and Arabs rather than directly from the Goths; Berber speakers could have dropped *v-* that they interpreted as the Berber genitive marker "of" in the expression "land of the Vandals." This was Vycichl's proposal in 1952a; see also Melvinger 1955:47, Halm 1989; for other proposals, see Krauss 1932:431ff. On other possible Gothic components in Judeo-Spanish, see Loeb 1885:248 and Mézan 1925:35.

The Jews alone may have preserved Go *swarts* since they were the first group that needed a term to designate the entire peninsula, since the Jews in both Christian and Muslim areas were essentially of the same North African stock and spoke one or more North African languages; the question of divided political control over the peninsula need not have interested the Jews. Jews frequently cut up space differently than coterritorial non-Jews. An example is Y *lite* "Grand Duchy of Lithuania" (encompassing Belorussia and parts of the Ukraine and Baltic lands) vs. G *Litau*, Lithuanian *Lietuva* "Lithuania." An additional impetus to use He *sfarad* indiscriminately for all regions of Spain might have been that most of the peninsula was actually unified, at least for a short while, under Muslim domination. Similarly, the Ashkenazic Jews still use He *aškənaz*/Y *aškenaz* indiscriminately to denote German and Slavic Jews whose cultures, until the 19th century, contained many elements in common; the assignment of a single term to Germans and Slavs in Medieval Hebrew simply reflects the fact that large parts of present-day Germany were inhabited by Germans and Slavs (Sorbs, Polabians; Wexler 1993c:106). The reconquest of most of Spain by the Christians in the

12th century would have had no effect on the meaning of *sfarad*, which could continue to denote the peninsula in its entirety (or without Portugal which was a separate kingdom).

Arabic geographical terminology differentiated Muslim and Christian regions for political and linguistic reasons; the Christians would be expected, for obvious historical reasons (i.e., the hope of regaining all Iberian territories from the Muslims) to use a uniform term for the once entirely Christian peninsula. Yet, the Christians appear to have lacked a general term for the entire peninsula until relatively late into the Reconquista period. For example, Lat *Hispania* denoted León and Castile under Christian control in the 11th century. In Christian parlance, Sp *España* denoted only Arab Spain as late as the 13th century; the Christian areas were called by local terms, for example "León," "Aragón," etc. (Baldinger 1972:45, fn 17). The absence of the Gothic toponym in Christian sources might suggest that the term was used primarily by Arabic speakers, though no Muslim attestation is known either.

During the Umayyad reign in Córdoba (929–1031), both Jews and Muslims used the Arabic term *afranjī* (~ He *[ʾIfrnjh)* to denote Christian residents of Catalunya and the areas north of the Pyrenees (J. Mann 1916–17:488, Ashtor 1:1960:285, fn 48, Glick 1979:235). The corresponding Spanish Christian term, *franco*, was applied generically to all residents north of the Pyrenees (ibid.:191), and has today become a popular Balkan Sephardic family name. It would be interesting to know if JSp *franko*/JAr *afranjī* ever became a designation for a resident of Christian Spain, in opposition to He *sfaradi*, which became narrowed to denote a resident of Muslim Spain; if so, in which locales? Avraham ben David ha-Levi Da'ud (Córdoba c.1110—Toledo 1180) used the term *sfarad* in his *Sefer hakabala* (1160–61) to refer to Christian Spain (N. Roth 1986:219). He *sfarad* "Spain," etc., is not a Sephardic family name, though it occurs, occasionally, among Ashkenazic Jews, for example, Y *sfard* (a sign of the bearer's Sephardic origin?).

While I find Bruckus' etymology reasonable, I cannot rule out an alternative theory that BibHe *sfarad* acquired the meaning Spain, based on formal similarity with Pun *i sephanim* "the island of rabbits," which is apparently the source of Lat *Hispania* (Baldinger 1972:15, fn 4, in his spelling). Ordinarily, dental and alveopalatal sibilants common to Punic and Hebrew have the same distribution in the two languages, which raises the question of whether the etymon was not *i šfanim*, as in Hebrew;

however, there is evidence that *s* and *š* merged in some dialects of Punic (Šifman 1963:23). The association of He *sfarad* with either He *i šfanim* or Lat *Hispania* could have taken place among Jews who were no longer able to motivate the epithet "island of rabbits" and hence, sought a Biblical Hebrew toponym of similar phonetic shape.

The popular view holds that Sephardic history begins with the Roman and Greek settlements in Spain, i.e., in the early Christian era. While there may have been Jews in Spain at this time, they probably did not contribute substantially to the formation of the "Sephardic" Jews. There is little reason to believe that the Muslim invasion of Spain encountered significant numbers of Jews still resident in the territory. In my view, the history of the Sephardic Jews properly begins in North Africa just prior to the Muslim conquest, and continues there and in Spain in 711. I also reject the view that derives some of the specificity of the Sephardic Jews from Palestine (Zimmels 1958, Mourant et al., 1978:51 and chapter 6 this volume).

Possible linguistic evidence for the claim that the Sephardic Jews had an earlier contact with Iberian Muslims than with Christians is the use of BibHe *kuti* "Cuthian" for Catholics in a Saloniki Judeo-Spanish text of 1568 (Karo 9a, cited by Bunis 1993a:27). This Biblical Hebraism might have been chosen either on grounds of phonetic similarity with Sp *católico* "Catholic," or because neutral unmarked BibHe *goy* "non-Jew; nation" had already been assigned to Muslims in Spain. In a Serbian Judeo-Spanish text from 1862 (Papo), "He" *goy* in fact denotes Muslims while "He" *ʿarel*, literally "uncircumcised," is used to specify Christians (Bunis 1993; Yiddish uses "He" *ʿarel* and *goy* mainly to designate Christians). The use of the neutral *goy* for Muslims could have arisen in Judeo-Spanish after contact with the Turks (Saloniki in the mid-16th century had a Turkish majority), though North African Judeo-Arabic also uses *goy* for "Muslim" (Leslau 1945b:71). The existence of *goy* in the meaning of Muslim in both the Balkan and North African Sephardic diasporas points to a possible Iberian Jewish usage.

Alongside the Berber-speaking majority, parts of North Africa had a minority Romance- (i.e., "neo-Latin"-)speaking population at the time of the Muslim conquest in the 7th century (Sittl 1882, M. L. Wagner 1936a, Lewicki 1951–52, Idris 2:1962:757 and chapter 4 this volume). The Moroccan geographer and cartographer, Abu ʿAbdullah Muḥammad ibn Muḥammad al-Idrisi (d.1166) wrote in 1154 that the majority of the inhabitants of Gafsa, Gabès, and Munastir (Tunisia) were "African

Romans" who spoke Latin (cited by Simonet 1888:xxxi, lxxv–vi, Esteban Ibáñez 1961:450 and Idris 2:1962:471). On the poor knowledge of Latin in North Africa, see Courtois 1945. The writings of Yehuda ibn Qurayš, a Jew of the late 9th and mid-10th century, from Tāhart, western Algeria, contains Romanisms (M. Katz 1950 and D. Becker 1984); this attests to the importance of the language in Algeria at that time, though of course does not necessarily mean that ibn Qurayš himself spoke a form of Romance (his name suggests a connection with the Qurayši tribe in Mekka, unless he acquired the name through association with Arabs who were themselves of Arabian descent).

Before the Arab invasion of North Africa and Spain in the late 7th century, the local Jewish communities were linguistically and culturally pluralistic. It stands to reason that in North Africa Romance- and Berber-speaking Jews first could have developed a merged culture (in both languages?) between the period of Roman settlement up until the Muslim invasion of the Iberian Peninsula in the late 7th century. (In Sicily before 1492 Arabic-speaking Jews also assimilated earlier Romance-speaking Jewish communities.) This merger may have included Greek regionally, for example, in coastal areas of North Africa. In Spain, the Jews also spoke a number of languages, for example, Latin and Greek (the latter on the southeastern coast), and possibly Gothic (also indigenous Iberian languages?). But since "Sephardic" involves the merger of Romance, Arabic, Berber, and vestigial Palestinian Jewish elements, there is no justification for identifying either the Latin-/Romance- (and/or Greek-) speaking Jews in Spain in the Roman and Byzantine periods or the Romano-Berbero-(Greek) Jews of North Africa as "Sephardic." In other words, *sfarad* is not always synonymous with "Spain" as far as Jewish history is concerned; moreover, it is a mistake to divorce the early history of the Iberian or Sephardic Jews from that of the North African Jews before 711, as is so often done.

I will call the two merged Jewries of pre-Islamic Spain and North Africa "pre-Sephardic" since they lacked the crucial Arabic (and in Spain, presumably also the Berber) ingredient—though, paradoxically, they probably comprised a stronger Palestinian Jewish component in their earliest stages of existence, thanks to the arrival of Jewish immigrants directly or circuitously from Palestine in the early centuries of the Christian era. They warrant the term "pre-Sephardic" since they very likely contributed to the establishment of Sephardic Jewry. To the best of my knowledge, no scholar has ever proposed that North African Jews entered Spain as speakers of Romance or neo-Latin (chapter 4 this volume), or that the cradle of Sephardic Jewry was in North Africa and not in Spain.

The coexistence of Berber, Arabic, and Romance that began in North Africa was preserved in Spain for several centuries, though the relative proportions of the mix changed through time and space. For example, there are no extant Berber records at all from Spain, though Berber (known in Arabic as *al-lisān al-ġarbī* or in Spanish as *algarabía*, both literally "the western language") was spoken in the peninsula, possibly becoming obsolescent in the 9th century (Lévi-Provençal 3:1967: 169). The 11th century witnessed a Berber language revival, especially in Granada, with the arrival of the Zenata Berbers from Morocco (on Berber toponyms in Spain, see Dubler 1943, de las Cagigas 1946a, Tovar Llorente 1946, Vycichl 1952a, Coromines 1972, Oliver Asín 1973, Bosch Vilá 1976, 1988, Glick 1978:160–61 and Barceló Perelló 1985; on a Berber substratum in North African and Spanish Arabic, see chapter 2 this volume). In Morocco, Berber was supplanted in many areas by Arabic. It is unclear when Moroccan Jews first became Berberophones or when the Judeo-Berber liturgical literature described by Galand-Pernet and Zafrani 1970 was written.

The extinction of Berber in Spain can be attributed to three factors:

(a) As in North Africa, Arabic became the language of culture and government because it was the *lingua franca* of the new Islamic realms linking the Iberian Peninsula with Asia and Africa.

(b) A shortage of Berber women in Spain may have obliged Berber men to marry indigenous Spanish women, with the result that offspring were rarely fluent in Berber (the same fate could, in theory, have overtaken Arabic, were it not for the administrative and cultural functions of the latter).

(c) The invasion of the Iberian Peninsula may have brought into contact a variety of mutually incomprehensible Berber dialects for the first time, thus inviting the use of Arabic or even Romance as *lingue franchi* or "common languages" (Coromines 1972:208).

It is conceivable that in the early 7th century Ibero-Romance-, and posssibly Greek- and Gothic-speaking Jews fled Visigothic Spain for North Africa. Given the rarity of colloquial North African Romance documentation, it is impossible to say how similar the two strains of Romance—Iberian and North African—were at that time. In any event, the migration of Iberian Jews southward into Africa during Visigothic rule presumably increased, at least temporarily, the importance of Romance among the indigenous North African Jews.

From the outset of the Arab settlement in North Africa, the Arabic language began to supplant Berber and Romance in many areas. With the arrival of the Judaized Arabs in North Africa in the late 7th century, Sephardic culture was created for the first time—particularly nourished now by the relatively more Judaized Iraqi, Yemenite, and Arabian descendants of converts to Judaism and Palestinian Jews (the first carriers of the Bible and Talmud to North Africa and Spain).

I conjecture that all three languages spoken by the North African Jews and non-Jews—Romance, Berber, and Arabic—were brought to the Iberian Peninsula. It is not unusual to find that coterritorial Jews and non-Jews differ in their language loyalties. It is conceivable that while North African Jewish and Berber immigrants to Spain shared the identical linguistic baggage, they could have differed in their linguistic preferences both before and after the invasion of the Iberian Peninsula, but the details are so far not recoverable. In any event, once in the Iberian Peninsula, both Jews and non-Jews were presumably subject to the same pressures of Arabization and subsequent Romanization, except possibly in princedoms under temporary Berber political control up to the 1100s.

There is one piece of evidence that suggests that indigenous North African Jews may have assimilated relatively quickly to Arabic after the arrival of the Arabs. The fact is that of the three religions practiced in North Africa prior to the coming of Islam—Christianity, paganism, and Judaism—only the latter survived alongside Islam (except for Egypt where Coptic Christianity has survived as a minority faith up to the present). Perhaps the survival of the Jews in North Africa was due in part to the fact that, as Arabic speakers from the Near East sharing the ethnic and cultural roots of the Muslim majority, they alone could constitute from the start an integrated segment of the newly emerging Muslim, Arabic-speaking society, while Christians and pagans, who had never before spoken Arabic or participated in Arabic culture, eventually lost their separate profiles in the Arab Muslim majority.

One very important piece of evidence in support of my hypothesis that Sephardic Jewry was born in North Africa shortly before it was transported to the Iberian Peninsula is that He *sfarad* was originally applied to North African Jews—prior to the migration of large numbers of Iberian Sephardim to North Africa beginning with the late 14th century.

The use of He *sfarad* to denote North African Jews is attested in the writings of Avraham ben Maymon (1186–1237, the Egyptian-born son of the famous Iberian philosopher, Moše ben Maymon, also known as Maimonides or the Rambam, 1138–1204), who in his *Milxemet elohim* called Nisim ben Ya'akov ben Nisim of Kairouan, Tunisia (also known as ibn Shahin, 11th century) "Sephardic" while Yeda'ya ben Avraham Bedersí (c.1270–c.1340) of Perpignan and Barcelona (according to his name, his ancestors possibly originated in Béziers, southern France) called the Egyptian Jewish scholar Sa'adya Gaon (882–942, a native of al-Fayyūm, an area that was possibly still Coptic-speaking at this time) "Sephardic" in a letter to Šlomo ben Adret of Barcelona entitled *Igeret hitnaclut* (found in the latter's *Responsa* 443; cited by Laredo 1944:358).

The significance of these examples is that they date from about a century and a half before 1391—the year when numerous Iberian Jews settled in North Africa in the wake of the nation-wide pogroms in the Iberian Peninsula. Hence, this usage of the term "Sephardic" cannot be attributed to the settlement of Iberian Jews in North Africa, or to the impact of Iberian Jewish scholarly works on North African writers, since the two authors cited earlier were not themselves North Africans. Conversely, the application of the term "Sephardic" to Sa'adya Gaon may not mean that the term *sfarad* was applied freely to all of North Africa Jewry; Sa'adya may have been "adopted" as a "fellow Sephardic" Jew by the Provençal and Catalan Jews, since his Judeo-Arabic translation of the Bible was well known in the peninsula and may even have been the basis of the very literal Ladino translations (better called "Ibero-Romance relexifications") of the Bible, which are first attested only in Italy and Turkey in the mid-16th century (unless we count the *Biblia de Alba*, prepared by rabbi Moše Arragel in the early 15th century as a manifestation of the Ladino tradition; for further discussion, see chapters 2, 4, and 6 this volume). Hence, I conclude that the use of the term *sfarad* to designate North Africa must be a vestige of the original meaning of the toponym, before it became linked exclusively to the Iberian Peninsula.

The date when "Sephardic" ceased to be the label for non-Spanish-speaking North African Jews remains to be determined; I suspect it happened after 1492 in North Africa, when the Iberian refugees sought to distance themselves from the indigenous North African Jews. After 1492, the Iberian Jews in North Africa were called (by non-Iberian Jews or as a Sephardic self-epithet?) He *məgurašim* "exiles" or JSp *forasteros* "outsiders" (this is parallel to the term *barrānī* > *marrano* discussed in chapter 2 this volume), while the indigenous Berber and Arab Jews were called in Hebrew *tošavim* "inhabitants." See also discussion of Tun"He" *baḥucim* "outsiders" in chapter 2, this volume (the latter root in non-Tunisian dialects of "Hebrew" is exclusively an adverb "outside"; its use here as a noun seems to be modeled on Ar *barrā* "outside": *barrānī* "outsider").

Another unanswered question that awaits study is the extent to which the Jews and Muslims (of Berber and Arabic origin both) who returned to North Africa brought back Berber cultural patterns and Berberized Arabic dialects to North Africa. The extent of Berber features retained by the Muslims and Jews could have differed in view of the fact that the Jews left Spain for North Africa beginning with the late 14th century while the Muslims came mainly in the late 15th through early 17th centuries. Future research is necessary to determine whether the folklore of the Iberian Arabs was as Berberized as that of the Iberian Jews.

The trilingualism in Romance, Arabic, and Berber that characterized North African Jewish society could have continued in the Iberian Peninsula after 711, though the written records make clear that Arabic early emerged as the dominant language of the Jews, both in the Muslim-dominated regions in the south and in the Christian north. There is also evidence that some Iberian Jews in the Muslim areas spoke Romance. For further details see the literature on the *muwaššaḥ*s of the 11th century written in Hebrew characters. An important change in the relative importance of Arabic and Romance characterized the Spanish Jewish communities after the 11th century, as more and more Jews began to shift from Arabic to Ibero-Romance (mainly Castilian). This is the first time since the pre-Sephardic communities in pre-Islamic Spain and North Africa that a Romance language emerged as the dominant language of the Sephardic Jews.

It would be interesting to determine whether Judeo-Spanish-speaking emigrés in North Africa after 1391 "converted" indigenous Arabic- and Berber-speaking Jews to Judeo-Spanish; eventually, most North African Sephardic Jews became monolingual speakers of Arabic (and marginally, of Berber?). Judeo-Spanish survived longest in the northwest of Morocco, where it became obsolete by the early 20th century, leaving a small residue of "semi-speakers" whose dominant language was standard Castilian. For further discussion, see the important description of Moroccan Ḥakitía by Benoliel 1926–52.

There is reason to believe that the Jewish population that resided in Spain after 711 was almost entirely of North African origin, though former Iberian emigrés to North Africa could have been included among them. Bachrach postulated a significant Jewish population in Visigothic Spain (1973:13), but there is no guarantee that these communities still existed in 711. The Arab historian Aḥmad Muḥammad ibn Musa ar-Razi (889–955) makes it clear that the North African Jews took the place of the previous Iberian Jews who no longer existed by 711 (his writings are also preserved in a Spanish translation from 1344; see Catalán Pidal 1975:262). As this comment was made almost two centuries after the Muslim invasion, it may reflect a contemporaneous belief that there were no Jews in Spain before 711 rather than the actual reality. For an opposite view, note the Medieval Christian charge that Iberian Jews aided the Muslims in their conquest of the peninsula (Baer 1:1961:22–23).

However, it is also significant that after the documentation relating to Jews in Spain during the Visigothic period, there is no mention of sizeable Jewish communities until the 9th and 10th centuries (in Muslim, Christian, and Jewish sources). One example is the characterization of Granada in 829 as *madīnat al-yahūd* "the city of the Jews" (Torres Balbás 1954:193 and Handler 1974:26). The first individual Jews to be recorded by name also date from this period, for example, the cortesans Ḥasday ibn Šapruṭ (Jaén c.910–970) and Šmuel ben Yosef ibn Nagrella ha-Nagid (Córdoba 993–1055, active in Granada), and the diplomat-slaver Ibrahim ibn Ya'qub (Tortosa, Catalunya 10th c; for further discussion, see the biographical details in Sáenz-Badillos and Targarona Borrás 1988:50–51, 108–109 and 53, respectively, as well as Strohmaier 1979 on ibn Ya'qub). A few other Jews who were identified by name in the 10th century hailed from Lucena (said to be largely populated by Jews) and Granada, with the geographical coverage gradually expanding in the 11th and 12th centuries to include Barcelona, Huesca, Toledo, and Tudela. On the existence of Jewish quarters in Zaragoza, Córdoba, and Toledo in the 10th century, see Lévi-Provençal 3:1967:353, 355, 365; for Córdoba, see also the remarks of ibn al-Faraḍi (962–1013), and Ibrahim (or Avraham Abu Yicxak) ibn Sahl (a Seville Jewish convert to Islam, c.1208–c.1260; ibid.:230, fn 1).

It is curious that the early Spanish Muslim writers rarely singled out the Jews in their detailed descriptions of the Iberian Muslim population, especially since it is unlikely, in view of the data given earlier, that the Jewish population was too sparse to merit separate mention (see ibid.:226). Stillman interprets the Arabic documentary silence as an indication that Arab historians were more concerned with the constant wars with the Christian north, and the Jews were probably a well-assimilated minority whose loyalty was not in question (1979b:54); these claims still do not account for the silence. I wonder whether the silence about the Jews was not a function of the belief among Muslim historians that the Jews were an integral part of the Berbero-Arab population and not a separate ethnic group that required a special mention (Lewicki 1951–52). Of course, why should Jews suddenly make their historical debut in Muslim historial writings in the 9th century? One reason might be that Judaism and Jewish culture were only then beginning to be conceived of—by Jews and non-Jews alike—as separate from Muslim religion and culture. This date did indeed mark the beginning of the end of the period of relatively free conversion from and to Judaism, of unfettered Jewish participation in Berbero-Arab culture and the beginning of Hebrew letters in Spain.

The association of Jews with Arabs is manifested variously in Christian literature; in addition to the Christian accusation that the Jews collaborated with the Muslim invaders in 711 (cited earlier), the Christians employed a common terminology for both Muslim and Jewish artifacts (chapter 5 this volume).

Thus, Sephardic Jews are unique among the various Jewish ethnic groups in that they underwent a *retrograde language shift* in the space of some 700 years—from Romance (and Berber) to Arabic and from Arabic (and possibly Berber?) back to (Ibero-)Romance. The Judeo-Spanish spoken by Sephardic Jews outside of North Africa today still shows Arabic (and to some extent also Berber) influences, some of which do not find immediate parallels in the Christian dialects of Ibero-Romance. As their languages of original written expression, the Sephardic Jews used Arabic, Ibero-Romance and, beginning with the 10th century, "Hebrew" (I purposely use quotation marks since what was called "Hebrew" by the Sephardic writers and by contemporary scholars was in fact Arabic or Ibero-Romance with a majority native Biblical, or less commonly Mishnaic, Hebrew vocabulary; this point is discussed in chapters 4 and 6 this volume). The "Hebrew" pronunciation and grammatical norms of the Sephardic Jews retain a number of markedly Arabic (and possibly Berber) features (chapter 4 this volume). Berber texts written in Hebrew characters are now found in Morocco, but their age is still uncertain. The most pervasive and long-standing Berber contribution to Sephardic Jewry appears to be in the domain of culture and not of language (chapter 4 this volume).

The Alleged "Hispanicity" of the Sephardic Jews

The Sephardic Jews today choose to identify themselves exclusively as transplanted Palestinian Jews who, from time immemorial, have been part and parcel of the Romance-speaking world; most non-native observers share this belief. In fact, the Sephardim, by virtue of their physical removal from Spain, have often been depicted (both by themselves as well as outsiders) as the most loyal bearers of 15th-century Iberian linguistic and cultural patterns at the same time that they are the heirs of relatively pure Palestinian Judaism. Here is a brief sample of recent formulations:

> [The Spanish Jews] left a Spain very Jewish; they went away very Spanish (de Madariaga 1946:25).
>
> While [the Ashkenazic Jews] were susceptible to any kind of superstition prevalent among their non-Jewish neighbours, [the Sephardic Jews] adopted only those practices which were regarded as being 'scientifically' well founded or approved of in the Talmud (Zimmels 1958:249).
>
> Without doubt. . .the reciprocal influence between Jews and Christians,. . .was much more significant in Spain than in any other country (Beinart 1987:11).
>
> [The Spanish Jews took with them] the love of Iberian languages, which they continued to express through speaking, writing, and singing in Ladino (Gampel 1992:34).

Gampel's use of the name "Ladino" to designate the spoken language is imprecise though it is widespread both among Sephardic Jews who speak Judeo-Spanish (known natively as Judezmo, Judyó, Jidyó and, in North Africa, as Ḥakitía) as well as among non-native observers; Ladino was originally the name given to the unspoken translation of Old Hebrew texts (see chapters 4 and 6 this volume). The confusion in the use of glottonyms is a function of the obsolescence of Judeo-Spanish and Sephardic culture in our days.

There are four facts that cast doubt on the claim that the Sephardic Jews had always been closely tied to Ibero-Romance language and culture prior to 1492:

(a) Sephardic folk culture and religious practices are primarily of Berber and Arab origin.

(b) The "Golden Age" of Sephardic Jewish scholarly output took place between the 9th and 12th centuries in the Muslim-dominated parts of the Peninsula and almost exclusively in the medium of Arabic (for example, in the Berber kingdoms that developed in the wake of the collapse of Umayyad Córdoba; see the biographies of Iberian Jewish scholars between the 10th and 15th centuries in Sáenz-Badillos and Targarona Borrás 1988).

(c) Christians tended to identify Iberian Jews and Muslims as members of a common linguistic and cultural community (see chapter 5 this volume).

(d) A form of Spanish became the primary language of most Sephardim only relatively shortly before their expulsion from the Kingdom of Spain in 1492.

The tendency in both the scholarly and popular literature to portray the Iberian Jews as *quintessentially* Romance-speaking—even though a considerable diminution in the number of Romance-speaking Jews must have taken place even before 711—is nearly universal. Beinart's statement blurs the distinctions between types of Jews; we need to distinguish between the relatively strong influence of Islam and Christianity on those Jews who practiced syncretistic forms of religion, and who eventually joined the Muslim and Christian fold (the so-called Marranos), and a relatively weaker Christian influence on the rank and file of the Jewish communities. Despite evidence of assimilation to Christian linguistic and cultural norms, the Iberian Jews and Marranos preserved a remarkable amount of their Berbero-Arab cultural patrimony. Beinart's imprecision is not universally accepted; for example, Martínez Ruiz believes that the contacts between Jews and Muslims in Spain were more intimate than those between Jews and Christians (1957:159; see also the discussion of Judaization in chapter 5 this volume).

Five factors account for the longstanding popularity of the "Hispanocentric" theme in Sephardic self-evaluations and in the scholarly literature:

(a) The belief in the "Hispanicity" of the Sephardic Jews finds its first expression in the writings of Spanish Christian travelers who encountered what they thought was an archaic but pure Castilian in the two Sephardic diasporas (de Illescas 1578 and de Haedo 1612). Contemporary Sephardic scholars blindly espouse these views (note the title of Benardete's book from 1963 or Séphiha [n.d.]).

On the widespread myth that contemporary Judeo-Spanish is a "conservative" or "archaic" language, see A. Alonso 1969:12, fn 11, Kunchev 1977:164, Díaz Mas 1986:104–105, Münch 1991:206, fn 31 and Minervini 1:1992:80, paragraph 3.3.1. Unfortunately, the examples cited for this claim are all features of Judeo-Spanish that are no longer found in Spanish dialects, for example, *š*, *ž*, *fižon* "bean," *fronya* "pillow case" (OSp *š*, *ž* > ModSp *x*, orthographically *j*, as in JSp *pašaro* "bird," *fižo* "son, boy" ~ Sp *pájaro, hijo*; Sp *frejol* "bean," *funda* "pillow case"). Judeo-Spanish looks "archaic" only when measured against the yardstick of contemporary Castilian phonology, morphology, and lexicon; in many other features, Castilian can be shown to be more "conservative" than Judeo-Spanish (Wexler 1977b:169–71 and 1993b). Analogous claims have been advanced periodically about the allegedly archaic roots of Sephardic balladry and music (for example, Seroussi 1991), despite repeated refutation (Bénichou 1968, especially 10, 30, 47, 84, 95, 240, 261, 273, 275, 313, 331, I. J. Katz 1973:243, Sánchez 1990).

Of course, the denial of the African contribution to Spanish ethnogenesis has also characterized Spanish intellectual circles for some time. Many contemporary Hispanists, in Spain and elsewhere, are almost totally oblivious to the fact that the African invaders of Spain were primarily Berbers and not Arabs, and that a sizeable part of the contemporary Iberian population must be of North African extraction. An extreme denial of the African invasion was given by Olagüe 1969—note also that his title singles out "Arabs" and not "Berbers." In his recent dictionary of Spanish history, Bleiberg has no entry for "Beréberes" (1979).

(b) The Sephardic Jews in both diasporas, who were almost exclusively Spanish-speaking, probably cultivated the image of "Hispanicity" as a means of preserving an independent profile vis-à-vis the indigenous Jewries (Wasserstein 1992). For similar reasons, the Jewish descendants of the Portuguese Marranos in Holland, Germany, and England retained Portuguese as their vernacular (until the early

19th century), never acquiring the Yiddish language of their Ashkenazic neighbors who far outnumbered them, and largely shunning intermarriage with the latter until recently. It is revealing that when Ashkenazic Jews in northwest Germany in the late 18th and early 19th centuries gave up Yiddish, they switched to standard German, while the coterritorial Portuguese Jews preferred to switch from Portuguese to the local Plattdeutsch (Low German dialect)—probably as a means of maintaining separateness from the Ashkenazim (Wexler 1987a:36, fn 72). Note also that the Iraqi Jews in India and southeast Asia preserved Arabic (apparently even to the extent of cultivating Muslim Arabic dialectal features in the emigration) and Iraqi cultural patterns from the late 1700s up to the present as a means of insulating themselves from the indigenous Indian Jewish communities (*idem.* 1983b).

(c) It is widely believed that the Sephardic Jews are descended from Jewish settlers who arrived in Spain during the Roman period.

According to the textbook explanation of Iberian Jewish settlement, the first Iberian Jews were the Latin- and Greek-speaking immigrants who came to the Peninsula in the early Christian era. The earliest documented Jewish presence in the Iberian Peninsula dates from the early centuries of the Christian era, for example, there are (Judeo-)Greek and Judeo-Latin inscriptions from the 3rd through 8th(?) centuries (*IHE*), as well as a reference to Jews in the proceedings of the church Council of Elvira that was convened in the early 4th century (Elvira is located in the southeast of the Peninsula, but there is no indication in the document where Jews resided). The Elvira Council document was clearly concerned by the pull that Judaism exercised on the indigenous pagan and Christian populations—to judge from admonitions to Christians to avoid contacts with Jews. This suggests a fairly substantial Jewish settlement in the Spanish lands at that time. On proselytism among the Jews, see chapter 2 this volume. There are myths in (much later) Jewish sources that Jews came to the peninsula with the Phoenicians in the pre-Christian period, but none of these claims can be corroborated. There are also scholars who believe that the distinctive features of the Sephardim (for example, their religious beliefs, their reading pronunciation of Hebrew) were actually brought as such from Palestine; this would provide the Sephardic Jews with a continous history of 2,000 years (Mourant et al. 1978:51).

While a Jewish presence in Spain during the Roman period is not in doubt, it is not at all clear that this settlement existed without interruption up to the North African invasion of 711.

(d) Castilian, which was spreading rapidly throughout the peninsula during the 13th through 15th centuries, affected almost all of the Jews by the early 15th century; Catalan-speaking Jewry had switched, by and large, to Castilian after the nation-wide pogroms of 1391 (Gutwirth 1989b:243). Arabic seems to have survived longest in Mallorca and Granada (the latter alone was under Muslim domination until 1492). The exiles of 1492 give no indication of carrying Arabic to the diasporas, except perhaps for those who hailed from the Kingdom of Granada. On the suggestion that Ibero-Romance dialects other than Castilian were imported to the Balkans, see M. L. Wagner 1914:100ff (in favor) and Wexler 1977b:168–70 (against). To cite Morley:

> when, in 1492, the Jews were expelled from Spain, they carried with them to their scattered asylums, the Spanish language, and Spanish tradition (1947:1).

As I will show, Morley may have been partly right about the language (though the use of Spanish among the Iberian Jews was relatively recent and probably coexisted alongside of a form of Judeo-Arabic that had an inordinately high Spanish lexicon, and has been mistaken for "Spanish"), but I believe his characterization of Sephardic culture was imprecise.

There are a number of potential indices of language shift that still have to be explored, for example, the use of Arabic names among the Jews in different parts of Christian Spain may give a clue to the status of Arabic in the Jewish community. Kraemer has recently suggested that the Arabic feminine anthroponym *Jamīla* was more common among Jews in Castile than in Aragón and Navarra (1991:265, fn 111); however, for this and other Arabic feminine names from Aragón from 1492, see Loeb 1884:70. The name *Jamīla* was never popular in Christian circles. The rare male name *Baḥya*, as in Baḥya (Abu Isḥaq) ben Yosef ibn Paquda (1040?–1110?) or Baḥya ben Ašer (13th century), appears to surface only in Aragón (Gonzalo Maeso 1960:483). In Christian documents, the Jews sometimes have names that could be derived from either Hebrew or Arabic, for example, JSp *Iusua Frances* (Zaragoza 1393; Blasco Martínez 1988:231) < He

Yəhošua' with He *š* > *s* (on the latter, see chapter 4 this volume) or from the Arabic surface cognate. It would be interesting to know if the "merger" of Arabic and Hebrew names into a common Spanish form made the former particularly attractive to Iberian Jews. For further discussion of the reliability of names in reconstructing Jewish migration patterns, see chapter 4 this volume.

(e) The illusion of an uninterrupted settlement history in Spain, beginning with Palestinian Jews of the Roman period and the primeval use of an Ibero-Romance speech form, is undoubtedly also supported by the important Sephardic contributions to Hebrew letters and Jewish religious literature beginning with the 11th century (even though this cultural and scholarly activity was in large part originally composed in Arabic, and later translated into Hebrew, Judeo-Spanish, and sometimes even into Latin). Despite the near total absence of Hebrew and Judeo-Aramaic documentation from the Iberian Peninsula prior to the 10th century, all scholars have also assumed that the Iberian Jews uninterruptedly used these two languages as the media of literature and liturgy.

It is easy to understand why so many scholars grasp so eagerly at this assumption, even though it has absolutely no factual basis: a hypothesis that a Hebrew-Aramaic liturgical tradition in Spain either did not begin until the 10th century or was in disuse for several centuries between the early Christian era and the 10th century calls into question the Palestinian Jewish ethnic stock of the first Iberian Jewish settlers.

Students of Iberian Jewish history after 711 who espouse the hypothesis of an unbroken chain of Jewish loyalty to Romance languages (in spite of the importance of Arabic in Iberian Jewish culture) make no attempt to conceal their bias. In assessing the linguistic preferences of the Jews in Muslim Spain, many scholars either treat the use of Arabic among the Jews and the production of a rich Judeo-Arabic literature as temporary or unworthy of special mention.

For example, Ḫaxen one-sidedly interprets the oft quoted remark by the Jewish poet Šlomo ibn Gvirol (or Gabirol, c.1020–c.1057) in Zaragoza in 1040 that "half [the Jews] speak Romance, the other Arabic" to mean that Romance was the dominant language of the Jews—i.e., "the Jews became arabized"; curiously, he does not say what their previous language was and why Arabic could not have been as dominant a language as Romance was for the poet (1980:72; see also Lévi-Provençal 1:1950:81, fn 1). Bunis cites the bilingual Romance-Arabic *muwaššaḥ*s, written in Hebrew characters by Andalusian Jews in the 11th century, as evidence that Romance was spoken by the Jews—but, strangely, not as evidence that Arabic was the spoken language of the Jews (1992:696–97). Scheindlin, in his comment that the Catalan and Aragonese Jews lost their "Arabic cast" (not "language?") by the 13th century, seems to be suggesting that Arabization was superficial and easily reversible (1992:54).

Even when scholars admit that the Iberian Jews became highly "Arabized," they do not conceive of Arabization as a block on the Jews' participation in Ibero-Romance language and culture; for example, Glick writes that "even highly Arabized Andalusi Jews were able to function in the Romance language" (1979:286; see also 171). Glick never says that "highly Romanized Jews were able to function in Arabic." Recently, Wasserstein has described the Iberian Jews as originally monolingual speakers of Latin/Romance (*sic!*), who later became bilingual in Arabic (1991:14). Corriente also seems to assume that aberrant spellings of Arabic in Jewish documents must mean that the Jews were part of those strata of the population most accustomed to lower registers of Arabic and Romance (1977:43, fn 53)—which would include many non-native speakers.

In two recent descriptions of early Balkan Judeo-Spanish (Judezmo), Bunis displays uncertainty as to whether the language developed in an Arabic or Ibero-Romance ambiance: [Judeo-Spanish] "originated in medieval Spain as the result of the interaction [*sic!*] between the Jews and their Christian and Muslim neighbors" (1991:8). Elsewhere, he suggests that the Jews brought Hebrew and Judeo-Aramaic to Spain (presumably as liturgical rather than spoken languages) and spoke Judeo-Greek; in Muslim-dominated areas of Spain, the Jews were naturally influenced by Arabic (1992:696–97). Blau suggests that Arabic succeeded in becoming a major medium of the Jews only because in Iraq it supplanted genetically related Aramaic, which had filled both colloquial and liturgical functions; in his opinion, in areas where the Jews did not speak Aramaic, for example, in North Africa, Arabic would have been unable to supplant the latter (1962:282; on the status of Aramaic in North Africa, see chapter 2 this volume). Blau makes no attempt to explain why the North African Jews *did*, in fact, become Arabic speakers. Does he assume that it was Iraqi Jewish emigrés who formed the new Arabic-speaking Jewries in North Africa?

Finally, for N. Roth, Arabization seems to be an accidental development, generated by the widespread coterritoriality of Jews and Arabs (both within and outside of Spain), by the fact that Hebrew and Arabic were so similar, and by the Jews' acquisition of an Islamic education (1983a:65). Coterritoriality is not at all convincing, since Yiddish speakers were coterritorial with Poles for centuries before a minority of Jews began to switch to Polish in the late 18th century, and Judeo-Spanish speakers lived in the Ottoman Empire for centuries before they ever became speakers of Turkish in large numbers.

Roth's claim that the similarity of Hebrew and Arabic was a factor encouraging the Jews to acquire Arabic is widely voiced. But Hebrew is beside the point since it was not the native language of any Jew and few could read it. The original so-called "Hebrew" output of these Jews was in fact an Arabic *grammar* onto which a genuine Old Hebrew lexicon had been grafted; hence, it is no surprise if Iberian "Hebrew" and Arabic turn out to have "similar" grammatical structures, differing only in their lexicons—the latter being the only non-Arabic element in Iberian "Hebrew."

It would be interesting to know how Iberian Arab Jews defined the relationship of their unspoken "Hebrew" to Old Palestinian Hebrew. For example, when Šlomo ibn Gvirol described the Jews as speakers of Romance and Arabic equally (discussed earlier), he also bemoaned the fact that Iberian Jews did not "know" (unspoken) Hebrew, i.e., he regarded Hebrew as a separate language. Conversely, in 16th-century Balkan Judeo-Spanish texts, He *lašon*, literally "language," is used to denote both Old Hebrew and Ladino (Karo 1568, cited by Bunis 1993:278). As I stated earlier, the two "languages" are indeed one and the same, since Ladino has a Hebrew syntax with a Spanish vocabulary. Despite the common language name, I doubt that Sephardic Jews in the 16th century ever regarded Ladino as a bizarre form of written Hebrew; the use of *lašon* for both Old Hebrew and Ladino may have been prompted by the identity of the texts and their common liturgical functions. The 16th-century definition contrasts with the 19th-century use of He *lašon* as a designation for Hebrew only (Papo 1862 and Bunis 1993 under *lašon*).

Most scholars ignore the important fact that Maimonides (1138–1204) himself, like the Spanish Arabs of his time, regarded Romance as Ar *ʿajamiyyat al-andalus* "the foreign language of Andalusia" (Meyerhof 1940:lxiv). In Christian parlance, Ar *al-ʿajamiyya* "the foreign language" became Sp *aljamía* (first attested in 1350), which denoted the corrupted Romance spoken by Muslims (*DCECH*). The Muslims also denoted Romance by the term *laṭīniyya*; on the preservation of this term by Jews—in the form *ladino*—to denote a "calque translation" (i.e., relexification) of Hebrew liturgical texts, especially the Bible, whose only Ibero-Romance component was the vocabulary, see chapter 6 this volume. Early on, the Spanish Christians abandoned the term *ladino* as a native glottonym, in favor of *romance*. OSp *ladino* also referred to Muslims who spoke Romance, and by the late 13th century, it appears to have acquired the meaning cunning, crafty, in addition to being the name of Old Spanish.

Though most students of Iberian Jewish history and literature eschew the Spanish term (but not necessarily the notion) *mozárabe* (< Ar *musta'rib* "Spaniard who was Arabized in language and culture but not in religion") in speaking of the Iberian Jewish context, some Hispanists have gingerly proposed classifying Jews who wrote in Romance under the term "Mozarabic" (Stern 1948). Cantera Burgos' coinage, "*judeomozárabe*" has never become popular (1957:18). Sp *mozárabe* first came into use in Christian León in the 10th century to designate any Arabized Romance immigrant from the south, regardless of religion or any Arabized Romance language or text. For discussion of the term and the Romance spoken by the group, see Baldinger 1972:33, 60, fn 37, Galmés de Fuentes 1977, Hitchcock 1981. Today the term "Mozarabic" is broadly used to denote Christians living in the Muslim regions who became attracted to Muslim culture and Arabic language and who wrote Romance (in various dialectal forms, all of them to varying extents Arabized) in Arabic characters.

In my view, the application of the terms "Mozarab(ic)" to Jews is inappropriate since most Jews (before the 12th century) were *by birth* Arabic, rather than "Arabized Romance" speakers. Jews who wrote Romance in Arabic characters include the Zaragozans Yona (Abu l-Walid Marwan) ibn Janaḥ (11th century) and Yona ben Yicxak ibn Biklariš (or Buklariš) (11th and 12th centuries; the Romanisms in his *al-Musta'īnī* were broadly utilized in the *DCECH*—where the author is referred to as Abenbeclarix), Yehuda (Abu l-Ḥasan) ben Šmuel ha-Levi (c.1070–1141) and Avraham (Abu Yicxak) ibn Ezra (1089–1164) from Tudela, Moše (Abu Harun) ben Ya'akov ibn Ezra from Granada (c.1055–after 1135), Ṭodros ben Yehuda ha-Levi Abul'afiah from Toledo (1247–1306) and Yosef (Abu 'Amr) ben Ya'akov ibn Ṣadiq from Córdoba (c.1075–1149;

see Trend 1959:425, 428 and Galmés de Fuentes 1983:19, 35, 293). Some of these Jewish authors preserve the earliest attestations of a number of Spanish words.

If the Jews acquired Ar *laṭīniyya* from the Muslims, it is tempting to assume that the calque language tradition that involved Ibero-Romance vocabulary and was denoted (at least since the mid-16th century) by the term JSp *Ladino*, may also have developed in Arab-dominated areas of the peninsula. Conversely, the Old Spanish meaning of *Ladino* as a "Latinized Spanish" also suggests a certain parallel with the Judeo-Spanish meaning and offers an argument for the claim that the Jewish *Ladino* tradition (if not the use of the name itself) may have been initiated by contact only with the Christian population. It is difficult to give a definitive answer to this question, given the extreme paucity of "translated" (i.e., relexified) Bible texts or even fragments from the peninsula in either Arabic or Romance, but there is some evidence to support the thesis that the Ladino texts (= Hebrew syntax and derivational patterns with an overwhelmingly Spanish lexical filler) were independent of the earlier Arabic (*Šarḥ*) "translations" (= Hebrew syntax and derivational patterns with an overwhelmingly Arabic lexical filler).

The evidence comes from the Arabic translation of the Bible by Sa'adya Gaon, which is known to have circulated in Spain; this translation deviated fairly broadly from the original Hebrew text. More literal translations also circulated in the Arab Jewish communities, including those of Spain, but only small fragments of these translations have survived (Wasserstein 1987, Tobi 1993). The first Ladino "translations" (the Istanbul Pentateuch of 1547 and the Ferrara Bible of 1553 in Latin characters) are far stricter literal translations of the Hebrew text, and hence, may have been inspired by literal Arabic "translations" other than that of Sa'adya. Alternatively, these literal adaptations of the Hebrew Bible may have developed first in a period of intensified Judaization. For a discussion of the interplay of literal renditions vs. relatively freer paraphrases of Old Hebrew texts, see Schwarzwald 1993a.

Arabic acquired important Jewish liturgical functions, while Hebrew was employed almost exclusively in the genre of poetry until the 15th century; for example, rabbi Yicxak ben Šešet Perfet or Barfat (Barcelona 1326–Algeria 1408), who migrated to Algeria in the early 15th century, expressed his regret that a secretary of the Jewish community in Teruel, Aragón knew little Arabic (cited by Neuman 2:1942:255 and Díaz Esteban

1975:97). This shows that knowledge of Arabic was crucial for Jewish communal activities in the late 14th century, at least in southern Aragón.

Gutwirth (1989b:241–45) presents interesting data to the effect that Judeo-Arabic texts, written in Hebrew characters, were prepared for Jews in Zaragoza in 1402 and in Calatayud in 1475; Beneveniste ben Solomon ben Lavi de la Cavallería from Zaragoza and Barcelona commissioned a book in Arabic in the early 1400s from Yehošua ben Yosef ben Vivas al-Lorki (c.1350–c.1419, a native of Lorca, Murcia). Gutwirth has also collected critical assessments of the Arabic language by 15th-century Iberian Jews. For example, Ašer ben Yexiel of Toledo said Arabic texts were too prolix and repetitive (Gutwirth neglects to note that the latter was a German immigrant to Toledo in 1305). While Toledo had been recaptured by the Catholics way back in 1085, ben Yexiel relates that, nevertheless, he had to learn to speak Arabic in order to perform his communal duties (Zimmels 1958:23). On the use of Arabic by Jews in Toledo, despite the absence of a large Muslim community in the late 12th and 13th cenutries, see Septimus 1982:126 fn 99 (with references). Yicxak ben Šešet Perfet (discussed earlier) also deplored the Arabic style of a document. A translation of Thomas Aquinas' Latin commentary on Aristotle's Metaphysics done by Avraham ibn Naḥmias in Ocaña, Castile in 1491 has the following phrase in the preface: "Arabic is not to be trusted."

At the same time, it is interesting to observe that the Church spread religious propaganda among the Jews only in Spanish, while Arabic was occasionally used alongside Spanish in the Christian missionizing efforts among the Muslims (Spiegel 1952:119).

An oblique indication of the primacy of Arabic among the Iberian Jews comes from the status of Arabisms in Judeo-Spanish. In comparison with Spanish, Judeo-Spanish is extremely poor in Iberian Arabisms. The explanation cannot be the expulsion of the Jews in 1492, since by this time, Spanish itself was already quite rich in Arabisms (Neuvonen 1941, Garulo Muñoz 1983, Maíllo Salgado 1983, Wexler 1989b, and chapter 6 this volume). I wonder whether the bilingual Jews were not hypersensitive about the retention of Arabisms as incipient bilinguals who were actively switching from Judeo-Arabic to Ibero-Romance speech and who felt that the retention of Arabisms would detract from their idealized "pure Spanish" norms.

A similar reluctance to use Arabisms characterized the Romance-speaking Muslims. For example, whereas the Arabic in the Romance of the Christians fell mainly in the semantic domains of the military and administration, the Arabic in the Romance writings of the Muslims was limited to Quranic and Islamic terminology (Hegyi 1978:306). This implies that the Jews and Muslims may have used fewer Arabisms in their Romance speech than the Christians themselves. An additional explanation for the small Arabic corpus in the Spanish of both the Jews and Muslims could be that the two minorities learned Spanish in areas where Spanish was relatively weakly Arabicized, for example, in Andalusia. In addition, I will argue later in chapter 6 that the low percentage of Arabisms in Judeo-Spanish could also reflect a partial language shift (i.e., relexification) from Judeo-Arabic to Spanish—involving the insertion of a fully Spanish lexicon.

Scholars are also ambivalent about the status of Arabic language and culture of the Jews resident in other Arab lands. Unlike the Spanish Jews, these have often been called *musta'rib* "Arabized" by scholars, as if to imply that they were not originally an indigenous populace (Idelsohn 1913:535, Tavil 1982:103, Leroy 1985:148). To imply that the Yemenite Jews originally had their own linguistic profile is tantamout to implying that Arabic was a second language for them.

Arabic would naturally be the first language of the Yemenite Jews if the latter were descended primarily from local converts to Judaism rather than Palestinian Jewish immigrants. Goitein subscribes to the view that Arabic became the dominant language of the Yemenite Jews (1934:xii; when?), but he rejects the claim that Yemenite Jews were largely descended from indigenous proselytes (1969:228; see also Ben-Zvi 1961:11). For Goitein, the Yemenite Jews were the "most intensively Arabized" of the Arabic-speaking Jews, though they still probably represented the "traditional Jew in the purest form" (3:1978:ix; on the origin of the Yemenite Jews, see chapters 1 and 2 this volume). For a discussion of Islamized Jews in Yemen in the 15th century, see Rosenthal 1980. Most Jewish historians imply that no matter the extent of intermarriage with non-Jews, the Jews outside of Palestine always remain identifiable as the descendants of Palestinian Jews (Zimmels 1958, passim and chapter 1 this volume).

Yet, if the bulk of the Jews in Spain and North Africa (and indeed in all non-Palestinian communities) descend in the main from indigenous converts, and not from Palestinian Jewish emigrés, then there is no justification in talking about their "Arabization" or "Romanization," etc., since the Jews would have been an indigenous population and thus native speakers of Arabic and Romance from the outset. To speak of "Arabized Jews" in Spain only makes sense if the latter were once speakers of a language other than Arabic. Only a minority of Iberian Jews spoke Arabic as a second language. Some of the Jews in the north of the peninsula (originally in the non-Castilian areas) could indeed have been the descendants of the Roman Jewish settlers, swelled in time by immigrants from Provence and other parts of Europe; these Jews would have presumably been Romance speakers. After 711, however, Jews in northern Spain would have become fluent in Arabic, thanks, no doubt, to the presence of North African Jews. For example, the well-known 10th-century Catalan diplomat and slaver, Ibrahim ibn Ya'qub, presumably recorded his visits to northern Europe in Arabic (they are preserved in this language in the writings of later Arab historians), but he might have been a native speaker of Romance, since his Arabic reveals Catalan substratal influence (Strohmaier 1979; on the use of Spanish by Iberian Jews, see Salomon 1973, Gutwirth 1980, 1986, 1988, and 1989a). However, the existence of Catalan patterns of discourse in ibn Ya'qub's Arabic need not prove he was a native speaker of Catalan; he might have been a monolingual speaker of the then extensively Romanized Catalunyan Arabic.

Towards a New Periodization of Sephardic History

Any periodization is, by definition, somewhat arbitrary and superficial, but the periodization schemes of Sephardic history that have been proposed in the literature tend to ignore the major linguistic and cultural transformations in Sephardic society. The quincentennial literature has produced three periodizations—for Iberian Jewish history (M. A. Cohen 1992:8), Iberian Hebrew literature (Scheindlin 1992:39), and Judeo-Spanish (Bunis 1992:696–706, 1993:17ff). These schemes emphasize three major milestones: the Muslim invasion of Spain in 711, the migration of the bulk of Iberian Jewry from Muslim to Christian areas after the 12th century, and the expulsion edict of 1492.

Cohen's periodization of Iberian Jewish history consists of four stages up to the expulsion edicts:

stage 1: the foundation of the Iberian Jewish communities up to the Muslim conquest of 711;
stage 2: the years from 711 up to the Almohade invasion of c.1150;

stage 3: the flight of Arabic-speaking Jews northward to the Christian domains between c.1150 to c.1350;
stage 4: the split of Jewish communities within Christian Iberia into Catalan, Castilian, Navarran, etc., communities, c.1350–1497.

Scheindlin also proposes a periodization of Iberian Hebrew literature partly based on considerations of migration and expulsion (given the absence of Hebrew literature from Spain before 711, Scheindlin begins his periodization at the point parallel to Cohen's second stage):

stage 1: c.900–c.1150, when most Jewish literary figures inhabited Arabic Spain;
stage 2: c.1100 and c.1300, a "transitional" period when Jews resided in both Muslim and Christian regions;
stage 3: c.1250 to 1492, when most Jews inhabited the Christian regions of the peninsula (he makes no attempt to distinguish between the Christian regions of Catalunya, Aragón, and Castile).

Though the stages of Judeo-Spanish in Bunis' periodization are not explicitly defined, the reader can easily extract the motivations for his trichotomous classification from his discussion:

stage 1: "Old Judezmo" (i.e., Judeo-Spanish), from the 11th century to 1492;
stage 2: "Middle Judezmo," from 1492 to the mid-18th century;
stage 3: "Modern Judezmo," from the early 19th century up to the present.

While Bunis' second and third stages are based on linguistic innovations (for example, growing Hebraization and Castilianization of the lexicon), the delineation of the second and third stages is entirely non-linguistic—the transplanting of Judeo-Spanish from an Ibero-Romance to North African Arabo-Berber and Balkan milieus. Bunis chooses the 11th century as his point of departure on the assumption that the Romance fragments in the bi- and trilingual *muwaššaḥ*s (written by Yehuda ha-Levi and others) are the forebear of Judeo-Spanish spoken by monolingual Iberian Jews. (My reservations about this assumption are discussed later in chapter 6.)

I should like to consider briefly the importance of the proposed milestones, especially the factor of expulsions/migrations. The new homelands of the Sephardim following the expulsions of 1492–98 exposed

Judeo-Spanish language and culture to altogether new influences, for example, Berbero-Arabic in North Africa, and Romaniote (Greek), and Ashkenazic influences in the Balkans; in some cases, the restructuring from the impact of the coterritorial North African and Balkan cultures was far-reaching. Max Weinreich, the eminent Yiddishist, was so impressed with the expulsion edicts that he proposed distinguishing between two periods in Sephardic history—"Sepharad I" (from the earliest settlements up to 1492), and "Sepharad II" (the diasporas outside of the peninsula). Weinreich also applied a terminology to the history of the Ashkenazic Jews that was based on voluntary migration out of the German lands: "Ashkenaz I" for the period when most Yiddish-speaking Jews resided in the German lands, and "Ashkenaz II" for the period when the center of gravity of Ashkenazic culture and population had shifted to the monolingual Slavic lands (1:1973:133).

But no event of migration seriously effected the ethnic make-up of the Sephardic Jews—which reached its final crystallization by c.1200 with the cessation of widespread proselytism; the latter fact never finds expression in any of the proposed periodizations. Despite the traumatic implications of the expulsions, the period 1492–98 hardly symbolizes a "new beginning" in Sephardic cultural history. The expulsion, as has been rightly noted, brought the Sephardim into close contact with Ashkenazic Jews. But the process of "Ashkenazicizing" Sephardic culture had its roots in the peninsula as far back as the early 14th century; this provides an important reason for choosing the early 14th century as a major roadsign in any periodization (see chapters 5 and 6 this volume). The Sephardim were receptive to Ashkenazic cultural influences in Spain, the Balkans, and even in North Africa (during the period of European colonial domination), as well as to North African Berber and Arab Jewish influences because they saw these influences as a means of Judaizing non-Jewish folk practices—a process that began in Spain over a century before the expulsion. For some comparative discussion of Judaization in the Sephardic and Ashkenazic communities, see chapter 6 this volume. The major process of intensive Judaization also finds no place in the periodization schemes.

Cohen's decision to take the year 711 as the boundary between his first and second stages is also unjustified, since this date, dramatic as it is for non-Jewish history, singles no radical transformation in the linguistic, ethnographic, or cultural profile of the Sephardic Jews; it had no serious impact on the mix of Berber-, Arabic- and Romance-speaking proselytes to Judaism, i.e., the Sephardic Jewry that was founded in North Africa must have continued, essentially unchanged, in the Iberian Peninsula after 711. At best, the invasion of 711 may have decreased the proportion of North African and Iberian Romance speakers among the Jews, while raising the importance of Arabic; in the Iberian Peninsula, the North African Jews remained carriers of an essentially Berbero-Arab culture—with the possible difference that contact with Berbers may now have been reduced in certain regions.

I see no particular merit in adopting Cohen's stages 3 and 4 or Scheindlin's stages 2 and 3 since the Arabic- (and Berber-?)speaking Jews who fled northward to the Christian areas to escape the discriminatory practices of the Almohade rulers continued to speak Arabic (and Berber?) for several generations, and even imposed their religious practices and culture on Romance-speaking Jews in the north, in many areas up until the 14th century. (Scheindlin recognizes that the removal of the bulk of the Iberian Jews to Christian regions did not spell the end of Judeo-Arabic; 1992:54.) Only by the late 13th and early 14th centuries did the bulk of the Iberian Jews shift to Castilian—at the height of the Judaization process in the peninsula. Bunis does not discuss the implications of his periodization, i.e., that if Judeo-Spanish begins with the migration of Arab Jews to Christian Romance-speaking areas, it must be the result of a shift from Judeo-Arabic.

Hence, it seems to me that the 13th and 14th centuries—as the *terminus post quem* for the language shift from Judeo-Arabic to some form of Spanish and the *terminus ad quem* for the exposure of Judeo-Berbero-Arab culture to Christianization and the process of heightened Judaization—represents the most significant milestone in Sephardic history. Yet, none of the three scholars surveyed above has given prominence to the late 13th and early 14th centuries for the reasons I have suggested, nor explicitly spoken of the language shift (though the importance of the latter was appreciated by Baruch 1923, Idelsohn 1923:1, González Llubera 1929:8, and Besso 1981:653–54); at best this date is implied in Cohen's and Scheindlin's broader cut in stage 3 and (the "transitional") 2, respectively.

Hebrew spellings of Arabic toponyms and native Hebrew words provide clues to the language shift from Arabic to Romance, as, for example, the loss of the distinction between "emphatic" *q* and "non-emphatic" *k*, a typical feature of Arabic phonology. An early example is the etymologically erroneous spelling of He *knafav* "his wings" as *qnfw* in an 11th-century Castilian Hebrew text (*IHE* 42). An early 14th-century Hebrew text from Tortosa has the spelling *'lksr* for Ar *al-Qaṣr* toponym (ibid.:277). The absence of He *q* suggests that the spelling may have been modeled on the Spanish pronunciation of the toponym, for example, *Alcazar* (ibid.:53–54) and that the scribes were native speakers of Romance and ignorant of Arabic pronunciation norms. Alternatively, the scribes may have been speakers of a Spanish Arabic dialect which had lost emphatic consonants (under Romance influence?), as is the case, for example, in the Judeo-Arabic of Tlemcen and Oran, Algeria today where /k/ and /q/ have merged into /k/ (ibid.:43, 54, fn 74—unless this is due to a Judeo-Spanish substratum; see also Garbell 1954 and chapter 4 this volume). Yet even the language shift from Judeo-Arabic to Spanish between the 11th and 14th centuries had limited importance, since it was not always accompanied by major changes in the ethnic and/or ethnographic structure of the community.

The Jews who left Spain and Portugal between 1492–98, as well as those who remained behind as converts to Catholicism (including the so-called Marranos—who preserved a unique social, if not religious, profile for about 150 years until they either dissolved in the greater Iberian society or emigrated), were almost all speakers of Ibero-Romance; yet, each group retained elements of the original Judaized Berbero-Arabic culture. In the Sephardic diaspora that took root in the Ottoman Empire after 1492, a Judaized Castilian koiné eventually became established (by the 1600s?)—among the Sephardic emigrés, as well as most of the Sephardicized indigenous Balkan Jews (of Ashkenazic [Germano-Slavo-Turkic], and Romaniote [Greek] origins primarily). Contact during some five centuries with Balkan Jews and non-Jews in Europe or with North African Berbers and indigenous Jews introduced the Sephardim to a number of new customs and probably new pronunciations of Hebrew, but does not seem to have eradicated much of their Berbero-Arabic heritage.

In conclusion, if I were to employ Weinreich's stages of "Sepharad," then the period from the genesis of the Sephardic entity in North Africa—with North African Latin, Berber, and Arabic as the three languages of the community—up to the early settlement of Spain, would constitute "Sepharad I." "Sepharad II" could define the period when the North African Jews in Spain shifted from their three languages to a predominantly monolingual use of Arabic. Finally, "Sepharad III" would mark the period that begins with the 11th century and probably continues until the expulsion where Judeo-Arabic was replaced by Spanish, either directly or indirectly through a transitory stage of highly Romanized (i.e., relexified) Judeo-Arabic.

4

The Berbero-Arab Roots of the Sephardic Jews

In chapter 2, I presented a variety of evidence attesting to mass and individual conversion to Judaism in the Near East and North Africa during the first millennium of the present era; it is primarily from these areas that the Iberian Jewish population was to draw most of its members. In this chapter, I will offer linguistic and ethnographic evidence to corroborate the venues of conversion that I postulated earlier. In the preceding chapters, I made two innovative claims:

(a) The "homeland" of the Sephardic Jews should be situated in North Africa in the 7th century, prior to the Muslim invasion of the Iberian peninsula, when a composite "Jewish" community consisting of Romance, Berber, and Arab proselytes and a minor Palestinian Jewish population was created for the first time.

(b) Of all the heterogeneous groups that participated in the formation of the Sephardic Jews, the Berbers appear to have played the most significant role.

The strongest evidence for a North African homeland comes from a handful of North African Latinisms and Grecisms in Judeo-Arabic and Judeo-Spanish, while the suggestion of a Berber provenience is motivated primarily by the strong Berber imprint in the folk culture of the Sephardic Jews which is identifiable even in our day. Judeo-Berber left no remains, but in the areas where it was spoken it must have been replaced fairly early by Judeo-Arabic or Judeo-Romance (by North African Latin and Peninsular Spanish). Nevertheless, Berber inevitably influenced both North African and Iberian Arabic, given the Berber origins of most of the Muslim population. To some extent, Berberized Arabic ultimately passed on Berber features to Spanish. Though Spanish-speaking Jews and non-Jews rarely differ in the inventory of Berber features, there are considerable differences in the details of distribution.

In contrast to language, the Berber impact on Sephardic folklore and religious practice is sizeable; it most likely was also impressive among the non-Jewish sectors of the population at one time, but the force of Arab Islam and Spanish Christianity succeeded in diminishing the Berber elements among the latter. Hence, the Iberian Jews may be the best living repository of early Berber folklore and religious practice. The retention of Berber cultural elements by Christians, Jews, and Berbers at a time when the three groups were rapidly adopting Arabic as their medium of speech and writing suggests that Arabization was much more penetrating in matters of language than in matters of culture and religion.

Evidence from Language

By themselves, linguistic data are not likely to be a conclusive means of determining the geographic or ethnic origins of the Iberian Jews, but against the background of attested proselytism in the Near East, North Africa, and Spain and ethnographic evidence, the language behavior of the Sephardic Jews can assume considerable importance in the reconstruction process. In chapters 4 and 5 this volume, I will examine a variety of linguistic data that lend force to the hypothesis of a non-Jewish proselyte origin of the Sephardic Jews: from Hebrew, Ibero-Romance, Arabic, and Berber, including the Jewish and Christian usage of a common Arabic vocabulary for Jewish and Muslim concepts.

The Status of Palestinian Hebrew and Judeo-Aramaic and the Determination of Sephardic Ethnic Origins

The glaring lack of evidence has not deterred many scholars from describing the Jews outside of Palestine as "linguistically, and therefore culturally separated" from their non-Jewish surroundings (Lewis 1984:77). The Jews' knowledge of written and liturgical Hebrew and Judeo-Aramaic is said to have played a major role in the active process of creating Judaized variants of coterritorial non-Jewish languages, such as Judeo-Arabic, Judeo-Spanish, etc. (on linguistic Judaization, see Wexler 1981a).

Here is a sample of views spanning over half a century:

> Although Hebrew was not the ordinary language of the Jews in the Diaspora, there must have persisted a knowledge of Hebrew, at least among their scholars (S. Katz 1937:64).

> Hebrew flourished in North Africa, especially in the first millennium after Christ. It colored the speech of the indigenous Jewish settlements and can be found in cryptic languages in Morocco (Vycichl 1952b:199).

> The Jews of Mecca and Medina [at the time of Muḥammad] hardly spoke an Arabic dialect of the kind of Yiddish or Ladino [*sic!*], but they must have used a variety of Hebrew names and abstract terms, particularly from the domain of their religious life and literature (Baron 3:1957:81).

> Hebrew [in the Islamic lands] of course remained but its use was limited (Lewis 1984:76).

> [Hebrew and Judeo-Aramaic] words with religious and cultural meanings must have been absorbed first, whatever the historical circumstances, since they had no foreign equivalents, and then fused in [Judeo-Spanish]. . . (Schwarzwald 1993b:40).

Bunis is of the opinion that the ancestors of the Iberian Jews brought both spoken Hebrew and Judeo-Aramaic with them to Spain (1992:697), though he gives no evidence for this claim. The very absence of Hebrew and Judeo-Aramaic in early Jewish diaspora society is one of the factors underlying my claim that the diaspora Jews are largely the descendants of proselytes to Judaism. If it could be shown that the earliest Jewish settlers in Spain spoke Hebrew or Judeo-Aramaic, then it would be possible to argue that they were very likely of Palestinian origin, or descended from Jews recently removed from Palestine.

The absence of spoken Hebrew and Judeo-Aramaic is not the only fact that arouses my suspicion about the Eastern Mediterranean Palestinian origin of the Iberian Jews. The rarity of a written Hebrew and Judeo-Aramaic tradition in Spain before the second millennium is no less striking. The language allegiance of the "Jews" stands in sharp contrast with that of the Romá (Gypsies), who, after about a thousand years of wanderings and dispersal throughout Europe and the Middle East, still preserve, in many communities, their native Indic language. In areas where Romani has been given up entirely, the Romá have often created a substitute "Romanoid" or "para-Romani" language—either by relexifying Romani to a coterritorial non-native language, or by relexifying a coterritorial non-Romani language to Romani vocabulary (in Spain this language is called Caló).

Unlike the Romá, the Jews declined to relexify their Palestinian languages to the coterritorial languages that they acquired in Europe and North Africa. For example, there is no evidence that either spoken Hebrew or Judeo-Aramaic was relexified to Greek, and that subsequently the latter was relexified to Latin, and so forth; in other words, there is no evidence that any of the spoken Jewish diaspora languages used a Hebrew or Judeo-Aramaic syntax, phonology, and phonotactics with a non-Semitic lexicon borrowed from the coterritorial non-Jewish languages. Nor did the Jews regularly create unique variants of non-Jewish languages solely by flooding the latter with mainly Hebrew roots; the only times this happened was when Yiddish speakers attempted to create a cryptic version of Yiddish that would be unintelligible to German speakers. For further discussion, see the Swiss Yiddish horse-trader's jargon, described by Guggenheim-Grünberg 1954 or "Modern Hebrew" (Wexler 1990b).

However, the comparison of Jews and Romá may be misleading if the latter led a more segregated existence from the coterritorial peoples (voluntarily or involuntarily) than the Jews; i.e., the social situation of the Jews might have predisposed them to greater assimilation with the coterritorial non-Jewish majority than was the case with the Romá, which would account for the linguistic assimilation of the Jews in the diasporas. The assimilation of the Jews to their non-Jewish environment may also have encouraged the creation of syncretistic religious expression, which, in turn, could have prompted a significant number of non-Jews to associate themselves with or formally join the Jewish community, whether in the context of intermarriage or otherwise, and Jews (of whatever ethnic origin) to join non-Jewish religious groups.

The fact is that during the first millennium the Jews did not preserve either of their Palestinian languages in speech and barely utilized written Hebrew in the diasporas, with the exception of Judaized Aramaic spoken in Iraq, Syria, Palestine and possibly Yemen—though these dialects were probably not all descended directly from the dialect spoken by the Old Palestinian Jews in their ancestral homeland. A striking piece of evidence that written Hebrew was unknown to most European Jews at the end of the 1st millennium comes from the biography of St. Cyril (Constantine), the Salonikan monk-missionary who brought a Slavic Christian liturgy to the Western Slavs in the 9th century. Cyril relates that he had to travel as far afield as the Crimea to find a Hebrew teacher. This suggests that perhaps the Jewish communities closer at hand in Greece, Bohemia or Italy, could not provide instruction in the language (Pritsak 1981:63). Thus, there is certainly no basis to the assertion that Hebrew attends the birth of a Jewish language and is one of its distinct components (as argued by M. Weinreich 1973[1980]:166, Bunis 1991:7–8 and Münch 1991:172, 203).

Three explanations can be proposed to account for the non-use of spoken or written Hebrew and Judeo-Aramaic in the early years of the European and North African diasporas. Let me begin with a consideration of spoken Hebrew and Judeo-Aramaic:

(a) The Iberian and North African Jews were not in the main descended from Palestinian Jewish refugees. Non-Palestinian converts would have felt little need to learn Hebrew and Judeo-Aramaic from the Palestinian Jewish emigrés. Hence, the minority Palestinian element in the North African and Spanish Jewish communities quickly abandoned Semitic languages in favor of Greek, Latin, and possibly other languages. (The same argument, *mutatis mutandis*, explains the absence of Hebrew and Judeo-Aramaic in Jewish communities in other parts of the world.)

(b) Palestinian Jewish communities speaking Hebrew and/or Judeo-Aramaic were indeed established in southern Europe sometime before the 3rd century A.D.—the approximate date of obsolescence of Hebrew in Palestine. However, these languages were soon replaced by a European language, usually Greek, and subsequently Latin, and left little or no trace. In this case, it would be possible, in principle, to argue for a Palestinian origin for most diaspora Jews.

The absence of colloquial Hebrew in the diasporas is important for establishing the chronology of Jewish settlement in southern Europe and North Africa. Colloquial Hebrew was abandoned in Palestine itself around the 3rd century A.D. We would then expect to find no use of spoken Hebrew in Jewish communities abroad founded after this date. Rome, during the early Christian era, is apparently the only place in Europe where a "synagogue of the Hebrews" is mentioned, i.e., a synagogue whose members claimed descent from a community of Palestinian emigrés or one in which Hebrew or Judeo-Aramaic was the language of prayer (Reinach 1882:143 and Wexler 1993c:22).

Conversely, the absence of Hebrew does not necessarily mean that the Jewish diaspora communities could not have been founded by Palestinian Jewish emigrés, who, I argue, arrived after the 3rd century, after Hebrew had become obsolete in most parts of Palestine; in that case they would have been speakers of either Judeo-Aramaic or Judeo-Greek. We know that Judeo-Aramaic was spoken, along with Judeo-Greek, by Jews in Palestine until the arrival of the Arabs in the 7th century, and that quite a few European Jewish communities were established in North Africa and Spain some time before the 7th century. Hence, if the Iberian and North African Jews had been of Palestinian origin, they should give some evidence of using Judeo-Aramaic. Since the absence of Judeo-Aramaic inscriptions in the diasporas suggests that this was not the case, I have to conclude that the bulk of the European Jews were not very likely the descendants of Palestinian Jews.

(c) The preoccupation with ferreting out traces of spoken Hebrew or Judeo-Aramaic among the diaspora Jews may be out of place. Indeed, Judeo-Greek, and to a lesser extent Latin, were also spoken by Jews in Palestine (note the massive Greek lexical, and also syntactic, component in Old Palestinian [Mishnaic] Hebrew and Judeo-Aramaic). A few Judeo-Greek and Latin inscriptions with Jewish content have been found in many parts of Europe and North Africa, including Spain, for example, the Judeo-Greek synagogue inscription from Elche in Alicante province, thought to date between the 6th and 8th centuries, contains one distinctively Judeo-Greek word—*proseuxē* "synagogue" (*IHE* 406–10 and Noy 1993:241), which in non-Judaized Greek only means prayer (see further discussion following).

Palestinian Jews who spoke Judeo-Greek could have retained this language when they settled in Europe and North Africa, given the international status of the language. If this scenario is true, then it becomes impossible to separate ethnic Jews from converts in the Greek-speaking diasporas.

Even if Palestinian Jewish emigrés did speak Hebrew or Judeo-Aramaic outside of Palestine, there is little chance that those languages could have been maintained for long outside of Palestine, since intermarriage with indigenous non-Jews (and even with Jews long settled abroad) would have greatly reduced the likelihood of passing on spoken Hebrew or Judeo-Aramaic to the successive generations. In summation, none of the evidence warrants the assumption that there ever were stages when the Jewish communities in Spain or North Africa consisted of a Palestinian Jewish majority. There is no basis to Bulliet's claim that before the Muslim invasion of Spain in 711, some Jews in the peninsula did speak a Semitic language (1979b:115).

The status of written Hebrew and Judeo-Aramaic in North Africa and Spain further strengthens my claim that the Sephardic Jews must have been largely of non-Palestinian stock. As I have already indicated, the use of Hebrew or Judeo-Aramaic on pre-Islamic North African and Spanish inscriptions is very spotty. The shipment of the Hebrew-Judeo-Aramaic Bible and Talmud from Iraq, Palestine and/or Arabia to Spain is not attested before the 10th century (see J. Mann 1916–17:486, 1918–19:151, 170, fn 163). There are no extant dated Biblical Hebrew manuscripts that were copied in Spain before the late 12th century (Baer 1:1929:1046, fn 6, 1054, Beit-Arié 1981:14, Scheindlin 1992:39, Sed-Rajna 1992:135). (A list of major Iberian and North African talmudic, biblical, and Hebrew language scholars, beginning with the late 10th century, was given earlier in chapter 2; see also the biographies in Sáenz-Badillos and Targarona Borrás 1988.) Pérès assumes that Álvaro of Córdoba, a Jewish convert to Christianity (d. 861–62), knew Hebrew (1962:726), but what is the evidence for this claim?

The *IHE* lists fewer than a dozen Hebrew inscriptions from Spain, believed to date from the 3th to the 8th centuries, seven inscriptions from the 10th century (the first dated one is from Calatayud 919: their #205), eight from the 11th century, and twelve from the 12th century; after this the number of inscriptions increases rapidly (Noy 1993). In Birnbaum's study of Hebrew paleography, the oldest Sephardic and North African manuscripts are dated approximately from the 9th and 10th centuries (1:1971:##231, 241). The oldest dated Hebrew Pentateuch manuscript, from Egypt, may have been composed in 930 (C. Roth 1953:28). The first occurrence of Hebrew in a rabbinical court document dates from 875 (from Cairo?; Weiss 1977:99). Finally, the trivial Hebrew component in Ibero-Romance languages stands in sharp contrast with the sizeable Hebrew (and possibly Judeo-French) component in German slang lists (known as Rotwelsch) after 1300 (see details in Wexler 1988, chapters 2–3); this fact suggests that even in the later years of Jewish settlement in Spain the indigenous Hebrew tradition was rather weak.

As far as original "Hebrew" prose is concerned, the earliest example is the correspondence between the Córdoba Jewish minister Ḥasday ibn Šapruṭ and the Khazar king in the 10th century. Original Iberian and North African "Hebrew" writing, unlike recopied Semitic Old Hebrew liturgical literature, is not of Semitic Hebrew origin, since its grammar is taken from the spoken language of the scribe—usually Judeo-Arabic or Judeo-Spanish (in the former case, "Hebrew" would of course be Semitic, but a different branch from Old Hebrew).

It might be argued that the virtual non-existence of either genuine Semitic Hebrew or non-Semitic (and Arabic Semitic) "Hebrew" texts between the 4th and 10th centuries in Spain and North Africa was due to the ravages of history. However, since other parts of Europe (for example, Italy, France, and the Germano-Slavic lands) also yield an impoverished harvest of "Hebrew" and "Judeo-Aramaic" texts before the 10th and 11th centuries (Italian "Hebrew" texts predate those of northern Europe by at least a century), I am inclined to believe these languages were simply not used by any European and North African "Jews" during the first millennium A.D. in any capacity. The Jewish cemetery inscriptions of Venosa in southern Italy, dated in the 5th and 6th centuries, also make scant use of "Hebrew" or "Judeo-Aramaic"—with orthographical errors (Lenormant 1882:202–203, 205 and Noy 1993).

In spite of the obviously interrupted transmission of written Semitic Hebrew and Judeo-Aramaic from Palestine to the European Jews, some scholars, nevertheless, assume interference from these two languages as the reason for several unique developments in Judeo-Spanish. For example, Gonzalo Maeso identified the similarity between Hebrew and Arabic as a factor stimulating the renaissance of Hebrew studies in Spain (1960:443). Biblical Hebrew and Arabic are "similar" because both languages are Semitic; Iberian "Hebrew" and Arabic are similar since both are Arabic in grammar! More recently, Bunis (1992:697) has suggested that Ibero-Romance-speaking Jews were able to preserve Arabic sounds (in Arabic loans) which were lacking in their native language more consistently than Christian speakers of Ibero-Romance, due to their knowledge of Hebrew, a cognate Semitic language with a similar sound inventory, thus, for example, Ar *ḥ* > JSp *x* in JSp *tarexa* "task" < Ar *ṭarīḥa* whereas Ar *ḥ* > zero in Sp *tarea* because Spanish lacked *x* at that time (now *x* exists and is spelled usually with *j*). Monolingual Arabic- and bilingual Arabic-Spanish-speaking Jews probably pronounced the voiceless pharyngeal Ar *ḥ* as such; as they became monolingual speakers of Spanish, *ḥ* must have become *x*. Alternatively, the Arabized Berbers and Berber Jews may from the very onset of bilingualism in Arabic have replaced Ar *ḥ* by *x*—as is illustrated by the pronunciation of *ḥ* in Arabisms in North African Berber. By the time most Iberian Jews had become monolingual speakers of Spanish, the latter itself probably had, in some regions, already developed *x* (< *ž*, *š*, etc.), which would have reinforced the *x* in Judeo-Arabic/Spanish Arabisms.

There is absolutely no need to introduce unwritten "Hebrew" into the argument, since its sound pattern was, by definition, a copy of the native Berber, Arabic, or Romance sound pattern of the users. As Garbell showed in her study of Iberian Hebrew pronunciation norms, the latter lacked an autonomous sound system that differed from the vernacular languages of the Jews (1954).

Both Old Judeo-Arabic texts and contemporary dialects show a relatively small corpus of Hebrew loans (though we lack a systematic quantitative and qualitative analysis of the Hebraisms and Aramaisms in Judeo-Arabic parallel to Bunis' comprehensive 1993 study of Hebrew and Judeo-Aramaic in 19th- and 20th-century Judeo-Spanish). M. Cohen has suggested that the closeness of genetically related Arabic and Hebrew (he means, I suppose, the Common Semitic lexicon retained in both languages) actually impeded the borrowing of a large number of Hebrew loans by Judeo-Arabic (1912:387). Is he implying that an alleged difficulty in identifying Hebraisms in Judeo-Arabic would have constituted a block to borrowing them?

The disinclination of Judeo-Arabic speakers to borrow Hebraisms—at least in the Middle Ages—may derive in part from the belief that Hebrew was a form of Arabic. For example, the Iberian Hebrew grammarian, Yicxak ben Yosef ibn Barun, who flourished in Zaragoza around 1100, sought Arabic and Judeo-Aramaic etyma for native Hebrew words (Wechter 1964), while his contemporary, Avraham ibn 'Ezra' (c.1089–1164), described Hebrew as unadulterated Arabic and derived many Biblical Hebrew words from Arabic (Weil 1968:ii–iii). Ibn Barun often interpreted Biblical Hebrew words in terms of the meanings of the Arabic cognates, for example, BibHe *'ɛmɛš* "last night" was linked with Ar *ams*—though the latter means yesterday in the daytime (see Eppenstein 1901:79 and fn 8, and my definition of Ladino as a form of Hebrew earlier in chapter 1). On the explanation of Aramaic words by reference to Arabic in 13th-century Toledo in the writings of Ramah (c.1165–1244), see Septimus 1982:15.

It would be instructive to investigate whether Hebrew terms used in Judeo-Arabic were integrated according to the sound pattern of Judeo-Arabic or replaced by cognates or similar-sounding terms in Judeo-Arabic. For example, talmudic He *ger* "stranger; convert to Judaism" is found in Iberian Sephardic writings and in various other Jewish diasporas, for example, Yiddish. Goitein discusses an Arabic letter of an Egyptian Muslim woman who sought to convert to Judaism in which the verb "convert" was *yuġayyirūki* "they will convert you" (Goitein 2:1971:310, 594, fn 49). This word could be derived either from JAr *ġ-yy-r* "change" or is an Arabic rendition of He *giyyer* "to convert"; see also AlgJAr *tġiyyər* "become Jewish" (M. Cohen 1912:394). But the existence of a merged paradigm, consisting of He *ger* and JAr *mġiyyir(īn)* in North African Judeo-Arabic, shows that cognate Hebraisms were not shunned by Arabic-speaking Jews (Leslau 1945a:72, 1945b:71).

Sala assumes that *š* was kept in Judeo-Spanish dialects wherever *ž* existed; in other dialects, *š* > *s*. He alleges also that *š* was more common in the Spanish of men, who had contacts with Ladino, on which the Hebrew influence was stronger. As I indicated earlier, there is barely any Hebrew lexicon in Ladino translations, but in terms of its grammar, Ladino is Hebrew. Also, women were said to be more likely to pronounce *s* for He *š* (1976:544). Sala's explanation of why He *š* > JSp *s* is not convincing, since *s* appears even when Judeo-Spanish dialects had *š* and *ž* natively—including pre–1492 dialects. I would ascribe the Old Iberian tradition of reading He *šin* (historically /š/) as /s/ to interference from Arabic (and possibly even Berber). The pronunciation of Hebrew *š* in Judeo-Spanish is extremely important since it reveals that the first attested Iberian Jewish reading tradition of Hebrew developed in a Berbero-Arabic-, rather than a Spanish-speaking milieu.

In the quotation cited at the beginning of this chapter, Vycichl expressed the view that Jewish or Judaized speech developed due to the (substratal and/or adstratal?) impact of Hebrew (see his term "colored"—*gefärbt*). This is a widespread misconception that can be readily refuted by two facts:

> (a) The volume of Hebraisms and Aramaisms in most Jewish languages, especially at birth or in their earliest attested stages, is very small. A substantial Hebrew-Aramaic component in a Jewish language can only be posited in much later historical stages, for example, Bunis' study (1993a) of Hebrew and Aramaic components in modern Judeo-Spanish reveals a considerably higher proportion and more variegated corpus than we can find in any texts of Iberian Judeo-Spanish.

I speculate that in all Jewish vernacular languages (with the possible exception of Yiddish, where Hebraisms may have been especially cultivated as a barrier against the Germanization of Judeo-Sorbian; Wexler 1993c) the Hebrew component did not grow in volume until the late Middle Ages, after Jews became relatively segregated or lived separately by choice from non-Jews in many parts of Europe and the Near East. The separation from the non-Jewish environment, that was both voluntary and enforced, brought about an increase in cultural and linguistic Judaization, one of whose manifestations was the Hebraization of the spoken Jewish language (for examples, see chapter 5 this volume).

The broken transmission of Hebrew in the diaspora can be vividly demonstrated by BibHe *hexal* "palace" (ultimately from Sumerian "large room"), used in Medieval Egyptian "Hebrew" in the meaning of ark for the Torah scrolls in the synagogue. Goitein cogently observes that since the Biblical Hebrew term is not attested in Talmudic Hebrew, its appearance in post-talmudic Jewish writings (in Hebrew or a Jewish language) must have another source. He proposed that Egyptian "Hebrew" might have acquired the Hebraism from Coptic *haykal* "sanctuary," itself possibly borrowed from Hebrew since Arabic was never in contact with Sumerian (2:1971:146); it is unclear to me why Goitein ignores the possibility of deriving the term, alternatively, from the Arabic surface cognate *haykal* "altar, temple, statue, huge beast, tall plant." The semantic overlap between Egyptian "Hebrew," Coptic, and Arabic suggests that the Egyptian Jews did not lift the term directly out of a Biblical Hebrew text, though they may have been inclined to accept Coptic *haykal*, etc., under the influence of Biblical Hebrew.

Another term connected with the inner architecture of the synagogue is Gk *ằmbōn* "pulpit," which first surfaces in Talmudic Hebrew in this form and again in Judeo-Greek from approximately the 3rd century A.D. (Krauss 1922:236, 351–52); the Grecism was also used in Latin and Coptic to denote the reader's platform in the church. In the 11th or early 12th century we encounter an entirely new Grecism in this meaning in the "Hebrew" composed by Judeo-Arabic speakers: JAr"He" *anbol* (in a Cairo Genizah document thought to originate in Ashkelon; Goitein 1961). Since this term is not known in Arabic, Goitein assumed the Jews acquired it directly from Gk *ềmboloi* "rostra in the Roman forum." The lesson of this example is that Talmudic Hebrew vocabulary was not as a rule continued in later stages of non-spoken "Hebrew"—until approximately the 2nd or 3rd century of the second millennium, when widescale Judaization processes in European and Arab Jewish communities introduced a host of written Old Hebrew words and expressions, partly due to an upsurge in talmudic and biblical studies. There is no trace of this term either in Iberian Judeo-Arabic or Judeo-Spanish.

Purely Biblical Hebrew terms for the pulpit appear in two Spanish synagogue inscriptions, for example, *migdal ʿec* (literally "wooden tower") in the El Tránsito synagogue in Toledo, built in the mid-14th century, and *migdal david* (literally "the tower of David") in the Córdoba synagogue, built in 1315 (Wischnitzer 1964:29, 34–35). I cannot find JAr *al-minbar* "pulpit" (used also in Yiddish and Judeo-French) in Iberian or North African Judeo-Arabic. The contemporary Judeo-Spanish practice is to denote the reading desk in the synagogue by the Hebraism *teba* (< He *tevah* "ark"; Bunis 1993a:26).

(b) If we eliminate the Hebrew and Aramaic component from a Jewish language, which is by and large localized in the lexicon and almost never in the syntax or phonology, the unique profile of the Jewish language vis-à-vis its non-Judaized cognate(s) is usually not significantly diminished. For example, the removal of Hebrew lexicon (or any other foreignisms not found in the cognate Christian source languages) from Yiddish or Judeo-Arabic would not produce standard German (or Sorbian) or Arabic, respectively. This proves that a prerequisite to linguistic Judaization is not a Hebrew or Judeo-Aramaic input. I shall return to this fact later in chapter 6 when I advance the hypothesis that proselytes (largely ignorant of Hebrew and Judeo-Aramaic) developed the "Jewish" languages—and not the Jews themselves. In particular, it is non-native speakers of Jewish languages and native speakers conversant in the cognate non-Jewish donor language(s) who naïvely believe that Hebrew and Aramaic are crucial to the Judaization process. I suspect this is because most words not shared by a Jewish language and its non-Jewish donor language are Hebrew; for example, the German Christian Yiddishist, Johann Christian Wagenseil, labeled Yiddish as "bad" German, a condition he thought was brought about by the Jews' excessive use of unspoken Hebrew (1699:7).

The linguistic facts presented earlier incline me to reject the widespread claim that despite the low educational level of most of the diaspora Jews in Hebrew and cognate studies at different historical periods, a written and liturgical Hebrew-language tradition was never interrupted in the Jewish community. The longevity of the unsubstantiated claim of a written and liturgical Hebrew tradition extending uninterruptedly from Palestine through the Iberian diaspora was guaranteed by the equally widespread, but also unsubstantiated, claim that a "Jewish people" of Palestinian origin existed in the diasporas. The belief of most Jews in the notion of a single and ancient Jewish people who possess a historical right to modern-day Palestine (though it is a right most decline to exercise) is probably the most important reason for the continued popularity of the "uninterrupted Hebrew tradition" theory, in spite of a growing body of facts to the contrary. There is a vicious cycle here: the belief in direct Palestinian Jewish antecedents was generated by the Judaization process, and the Judaization process was, in turn, stimulated by the belief in Palestinian Jewish origins.

Scholars have long noted that in Muslim Spain, where Iberian "Hebrew" documents first surface in the 10th century, the language was almost exclusively limited to the genre of poetry; in most other forms of written discourse, the Jews wrote Arabic (usually in Hebrew characters). (In my terms, the Iberian Jews wrote poetry in a form of "Arabic" that was heavily infiltrated by Hebraisms, not in Semitic Hebrew.) Even after the start of a written "Hebrew" tradition, and the reception of the Hebrew-Aramaic Bible and Talmud, Jewish scholarly writing in Arabic often ignored Hebrew terms even when the latter were available. For example, the Córdoba-born philosopher, Maimonides (1138–1204), despite his knowledge of Biblical Hebrew, chose not to include Hebrew terms in his multilingual medical glossary (Meyerhof 1940:lxv). Of course, the Hebraisms might have been removed by later Muslim authors who recopied the text (Joel Kraemer, personal communication); if Romance and Berber terms in Maimonides' text were not eliminated by the copyists, that is because they were probably technical terms familiar to all Iberian Arabic-speaking scholars of the time. However, in contrast, a North African Muslim contemporary of Maimonides, al-Idrisi (d.1166), included Hebrew terms in his writings (as a result of his contacts with Jews in Palermo, Sicily?).

In Simonssohn's opinion, Hebrew became popular in Europe after the 8th century with the "Orientalization" of the prevailing Judeo-Greco-Latin culture. This was made possible by the migration of Iraqi and other Arabic-speaking Jewish scholars to Europe and by the forging of closer ties between European and Asian Jewish communities (1974:850–54; and chapter 2 this volume). The exodus of Jews from Iraq followed the Arab invasion which imposed Arabic on the newly conquered territories and caused considerable dislocations in the indigenous societies. The Muslim migrations from the Arabian Peninsula may also have included local Jews. Aramaic was eventually supplanted by Arabic everywhere except in the northern areas of (modern-day) Iraq, Syria, and Iran and in southeastern Turkey (i.e., in "Kurdistan") where a minority Christian and Jewish population continues to speak dialects of Aramaic up to the present day.

Religious writings in Judeo-Aramaic, already unintelligible to Jews living in North Africa, Europe, and Hellenized Asia, now became less intelligible to Near Eastern Jews, as Aramaic lost its position as the spoken language of most of the Western Asian Jews. The language shift from Judeo-Aramaic to Arabic ultimately could have given an impetus to the renewed use of "Hebrew" as a written language, which would account for its preferential ranking over Judeo-Aramaic as a liturgical and literary language (no Jewish nationalists in the late 19th century ever proposed a "revival" of Judeo-Aramaic; see also Baron 5:1957:250). Baer assumes that the use of "Hebrew" in Spain was intended to replace written Judeo-Aramaic (1:1929:1046, fn 6), but there is no evidence that the latter was ever spoken or written in that territory prior to the early second millennium. Yehuda ibn Qurayš of Tāhart (western Algeria) wrote to the Jews of Fès in the 10th century that they should not neglect the study of Judeo-Aramaic, since the latter could lead to a better understanding of Hebrew and Arabic (Zafrani 1967:179); ibn Qurayš probably had in mind written Aramaic.

International contacts between Jews could also have stimulated the use of a common written "Hebrew" as a *lingua franca*. Finally, the interest in elevating either "Hebrew" or "Judeo-Aramaic" to the position of a literary and liturgical language might have been modeled on the practice of the Muslims and Christians, both of whom were codifying their own religious languages—Classical Arabic and Medieval Latin—in the 8th and 9th centuries (on the "artificiality," i.e., non-descendability of Medieval Latin from some form of spoken Latin, parallel to the relation between "Medieval Hebrew" and Old Semitic Hebrew, see Wright 1982, 1992, and Horvath and Wexler 1994). Curiously, the codification of written Arabic and much of the early literature in this language was due to non-Arab scholars (Bulliet 1979b, chapter 6)

It is conceivable that Aramaic enjoyed less prestige than Hebrew among the Jews since the language was not used exclusively by Jews; aside from some Christian populations in the Near East who spoke the language and used it as a liturgical language (for example, the Jacobites, Maronites, Nestorians), forms of Aramaic were the liturgical language of a number of Christian groups during the first millennium in Pakistan, southwest India, and the Sinkiang province of western China.

Another index of the rarity of an early spoken/written Hebrew or Judeo-Aramaic tradition in North Africa and Spain is the paucity of Hebrew or Judeo-Aramaic loanwords in Berber and North African Arabic (I noted the same phenomenon in Spanish earlier). This fact suggests that Hebrew was unknown to the indigenous Jews until relatively recently. Berber dialects appear to have no Hebraisms that are not also found in coterritorial Arabic (Vycichl 1972), despite the fact that Berber-Jewish contacts date from pre-Islamic times. It is difficult to identify pre-Islamic Berber borrowings from Hebrew due to the possibility of positing an alternative Punic etymon. For example, Ber *armūn* "pomegranate" looks on the surface like it might be < He *rimmon* (Ar *rummān* is excluded on phonological grounds), but Colin prefers to posit a Punic etymon for the Berber term for two reasons: the Romans called the fruit *punicum malum* or *punicum pomum*, ascribing it to the Phoenicians, and the term is found only in Eastern Berber dialects (in present-day western Egypt, Libya, and Tunisia) which were exposed to Punic influences (1927:88–89; however, Mercier 1907:89–90 and fn 1 opted for a Hebrew etymon for Ber *armūn*). On Punic influences on Berber, see also Vycichl 1952b.

Most Jewish communities have traditionally developed an unspoken language of Bible "translation" that consists of the syntax and derivational properties of the Biblical Hebrew text with a lexicon which is derived from the Jews' spoken language. In the Iberian milieu, the translation language was called in Judeo-Arabic *Šarḥ* ("explanation") when the lexical filler was derived from Arabic (the name was also used in other Judeo-Arabic-speaking societies), and in Judeo-Spanish *Ladino* ("Latin, the intelligible language") when Castilian lexicon was used. Recently this glottonym has been used, by native speakers and non-natives alike, in violation of historical practice, to designate spoken Judeo-Spanish. Almost all scholars have regarded the *Šarḥ* and Ladino as unspoken "calque" variants of Judeo-Arabic and Judeo-Spanish, respectively (two examples are Blau 1965 and Séphiha 1973). Yet, it stands to reason that if the syntax and derivational patterns of the "calque languages" are Old

Semitic Hebrew, and only the lexicon is Arabic or Spanish, then there can be no such phenomenon as a "calque" variant of Judeo-Arabic or Judeo-Spanish. While the definitions of Blau and Séphiha continue to reverberate through the literature, there have recently been some encouraging signs of dissatisfaction over the status of Ladino as a "language" and its genetic classification, especially among German scholars:

> . . . I also prefer to speak of *Ladino texts* and of a *Ladino* process, not of *Ladino* (Busse 1991b:47; see also his critical remarks, 40–51).
>
> Ladino is thus indeed not an independent language alongside Judeo-Spanish, but a 'sort of text' (Kohring 1991:122, fn 29).
>
> *Ladino*, which is no written language, but rather only a language style, i.e., the translation style of traditional interlinear Bible versions (Münch 1991:215).

I would go one step further than Busse, Kohring, and Münch, and claim that if the calque texts have a Hebrew syntax and derivational structure, and only the original Biblical Hebrew lexicon has been relexified to Arabic or Spanish, then the *Šarḥ* and Ladino texts are, genetically, unspoken dialects of Biblical Hebrew, and as such are Semitic languages with unusual non-Semitic lexicons. Alternatively, since the *Šarḥ* and Ladino texts were originally closed corpera, it may even be more proper to call them "linguistic fragments" rather than "languages." In any case, it is clear that their grammars do not come from the spoken languages of the Jews who composed them (Horvath and Wexler 1994).

Hence, what is commonly called "Medieval Iberian Hebrew" (i.e., original texts composed in Spain, as opposed to copies of genuine Old Hebrew literary or liturgical texts) is genetically either Judeo-Arabic or Judeo-Spanish with a Hebrew lexicon; what are commonly called "Judeo-Arabic" or "Judeo-Spanish calque translations" of Old Hebrew are in reality not "translations"—but dialects of Old Hebrew which are extremely bizarre by dint of their almost entirely Arabic or Spanish lexicon.

In some Jewish communities, a genuine old Semitic Hebrew text (for example, from the Bible) is even replaced by a pseudo-"Hebrew" paraphrase, which utilizes primarily the grammar of the scribe's spoken language. For example, Sephardic Jews in Corfu sometime after the 16th century relexified a Ladino text (itself relexified Biblical Hebrew) to "Hebrew" (Corré 1971:2–3, 113–19).

A comparative study of non-native Hebrew inscriptions from different speech communities would reveal a multiplicity of grammars—with the only feature common to them all being the Hebrew lexical filler. Early European examples of non-Semitic "Hebrew" are a bilingual Hebrew-Latin epitaph from Venosa, Italy, dated between the late 5th and early 6th centuries. The "Hebrew" text reads *šlwm ʿl bnyryqy'ny* /šalom al Benericianus/ "peace on Benericianus" where the proper name carries the Latin dative ending *-i* (Noy 1993:106–107; see also a second text from Venosa with the same dating and a text from Taranto, 7th or 8th century, ibid.:108–10 and 154–57, respectively). The trilingual Tortosa inscription (5th or 6th century?) also reveals a Latin or Greek genitive ending in the Hebrew inscription (ibid.:247). The Latin writing system has even resulted in the writing of correctly formed Hebrew letters from left to right rather than the reverse; an example from Sardinia, 4th or 5th century, is discussed by ibid.:232 (see also 69).

There are no extant Judeo-Arabic or Ladino texts from the peninsula (the earliest Ladino text is the Istanbul Pentateuch of 1547), but many scholars believe the Ibero-Romance calque tradition existed in Spain as early as the 13th century (see, for example, Busse 1991b:40–45, Kohring 1991:122, fn 29 and Münch 1991:215). The Judeo-Arabic *Šarḥ* text was known in the peninsula, since occasional fragments are quoted, even by Muslim writers, but no complete texts have survived.

The existence of "Spanish" or "Arabic translations" of the Hebrew Bible allows me to draw two important inferences:

(a) The Hebrew Bible text must have been available to the Iberian Jews who first devised Ladino; but this is not necessarily the case with the Spanish Arabic *Šarḥ*, which could have been imported ready-made (in the absence of the Hebrew original) from North Africa and the Near East. A thorny question that requires increased study is whether the Ladino texts were modeled on the Arabic *Šarḥ*, either the relatively free version composed by the Egyptian-born Saʿadya Gaon (882–942), known by the synonymous JAr *Tafsīr*, which became popular among Jews throughout the Arabic-speaking world, or the more literal versions done before and after Saʿadya, of which only fragments survive. It would be interesting to determine to what extent Saʿadya's translation was understandable to speakers of other Judeo-Arabic dialects (on differences between his text and Algerian Judeo-Arabic, see M. Cohen 1912:400).

For example, the Spaniard ibn Ḥazm in the 11th century quotes from the Arabic translation of the Mishnah and there is some reason to believe he was familiar with Sa'adya's translation of the Bible into Judeo-Arabic (Y. N. Epstein 1950:24, Tritton 1958:392, Wasserstein 1987:371, Tobi 1993). Since the latter's translation into Arabic departs from the word order and derivational norms of Hebrew, which is unusual in Jewish Bible "translations" in the Middle Ages, the far more literal Ladino "translations" may have been modeled on other Judeo-Arabic texts which followed the syntax and derivational rules of Biblical Hebrew more rigorously. If it could be shown conclusively that this was the case, then Ladino texts would establish the existence in the Peninsula of Arabic translations (i.e., paraphrases) other than the one done by Sa'adya. Arragel's relatively literal translation into Spanish from 1422–33 may be related to Judeo-Arabic translations that are not based on the translations by Sa'adya. I know of no systematic comparisons of the *Šarḥ* and Ladino texts.

(b) The first Ladino "translations" could not have arisen until most Iberian Jews had switched to Spanish—sometime between the 11th and 14th centuries. Hence, I agree with those scholars who have suggested, up to now without convincing argumentation, that the Ferrara and Istanbul Ladino "translations" probably enjoyed Iberian forebears. Given the lateness of the extant Ladino texts (even if I assume that the ***Biblia de Alba*** of Arragel 1422–33 is part of the Ladino tradition), it may be plausible to posit the Ashkenazic scholars who came to Spain in the 14th century as the inspiration for the Ladino translations ("Yiddish" parallels existed by this time).

Since most *Šarḥ* and early Ladino Bible texts follow the syntactic and derivational patterns of Old Hebrew, they are largely unintelligible to speakers of (Judeo-)Arabic and Spanish; hence, the claim that ignorance of Old Hebrew was the reason for the creation of these texts is unconvincing. The calque texts reflect the low prestige of Old Hebrew and Judeo-Aramaic vis-à-vis Judeo-Arabic and Judeo-Spanish.

Spoken Jewish languages tend to utilize free paraphrases of Biblical Hebrew expressions, rather than literal renditions. For example, while Biblical Hebrew phrases were being "translated" literally into Ladino, the same phrases surfaced in colloquial Judeo-Spanish in a looser translation. This fact raises the question of whether the latter were not of immediate Christian (or Muslim) origin since they suggest ignorance of (or disinterest in) the original Hebrew expressions. Another question that requires study is whether the colloquial Judeo-Spanish renditions of Biblical passages are earlier or later than the corresponding Ladino forms. Compare, for example, BibHe *šalax laxmexa al pne hamayim ki berov hayamim timcaenu* "cast your bread upon the face of the waters, so that you will find it at the end of the days," which appears as Lad *solta tu pan sovre fases de las agwas ke en mučedumbre de los dias lo ayaras*, but as JSp *eča un pan ala mar, al kavo del anyo lo toparas* (Bunis 1991:22). Such "paired" examples are known from all Jewish languages and deserve a careful, comparative, study.

A further index of the recency of Hebrew studies among the Sephardic Jews is the quality of written "Hebrew" in non-scholarly materials. When mistakes are uncovered in Iberian "Hebrew" materials, they are often attributed to the unfamiliarity with the language of the alleged non-Jewish scribe or Marrano convert to Christianity, rather than to the ignorance of the Jews themselves. An example is K. Katz's analysis of the misspelled Hebrew inscription on a Passover Seder plate, possibly from Valencia, dated approximately 1450, which contains the vocalized inscription *sɛder pɛsah maccā' mārōr* "the Passover seder, unleavened bread and bitter herbs" instead of the correct spellings *sedɛr, pɛsaḥ*, and *maccāh* (1968:187, 190, illustration #160). Yet, it seems to me that if a non-Jew had confused ' and *h* (the confusion of *h* and *ḥ* is less surprising, since the shapes of the two letters are very similar), his Jewish patrons would have insisted on corrections. Furthermore, how would a non-Jewish artist, presumably ignorant of the Hebrew alphabet, have known to replace the letter *he* /h/ in *maccāh* with *'ayin* which has an entirely different shape? Might he have been supplied with an incorrectly spelled text by his Jewish patrons? If the artist were indeed a Jew, the errors would suggest that in the latter's pronunciation of Hebrew ' had no phonetic value and that *ḥ* had merged with *h*. Such errors could only reasonably be expected from a Jew who was unfamiliar with Arabic; in other words, the Valencian Jewish artist (if the provenience of the dish is accurate) could have been an Ibero-Romance-speaking settler from a more northerly area.

For other misspellings in Hebrew inscriptions from Castile in the 11th century, see *IHE* 42. A poem by the Toledo-born poet Ṭodros ben Yehuda ha-Levi Abul'afiah (1247–c.1306) states that Arabic and Spanish sufficed for the Jews, while Hebrew was unnecessary (Baer 1:1961:239); see also the famous poem by Šlomo ibn Gvirol from Zaragoza 1040 that the Jews spoke only Romance or Arabic which I cited earlier in chapter 3. According to Baer, ignorance of Hebrew in the Jewish communities of Aragón propelled the cantor to assume the leadership of the service in the synagogue (ibid.:313, 432, fn 40; see also Freehof 1962). Conversely, the German rabbi Ašer ben Yexiel (c.1250–1327) who emigrated to Toledo from Köln in the early 14th century, claimed that his Hebrew was poorer than that of the indigenous Jews. For further discussion on the recency of Hebrew studies among the Ashkenazic Jews at this time, see Wexler 1993c, chapter 7. It stands to reason that Hebrew scholarship in Spain could have varied greatly from locale to locale, but not all the details are known.

There is also some indication that Hebraisms were integrated into colloquial Judeo-Ibero-Romance without regard for the original Hebrew phonological or orthographic norms. For example, He *bet din* "rabbinical court" (literally "house of judgement"), sometimes Arabized by an accreted definite article, became an animate noun in 13th-century (Judeo-) Ibero-Romance, see, for example, Sp *vedín, albedín(o)* "rabbinical judge" (cited by Malkiel 1983:18 from the *Libro de los fueros de Castilla* 13th century; see also Garbell 1954:672, Steiger 1956–57 and chapter 4 this volume).

Errors in depiction of Jewish ritual scenes in illuminated manuscripts have also been ascribed to the ignorance of gentile artists. In the Leipzig *Maḥzor*, an illuminated Jewish prayer book produced in southwest Germany between 1310–30, a Jewish male is portrayed wearing a *ṭallit*, or prayer shawl, with red stripes (see the illustration in Krüger 1968:37, Metzger and Metzger 1982:142, #197). Usually the stripes on the *ṭallit* were depicted as blue or black and this color preference continues in force today (though red stripes are occasionally encountered, too). Metzger and Metzger wrote the following comment: "The red stripes that appear in the Leipzig Maḥzor can only be due to an unexplained fantasy of the painter" (ibid.:150). Yet, the Metzgers make no comment on the red stripes on the prayer shawl depicted in an Italian manuscript from Florence 1492 (ibid.:142, #197). Given the widespread belief among northern European Jews that the color red afforded protection against the evil eye (a superstition shared with many coterritorial peoples), it would not be surprising to find a prayer shawl with red stripes. The color red was to some extent extirpated from Jewish use by the rabbis who appreciated the non-Jewish functions of the color. Curiously, the Talmud also ascribes similar functions to the color red; apparently, the authority of the Talmud was insufficient to persuade the diaspora rabbis to keep red stripes on the prayer shawl. On the status of the color red among the Ashkenazic Jews, see Wexler 1993c:160–61 and on Judaization, chapter 5 this volume. This example shows how important it is to recognize that while the Judaization process required citations from the Talmud, not all possible Talmudic precedents were welcomed by the Sephardic or Ashkenazic rabbis.

The status of spoken Aramaic among North African Jews is difficult to reconstruct since non-Jews also used the language and there are few written records. Conceivably, speakers of Aramaic could have accompanied Arabs in their westward migration to North Africa and Spain. If the language were spoken, albeit briefly, in North Africa, was it brought from Palestine, Yemen and/or Iraq? There is some indication that Aramaic may have been spoken in parts of the Central Mediterranean (for example, in Malta) and parts of southern Europe in the first half of the first millennium, but not necessarily by Jews (see Fitz 1972 on the use of Aramaic among Syrian soldiers in the Roman city of Intercisa, contemporary Dunaújváros, Hungary). Spoken Judeo-Aramaic in Egypt in the pre-Christian period had given way to Greek and Coptic.

Both Eastern and North African Arabic dialects have a minor Aramaic component. Aramaisms which surface in North African Arabic dialects could have been brought either as loans in the Eastern Arabic dialects newly brought to North Africa (these loans were obtained from direct contact with speakers and through literature), or acquired from North African dialects of Aramaic (spoken by Jews exclusively?).

The geography of an Aramaism in Arabic is the best clue to the most likely place of borrowing. An example of a pan-Judeo-Aramaism in Arabic is *ṣallā* "pray," *ṣalā* "prayer," though Judeo-Arabic appears to be unique in the semantic calibration of the root, see, for example, JAr *ṣlā* "synagogue" and discussion below. If this term entered Arabic directly from a Judeo-Aramaic source, then we could postulate contact in a variety of locales: Arabia, Iraq, Palestine, or Syria. SpAr *gavn* "disposition, talent" (de Alcalá 1505) and MorAr *jawn* "color" (Bencherifa 1971, #1225) may have come from the Aramaic substratum of Syrian Arabic (Corriente 1977:153; Hebrew also has *gavɛn* "hue").

Only occasionally are we in a position to posit the relative chronology of the diffusion of Aramaisms from east to west, for example, Ar *nā'ūra* "water wheel," of Aramaic origin, appears to have been unknown in North Africa in the 10th century, to judge from the contemporary writings of the Jerusalem-born geographer al-Maqdisi (or al-Muqaddasi; see Fraenkel 1886:134 and Fück 1955:167). The existence of *(an)nora* (1148), *(an)noria* (c.1280), *alnagora* in Old Spanish—surface cognates of BalJSp *naoria, anyaora* (the latter variant appears in Karo 1568:18a, cited by Bunis 1993a:22)—suggests that this Aramaism entered North African Arabic in a later wave, say with the banu Hilal or Ma'qil Bedouins after the mid-11th century. For further variants in Spanish and Judeo-Spanish, see Steiger 1932:287 and Wexler 1988:51. It is tempting to suppose that the distinctiveness of the Judeo-Spanish reflexes with *-ao-* reflects independent channels of diffusion of Arabisms for Jews and non-Jews or at least compensatory lengthening among Jewish speakers for the lost ʿ (which eventually > *g* > zero); the latter case suggests that the Jews may have pronounced Ar ʿ in Arabisms longer than most non-Jews.

It is difficult to reconstruct the source of Aramaisms in North African and Iberian Arabic dialects which are not found in Eastern Arabic dialects—past or present. One example is *qalʿa* "castle, fortress" (with initial stress in Classical Arabic and final stress in Spanish Arabic) ~ EAr *ḥiṣn* (attested in Arabia, Syria, and Palestine, and also very marginally in Spanish toponyms: Colin 1931:13); the existence of Ar *qalʿa* in Iranian, see, for example, Per *ġäl'e*, suggests that the term may once have been known in colloquial Eastern Arabic as well (Fück 1955:169). A similar problem attends the anaylsis of Greek components in Arabic dialects. For example, Gk *pandokeíon* "inn" surfaces as *funduq* in Syrian, Egyptian, and North African Arabic—all once spheres of Byzantine influence (ibid.); this sort of geography complicates the identification of the venue of the borrowing, i.e., the choice is between a local Greek source (in more than one locale) or an imported Eastern Arabic intermediary for the Greek root in North African Arabic.

In 1913, Marçais discussed an Aramaism in North African Arabic dialects that is apparently unattested in Eastern Arabic; in his view there might be grounds for suspecting that the Aramaism diffused to Arabic through a Jewish intermediary. The word, MorAr *xalaqṭīr, xanaqṭīra* (Tangiers) "white magic, incantation formula or the ceremony in which the incantation is recited," first attested in the 7th century, is ultimately from Gk *xaraktēr* "magical sign" (the Grecism is also found as Lat *character* "sign, written magical formula"). Marçais doubted that the Grecism entered Arabic directly and posited instead a Judeo-Aramaic intermediary, *kəlaqṭerin* "image; type" (borrowed from the synonymous variant Gk *xaraktērion*). He based his preference for a Judeo-Aramaic carrier on the dissimilation of *-r-. . .-r-* > *-l-. . .-r-*, which is typical of the latter. But, as Marçais himself observed, dissimilation is also attested in Greek, for example, *xalaktēras* (ibid.:202). I doubt the necessity of an Aramaic carrier on formal grounds, and especially since there is so little sure evidence of a (Judeo-)Aramaic presence in North Africa. I would hope that specialists in the future would address this question systematically.

On the status of Arabic and Spanish among the Iberian Jews, see chapter 3 this volume.

Jewish Onomastics as a Reflection of the Ethnic Origins of the Sephardic Jews

In chapter 1, I discussed the relative status of Arabic and Romance among the Iberian Jews; I return to this question now by examining the extent to which names might serve as an index of the ethnic affiliation, linguistic allegiances, and geographical origin of the bearers. Though names have to be used with great caution due to the facility with which they can spread from one territory to another, they can offer, nevertheless, valuable clues. On the ease with which names can spread, in the absence of the donor language, see Kraemer's discussion of Ar *Jamīla* in chapter 1 this volume.

Goldberg emphasizes, quite rightly, that contemporary Libyan Jews who have Berber surnames need not necessarily be descended from Berber converts to Judaism. He believes itinerant Libyan Jewish peddlars could have acquired Berber names from their Berber patrons (1972:245, 250–51, 254). However, the existence of so many Berber elements in Jewish names from Morocco to Libya (for Tunisia, see Eisenbeth 1936 and D. Cohen 1:1964:1), makes it unlikely that Goldberg's explanation can account for all or most Berber names.

The lesson of Goldberg's data is that we need to find historical and ethnographic evidence to corroborate the tentative conclusions reached solely on the basis of linguistic data. Thus, Bulliet's suggestion that Arabic names can serve as a reliable index of the relative chronology of conversion to Islam (1979a, 1979b) and Abbou's statement that Moroccan Muslims who bear Jewish surnames must have been Jewish converts to Islam (1953:396) are overly simplistic. Iberian Christians who did not convert to Islam also bore Arabic names in Muslim Andalusia (for examples from the 9th through 11th centuries, see Menéndez Pidal 1929:441, Zayat 1948:5, Stern 1949, Lévi-Provençal 3:1967:217). Slavs, too, who were originally brought to the peninsula to be slaves of the Muslim rulers usually received stereotyped Muslim names, though the bearers were not always fluent in Arabic (ibid.:2:1950:125, Canard 1958:23, 131, fn 269; on Slavic-Jewish contacts in Spain, see chapter 2 this volume).

Unlike Arabic names, which were shared by the entire population, Berber names tend to be the exclusive property of Berbers. There are a number of Berber names attested among Moroccan and Iberian Jews, for example, *Yosef ben Yehuda ben Ya'akov ibn 'Aknin*, born in Barcelona c.1150, died in Fès in 1220 (Wasserstein 1985:221, fn 81 suggests he may have been born in Morocco). Another possible example is the first component of the name *Dunaš ben Labraṭ ha-Levi* (c.920–c.990; Sáenz-Badillos and Targarona Borrás believe he was born in Baghdad and educated in Fès, 1988:44), but a Berber personal name would support the view that the latter was a native of North Africa—unless he acquired the name *Dunaš* after emigrating from Baghdad to North Africa (Rabin 1971). Another bearer of this name was the philologist *Dunaš ben Tamim* (c.900–960), who probably hailed from Kairouan, Tunisia. The name *Dunaš* has also been defined as Arabic (Zunz 1837:44). The fact that the name disappears from all records after the 10th century may cast light on the relative chronology of the de-Berberization process.

The surname of *Yicxak Nafūsī*, who settled in Aragón in the late 14th century, points to a Libyan Berber origin (Hiršberg 1963:324). See also the example of *Janūnī* in Eisenbeth 1936:131 (cited also by Goitein 3:1978:491, fn 58). Further Berber examples, *Azoulay, Ergas, Verga(s)*, are discussed by Eisenbeth 1936:89, 124. Note also that the Berber prefix *o-, u-* "son of" appears with the Jewish surname *Ohayon* in Fès 1494 (Zafrani 1968:125) and Portugal before the expulsion of 1498 (Laredo 1978:235); it is unlikely that an Iberian emigré to Fès would have acquired the Berber prefix in just two years of residence there. The Berber name with this prefix is currently very common among North African Jews, but noticeably not among Balkan Sephardim, except occasionally without the Berber prefix (ibid.:575–76 and Elazar 1966:156). This shows that Iberian Jewish names became "de-Berberized" in Spain prior to the expulsion, probably after the 12th century with the waning of Berber hegemony in Spain; in North Africa the prefix might have been restored under the pressure of coterritorial Berber Jews. But there has also been partial Hebraization in North Africa of Ber *Ouhaïoun* (in a French spelling) > *Benhayoun* (Hamet 1928:29, 52–53).

Though Jewish names have to be used with caution in reconstructing ethnic origins, they can still be a reliable indication of migration, as well as language preference or shift, provided we can identify formal changes in the names over time or systematic differences between coterritorial Jewish and non-Jewish variants of a common anthroponymic corpus.

For example, names connected with nonlocal toponyms can give some idea of migration history, though not necessarily that the bearers were descended from non-Jews. Thus, some names allow us to reconstruct migration from the Near East to North Africa to Spain (see the examples of *Dunaš* and *Nafūsī* cited earlier). A problem with names derived from toponyms is that the latter may indicate the place of residence (sometimes very brief) of the bearer or the origin of an ancestor, rather than his own origin. These possibilities are even alluded to in the responsa of

Hay Gaon of Pumbedita, Iraq (d. 1038). The same problem of interpretation attends the surnames borne by Muslims (H. J. Cohen 1970:24–25 and Kedar 1973:128–29).

The danger of using family names as an index of geographical origin is dramatically illustrated by the uniquely Ashkenazic Jewish family names *Blox* and *Valax* (usually spelled *Bloch, Wallach*). These two variants are derived from a single Celtic ethnonym (related to Eng *Welsh* and the second component of *Cornwall*), which, in German and Slavic languages, came to designate a Romance language or group (for example, G *Welsch*, Sl *vlax, volox*, etc.), and by extension an "incomprehensible language" (as in G *Kauderwelsch*). It would be rash to assume a Celtic or Romance ethnic component in the Old Ashkenazic Jewish community, though a Romance or "non-indigenous" land of origin (from the point of view of Germans and Slavs) for these Jewish name-bearers may not be a farfetched assumption.

Finally, we must keep in mind that quintessential Jewish names may not always point to membership of the name-bearer in the Jewish community, for example, a certain *Mosé Cohen* is cited in a Seville Christian document of 1453 as a "Morisco" (K. Wagner 1978, #5). The person in question may have been either a Jewish convert to Islam or an Arabic-speaking Jew miscategorized by the Christian scribe.

The anthroponyms of Iberian Jews before the expulsion which were constructed from toponyms are overwhelmingly of Arabic origin—except for a modest number of Romance names which coexist alongside Arabic names in Catalunya or Navarra (and usually known only from Christian documents).

For example, the common Balkan Sephardic name *Alkalay* (used also by North African Muslims) seems to have developed as a denotation of a person who resides in or comes from a town that has Ar *al-qalʿa* ("the fortress") as one of its components (for example, Sp *Alcalá de Henares, Alcalá de Ayub*, etc.) or, alternatively, from Ar *al-qilāʿ* "castles," the Arabic designation for Castile (< Sp *castillo* "castle"), i.e., a Jew from Castile, assuming that Ar *qi* became Sp *qa* by assimilation to the final *-á*. There is no sound change of *i* > *a* in Arabic, and the final stress on Ar *qalʿa* in both the Spanish and Judeo-Spanish anthroponym reflects the stress placement in Spanish Arabic vs. initial stress in standard Arabic. JSp *-y* < JAr *ī* "person from." Christians could also name themselves after towns with the component *Alcalá*, but they utilized the Romance preposition *de* rather than the Arabic derivational suffix *-ī*, for example, *de Alcalá*. The longevity of surnames derived from toponyms with the Arabic suffix deserves special mention, for example, *al-Lorki* "person from Lorca, Murcia" was in use up to the 15th century.

In the Balkan Sephardic diaspora, names with *-í* are common, for example, BalJSp *Eskaloní* < *Escalona*, the province of Toledo, *Nagiarí*, *Najarí* < *Nájera* (Saporta y Beja ms). For further examples, see Sachs 1934:394–95, 398, M. L. Wagner 1934:239–40, Abbou 1953:81, Martínez Ruiz 1960:110 and Lapesa 1965:108; for further examples with *-í* based on North African toponyms which differ from Muslim forms, see Hamet 1928:27. See also IstJSp *Algranti* (< *Granada*) and SalJSp *Nefusí* < a Libyan placename, and JAr *Nafūsī* discussed earlier. In the Ibero-Romance speech of Christians, Ar *-í* is often found, but not in toponymic or anthroponymic functions, for example, Sp *valencí* "type of grape" (Salvador 1958–59:48; other examples are given in Wexler 1988:60–61) vs. AlgMAr *Balensi* surname < Sp *Valencia* province name (Parzymies 1979:117).

Algerian Muslim family names derived from Iberian toponyms, such as *Andalusī*, *Ġarnāūṭ* (< *Granada*), *Balensī*, *Kartubī* (< *Córdoba*), are relatively few in number, despite the fact that substantial numbers of Andalusian Muslims settled in Algeria in the early 17th century (ibid.). Among Moroccan Muslims, the province of Murcia gives rise to the surname *Almorsy* (Hamet 1928:51).

Very often, Arabic-speaking Jews and non-Jews used different forms of the same personal names; this fact provides us with a fairly reliable means of identifying Jews. Many distinctive Jewish forms of non-Jewish names appear to have been created *in situ*.

For instance, in Jerba, southern Tunisia, Jews have distinctive forms of BibHe *Avraham*, *Mošεh*, *Yosef* in Judeo-Arabic, for example, *Braham*, *Muši*, *Yušif* ~ MAr *Ibrāhīm*, *Mūsa*, *Yūsef* (Udovitch and Valensi 1984:28; there is sibilant confusion in this dialect, so that *Muši* cannot be derived directly from He *Mošεh*). In other regions, for example, Morocco, *Brahim* is a Muslim name (Kjamilev 1968:102). It would be useful to determine where in the Arabic-speaking world Jews and non-Jews have created variants of common names. Schacht suggested over half a century ago that Christians in Spain used standard Muslim names without differentiation, in contrast to a separate communal profile for the two religious groups in Egypt, Syria, and Iraq (1931:173; unfortunately, his examples are not defined according to ethnic or religious group).

Ethnic differentiation in anthroponyms could have three explanations: the existence of different names borne by Jews and non-Jews might imply the existence of communally differentiated dialects in a given locale, that the Jewish settlement was of considerable antiquity, or that the Jews brought these names from another region where they were not originally a distinctive mark of Jewish origin.

The pair He *Avraham*/Ar *Ibrāhīm* might be an example of ethnic differentiation. Among Iberian Muslims the name surfaces as Sp *Hibrahen*, *Ybraen* or *Ibrahim* (see the 16th-century Christian text from Soria discussed by Harvey 1981:2–3); in an Andalusian Arabic source from the late 16th century, the name assumes the form *Abrāhīm* (Corriente and Bouzineb ms, #1494). The latter form is also frequently attested among Jews, for example, Lat *Abrahim* (Barcelona 1279) or Lat *Abraffim* (Sitio de Belaguer

1280; D. Romano 1956:249); on the change of Ar, He *h, x, ḥ* > *f* in some Ibero-Romance dialects, see Wexler 1977b:175ff. *Abrahim* also surfaces as a Jewish name in 13th-century Marseilles and Bougie, Algeria (Loeb 1888; see also examples in Luis Lacave 1971:87 and Peñarroja Torrejón 1990:174, 217). For the undated variant *Ebrahim*, see González Palencia 3:1930:940 and Peñarroja Torrejón 1990:362. The non-canonic forms are not attested in Arabic or Hebrew documents that follow standard Arabic and Hebrew orthography, respectively; only the Romance texts reveal the actual pronunciation of the name. Brockelmann assumed that He *Avraham* > Ar *Ibrāhīm* through the intermediary of Aram **Abrāhīm* (1908:256).

Other names that may be revealing of the ethnic origins of the Iberian Jews are names connected with practitioners of Jewish ritual. Here the question of interest is what language is chosen for the names.

For example, the animal slaughterer, who performs his task according to a Jewish religious ritual, is ordinarily named in Ashkenazic circles by He *šoḥeṭ*, as in family names such as Y *Šoyxet[man]*. The profession also serves as a family name in Spain, where an Arabic root is used, for example, JAr *lḥḥ'm* /laḥḥām/ "butcher" is the basis of the names *l'gym* /lagim/ and *l'gwm* /lagum/ (Sagunto 1358; Baer 1:1929: 208, IHE 314). In view of the fact that there is no *equivalent* Romance name for this profession either among the Iberian Jews or in the Sephardic diasporas, I assume tentatively that in Sagunto (on the Valencian coast) the function of ritual slaughterer may have been performed originally, or primarily, by Arabic-speaking Jews. If so, may I assume that Ibero-Romance-speaking Jews in the late 14th century were generally more lax in their observance of Jewish ritual and, hence, relied on Arabic-speaking Jews to supply ritual slaughterers? The voicing of the medial *ḥ* to **ġ* > *g* is typical of Ibero-Romance dialects (see Lat *vita* "life" > Sp *vida* and discussion of Lat *rūta* in this chapter). Corriente also observes the possibility of voicing *ḥ* > ʿ in Iberian Arabic (1977:57; for Algerian Muslim Arabic, see Marçais 1911:266). See also JPr *sagatar*, Ferrara JIt *sagonnar* "slaughter ritually" < He *šaḥaṭ* (discussed in Wexler 1988:71, 105). In non-Arabic-speaking Sephardic communities, He *ḥ* becomes zero, for example, JSp *Çimá* female name (1492) < He *śimḥah* "joy" (Carrete Parrondo 1991:40; on this name and its form in Judeo-French and Yiddish, see Wexler 1988:97–98).

Similarly, the surname formed from the term for ritual meat cleaner or porger in Spain also seems to be exclusively of Arabic origin, for example, *'ln'qwh* /alnaqāwa/ (Toledo 1341:*IHE* 107), *'nq'wwh* (Tlemcen 1442: ibid.:47), *Anacahva* in a Christian manuscript from Toledo 1404

(Baer 1/2:1936:246) (on the dual rendition of the Arabic definite article *al-*, see later this chapter). Hamet's derivation of the name *Ankauoa* from Ber *in* "from" and a toponym (1928:39) is unconvincing. Goitein cites JAr *munaqqī* "cleaner of meat" (2:1971:570, fn 36), but without mention of place and time of writing. Note also MorAr *naqawa, tenqiya* "cleanliness" (Tedjini 1923 and Sobleman and Harrell 1963, respectively). IrJAr *linqawa* denotes debris taken from the meat in the cleaning process (Ben-Ya'akov 1985); Iraqi Jewish women use this root while men are said to prefer the Hebraism *n-q-r* (ibid.:136). See also the discussion of JSp *purgar* in chapter 5 this volume.

Significantly, I can sometimes plot the language shift from Arabic to Romance, *grosso modo*, on the basis of the changing forms of Jewish names derived from Iberian toponyms, though I recognize that the switch from an Arabic to a Romance form could have come about long after the name-bearers had become Romance speakers. A systematic study of such name changes throughout the peninsula should be a major desideratum of Judeo-Ibero-Romance linguistics.

Some Arabic names derived from toponyms begin to assume Romance forms among Iberian Jews in the late 14th century, for example, *Axibil* (1321), *Axivil* (1352) < Ar *Išbiliyya* "Seville" vs. *de Sibilia* (1372) and *Sevillano* (late 15th century) < Sp *Sevilla* (Wexler 1993d:214, citing examples from Christian Romance documents); see also contemporary Mor (Fès) JSp *Sivilya*. In the Hebrew inscription accompanying parallel Arabic and Spanish texts on the sarcophagus of Fernando III from 1279 in the Cathedral of Seville, the city was still called by the Arabic form, see He *'šbylyh* (*idem*. 1984:44). Further examples from Hebrew inscriptions are given by *IHE* 101, 139, 172, and Zunz 1823, the pioneering study in Spanish Jewish toponyms which retains its interest to this day.

The toponym Ar *al-Qaṣr* appears in a Hebrew inscription from Tortosa, early 14th century, as *'lksr* /alkas(a)r/, which reflects the Spanish pronunciation, see Sp *Alcazar, Alquázar, Alcocer*; the variant Arabized spelling *'lqcr* is also attested. The *IHE* 277 unjustifiably calls the first example a "bad" Arabic spelling. Curiously, the city of Calatayud was rendered in Hebrew sources of the late 15th century in the Castilian manner, for example, *ql'ty[wd]* (de las Cagigas 1946b:87 and Luis Lacave 1971:81), though a Latin document from 1283 has *Calataiubii*, which is closer to Ar *qal'at 'ayūb* (Baer 1:1929:137). Zaragoza is spelled both in the Arabic and Castilian manner in a Hebrew document from Aragón from 1465 (Luis Lacave 1971:49, 79). See also He *Barcelonah* with *c* = /c/ (still the current norm) ~ Cat *Barcelona* with *c* = /s/ vs. Moz *Baršilūna*/*Barj-* (late 9th century: Peñarroja Torrejón 1990:120–21) and the Iberian Jewish surnames *Albaršiloni* Denia, 11th century (Eisenbeth 1936:91), and contemporary Oran *Baršilon* (~ ModstAr *Baršilūna*).

Many well-known Ibero-Romance family names that are derived from Iberian toponyms surface for the most part in the diasporas and are rarely attested in the peninsula before 1492.

Examples are *Marciano* in North Africa (< the province of *Murcia*) and *Toledano*, which is extremely common in both diasporas. A variant of the latter, *Toledo*, first known to me from Istanbul 1755, is less common. For pre-expulsion examples in Christian documents from Seville 1480 and Burgos 1487, see K. Wagner 1978, #161, and López Mata 1951:381, respectively. In addition, there are a number of Iberian Jewish converts to Christianity in the 15th century who bear the name *de Toledo* (Castro 1984:472, fn 40, 477). As far as I know, neither name is common among Christians, though *Toledano* surfaces occasionally among Iberian Muslims; see examples in a Romance manuscript with Aragonese features from 1467, written in Arabic characters (ms DS, line XV–2, in Lincoln 1945:114) and in Seville documents from 1475 and 1502 (K. Wagner 1978, ##131, 404). Hence, Abbou's assertion that Moroccan Muslims who bear the names *Toledo* and *Tredano* are descendants of Jewish converts to Islam (1953:81, 396) is unconvincing (see also earlier discussion of *Alkalay*).

The lateness of *Toledano* is also suggested by the folk etymology for this city, for example, JSp *Toledo no* "Toledo no," exhorting Jews not to return to Spain; this novel etymology was given by Toledano (1911:74, fn 5, and cited by Gutwirth 1986:348, fn 8), but I am ignorant of its age. (This folk etymology shows that the popularity of the surnames *Toledano, Toledo*, at least among Jews, is mainly a post-expulsion phenomenon.) But N. Roth cites the folk etymology proposed by Avraham ibn Da'ud (Córdoba c.1110–1180) that *Toledo* is related to BibHe *ṭalṭel* "thrust out" which occurs in the phrase *məṭalṭɛlxa ṭalṭela* "thrust you out with a (mighty) thrust" in Isaiah 22:17 (1986:191).

In North Africa, Jewish surnames based on Iberian toponyms may surface in both Arabic and Romance forms, for example, *Saragosti* (contemporary Tunis) ~ *Saragossi* (15th and 16th centuries: Eisenbeth 1936:170, Laredo 1978 and León Tello 1979:134), BalJSp *Saragussí* (Saporta y Beja ms). However, the first variant may have been created anew under Tunisian Arabic influence. Arabic surnames used by Balkan Jews either continue Iberian names or were inspired by contact with Turkish Arabisms (for example, *Aben-Ezra, Aven-Yaeš, Yahya*, cited by Molho 1950:71). Similarly, the designation of Balkan synagogues by Iberian topomyms is no sure clue to the Iberian origins of the founders of the congregations (Wexler 1977b:168–69).

The coining of new toponymic surnames in North Africa and the Balkans involving Castilian forms is not necessarily evidence that Sephardic Jews in the diasporas sought to emphasize their links with Christian Spain, i.e., to give expression to their "Hispanic" origins (chapter 3 this volume). The attempt at "Castilianization" outside of Spain may rather have been an attempt to retain a unique profile in areas also populated by non-Iberian Jews. This voluntary Castilianization stands in sharp contrast to Ashkenazic naming practices in the 18th and 19th centuries, when Christian authorities in Germany and Austria forced the Ashkenazic Jews to assume German surnames, very often of non-Jewish invention. At various periods of history, both the Sephardim and the Ashkenazim have often imitated the linguistic norms of Spanish and German speakers, respectively.

Significantly, while Arabic names very quickly became extinct among Christians after the Reconquista, Jews continued to bear Arabic names up to the expulsion and in the diasporas. Royal ordinances forbidding Jews and Muslims from having Christian names might have encouraged the practice among these two minorities to use Arabic names (for example, the decrees of Seville 1268, Valladolid 1313 and 1351 and Toro 1371, cited by Baer 1/2:1936:60, 133, 206–207). Hence, Arabic names cannot be a sure sign of the native language of the bearers, even in Christian-dominated areas.

Another reason why Jews might have retained Arabic names was that otherwise it would have been impossible to keep track of agnatic lineage (i.e., kinship through male descent or on the father's side), assuming that consanguinity remained a powerful social force (Glick 1979:140–41 makes this point in reference to the "Moriscos," Muslims who resided in Christian areas; on agnatic lineage, see also Gutwirth 1985a:87). A question for future research is whether agnatic lineage was retained equally by Jews and Muslims. For example, there is reason to believe that by the mid-10th century, the majority of Andalusian Muslims would have consisted of new Muslim converts who had, presumably, little concern for tribal issues. Conversely, Christian converts to Islam in León in the 9th century did take Arabic tribal names beginning with *benī* along with agnatic forms of kinship (Glick 1979:187–88). Note the Jewish practice of using the Arabic anthroponymic formula *ibn* {*X*}, literally "son of {X}," in which {X} is not the father's name (i.e., *ibn* is not a patronymic) but the name of the head of the family, for example, the father of a certain *Menaxem ibn Zerax* of Navarra (d. 1385), literally "Menaxem the son of Zerax," was *Aharon* (Lešem 1972:57–59). Often the Jewish name contained both patronymic and clan information, for example, Yehuda (Abu l-Ḥassan) ben Yosef ibn Ezra (Granada, 12th century), Šlomo (Abu l-Rabiʿ) ibn Yaʿiš (b. Seville-d. 1345), David ben Yosef ibn Yaḥya (1465–1543). On Spanish Christian names with *ibn* in the 10th century, see Menéndez Pidal 1929:535–36. The formula *ibn* {*X*} still survives in the Balkan diaspora, as in *Aben-Ezra, Aven-Yaeš* (Molho 1950:71), which is a warning not to assume that names that originally denoted agnatic lineage need do so indefinitely. Lešem notes that Arabic *ibn* "son of" is often abbreviated in Jewish sources to *n'* (spelled in Hebrew with a final *n*) which seems to follow Arab norms; a Hebrew abbreviation would be ״ (1972:57).

Finally, the distribution of Arabic names among Iberian Muslims and Jews needs a close study. In areas where Jews tended to have Arabic names, for example, in Zaragoza in the late 14th century, we sometimes find Romance names in use among Muslims (Blasco Martínez 1988:226). Conversely, Peñarroja Torrejón suggests that Romance names were more common among Jews than among Muslims in Valencia (1990:93, fn 125). These facts raise the question of whether Jews and Muslims differed in the pace of their linguistic Romanization and/or Christianization. In the case of Valencia, the Jews may have come to this region from other territories and so could have differed from the coterritorial Muslims who were probably of local origin. A systematic comparison of crypto-Judaism and crypto-Islam in the peninsula might also shed light on this question. The discussion of women as practitioners of crypto-Judaism and crypto-Islam was mentioned earlier in chapter 2 this volume.

Jewish Migration from North Africa to Spain as Reflected in North African Latin and Greek Elements in Judeo-Arabic and Judeo-Spanish

I observed earlier that after the Arab conquest of North Africa in the late 7th century, Romance speech persisted in some parts of the territory as late as the 12th century. North African Romance elements entered Berber and the newly-forming North African dialects of Arabic—either directly or through the intermediary of Arabic and Berber, respectively. I submit that Judaized Latin terms may also have penetrated the Arabic speech of North African Jews prior to their migration to Spain after 711. A few Grecisms (not unique to Judaized dialects), some denoting aspects of Jewish religion and culture, also circulated among Jews in North Africa and these too were deposited in Iberian (Judeo-)Arabic and (Judeo-) Spanish. To the best of my knowledge, no one has ever made this claim before.

Greek was not the major language of the North African Jews after the 2nd century A.D., so I assume that the Grecisms must have been incorporated in the North African Latin of the Jews, just as many Grecisms were used in the Latin of the Jews in Rome (where the local Jews probably spoke Greek as late as the 4th century; on Judeo-Greek inscriptions in North Africa, see Solin 1980:326–27).

North African Latinisms in (Judeo-)Ibero-Romance and/or Iberian (Judeo-)Arabic can be tentatively identified whenever the forms and/or meanings cannot be smoothly derived through the customary channels of transmission to Ibero-Romance from colloquial Iberian Latin or the written Iberian Latin cult language. Non-orthodox channels of transmission almost always presuppose an Arabic intermediary carrier. It also occurs to me that, in principle, some deviant Romanisms in Iberian and North African Romance and Arabic might conceivably be ascribed to the Mediterranean Lingua Franca, or Sabir, first attested in the 16th century (Schuchardt 1909). While this date is too late to be relevant for us, the Jewish and Muslim data offer support for the view that the genesis of Lingua Franca was several centuries earlier than the first attestation of the language.

There is no comprehensive study of the Romance elements in Ibero-Romance that might be from North African Latin, even though quite a few examples have been discussed in the literature.

For example, Spanish preserves a reflex of Lat *quercus* "cork-soled shoe" in the form *alcorque* (15th century), which was probably not inherited directly from Latin, to judge from the /k/ and Ar *al-* "the" (*DCECH*); Sp *alcorque* must have been received via SpAr *qurq*, still attested, in the forms *qọrq, gurg*, etc., in rural Algerian and Tunisian Arabic and in Maltese; the oldest Iberian attestation of the Latinism comes from the writings of the Almerian Jew Yona ben Yicxak ibn Biklariš, c. 1106. For further details, see *DCECH*, as well as Simonet 1888:131, Colin 1931:26, fn 3, Glick 1979:229.

Latinisms in North African Arabic which differ somewhat in form and/or meaning from the Ibero-Romance cognates are an important tool for reconstructing the outlines of North African Latin. Sp *camisa* "shirt" (899) < Lat *camisa* (< Celtic < Germanic; *DCECH*), while the North African Arabic and Berber congeners point to a form with *i* after *s*, for example, AlgJAr *qməjjä* (M. Cohen 1912:420), AlgMAr *qmejja* (Ben Sedira 1910) and Ber *taqmižt* < Lat *camisia* (Schuchardt 1918:59). In Spain itself, Arabic followed Ibero-Romance forms without the second *i*, to judge from Granadan Ar *camíz* (Torreblanca 1982:458–59), unless this should be derived from stAr *qamīṣ* (Simonet 1888:lxvii, fn 2, lxxv, fn 3).

In most Ibero-Romance dialects Latin intervocalic voiceless stops early became voiced. For example, AlgJAr *rūtä* "rue (a woody herb with yellow flowers)" (with a surface cognate in Andalusian Arabic) cannot be derived smoothly from Sp *ruda* (1399; M. Cohen 1912:422–23, *DCECH*); the presence of the voiceless stop in *rūtä* indicates either that Arabic took the term directly from Latin, or from an Iberian dialect which preserved intervocalic *t* until the time of the borrowing. Since the voicing of Latin intervocalic *t* > *d* is attested in Castilian documents as early as the 9th and 10th centuries and so must have already taken place by the time of the first contacts between Spanish and Arabic (Menéndez Pidal 1929:247–65), the most attractive hypothesis is that Algiers Judeo-Arabic continues the North African Latin form with *-t-*, which could have been brought to Spain as early as the 7th and 8th centuries, and then was brought back to Algeria from Spain sometime after 1391.

A contemporary Balkan Judeo-Spanish Arabism which also optionally preserves the original unvoiced stop (corresponding to only a voiced consonant in the Spanish surface cognate) is JSp *taleka* ~ *talega* "bag for carrying the phylacteries and prayer shawl" (Bunis 1993a:148) vs. Sp *talega* "bag, sack" (1202) < Ar *taʻlīqa*. A /k/ is still found in Cat, Arag *taleca*, Mal *talec*, but the latter do not contribute to Judeo-Spanish and are thus irrelevent for us. This particular artifact appears to be uniquely Jewish, since there are no parallel artifacts in Islam or Christianity. For further discussion of synonymous *korača* < Latin, see chapter 5 this volume.

A few of the Romance words in Judeo-Romance that are not attested in other (non-Arabized) Ibero-Romance dialects may also come from North African Latin.

For example, the *Kharjas* have the word *mamma* "mother" that appears in both Greek and Vulgar Latin (Armistead and Monroe 1983:190); Mozarabic (the Arabized Romance spoken in Muslim Spain by Jews, Christians and Muslims—see earlier discussion in chapter 3 this volume) also has a double *m* (ibid.:183). Another example might be BalJSp *barvés*, IstLad *barbez* (Kuli 1730), Mor (Alcaz) JSp *barbej, -l* "sheep" < Lat *vervex*; Spanish uses *carnero* (1049) < Lat *carnārius* (Martínez Ruiz 1980) instead, but Lat *vervex* does appear in Spanish Latin, Catalan, and in a placename in Aragón (García de Diego 1921:409–10). A non-Castilian source of JSp *barvés*, etc., say Catalan, is not attractive since the Romance component of Judeo-Spanish is almost entirely of Castilian origin. Other potentially unique Latinisms in Judeo-Spanish include JSp *končéntu* < Lat *conceptus* "conception" vs. learned Sp *concepto* "concept" and Arag *concieto* "appetite of a pregnant woman," Arag (Alto Ribagorza) "desire to be pregnant" (Malkiel 1955:65; the latter was also discussed by M. L. Wagner 1953:359) and MorJSp *regist(r)o* "shame, modesty, shyness" < Lat *gestŭs* "pose, movement of the body" (Benoliel 1926:505) vs. the Latin cultism that is the basis for Sp *registro* "registration, record, search" (*DCECH*). For other unique Romance strata in Judeo-Spanish which Malkiel attributed to an "early" stratum (but without suggesting a North African Latin origin), see his 1947:286 and fns 72-3; for a discussion of Judeo-Spanish reflexes of Lat *intermittere* "interrupt," see *idem*. 1955:52.

Mozarabic also had a unique corpus of Arabic Latinisms; this is evident from an examination of Mozarabic texts and from the form of some Arabic Latinisms that were diffused to Spanish from Mozarabic dialects. In principle, some of these Latinisms could have been derived from North African Latin and brought to Spain by Arab and Berber speakers (see Martínez Ruiz 1976).

Examples are Lat *campania* "arable land, countryside" > Moz *kanbāniya* > Sp *campiña* (García Gómez 1977:xii); Lat *crocus* "safran" > SpAr **al-qúrqa* (> Moz *qrūqo* (in the writings of ibn Biklariš, see earlier) > Sp *ancorca* (1680, with an unexpected form of the Arabic definite article; an Old Catalan surface cognate dates from 1455; see *DCECH*). For further discussion, see also Baldinger's derivation of Pt *cotoudo* "elbow, cubit" < Moz *qubṭél, -al* < SpAr *qobṭal* < Lat *cubitālis* (1972:75–76; see also Steiger 1932:153–54); the *DCECH* derives Sp *cotobelo* "opening in the bridle bit" from the same Latin etymon. AlgJAr *qǭbṭ ăl* "elbow" must have been brought back from Spain, since Algerian Muslim Arabic has the Latinism in the form *ko*^{u}*ṭ* (M. Cohen 1912:426–27). See also the etymologies proposed by the *DCECH* for Sp *escarlata* "scarlet cloth," *espinaca* "spinach" and *endibia* "endive."

The *DCECH* derives Sp *garbillo* "type of matweed sieve" (in the Castilian of Almería, Murcia, and Valencia) < Cat *garbell* "sieve" < Ar *ġirbāl* < Lat *crībellum* "small sieve." The Latin root is the basis of MorAr *kerbálo* (west of Ceuta) and MorJSp *gerbállo* (with geminated *l*; see Benoliel 1926:534, 1928:194). While the former might be a vestige of North African Latin, the Moroccan Judeo-Spanish Arabism (by virtue of its *g*-) appears to have been brought back to North Africa from Spain.

Linguistic data can also give clues to the diffusion of Iberian Judeo-Arabic and Judeo-Spanish to North Africa after 1391, as well as to movements of Jews and Muslims from Spain to North Africa. A task for the future will be to study systematically the differential impact of Iberian Arabic and Romance on North African Arabic and Judeo-Spanish.

Words like Sp *sera* "basket made from esparto grass" are the basis of my claim that North African Latinisms could have been secondarily diffused from Spain to North Africa. *Sera* appears in Iberian and North African Arabic as *šayra* (10th century). The *DCECH* rejected a Berber origin for *šayra* in favor of a pre-Roman Hispanic source for Sp *sera*. Another example of a pre-Roman pan-Iberian term may be Sp *abarca* "leather sandal," which > SpAr *parġa*; Spanish has borrowed back the Arabic form as *alpargata*, *-e* "cord sandal." It is significant that Alg, Mor (Fès) JAr *pəlġä* "slippers" has *p*—which attests to an Iberian Judeo-Arabic origin, since coterritorial North African Muslim Arabic dialects have the word exclusively with *b*- (*p* is ungrammatical in these dialects), for example, Mor, AlgMAr *bəlġa* (M. Cohen 1912:420, Brunot 1936:6).

It is noteworthy that a number of Latinisms suspected of having a North African etymon or of reaching Castilian through a Mozarabic carrier denote folk customs or beliefs; some of these are preserved in texts written by Iberian Jews and/or surface in contemporary North African Judeo-Spanish or Judeo-Arabic.

An example is Moz *jibsiyāgo* "certain days of the year considered dangerous or unhappy" (in a Jewish source, rabí ben Zaid, 961) vs. Sp *aciago* "of ill-omen" < Lat *aegyptiacus* "Egyptian" (Simonet 1888:163, *DCECH*); Sp *cambuj* (1607) "mask made of linen cloth placed on newly born boys in order that they hold their head to the right" < Moz *qapūč* < SpAr *kanbūš* < Latin (*DCECH*). Finally, to cite an example of a pan-Judeo-Spanish term, see Lat *papāver* "poppy," reshaped under the influence of Ar *ḥabba* "grain of cereal" > Moz *ḥabapáwra* > Sp *amapola* (c. 1400); see also BalJSp *xanapoya* (M. L. Wagner 1931:244) and MorJSp *maxapola* (Benoliel 1926:527, 1928:218; on the change of *b*- > *m*- after metathesis, see the etymology proposed for Sp *marrano* by Malkiel, which I discussed in chapter 2 this volume).

It is extremely difficult to gauge the volume of Latinisms in Spanish and Judeo-Spanish that might have been received through an Arabic intermediary.

For example, SalJSp *kandil*, TunJAr *kandīl* "oil lamp burned in honor of the deceased" (D. Cohen 1:1964:46; see also chapter 5 this volume) could either be from Ar *qandīl* "oil lamp" (< Medieval Gk *kandíli* < Lat *candēla* "candle") or from Arabized OSp *candil* (first attested c. 1400); see also BalJSp *kandela* "candle" < Sp *candela* c. 1140, inherited from Latin (*DCECH*, Bunis 1993a:271, 331).

It is also difficult to decide whether Latinisms in Berber and North African Arabic were received directly in both languages, or whether one of the target languages was the immediate source of the other. Relevant are the discussions of the Latin names of the months by Esteban Ibáñez 1961:453–55, and of Latinisms in Berber by Schuchardt 1918 and Rössler 1962.

Greek words that are known uniquely in North African Judeo-Arabic could conceivably be pre-Islamic Greek or Latin substratal elements. The impact of Greek and Latin on North African Berber also raises the possibility that the latter played a role in diffusing Grecisms and Latinisms to Ibero-Romance. On Tamasheg Berber as a colloquial carrier of Grecisms and Arabisms to West and Central African languages, see Wexler 1980.

For example, Gk *leúkē* "white poplar" surfaces as *lawq* in Medieval Judeo-Arabic poetry from North Africa (Mainz 1949:77, verse 8; Colin 1970:229); aside from Malt *lūq*, I am not aware of the presence of this Grecism in any other North African Arabic dialect. Possibly related is the Moroccan (and other?) Judeo-Arabic family name *(Al-)lūq*, which Laredo derives from two placenames, Lugo (Galicia) and Lluch (Mallorca; 1978:273). The problem with Laredo's first derivation is that few Jews resided in Galicia before 1492. Another example is Gk *mēlōtē* "lambhide" > Ar *mellūṭa* > OSp, OPt *melota, -e* "monk's garment made of hide"; the Grecism also > Lat *melota, -e(s)* > Sp *marlota* "luxurious Muslim clothing" (Baldinger 1972:66–67).

Interrupted transmission also characterizes a number of Iberian Latin toponyms in Spanish, for example, Lat *Gades* > Ar *Qādis* > Sp *Cádiz* (Torreblanca 1982:449, 453, Galmés de Fuentes 1983:24, fn 16); AndLat *Iliberri* > Ar *Ilbira* > Sp *Elvira* (Cabanelas Rodríguez 1992:133). The existence of merged vocabularies in Spanish and Spanish Arabic, consisting of one another's loanwords attests to the extent of bilingual interference in both directions (Glick 1979:81 cites the example of wheat terminology).

Continuing the discussion earlier of a possible North African Romance component in North African and Iberian (Judeo-)Arabic, I shall examine in some detail three Iberian Jewish terms for synagogue. These terms demonstrate strikingly the methodological difficulties that attend linguistic as well as historical and ethnic reconstruction:

(a) JGk *proseuxē* (literally "prayer") is attested once in a Greek synagogue inscription from Elche, Alicante, 6th through 8th centuries;

(b) Lat *schola* (literally 'school') surfaces in the (Judeo-)Catalan and (Judeo-)Aragonese reflexes of the root from the 13th through 15th centuries;

(c) Lat *synagōga* is used in (Judeo-)Spanish, (Judeo-)Portuguese, and in Iberian Arabic in the 13th through 16th centuries, in a variety of syncopated forms, for example, JSp *sinoga*, *esnoga*, etc., SpAr *šnūġa*, etc.

JGk *prosuexē* was first attested in the writings of Flavius Josephus (36–c.105) and in the New Testament (1st and 2nd centuries A.D.; see Wexler 1987b:19–24). The habit of designating the synagogue by the root for prayer is typical of Afro-Asian Jewish languages, and thus may have its roots in Palestinian spoken Hebrew or Judeo-Aramaic (Wexler 1981c; on the existence of a shared old colloquial Hebrew stratum in some Jewish languages, see chapter 4 this volume). In non-Judaized Greek, *proseuxē* denoted preparation (for war).

If JGk *proseuxē* was introduced into Spain through oral channels, then I would suggest às the carriers either Jewish immigrants from Rome in the early Christian era or North African Jews after 711 who could have acquired the word from North African Greek or (Hellenized) Latin; the Grecism is not found in North African Latin sources, but is attested in the writings of Juvenal in the form *proseucha* (ibid.: 118). Alternatively, *proseuxē* raises the possibility that the Iberian Jews were heirs to Judeo-Greek literature, for example, the Septuagint translation of the Hebrew Bible, though the latter is not found in Spain or North Africa, and the Sephardic Jews after 711 probably had no contact with spoken Judeo-Greek.

A piece of evidence supporting a North African venue for JGk *proseuxē* might be the Jewish use of Ar *ḥ-ḍ-r* "prepare, be ready," see BosJSp *las xadras* "month before Passover when women prepare house" (Baruch 1930:148, fn 8, S. Romano 1933, Crews 1960:74–75), SalJSp *xaδrá* "eve of a major religious holiday," *xaδrár* "make preparations for the celebration of a major holiday." Only MorJSp *alxadrar* "be ready, assist in" (now) lacks Jewish ritual associations (Benoliel 1927:569). See also MAr *ḥaḍrā'* "celebration of drinking and eating" (Freytag 1830), *taḥḍīr* "preparation of food," *ḥaḍīra* "floor for drying dates" (Wehr 1971) and Gurage *ḥaḍra* "gathering at which prayers are performed and food is taken" (Leslau 1979:332). Might *ḥaḍra* have originally denoted the festive meal on Friday night, the beginning of the Jewish Sabbath, before developing its present more general meaning? The use of this root with a ritual meaning is also found in Malt *maħdar* "place where the married couple meet their parents on the day of the marriage."

In this example, the Judeo-Spanish infinitive belongs to the class of *-ar* verbs; this is in contrast to other Hebraisms and Arabisms which are assigned to the infinitive class in *-ear*. The distribution of the two endings deserves a special study, especially since the choice may reflect chronological differences. Sometimes Judeo-Spanish and Spanish differ in the choice of endings with Arabic verbs, for example, Sp *harbar* "work with haste, poorly" (c. 1500) vs. MorJSp *xarbear* "ruin, spoil; perforate; search; make untidy" < Ar *ḥ-r-b* (see references in Wexler 1988:74, fn 393, and the discussion of Coromines et al., 3:1982:1014, fn 5). On the other hand, MorJSp *xarbear* might be a post-1492 borrowing from coterritorial Moroccan Arabic.

A North African source of Gk *proseuxē* becomes more compelling when we note that MorJAr *ṣlā* "synagogue" is, like the latter, also derived from the word "prayer" (ultimately, this pan-Arabism is of Aramaic origin). Nowadays in North Africa JAr *ṣlā* is found in Morocco and Libya, as well as in the Judeo-Arabic of Yemen and Iraq; occasionally, we also find *knīs(a)* (*knīs* is the standard Muslim Arabic term everywhere). JAr *ṣlā* has surface cognates in non-Jewish dialects of Arabic but only in the meaning of prayer, for example, written Ar *ṣalā*, plural *ṣalāwāt* (already attested in the Quran; Lane 1863–93), MorMAr *ṣḷā* "prayer" (Westermarck 1:1926:134).

To argue that MorJAr *ṣlā* was modeled on JGk *proseuxē* is, however, problematic, since the Greek pattern of discourse never reached Iberian Arabic or Judeo-Romance either as a loan or a loan translation. The fact that *ṣlā* is unknown in parts of Jewish North Africa as the term for synagogue (where we get *šnūġa*), suggests that *ṣlā* might have been an Eastern Arabic innovation (Yemenite and Iraqi Judeo-Arabic) which reached North Africa after the waves of Bedouin migration in the 11th and 12th centuries, too late to take root in Spain (for Moroccan Judeo-Arabic data, see Stillman 1981:248 [Sefrou] and Heath and Bar-Asher 1982:49 [Tafilalt]; for Libya, see Goldberg 1983:91, for Central Yemen, see Goitein 1934:143, 173). An Eastern Arabic source for JAr *ṣlā* "synagogue; prayer" (as well as for non-JAr *ṣ[a]llā* "prayer") is persuasive since the root comes ultimately from Aramaic—the language of the Jews in Palestine and Iraq, and possibly also Arabia (chapter 3 this volume).

On the surface the broad geography of MorJAr *ṣlā* beyond the confines of Morocco is a powerful argument against deriving the term from a North African Greek prototype; however, I have a reservation about linking African and Asian instances of JAr *ṣlā* in a common isogloss. Even if MorJAr *ṣlā* is not from North African Greek, it might still have independent, indigenous roots. While MorAr *ṣlā* is not used in the meaning of a house of prayer, West African languages spoken by Muslims do use this root to denote the mosque, which they presumably borrowed from Moroccan or Algerian Arabic, for example, Fula *dabsala* "straw mosque" (Gaden 1909), Hausa *masallāci* "mosque" (*ma-. . .-ci* is probably a native derivational process rather than a loan from Ar *muṣalla* "place of prayer"; Wexler 1980:541). West African languages spoken by a predominantly Muslim population also have Ar *masjid* "mosque," for example, Manding *misidi*, etc. The latter is reminiscent of AlgAr *msid* "school" or Mauretanian Ḥassanīya Ar *msīd* (ibid.:541, fn 43, chapter 2 and discussion to follow this volume).

Thus, while the development of "prayer" > "synagogue" is typical of Jewish languages (possibly based on BibHe *bet tfillah*, literally "house of prayer"; on this and other Biblical Hebrew terms for a Jewish house of prayer, see Wexler 1981c), MorJAr *ṣlā* may be altogether independent of Iraqi and Yemenite JAr *ṣlā*, or of Biblical Hebrew, Judeo-Aramaic, and Judeo-Greek patterns of discourse. The African Arabisms allow me to entertain the hypothesis that the shift of "prayer" > "house of prayer" might have been a unique Moroccan *Muslim* innovation which spread south with the diffusion of Islam into West Africa. Subsequently, the use of *ṣlā* to denote the mosque became obsolete in North African Arabic—surviving only among the Moroccan Jews. I cannot rule out the possibility that the "conservativeness" of Moroccan Judeo-Arabic in retaining this term was prompted by the pan-Judeo-Arabic tradition of naming the synagogue by "(house of) prayer"; in other words, the non-Jewish *ṣlā* was amenable to Judaization (supported as it was by Biblical Hebrew). Alternatively, Moroccan Jews may have acquired *ṣlā* from direct contacts with Islamized (and Judaized?) black Africans.

To conclude, a hypothetical MorMAr *ṣlā* "mosque" might have been supplanted by Ar *knīs* or *knīsa* (the latter now denotes the church as a rule), under the impact of Classical Arabic or the Arabic spoken by the banu Hilal Bedouins who swept into North Africa in the 11th and 12th centuries.

SpAr *knīs(a)* denotes variously the mosque, synagogue, and church, and could be of literary Arabic origin. Examples are IbAr *kanīsa* "church/synagogue" (from Abu ʿUbayd ʿAbdullah ibn ʿAbd al-ʿAziz al-Bakri, 11th century, Córdoba; Idris 2:1962:194, fn 2), MorAr *kanīsa* "synagogue" (15th century, Touat, Tamanṭīṭ, southern Algeria; *idem*. 1974:190; see also Hunwick 1985:173). Gottheil also has one example of *kanīsa* for synagogue in an 11th-century Cairo Judeo-Arabic Genizah document, alternating in the same text with *knīs* (1907:487). Ar *knīs(a)* in the meaning synagogue deserves a comprehensive study. For example, when did *k-n-s* undergo bifurcation into *kanīsa* "church" and *knīs* "synagogue?" The coexistence of *knīs* with *ṣlā* in Yemenite and other Judeo-Arabic dialects (cited by Goitein 1934:143, 173, and 2:1971:453, fn 52) may reflect multiple origins of the local Jews. Italian Jews in the 14th century also used It *muskita*, *miskite* "synagogue" ~ OIt *moschéta* (14th century), *meschita* < Ar *masjid* "mosque" (14th through 17th centuries; Wexler 1981c:123). If JAr *knīs* is not a borrowing from Muslim Arabic, it could be an adaptation of written He (*bet*) *knɛsɛt* (< Judeo-Aramaic).

Within Ibero-Romance, reflexes of Ar *knīs* surface only in Portuguese, if this is the source of Pt *genesi(m)* "room or school where rabbis expound on the Bible; tribute paid by Jews for religious schools" (Freire 1939–44) and contemporary Marrano Pt *geneses* "Jewish religious school" (*Ha-Lapíd* 2, 1928, no.11). This example suggests either the lack of a North African Judeo-Greek impact on the Portuguese Jews or a much later origin for the latter, say in the 10th and 11th centuries.

There are other Arabic terms for synagogue, but they seem not to be used by Jews, for example, EgAr *maḥfil* "synagogue; synode; cortège" surfaces as Sp *manfla*—but in the meaning of brothel (late 16th century); SpAr *maḥfal* "reunion" is attested since the 11th century (*DCECH*). In Spain, ClAr *jāmiʿ* "mosque" assumed the meaning of church as well, for example, ValAr *gímee* (1566; Steiger 1932:188, 325, 375).

The use of Lat *schola* "school" to denote the synagogue is characteristic of Judeo-Romance beyond Iberia, for example, the Medieval French and Italian writings of the Jews, and probably has its roots in JGk *sxolē* "school, synagogue," first attested in the latter meaning in the New Testament, Acts 19:9 (Wexler 1993c:102–104). This raises the possibility that *schola* was used in this meaning in colloquial Judeo-Latin and Judeo-Greek. The latter is probably the source of Y *šul* and JSl *škola* (Wexler 1981c:123–27 and 1987b:124–28).

Significantly, *schola*-reflexes surface in regions of Spain that were settled by Jews centuries before the Muslim invasion in 711. Jews of course resided in other areas of the country at this time, but we have no idea how they denoted the synagogue, except for JGk *proseuxē* in Alicante.

It is unlikely that the Catalan and Aragonese Jews inherited *schola* from the original Roman Jewish settlements in those areas; the late attestation of the term everywhere—from the two centuries prior to the expulsion of the Jews in 1492—speaks against a pre-Islamic borrowing. It makes more sense to suppose that *schola*-reflexes diffused from Provençal south into Catalan, Aragonese, and marginally Valencian territory (and possibly north into France), but, curiously, not into (Judeo-)Spanish. The absence of a Judeo-Spanish reflex is surprising, since large numbers of Catalan-, Aragonese- and Valencian-speaking Jews began shifting to Castilian in the late 14th and 15th centuries. This fact suggests that the non-Castilian Ibero-Romance Jews in the northeast of the peninsula exercised little impact on the shaping of Castilian Jewry—at least linguistically (on differences among Castilian, Valencian, Aragonese, and Catalan Jewries in the practice of ritual, see chapter 5 this volume).

In addition to Ibero-Romance, syncopated reflexes of Lat *synagōga* also appear in Judeo-Provençal, for example, *esnogue, esnoga* (M. Cohen 1912:423, Blondheim 1925:115–19), but I presume that the latter is a late loan from Judeo-Spanish or Marrano Portuguese. Valencia constituted a mixed zone with reflexes of both forms, for example, Val *la escola o sonagoga* (1412–14; Hinojosa Montalvo 1978:302). The coexistence of two or more terms for synagogue suggests the words may originally have denoted two different sorts of prayer houses, much like Eng *shul* "orthodox synagogue" (< Y *šul*), *temple* "reform synagogue" and *synagogue* "conservative synagogue." Lida de Malkiel suggested that Lat *proseucha* (< JGk *proseuxē*) denoted a small Jewish house of prayer, in opposition to unmarked *synagōga* (1962:100, fn 7); the suggestion is plausible, but the glosses may have to be reversed, since Balkan Judeo-Spanish reflexes of Lat *synagōga* developed the meaning of "women's section of the synagogue"—i.e., a small version of the male synagogue, for example, SarJSp *znugita* with a diminutive suffix (Crews ms, Saporta y Beja ms; chapter 2 this volume).

While Christians certainly received Sp *sinagoga* < Lat *synagōga*, I doubt that the latter can be the immediate source of the syncopated surface cognates, *esnoga*, etc., the only forms used by the Jews. It is counterintuitive to suppose that the Jews would borrow a Christian term for synagogue; rather it was the Christians who got the syncopated term from the Jews. Furthermore, the syncopated form is often more colloquial in Christian parlance than Sp *sinagoga* and the normal term when referring to specific synagogue buildings. The Inquisition protocols have both the spelling *xinoga* [š-] (Toledo 1489; Beinart 1980:291) and *s-* (Toledo; León Tello 1979:426). Mozarabic sources uniformly show an initial *š-* in this root. In Arabic sources, the plural can be formed optionally with a "broken plural" (discussed later this chapter), for example, *šanā'iġ* ~ *šunūġāt* plural (see also *xonoga*, plural *xonoguit*, in de Alcalá 1505, cited by Griffin 1960:128, according to whom the initial consonant clearly reveals Mozarabic influence; see also Malkiel 1983:34–35). The *DCECH* notes that many Arabisms with the canonic shape CCV- acquire a prothetic *e-* in Spanish (2:1980:661).

As to the geography of the terms, there are two reasons underlying my belief that the Jews acquired Lat *synagōga* in North Africa, though it could become syncopated either in North African or Iberian Arabic. The term was used in its full form in North

African Latin by Jews and non-Jews alike, and in a syncopated form in North African and Iberian Muslim Arabic and Judeo-Arabic. At least two scholars have suggested that Ar *šnūġa* < Gk *synagōgē*: M. Cohen 1912:391, 423, and Leslau 1945a:74, fn 23. Malkiel also regarded the Spanish use of Gk *synagōgē* as a reflection of the influence of Alexandrine Greek culture on the Jews (1983:39); this characterization of Jewish culture may be appropriate for Roman and Hellenistic Egypt, Palestine, and Asia Minor, but I am not sure if it was also true of North Africa at the time of the Arab invasion.

There is considerable evidence that unsyncopated Lat *synagōga* was used in North African Jewish, Christian, and possibly pagan sources from the 2nd to the 6th centuries, for example, on a 4th-century Judeo-Latin inscription from the synagogue at Ḥammam-Lif (Roman Naro) near Tunis, as well as by Christian authors, for example, Tertullian (late 2nd century), St. Augustine (early 5th century), and the Byzantine Emperor Maurice (end of 6th century; Monceaux 1902a:5, 17, 25, 27). Gk *synagōgē* and Lat *synagōga* were not generally used by Jewish authors to designate the synagogue building—only the Jewish community. The semantic shift of Gk *synagogē* "community" > "synagogue" was characteristic only of Christian usage in European languages. In contrast, as I noted earlier, Judeo-Greek preferred *proseuxē* from the word "prayer"—which is a common Afro-Asian, and in part, European Jewish pattern of discourse (Wexler 1981c). Two instances of the term in the meaning synagogue in Hellenistic Jewish communities come from the Theodotos inscription in Jerusalem (thought to date from the late 1st century A.D.) and from Berenike, Cyrenaica (now Libya; see Weill 1920:30 and Lifshitz 1967, #100, respectively, and Wexler 1981c:109).

The origin of the syncopation, or haplology, needs to be established. Malkiel assumed that Lat *synagōga* became syncopated on Spanish territory since haplology in Spanish usually involved Latin roots, though he recognized the existence of phonological problems with this particular word (1983:38). A possible problem with Malkiel's suggestion is that other Spanish Grecisms ending in *-ōgē* undergo no haplology, for example, Gk *isagōgē* "introduction," *paragōgē* "addition of a letter or syllable to a word" > Sp *isagoga*, *paragoga*, unless the latter were much later Spanish cult loans from Latin. I suggest that Lat *synagōga* became syncopated to Ar *šnūġa* in North Africa or very early in Iberian Arabic; for example, Córdoba Ar *šanūġa* and Elvira Ar *'lšnyra* "synagogue" 9th century (Idris 1974:174, citing al-Wanšariši d.1508, and Agnadé 1986:63, fn 91, respectively; the *DCECH* also sites two toponyms *La Sinòga* from Lérida, under the entry *acta*). Conversely, Brockelmann noted examples of haplology in Arabic involving dentals, for example, *istaṭāʿa* "he could" > *isṭāʿa* (1905:630, 1908:262). Haplology in Arabic is easily motivated by the fact that the excessive length of Lat *synagōga* violated permissible Arabic canonic shapes.

M. Cohen specifically rejected the hypothesis of Arabic haplology in our word (1912:423), on the grounds that *š* establishes a Spanish source for the Arabism (ibid.:423). It seems to me that we can posit a North African Arabic origin for the syncopation, since the change of Lat *s* > Ar *š* points to Arabization—either of a Latinism in North Africa, or of an Ibero-Romanism in Spain. When this term was borrowed by Spanish-speaking Jews and Christians, it assumed the form JSp *(e)snoga* ~ Christian *sinoga*, etc. For details, see Malkiel 1983; on the semantic development of BalJSp *eznoga*, SarJSp *znugita* "woman's section in the synagogue," see chapter 2 this volume. This is tantamout to claiming that *sinoga*, etc., and *sinagoga* reached Spanish through two paths of diffusion.

Among Arabic-speaking North African Arabs and Jews, *šnūġa* is sporadically attested in Algeria, among Muslims in Tlemcen (M. Cohen 1912:423), and Jews in Oran (Corré 1991:42; see also Malkiel 1983:29 and fn 64, 36–37). It is also known in the Judeo-Arabic of Debdou (in the Atlas mountains of Morocco, about 80 miles east of the Algerian border). Writing in the early 19th century, Borrow cites the (Spanish?) form *šenoura* without a gloss (1869:28), which suggests the term was still widely known at this time. The geography of the occasional *šnūġa* forms in North Africa does not point to a relic form from North African Latin and Arabic, since most of the locales in which it surfaces were settled by Iberian Jewish refugees between 1391 and 1492. Hence, I view NAfrJAr *šnūġa* as a "returnee" from Spain—i.e., an Old North African Arabic term used in Iberian Arabic. Oran had no organized Arab Jewish communities before the 13th century, i.e., a century before the arrival of the first Spanish Jewish emigrés in 1391, while Tlemcen was a major Judeo-Berber center in the 10th and 11th centuries that had contacts with Iraqi Jewish scholars, was destroyed by the Almohades in 1146, and regained a Jewish population only in 1248, with Spanish Jews arriving after 1492. Hence, I conclude that NAfr(J)Ar *šnūġa* died out in its North African homeland after 711, only to be subsequently revived in a few locales thanks to Sephardic returnees to Africa.

It is a puzzle why some Iberian Arabic sources qualify *šnūġa* with the phrase "of the Jews." For example, the poet Ibrahim ibn Sahl (d. 1251 or 1260), a Seville Jewish convert to Islam whose use of wine rendered his adherence to Islam suspect (on syncretistic religious practices, see chapter 2 this volume), uses the expression *šnūġāt al-yahūd* (Lévi-Provençal 3:1967:230, fn 1), as if to imply that there were also non-Jewish "synagogues" as well. Or perhaps the term was at that time not yet in common use among Spanish Muslims, who might have preferred *knīs(a)* (discussed earlier). In any event, ibn Sahl's evidence suggests that Iberian Jews did use the term. The relative productivity of JAr *šnūġa* needs to be studied; it is interesting that Maimonides uses the expression *bet alknεsεt* in his Judeo-Arabic writings (due to similarity with Ar *knīs[a]*?; see Blau 1958:190, fn 40).

In summation, if NAfr(J)Lat *sinagōga* > NAfr(J)Ar *šnūġa* > (J)Sp *(e)snoga*, etc., then we have here an invaluable example of an early North African Latinism/Arabism brought by the first wave of Jewish settlers to Spain. Later migrations of Bedouins to North Africa, and in part to Spain in the 11th and 12th centuries, may have deposited the EAr *ṣlā* in Moroccan Judeo-Arabic.

In future we need to look for other isoglosses that divide up North African Judeo-Arabic and Judeo-Spanish dialects in a similar manner. A similar configuration is provided by the Judeo-Spanish term for "cemetery." Reflexes of the euphemism He *bet xaim* (literally "house of life") surface in Spain, Algeria, and Tunisia (and Balkan Judeo-Spanish) vs. MorJSp *meʿara* (literally "cave"), found also in Yemen (in North African Muslim Arabic, the latter denotes specifically a Jewish cemetery). It is unclear whether NAfrHe *bet xaim* is a new introduction from Spain or an older indigenous innovation. An isogloss linking Morocco and Yemen raises the possibility of an Eastern Arabism deposited in the wake of the Bedouin migrations across North Africa during the 11th and 12th centuries. Another open question is whether the linguistic differences reflect differences in burial practices.

There are three conceivable explanations for the change of *s* > *š*:

(a) Bilingual Arabs, both in North Africa and Spain, interpreted Sp *s* as closer to their *š* than to *s*; conversely, Ar *š* appeared to Romance speakers as closer to their own *s*. In both directions, most bilinguals applied the principle of the "shortest phonetic path" between the two sound systems. On the change of OSp *s* > *x* [š] due to Arabic influence, see Baldinger 1972:87, fn 72.

(b) In the case of the Jews, the concept of the "shortest phonetic path" between two languages may not always be relevant.

Even though the replacement of He *š* by JSp *s* looks like the change of Ar *š* > (J)Sp *s* that I cited earlier, it may have been motivated by etymological rather than phonological considerations. In other words, He *š* > JAr *s* on the basis of cognate correspondences, such as He *lašon* = Ar *lisān* "language." Garbell's claim that under the influence of Spanish, He *š* > *s* in the Sephardic pronunciation of Hebrew is unconvincing (1954:696), since pre-expulsion (Judeo-)Spanish and Catalan both had *š* in their native sound patterns.

The etymological argument is not weakened by the few cases where Judeo-Spanish also has *š* in Romance terms ~ Sp *s*, for example, BalJSp *šastre* "tailor" ~ Sp *sastre*, JSp *(mwerte de) šapetanya* "sudden (death)" (18th century; Armistead and Silverman 1990:24–25, 30, fn 15) vs. SalJSp *supetanya, so-* ~ Sp *supitaño* (13th through 18th centuries) < Lat *subitaneus*. JSp *š* in these Romanisms could be due either to dissimilation (in the case of Sp *sastre* ~ JSp *šastre*) or Mozarabic influence; note, for example, Gk *asfaragos* "asparagus" > AndAr *isfaraj* but Moz *ešparrago* 11th and 12th centuries ~ ModSp *espárrago* (A. Alonso 1969:39). On Mozarabic features in Judeo-Spanish, see chapter 5 this volume.

Among Arabic-speaking Jews, including those in Spain, He *š* > JAr *s*, for example, Tafilalt (southeast Morocco) JAr *d-r-s* "sermonize" < He *daraš* (Heath and Bar-Asher 1982:43 and Benoliel 1926:343). The data are hard to interpret given the sibilant confusion in all components of these Jewish dialects of Judeo-Arabic, the age of which is not datable with certainty (Zavadovskij 1962:41). In theory, JSp *darsar* "sermonize" might also be from cognate Ar *darasa* "study," *darrasa* "to lecture"; however, since Balkan Judeo-Spanish dialects have *druš* "sermon" with *š* (see also TunJAr *drāš* "disputes" vs. *ḍrāš* "funeral oration," cited by D. Cohen 1970:157), it may be expedient to derive the verb directly from Arabic. However, a Hebrew source could still be maintained, since He *š* also > JAr *s*. The divergent treatment of He *š* in the verb and noun could then be explained by different chronologies of borrowing: the verb might have been borrowed by Iberian Judeo-Arabic speakers (hence *š* > *s*), with the noun borrowed when the Iberian Jews were mainly Spanish-speaking, thus He *š* could be retained intact. Another fact that might show that JSp *darsar* is old and from Hebrew is its assignment to the conjugation class *-ar*; new Arabisms (and other non-nativisms, except for Hebraisms) in Judeo-Spanish tend to be assigned *-ear* (for Morocco, see Benoliel 1926:361–63 and the discussion above).

Finally, it is not unreasonable to propose that JSp *darsar* < Arabic while forms with *š* < Hebrew, since there are cases of etymologically mixed paradigms in Judeo-Arabic consisting of Arabic and Hebrew cognates, for example, AlgJAr *bəzza* "humiliate" < Algerian Arabic (~ ClAr *baδδa*), but the noun "humiliation" can be either < AlgMAr *təbzīä* or < AlgJAr "He" *bizzui, bəzzåyọn* (< He *bizui* "deprecation, denigration," *bizayon* "disgrace, shame, contempt"; M. Cohen 1912: 401).

Lat/Sp *s* > (J)Ar *š* > (J)Sp *s* (Galmés de Fuentes 1983:235), though there are exceptions, for example, IbAr /santibaṭr/ "Saint Peter" (13th century; Torreblanca 1982:448) vs. *šant mariyya* (Corriente 1977:125). In other words, we may be dealing with a retrograde sound shift, from Lat/Rom *s* > (J)Ar *š* > (J)Sp *s* (on this phenomenon in general, see U. Weinreich 1958). For example, Pt *serife* < Ar *šarīf*; Pt *alvíçara* < SpAr **al-bíšra* "tip for good news" (Corriente 1977:50). If the Iberian Jewish family name *ibn Migaš* found in Granada, 11th and 12th centuries, is of Greek origin (a possibility I raised earlier in chapter 2), then *s* of Greek origin also participated in the change to JAr *š*.

(c) A final possibility is that the Jews may have first formed their pronunciation of Hebrew as Berber-speakers, and preserved this pronunciation norm when they became Arabic speakers. If so, we could put a rough date on the rise of Hebrew studies in North Africa. According to 'Ali ibn Ḥazm (994–1064), who was the grandson of a Spanish Christian convert to Islam (cited by Pérès 1950:293), the Berbers spoke Arabic "badly"; he also suggested that Ar *š* > Ber *s* (D. Cohen 2:1975:25). Other scholars have also assumed that the Berbers were the most active agents of phonetic and morphological change in Andalusian Arabic (Marçais 1906a:152–53, Pérès 1950:298).

Latin loanwords with *s* appear in Berber with *š*, for example, Lat *secāle* "rye" > Ber *šqālya* "type of rye with very flat grain"; Lat *sapīnus, sapīnea* > Ber *šbényä* "an indeterminate conifer, maybe juniperus sabina" (Marcy 1936:38–39). Hence, I could ascribe JAr *s* for He *š* (as well as later JSp *s* for He, Ar *š*) to Berber speech habits. D. Cohen tentatively ascribed the sibilant confusion in the Judeo-Berber *Haggadah* text studied by Galand-Pernet and Zafrani 1970 to Judeo-Spanish influence, given the settlement of the latter in Judeo-Berber-speaking areas (1971:413); but Berber sibilant confusion may be too recent to be relevant to the present discussion. A difficulty with the Berber connection is that it is not clear whether there are other unambiguous Berber substratal features in (Judeo-)Arabic. The shift from *š* > *s* also characterizes Punic loans that entered Berber. Vycichl gives examples, though without explicit mention of sibilant confusion, for example, Pun **rūš* "head, cape" surfaces in North African toponyms as *rus-*, as in *Ruspina* at Munastir south of Susa (Tunisia; 1952b:201); but could Ar *rās* "head, cape" have influenced the form of the toponym?

Another Latinism with initial *s* > Ar, He, Moz *š* is Lat *senior* "senior; a minor church official who is inferior to a deacon"; in Jewish sources Lat *senior* was the title of a synagogue elder. A North African source is also plausible for this Judeo-Spanish Latinism, given the existence of Lat *senior* "priest, prior, cleric lower than deacon" in sources from Kairouan, Tunisia from the 6th to the 11th centuries (Courtois 1945:118–19).

The Latinism also became a Jewish personal and family name, for example, He *šny'wr* (*IHE* 367—possibly from the 14th century; Baer 1/2:1936:281 gives He *šynywr*). The name was known in North African Judeo-Arabic, to judge from *šanyūr* in a Genizah document (of unknown origin) from 1107 (Goitein 2:1971:130). A Valencian Romance manuscript in Arabic characters from the late 16th century has *šinyur* (see the Inquisition trial of Baltasar Alaqua; Galmés de Fuentes 1983:36); this form is similar to JSp *sinyor*; Simonet gives Moz *šeñor* [šannor] (1888:590). While MalJAr *al-šnyūrs* (14th century) takes a Romance plural and the Arabic definite article (Millás Vallicrosa and Busquets Mulet 1944:286), the term may have been regarded as an "Arabism" by Mozarabic speakers, since it takes an Arabic broken plural, for example, *sanānīr* (Toledo, 12th and 13th centuries; González-Palencia 1:1926:133, 139; see also Galmés de Fuentes 1983:112), and *šanayānīr* (Jaca 1224; Bosch Vilá 1954:193 and fn 18). The word is also a personal and family name in Yiddish, for example, *šneer*, spelled as if it were He *šny'wr*—presumably because the unfamiliar Romanism was interpreted by many speakers, despite the resulting ungrammaticality, as He "two light." The Yiddish name may have been inherited from the Balkan Latin substratum of the Jews who first settled in the Germano-Sorbian lands by the 9th and 10th centuries at the latest.

I believe that Minervini was the first to note that the spelling of Lat *senior* in Judeo-Spanish varied with the meaning (see 1:1992:59 and the contrast in 2:1992:154, lines 28 and 30—citing a late 15th-century text from Zaragoza): *synywr* "sir, mister" (*DCECH* notes that in Latin and Spanish up to the 14th century, *senior/señor* had both masuline and feminine gender, but there is no trace of a common gender in any Jewish language) vs. *šynywr* a Jewish male personal or family name. I do not agree with Minervini's suggestion that the multiple spellings represent simply the desire to distinguish the two homophones orthographically. In my opinion, the divergent spellings suggest two pronunciations of two chronologically distinct strata. While the Hebrew letter *šin* did indeed denote both /s/ and /š/ among the Iberian Jews, I assume that the anthroponym was in all likelihood pronounced by the Jews as *šneor* or *šenyor* (as suggested also by the Yiddish datum). Lat *senior* as an anthroponym may have been acquired first by Romance- and/or Arabic-speaking Jews in North Africa prior to the Muslim invasion of the Iberian Peninsula in 711. From Spanish the Iberian Jews later borrowed the second variant, now JSp *sinyor* "sir, master," which is almost identical with the standard Spanish form.

Toledo Mozarabic has only *š* in this root, for example, /šannor/ "sir" and apparently no male name from the word (Galmés de Fuentes 1977:205, 1983:112); *š* is also found in the pronunciation of this word in "Moorish Spanish" dialogue recorded in Spanish literature of the 17th and 18th centuries (Gilbert 1980:76). Significantly, Lat *senior* is rare in Moroccan Judeo-Spanish anthroponyms, which suggests that the anthroponym, assuming it existed at all, may have become obsolete after the Jewish migration to Spain in 711—i.e., it was obliterated by new naming practices that never spread to the Iberian Peninsula; in fact, in Spain, the name (including the Hispanized compounds *Ben Senyor, Bon Senyor*) seems to be far more productive in Catalunya and Aragón than in Castile (Laredo 1978:893–97; see also my discussion of Arabic names in Judeo-Spanish earlier in this chapter). A topic for future research is to determine whether old forms of Iberian Judeo-Arabic that became obsolete in the Muslim-dominated areas, nevertheless survived in the far northeast of the peninsula, early under Christian domination.

Another Spanish ecclesiastical term, this time from Greek, that might also be of North African origin, to judge from the narrow meaning of the term, is Sp *papaz* "Christian priest in North Africa" (which *DCECH* derives through an Arabic intermediary). Conversely, JSp *papás* "priest" may be a much later loan from Balkan Greek. Schuchardt noted the first attestation of the term in the *Lingua franca* described by de Haedo in 1612 in Algiers (Gilbert 1980:79–81).

I know of one Hebraism that surfaces both in North African Hebrew and Spanish Latin, and in all subsequent Jewish languages, which may have acquired its form in North Africa. I am referring to He *rabbi* "rabbi" (literally "my teacher"), found on a Hebrew inscription from Volubilis, Morocco, 2nd and 3rd centuries (Laredo 1954:168; for Italian Latin examples, see Frey 1:1975, #611; Baron 5:1957:400, fn 3). For further discussion, see also SpLat *rebbites* (Mérida, Extremadura, possibly 6th century), discussed by C. Roth 1948. The latter's suggestion that this word is evidence that the Spanish Jews then had close ties with Palestine is unwarranted. In Judeo-Arabic the Hebraism now has the form *ribbī* "rabbi" (for an example from a 13th-century Spanish Arabic text, see Bencherifa 1971, #642 and Corriente 1977:25). SpAr *rabi* was glossed as teacher by de Alcalá 1505 (ibid.:79). Note also the discussion of JSp *rebissa* "rabbi's wife," also of possible Judeo-Greek or Judeo-Latin origin, in chapter 2 this volume.

BalSp *ribi* ~ *rubi* "religious teacher" could both be from Arabic, since Ar *a* > *u* in the environment of labials, for example, Ar *rabbī* > *rubbī* "my Lord"—a cognate of He *rabbi* (Lebedev 1977:34). While the raising of *a* > *e* is typical of Latin and Arabic (Wexler 1988:17–20), *a* > *i* is typical only of Arabic (the so-called *imāla*). There is no way to determine whether the Arabic pronunciation of this word with *i* is due to an earlier Judeo-Latin pronunciation. Conversely, TunJAr *ṛāb* "rabbi-saint cult" looks like a later loan < He *rav* "rabbi, teacher" (with the replacement of *-v* > *-b* under Arabic influence) vs. older TunJAr *rəbbī* "religious teacher, rabbi" (D. Cohen 1:1964), reflecting either Arabic *imāla* or a Judeo-Latin form. The use of a Hebraism to denote the rabbi-saint who is the object of veneration might have been a conscious attempt to Judaize a local non-Jewish custom (see chapter 5 this volume). TunJAr *rəbbī* is probably original to the dialect since a foreign rabbi is called by a different word altogether in North African Judeo-Arabic, for example, *ḥaxām* < He *ḥaxam*, which is probably a loan from Judeo-Spanish (M. Cohen 1912:392).

Judeo-Greek and Judeo-Latin terms, if they are translations of Old Hebrew and Judeo-Aramaic patterns of discourse, may enable us to plot the extent to which Palestinian Jewish culture was retained in the diasporas. The fact that almost no Judeo-Greek or Judeo-Latin expressions appear in the languages of the Sephardim either as loans or as models for loan translation suggests a break in the transmission from Judeo-Greek and Judeo-Latin to the North African and Iberian Sephardim. For example, there is no trace of JLat *coena pura* "Friday," literally "pure meal," that is found in the North African Latin writings of Tertullian (late 2nd century), Ticonius (late 4th century), and Augustine (early 5th century). The expression survives only as Sard *kenáƀura* "Friday" (Sittl 1882:151, M. L. Wagner 1920b:619–20, Bonfante 1949:173, fn 7, 175, fn 15). The island had close contacts with Africa; see also M. L. Wagner 1956 for discussion of a Berber term used in Sardinian.

Y *čolnt* "Sabbath food cooked on Friday to avoid the prohibition of working on Sabbath" is probably of North Italian or Balkan Romance provenience (Wexler 1992:45, 84, 110, where I reject the near universal derivation of the unique Yiddish Romanism from Judeo-French). The ultimate model may be synonymous He *ḥammin*, which is also used in pre-expulsion Iberian documents; there is no surface cognate of Y *čolnt* in Judeo-Spanish, though the Judeo-Latinism (or Hebraism) might be the basis of MorJAr *sxīna* < "hot" (feminine singular) which also designates the Sabbath food; the latter is unknown in Iberian Judeo-Spanish, though this is the basis of OSp *zahinas* "porridge" feminine plural (1495). I have no direct evidence that the term or the concept denoted were known in North African (Judeo-)Latin.

On the pair Ar *adefina/sxīna* as a mirror of Jewish settlement history in Spain, see chapter 4 below; for Ethiopian congeners of *adefina*, see chapter 2 this volume.

As I noted earlier, JGk *paraskevē* "Friday" (~ Gk "preparation"), probably modeled on JAram *'aruvta'*, *'ɛrɛv* (literally "evening") is unknown in Spain (Wexler 1987b:19); the Aramaic expression is found in pre-Islamic Yemeni Judeo-Arabic (Kister and Kister 1979:234 and fn 16). Might I assume that Friday evening was once not regarded by the Sephardim as the beginning of the Sabbath, and hence, had no special function? Might the Muslim choice of Friday as the day for weekly prayers in the mosque have influenced the Jewish practice of commencing the Sabbath on Friday eve? The fact that Y *fraytik* "Friday" was taken from German, and not from Hebrew or Judeo-Aramaic makes me think that the Ashkenazim may also not have originally commenced the celebration of the Sabbath on Friday evening—as is universal today. The word "Friday" can denote a holiday in some German and Russian dialects—presumably a borrowing from the Jews—but the examples are, unfortunately, undatable (Wexler 1987b:22–23).

There is evidence that North African Sephardim may have also brought Grecisms with them to the Iberian Peninsula that do not designate Jewish ritual. Where such examples differ from the non-Jewish surface cognates, they might allow us to posit separate channels of diffusion of Grecisms to the peninsula, for example, the Christians received Grecisms from learnèd Latin or another European language (some of which were subsequently deposited in Judeo-Spanish), while the Jews received Grecisms from North African Latin. The following examples illustrate this category of Grecisms.

For example, Gk *stafylínos, stafinari* "carrot" is found in both Iberian Arabic and (Judeo-)Spanish, but the Judeo-Spanish reflex differs slightly from the surface cognate in most forms of Ibero-Romance: JSp *safanoria* has numerous parallels in the south Mediterranean, for example, SpAr *isfannāriya* (Martí 13th century), *safannariyat, isferníya* (de Alcalá 1505), Val *çafanoria* (Colin 1970:230). Since uniquely Valencian components are unknown in the Ibero-Romance component of Judeo-Spanish, to the best of my knowledge, there is no point in proposing that Val *çafanoria* is the source of JSp *safanoria*, despite the formal identity.

I can presume either that Judeo-Spanish got its Grecism from North African (Judeo-)Arabic, or that the Judeo-Spanish Grecism was originally identical to the Spanish congener, and that the formal changes that affected the Spanish Grecism postdate the expulsion of the Jews in 1492. Unlike Judeo-Spanish, Spanish has metathesis in *zanahoria* (*h* < *f*) and in some other Arabisms, for example, Sp *adelfa* "rose-bay" vs. SalJSp *adefla* "bile, bitterness" < SpAr *dafla* (~ ClAr *difla*); note also metathesis in MorAr *delfa* (see also Wexler 1988:50–51). AndSp *zanahoria* "carrot" coexists with the solitary *ahenoria* in Seville. The presence of the unmetathesized form in two Castilian dialects—Andalusian and Judeo-Spanish—as well as in Catalan and Valencian, suggests that this variant was once more widespread in Castilian at large (see also OSp *çahanoria* 1330 or 1335; *DCECH*). The picture in Spanish is also mixed in the case of Ar *al-ḥabaq(a)* "basil," see PtLad *alhabaka* (Ferrara 1553), JSp *alxabáka* ~ OSp *alhabeca, alhabega* (Murcia dialect, c. 1560 and still attested in Albacete) vs. ModSp *albahaca*; see also unmetathesized OPt *alfábega, alfávega*, ModPt *alfavaca* (since the 16th century—possibly via Castilian), NPt *alfádega, arfádiga, orfádiga*, Cat *alfab(r)ega* (Blondheim 1925:149, Steiger 1932:216 and Wexler 1977b:182).

Conversely, MorAr *delfa* suggests that metathesis in Spanish Arabisms may have begun in North African Arabic dialects. The argument of the *DCECH*, that the metathesis in MorMAr *defla* points to a Mozarabic source, is unconvincing (why should there have been Mozarabic influence on Moroccan Arabic?). The chronology and origin of metathesis are unknown to me, though a late 16th-century Arabic translation of a Spanish text (studied by Corriente and Bouzineb ms) reveals *isfarniyā*, with a unique form of metathesis (see also North African data following).

Most North African Arabic and Berber dialects have since replaced this Grecism, which was unknown in Eastern Arabic, with new forms that never reached Spain. The Greek term was once known in Morocco, for example, Muḥammad ibn Hišam as-Sabti (of Ceuta, Morocco, 12th century) cited dialectal NAfrAr *safannāriyya*. The pace of replacement of the Grecism varied widely, to judge from the fact that Tangiers Arabic in the 18th century still had *sefrāniyya*, while Fès had *ṣəfrāniyya* with *ṣ* induced by the root *ṣ-f-r* "yellow." Some Berber dialects in the northern Middle Atlas, in the vicinity of Fès, also have *ṣəfrāniyya* (Zemmūr) and *sfannār* (Bni-Mṭīr); see also Mrāzīg (south Tunisia) *sənnārya*, Ber (EConstantine and Aurès) *sənnāriyya* (Mercier 1907:92). The Grecism is still preserved in Central and Eastern North Africa, for example, Tripoli and TunAr *sfənnārya* (the basis for Malt *sfunnārîya*).

There are a variety of innovations in areas of North Africa that have replaced the Grecism, for example, Central and EAlgAr (except for Djidjelli) *zrūdiyya* (> Kabyle Ber *zrūdga*). In Morocco the popular form among Arabs and Berbers both is *ḥīzzo*, of possibly Berber origin (Heath and Bar-Asher 1982:49, 78 cite *xizzu* "carrots" in Tafilalt Judeo-Arabic), while the Muslim dialect of Tanger has *ža'ɛda*—applied to a variety of plants. (The form *ḥīzzū* was known in Marrakech in the 16th century, to judge from the testimony of the Moroccan botanist al-Ġassani.) According to Colin, AlgAr *zrūdiyya* was derived from the name of the village Zrūd near Kairouan, Tunisia that was famous for its vegetables, especially carrots (1930a:125). The term was first mentioned by Abu 'Ubayd 'Abdullah ibn 'Abd al-'Aziz al-Bakri (d. 1094 Córdoba). This date is important since it permits us to connect the staggered obsolescence of the Grecism in North Africa with the invasion of North Africa by the non-Hellenized Bedouins in the 11th and 12th centuries.

Another possible unique North African Grecism might be JSp *abutargo* "roe." The *DCECH* derives Sp *botarga*, first attested in the late 16th century, via the intermediary of Italian comic literature; the Grecism also begins with *b-* in other European target languages. The late chronology in Spanish could rule out a common source for the two surface cognates; note also the differences in gender—feminine in Spanish, masculine in Judeo-Spanish. Besides Judeo-Spanish, a masculine gender is also found in the Portuguese and Occitan surface cognates. Arabic cannot be the immediate source of the Judeo-Spanish Grecism, since the latter has *baṭraḥ(a)*. Crews (ms) notes that in Greek roe is denoted variously as *buttágra, butárga*, and *augotáraxo*; the latter could conceivably be the source of JSp *abutargo* (in the Balkans after 1492?). The Grecism is also attested in Coptic as *pitarixon* (*DCECH*).

It might seem attractive to derive JSp *a-* in the word for roe from Ar *al-*, the definite article, which could eliminate the need of a direct transmission from North African Greek (though *a-* might have been added much later, see later this chapter).

But this suggestion is problematic since assimilation of the lateral to the first consonant of the noun (and subsequent gemination of the latter) is only possible in Arabic before dental and alveopalatal consonants, never before a labial. An initial *a* instead of the expected *al-* before an Arabism beginning with *b-* is very rare in Spanish, for example, *(a)bellota* "acorn" (the long form is found in the *Cancionero de Baena*, late 14th or early 15th century, and in 16th-century Spanish texts) < Ar *ballūṭa*. The Judeo-Spanish surface cognate begins with *b-*, though the form *arvellota* (< Ar *al-*) is also known in Balkan Ladino (Blondheim 1925:148, Steiger 1932:179). In post-1492 Judeo-Spanish there are instances of *al-* attached to Romance words, especially those whose root originally began with *a-* or *l-*, for example, JSp *a(l)viyana* "hazelnut" < ~ Sp *avellana* < Lat *abellana (nux)*, but note also Seville Sp *arvellana* (M. L. Wagner 1936b: 170).

Occasionally in Judeo-Spanish and Spanish there are cases where *al-* is not assimilated to the following dental or alveopalatal consonant, as is required by Arabic grammar, for example, JSp *a(l)safrán* "safran" (Crews 1961:17) ~ OSp *(a)çafran*, ModSp *azafrán*. Hence, I will tentatively regard JSp *abutargo* as a "unique Grecism," possibly diffused to the Iberian Jews through a North African conduit.

Many scholars have proposed that a few other Grecisms in Judeo-Spanish that denote aspects of Jewish ritual should also be derived from Judeo-Greek, but I doubt that a unique Judeo-Greek source can be maintained. For example, SalJSp *meldar* "read," AlcazJSp *mendar* "read Hebrew books" (Martínez Ruiz 1963:87, fn 42), is treated popularly as a Hebraism and is derived < He *lamad* "he learned" (on the widespread Jewish habit of making homophonic translations, see Blondheim 1925:145ff and Banitt 1985).

Surface cognates of JSp *meldar* exist in Judeo-Italian, Judeo-Provençal, Judeo-French. These facts lend support to the hypothesis, proposed by Blondheim (1925:75–79), that there once was a Judaized form of Latin and that JSp *meldar*, etc. comes from a Judeo-Latin Grecism. While the Grecism may have been unique to Judeo-Latin and to a number of non-Iberian Judeo-Romance languages, I prefer to derive JSp *meldar* (with Old Judeo-Catalan surface cognates) < cognate Cat *maldar* "make a special effort to attain" (1988:27–29). I presume the Catalanisms made their way into Judeo-Spanish when Catalan-speaking Jews moved in large numbers to Castile after 1391.

Other allegedly unique Judeo-Grecisms in Judeo-Spanish include MorJSp *talamon* "wedding canopy, (chair used in) the religious ceremony on the eve of a circumcision" (J. Pimienta 1991:110, fn 94, Anahory-Librowicz 1993:292), BalJSp *talamo* "nuptial dais" < Gk *θalamos* and *aladma*, etc. "excommunication" < Gk *anaθēma*, found in a number of texts from non-Castilian areas between the 13th and 15th centuries, for example, Aragón (discussed at length by Ekblom 1942–43 and Malkiel 1946; Wexler 1988:25–26). Most of these Judeo-Romance Grecisms are not encountered in non-Romance Jewish languages, except *talamo*, which surfaces in Western Yiddish (Wexler 1987b:30, 35). However, I prefer to derive JSp *talamo(n)* from cognate Cat *tàlem*, which has Christian religious connotations (Wexler 1988:32–35; for Catalan details, see also Coromines et al., 5:1985:389–92). In contrast to Ekblom and Malkiel, I regard *aladma* as an Arabism. For further discussion, see chapter 5 this volume.

Finally, if Judeo-Spanish is *not* derived from Latin directly, but is rather a form of Spanish that was Judaized between the 11th and 14th centuries in the peninsula, then there can be no talk of a direct "Judeo-Greek" substratal component in Judeo-Spanish. My reservations about positing a Judaized form of Latin will be presented later in chapter 6 this volume.

The Arabic Imprint on Judeo-Spanish and Judeo-Spanish "Hebrew"

There is a substantial Judeo-Arabic imprint in Judeo-Spanish, but the converse is not true. The quality and quantity of the Arabic imprint in Judeo-Spanish and Spanish are radically different. Christian Spanish (in most of its dialects) displays an Arabic imprint in the lexicon, which greatly exceeds that of Judeo-Spanish, but the latter, especially in its earliest attestations, also had an Arabic imprint in the syntax and phonology. The reasons for these differences must be sought in the dissimilar external histories of Spanish and Judeo-Spanish. The Christians appear on the stage of recorded history as speakers of Ibero-Romance; they became speakers of Arabic as a second language after the 8th century in areas ruled by Muslims; by the mid-11th century, as a function of the Reconquista, the Christian population reverted to a state of monolingualism in Ibero-Romance. I disregard here bilingualism in two or more Ibero-Romance languages. For the overwhelming majority of Iberian Jews, Arabic, and/or Berber were the native languages up until the 11th century; subsequently, Ibero-Romance speech was acquired as a second language, and ultimately Judeo-Arabic was given up altogether.

An important question for Jewish linguistics is to determine how and when Arabic- (and Berber-)speaking Jews became speakers of Spanish. The language switch from Judeo-Arabic to Spanish could have been either complete or partial. A complete shift to Spanish means that the Jews acquired total mastery of the target language, though some of the first Jews to learn Spanish might have had only an imperfect control of the language, as is typical in immigrant societies. Physical removal from Arabic-speaking locales would have ensured the rapid switch of the Jews to the coterritorial Ibero-Romance speech of the non-Jews, with the possible retention of a small unique Jewish vocabulary (from Arabic and Hebrew), mainly linked to the semantic domains of Jewish cultural and religious expression. Theoretically, the gap between the Spanish speech of Jews and non-Jews could have widened if Jewish settlement patterns led to changes in the dialectal makeup of the speech of the Jews, or impeded the spread of innovations from the Christian majority to the Jewish minority.

In the event of a partial language shift to Spanish, the Sephardic learners would have acquired the lexicon of Spanish but only some of its syntactic and phonological rules, mainly via the lexicon. Hence, they would have been using an Arabic grammar, onto which a Spanish lexicon had been grafted. Strictly speaking, a "partial language shift" is no language shift at all, since only "relexification" of the speaker's language is involved. Partial language shift takes place when the learners are poorly exposed to the native norms of the target language, for example, if the Arab Jews learn Spanish from one another, or from Arabic-speaking Muslims who themselves had acquired only an incomplete mastery of Ibero-Romance speech; these conditions are satisfied whenever Spanish-speaking Christians constitute a minority of the local population. But it is important to note that if the Jews were reluctant to acquire the target language, they could have performed a partial, rather than full language shift, even in close proximity to a large body of native speakers of Spanish.

The Judaized Spanish that is spoken presently in the Balkans, Turkey, and Israel is a slightly Judaized form of Spanish. But this fact does not refute the possibility of an original partial language shift—at least for certain segments of the Iberian Jewish population. Conceivably, some members of the first generation(s) of Iberian Jews who were exposed to Spanish might have acquired only Spanish lexicon, while still maintaining Arabic grammar; subsequently, this relexified Judeo-Arabic was replaced by standard Spanish. Jews speaking standard Spanish and relexified Judeo-Arabic with Spanish lexicon most likely lived side by side in the same communities. Eventually, Jewish speakers of Spanish could have minimally Judaized their speech, either by retaining vestigial Judeo-Arabic and Arabized Hebrew elements from their ancestral language or by borrowing from relexified Judeo-Arabic (on the use of Christian Spanish in the Balkans in the 16th century see, Bunis 1993b: 537–40).

As I suggested in chapters 3 and earlier in this chapter, a partial language shift was also carried out on the level of written expression, for example, when Hebrew lexicon was lifted out of the original Biblical Hebrew texts and replaced with Judeo-Arabic or Judeo-Spanish lexicon. The relexification of Biblical Hebrew vocabulary even led to the elimination of Hebraisms that were used in colloquial Judeo-Arabic and Judeo-

Spanish. As I had occasion to note earlier, I define Ladino and the *Šarḥ*, contrary to the *opinio communalis*, as bizarre forms of Hebrew genetically unrelated to Spanish and Arabic, respectively. Because of the predominance of Arabic or Spanish vocabulary in the "calque translation," the relexified language "appears" in the eyes of most users and neutral observers to be related to the language donating the vocabulary, for example, Ladino was, not surprisingly, traditionally assumed to be a form of "Spanish." Further discussion can be found in chapter 6 this volume.

Evidence for a partial language shift comes from the nature of the Arabic imprint in Judeo-Spanish and in the Hebrew pronunciation norms of the Iberian Jews. The retention of Arabic norms in the pronunciation of Hebrew, for example, suggests that the phonological system of "Judeo-Spanish" was Arabic and not Ibero-Romance. I will discuss the Arabic imprint under the following headings: Iberian Judeo-Spanish Arabisms which are Unique in Inventory, Form, or Meaning; The Arabized Pronunciation of Judeo-Spanish and Judeo-Spanish "Hebrew"; Arabic Grammatical Processes in Judeo-Spanish and Judeo-Arabic/Judeo-Spanish "Hebrew"; The Copying of Arabic Patterns of Discourse in Judeo-Spanish and Judeo-Spanish "Hebrew"; The Common (")Hebrew(") and (")Judeo-Aramaic(") Corpus of Judeo-Arabic and Judeo-Spanish. The Berber impact on Iberian (Judeo-)Arabic and (Judeo-)Spanish will also be discussed. On the recalibration of Muslim Arabic terms and names in Iberian (Judeo-)Spanish and Judeo-Arabic, see chapter 5 this volume.

Iberian Judeo-Spanish Arabisms which are Unique in Inventory, Form, or Meaning

Judeo-Spanish has a small number of Arabisms which are closer in form and/or meaning to the Arabic etyma than the surface cognates in the Spanish spoken by Christians, and a very small corpus of Arabisms which are unattested in the latter altogether.

Here, I will give examples of unique Arabisms that enjoy attestation in Iberian Judeo-Spanish, or both Balkan and North African Judeo-Spanish (a distribution that establishes with some certainty the Iberian origin of the Arabisms), and Arabisms in either Balkan or North African Judeo-Spanish where a later non-Iberian Arabic impact can be ruled out (Turkish Arabisms in Balkan Judeo-Spanish can almost always be identified from their form and/or meaning, and hence, pose less of a problem than Moroccan Arabisms acquired after 1391). Arabisms with no religious connotations of any kind that have acquired Jewish connotations in Judeo-Arabic and Judeo-Spanish are discussed later in chapter 5.

Examples of Arabisms attested in Balkan Judeo-Spanish and Ladino that are not found in Spanish itself are IstLad *alamimes* "turbans" < Ar *al-'imāma* (Kuli 1739, see Crews 1957:226); Mac (Bit) JSp *alxasarear* "bewitch," SalJSp *alxasaras* "intrigues" < Ar *saḥara* "bewitch" with an accreted Arabic article (that shows that the verb was derived from an underlying noun) and metathesis (Wexler 1988:52). Metathesis is unusual in Judeo-Spanish; the Moroccan Judeo-Spanish congener also has metathesis, but not Moroccan or Iberian Arabic (Martí 13th century for the latter).

JSp *alxad*, Mor (Alcaz) JSp (*el día de*) *aḥad* (Martínez Ruiz 1963:103, fn 126), and *el ḥad* (ibid.:109, fn 168) "(the day of) Sunday" ~ IbMSp *diyah dā-l ḥadd* 1467 (Hoenerbach 1965:154.15). MorJSp *letrea* ~ SalJSp *alitréa* "vermicelli" < Ar *aliṭriyya*, ultimately < Greek (Kuli 1730, Crews ms). The talmudic Hebrew surface cognate, *'iṭriah*, is not preserved in any Jewish language. For further details, see the discussion of BibHe *hexal* earlier in this chapter. Sp *aletría* is known only since 1607, hence I assume that Judeo-Spanish and Spanish acquired the Grecism through independent channels and at different times: via Arabic > Judeo-Spanish (earlier) vs. via Catalan > Spanish (later); otherwise, I would have to argue that the Judeo-Spanish forms show that the Grecism was known in Spanish some time before 1607 (on the Catalan intermediary for Spanish, see Baldinger 1972:77 and Coromines et al., 1980ff.)

Ar *maḥa, maḥā* "efface, cancel, dispell, remove (diseases), obliterate; (God) cancel sins" appears to have been used only by Jews and Muslims in Spain; see also Mac (Skopje) JSp *amaxar* "cure" < "soak off magic formula in water," and MSp *amaxo* "divine pardon, divine grace," *amaxara* "he will soak off, he will pardon" (Harvey 1960:70, 72) vs. Sp *majo* "fastidious (person)." Galante also cites IstJSp *rio maxo* "quiet river" in a proverb (1902:445). The root *m-ḥḥ-y* "wash away" is also attested in Judeo-Aramaic (Morag 1988:50), which is a rare example with a geminated *ḥɛṭ*; gemination is also found occasionally in the Syriac cognate. A Judeo-Aramaic etymon is conceivable but unlikely, given the Arabic data and the rarity of Aramaisms in Judeo-Spanish (see earlier this chapter; for additional examples and details, see Wexler 1988:47–52).

Occasionally, Spanish and Judeo-Spanish appear to have borrowed different forms of the same Arabic root.

For example, Sp *dolama* "hidden defects of horses" (1613) < Ar *ẓulāma* "prejudice, damage, harm" vs. IbLad *adolmar* "do violence" (Arragel 1422–33), Ferrara PtLad *adolme* "injustice, violence" (1553) < Ar *ẓulm* (Blondheim 1925:41, Steiger 1932:170, the *DCECH*). Note the relatively late date of the Spanish attestation in comparison with the pre-1492 Iberian Ladino source.

In one case Judeo-Spanish and Spanish retain chronologically distinct forms of a common Arabism.

For example, OSpAr *al-'arz* > MorJSp *alarzel* "larch tree," Ferrara PtLad *alarze* (1553), while a newer SpAr *al-'erz* > OSp *alerce* (1475—this is also the contemporary form), *alerze* (de Alcalá 1505, Dozy and Engelmann 1869:98, M. L. Wagner 1920a:545, 1931:235 and fn 1).

Occasionally Jews and Muslims differed considerably from Christians in the frequency of use of common Arabisms.

An example is Sp *timar*, OSp *(a)tamar* "complete" < Ar *tamm* "complete" that appears in the *Cancionero de Baena* (late 14th or early 15th century). In the Spanish writings of Jews, for example, in the *Coplas de Yosef* (first half of the 14th century) and the *Proverbios morales* 1355–60 of Santob de Carrión (Šem Tov ben Yicxak Ardutiel), we find *atemar* (M. L. Wagner 1920a:546, González Llubera 1935:5 and fn 9, 1947:45). The term is also attested widely in late Muslim aljamiado texts, for example, in *Las leyes de Moros* (14th and 15th centuries).

A number of Arabisms in Judeo-Spanish are closer in form to the Arabic source etyma than the Spanish surface cognates. However, in most cases, I cannot use these facts to claim that Jews were more knowledgeable about the Arabic etyma (for example, because they were more often bilingual than the coterritorial Christians) or were more careful to resist Ibero-Romance encroachments on the structure of the Arabic loans. The greater formal distance between the Arabic etyma and their Spanish reflexes may have been due to later phonological changes in Spanish that were not shared by Judeo-Spanish. For example, MorJSp *alxabaka* "basil" < Ar *al-ḥabaqa* (ordinarily *ḥabaq* in Arabic) lacks the metathesis characteristic of Sp *albahaca*. The Iberian Arabic origin of the Moroccan Judeo-Spanish Arabism is clear from two facts: the word also surfaces in contemporary Balkan Judeo-Spanish where there is no possible interference from a Turkish Arabism, and coterritorial MorAr *el-ḥabaq* (ending in a consonant) is not a likely source of the Moroccan Judeo-Spanish Arabism. Moreover, Christian dialects of Ibero-Romance other than Castilian have the Arabism without metathesis.

Ar *kuḥl* "antimony" appears in two Saloniki Judeo-Spanish books of the mid-16th century with *h* and *x* in place of Ar *ḥ*, for example, *alkoholes* "alcohols" (ibn Pakuda 1569:25b) vs. *alkoxolarse* "apply kohl to the eyes" (Karo 1568:55a, both cited by Bunis 1993a:21, fn 7). The earliest Spanish attestations are *alcohol* (1278) and *alcoholar* (1298), respectively (*DCECH*). I draw two conclusions from the Judeo-Spanish doublets: that the pronunciation of Iberian Judeo-Spanish Arabisms maintained its distinctive features (JSp *x* vs. Sp *h*, now phonetically zero) for several centuries, which presupposes a certain amount of physical separation of the two Iberian speech communities or at least unreceptivity of some Jews to Christian Spanish norms, and the de-Arabization of Judeo-Spanish phonology must have varied with the speaker. This is consistent with my view that Arabic-speaking Jews made both partial and full language shifts to Spanish (see also chapter 6 this volume).

Another example of JAr *x* ~ zero in Spanish is MorJSp *alxádža* "jewels," which may be of Iberian Arabic origin, because of the accreted *al-* (vs. MorAr *ḥádža* "necessity, thing"; Martínez Ruiz 1966:50). Unlike Judeo-Spanish, Sp *alhaja* /alaxa/ is now quite distant from the original Arabic form, but this is because of phonological changes in Old Spanish, for example, Ar *j* > OSp *j* [dž] > *x* and Ar *x* > OSp *f* or *zero* (orthographically *h*; see Steiger 1932:192), rather than a greater Jewish fidelity to the Arabic source form. Often /x/ is retained in Judeo-Spanish in Hebraisms and Arabisms but lacking in Ibero-Romance Arabisms (/x/ was unknown in Spanish dialects at the time), for example, JSp *alxenya* "henna" < Ar *al-ḥinnā'* vs. Sp *alheña* (Yuhas 1989:204); JSp *tarexa* "task" < Ar *ṭarīḥa* vs. Sp *tarea*.

One Arabism common to both Judeo-Spanish and Spanish that has a different meaning in the two target languages holds special interest, especially in the context of staggered migrations from North Africa to Spain. That is IbJSp *adafina, adefina* "food cooked on Friday to be consumed on the Sabbath, when all work is proscribed by Jewish law" (for early 15th and early 16th-century Inquisition attestation, see Beinart 1:1974:115, 482, 545, 577; 3:1981:433; see also Cooper 1993:104, and earlier discussion in this chapter).

Ar *d-f-n* means only to hide, conceal; in Spanish the Arabism has the meanings exquisite dish (*Libro de buen amor* c. 1330) and secret (*Cancionero de Baena*, late 14th or early 15th century). In theory, the semantic differences could have developed as contact between the Jews and Christians or Jews and Muslims diminished. For example, Avalle Arce thinks the term came to denote a Jewish dish only at the end of the 15th century (1946:146). Spanish writers in the late 15th century use the alleged Jewish penchant for consuming Muslim foods as a weapon of invective against Jews (Gutwirth 1985b). The Inquisition protocols regarded *adafina, adefina* as a typical Jewish food (see the novel entitled *La lozana andaluza* 1528 by the Jewish convert Francisco Delicado, discussed by Espadas Burgos 1975:541, 545, 551). The meaning of exquisite dish makes an immediate parallel with "Sabbath food" that raises the question of a possible Muslim origin for the Jewish food custom (for a genuine Old Palestinian Jewish precedent, see later discussion this chapter of He *ṭaman*). Indeed, according to Gutwirth 1989b:246, fn 30, the writings of the Jewish convert Cota indicate that the Jews and Muslims ate similar foods.

The Arabism is now found only in Moroccan Judeo-Spanish, along with a derivative, for example, Mor (Alcaz) JSp *dafinero* "receptacle for making *adafina*" (Martínez Ruiz 1963:103, fn 127); see also Benoliel's variant *adafinero* (1927:566). According to M. L. Wagner 1914:145 and 1920a:544, *adefina* was formerly known in Turkish Judeo-Spanish, but I lack other confirmation of this. Bunis cites a Hebrew translation equivalent for Balkan Judeo-Spanish, *xaminero* < He *ḥammin* "Sabbath food" plural < *ḥam* "hot" (1993a:37). The Hebrew food term is attested in Iberian Judeo-Spanish writings and in a number of Jewish languages, alongside native terms (Yehuda ben Barzilay al-Barceloni, 11th and 12th centuries, used *ḥammin* to mean "hot food"), for example, YemJAr *ḥammim* for "Sabbath food" (Goitein 1931:367) with the more usual plural ending *-im*.

I know of only Portuguese forms of the Arabism without the Arabic definite article, for example, Pt *defina* (from the late 15th or 16th century, presumably in a text composed by L. Enriques, a converso; see Mendes dos Remédios 1927:243 and Benoliel 1926:211). For further discussion, see also MorJSp *dafina* in the next paragraph. Freire distinguishes between ModPt *adafina* "Jewish food" and *dafina, defina* "(dish made from) coagulated pig's blood" (1939–44)—further support for a non-Jewish origin for meanings associated with food.

It is significant that Ar *d-f-n* has two semantically and formally distinct reflexes in Algiers Judeo-Arabic, for example, AlgJAr *dfīna* "food" vs. *tfīna* "funeral"; see also MorJSp *dafina* "Sabbath food" (Benoliel 1928:52) vs. MorAr *tfīna* "burial." These data establish that AlgJAr *dfīna* and JSp *adafina* were brought to North Africa from Spain, while *tfīna* was an indigenous loan; further support for this claim is the fact that MorJSp *adafina* lacks assimilation of the Moroccan Arabic definite article *el-* before *d-* > *edd-*, which would be expected in Arabisms taken from coterritorial Moroccan Arabic. Moreover, in contrast to Iberian and Algerian Judeo-Arabic, Moroccan Judeo-Arabic uses native *sxīna* (< "hot") to denote the Sabbath food, that appears to be a loan translation of He *ḥammin* "Sabbath food."

Since the Arabism denotes a Jewish cultural artifact, the meaning Sabbath food may be pre-Iberian, but it is difficult to determine the chronology of JSp *adafina*, etc. In earlier writings (1978, 1988:48–49) I argued that *adafina* may have translated He *ṭaman* "hide" in the Talmudic Hebrew expression *ṭaman ɛt haḥammin* "he hid the Sabbath food" (i.e., allowed it to simmer in a pot for twenty-four hours). The concept of He *ṭaman* might be the basis of terms in other Judeo-Arabic dialects, for example, YemJAr *kubānäh* "Sabbath food made from millet" (< Ar *k-b-n* "hem"), IrJAr *t(ə)bīt* (< Ar *b-t* "take shelter at night"). What weakens the hypothesis of a talmudic Hebrew model for these food terms is that Ar *d-f-n* denotes food in a number of Muslim Arabic dialects outside of Spain, for example, Syrian, Iraqi Ar *madfūna* "stuffed food," ClAr *dafīn* "flesh meat buried in rice" (Lane 1863–93, citing a source from the 12th century); the Arabism is also used in a number of Ethiopian languages to denote a bread of inferior quality (chapter 2 this volume), and the use of the concept "hide" is restricted to Judeo-Arabic and its Judeo-Spanish satellite; I can only cite one instance where "He" *ṭamun* "concealed" was used in Ashkenazic Hebrew to denote the Sabbath food—in the writings of the 14th-century Slavic-speaking rabbi Iserlin (Lunski 1924).

These facts raise the possibility that the use of "hide" is purely an Arabic innovation; this could even be the source of Y"He" *ṭamun* in the writings of Iserlin (see the arguments for a Turkic component in early Yiddish in Wexler 1993c:126). Hence, the use of the concept "hide" in the talmudic Hebrew expression and Judeo-Arabic could be coincidental; given the break of about half a millennium between the writing of the Talmud and its transmission from the Near East to North Africa and Spain, the expression *ṭaman ɛt haḥammin* might not have been well known until several centuries after Arabic became the language *par excellence* of the North African and Iberian Jews. Also, the variety of terms in Judeo-Arabic, despite their semantic common denominator, points to relatively late creations.

The presence of *sxīna* in Moroccan Judeo-Arabic vs. *adefina* in Moroccan Judeo-Spanish offers yet another example of the two-tiered transmission of Arabic from North Africa to Spain that I discussed earlier. *Adefina* could have been the earliest term to be imported into North Africa and Spain, while the Moroccan regionalism *sxīna* was an innovation of later date that failed to reach Spain. In the territory between Algeria and Libya, the Sabbath food is denoted in Judeo-Arabic by reflexes of *d-f-n*. I have no way of knowing whether *sxīna* ever circulated in these areas as well; if so, it could have been supplanted, at least in Algeria and Tunisia, by reflexes of *d-f-n* when the Judeo-Spanish refugees settled there after 1391. Conversely, MorJAr *sxīna* could be quite old, if it is a translation of colloquial OHe *ḥammin* "Sabbath food" < "hot"; a translation of "hot" is found in Y *čolnt*, which I derive from either Italian or Balkan Latin. The traditional view is that Y *čolnt* is a borrowing from

Judeo-French; Ben Moše, a resident of Prague and Meissen in the early 13th century, claimed that this was the name of the Sabbath food in France (Kupfer and Lewicki 1956:203), but to the best of my knowledge, the term is not found in any native Judeo-French text. Ben Moše may have simply been applying his Yiddish term to the parallel French Jewish food. I know of no term "Sabbath food" derived from the root "hot" in any form of Judeo-Ibero-Romance, hence, the Judeo-French and Yiddish data do not make a convincing case for reconstructing the meaning Sabbath food for *JLat *calentem* "warming." On possible non-Jewish Romance models for the Sabbath food in Judeo-French and Yiddish, see Wexler 1992:48, fn 108.

On JSp **alminbar*, see chapter 2 this volume; on Arag, etc. *aladma*, etc., see chapter 5 this volume; on JSp *xazino* "sick," see chapter 5 this volume; on JAr *n-q-y*, see earlier this chapter.

To conclude, it appears that most Arabisms in Judeo-Spanish were, by and large, not very different in form and meaning from the Spanish surface cognates. Thus, Judeo-Spanish must have received the bulk of its Arabic corpus indirectly from Christian Spanish rather than directly from Judeo-Arabic. Furthermore, as I noted earlier, the volume of Arabisms in Judeo-Spanish is considerably smaller than the Spanish corpus, while the Judeo-Spanish corpus of unique Arabisms is even smaller.

Considering the Arabic-language background of the Iberian Jews, the relatively small corpus of Arabisms in Judeo-Spanish can have three explanations:

(a) The Jews departed Spain before most of the Arabisms now in use in Spanish were accepted.

(b) The Jews acquired Spanish in areas of the country where the volume of Arabisms was relatively low, for example, Andalusia.

(c) As speakers of Judeo-Arabic in the midst of a language shift, the bilingual Jews might have been anxious to avoid the use of words from their former language.

The first explanation is not acceptable, since Spanish had acquired the bulk of its Arabisms by the 13th century (Neuvonen 1941); an Andalusian parallel is not convincing since this area was settled by speakers from the north after the exodus of the Jews (Garulo Muñoz 1983 and Wexler 1989b). The third explanation is attractive, since in cases of partial language shift or relexification, the native lexicon is usually given up in bulk. Yiddish provides a parallel case, assuming that it is relexified Sorbian; the actual Sorbian lexicon in Yiddish, in contrast to syntactic and phonotactic phenomena, is quite small. For further discussion, see chapter 6, this volume.

The Arabized Pronunciation of Judeo-Spanish and Judeo-Spanish "Hebrew"

"Hebrew" words in Judeo-Spanish and in "Hebrew" texts written by Judeo-Spanish speakers, which have surface cognates in Arabic, often underwent formal changes under the influence of the latter.

For example, JSp *midrasas* "schools" Tudela 1363 < He *(bate) midraš*, literally "houses of study," has a Spanish feminine plural marker (Kayserling 1861:208); the expected plural would be **midrases* since the noun is masculine in Hebrew (MacJSp *midrašis* cited by Bunis 1993 is masculine). The change in gender suggests reshaping under the influence of cognate Ar *madrasa* "school," plural *madāris* (or synonymous Sp *escuela?*). Solà-Solé and Rose cite the example of Sp *çedaquin* "righteous people, saints" in a 15th-century Valencian Christian text (1983:200–201, line 14); this is either an accidental distortion of He *cdyqym* /cadikim/ (*cadiq* singular) or reflects interference from cognate Ar *aṣdiqā'* or *ṣudaqā'* "friends"—with broken plurals (the singular is Ar *ṣadīq*, see later this chapter).

In He *hclmydynh* /hacalmedina ~ hacalmidina/ "the magistrate" < Ar *ṣāḥib al-madīna*, literally "companion of the city" (Teruel 15th century; Díaz Esteban 1975: 105–106, line 121), the spelling *-mydynh* may reflect the raising of *a* > *i* in Arabic, known as *imāla*, which is characteristic especially of Granadan Arabic (see the discussion of Ar *majūš* in chapter 2 this volume) vs. He *mədinah* and stAr *madīna* (on this root see below this chapter). The spelling of *c* for Ar *ṣ* follows the sets of correspondences obtaining between Hebrew and Arabic (vs. Lat *zavalmedina* Zaragoza 1180; Baer 1:1929:38), and is independent of the contemporary Balkan Judeo-Spanish dialectal pronunciation of *cade* as an affricate /c/—for example, in Bosnia and Bucharest. This latter feature may be due to recent Ashkenazic influence (Crews 1962:89–90, fn 12); in other Judeo-Spanish dialects, *cade* has the value of /s/—originally /ṣ/? If the choice of *cade* was a reflection of Arabic-Hebrew cognate relationships that determined the spelling of Arabisms in Hebrew characters, then it was not an accurate reflection of phonetic reality. On cognate pairs involving He *š* ~ Ar *s*, see earlier this chapter.

In principle, the form of a Hebrew word could be influenced by the Spanish surface congener rather than by the Arabic cognate. In the case just cited, if He *-mydynh* were to be read /medina/, it would resemble Sp *medina* (meaningless in Spanish, but common in toponyms, see for example, Medina del Campo). But this interpretation is unlikely, given the Arabic rule of *imāla* and the lack of sure cases of Spanish interference (see chapter 5 on Spanish Christian influences on Judeo-Spanish language and Sephardic culture). Conversely, the Hebrew spelling of Romance in some texts does follow Romance pronunciation norms rather than Arabic orthographic norms, for example, Jews have *ly, ny* for [l', ñ] in Hebrew characters, while the Muslims spell the latter with *ll, nn* (with the diacritic for gemination, *tašdīd*; Spiegel 1952:116). Future research is needed to determine whether Jews and Muslims reacted differently to the impact of Spanish.

Another instance of Ar *imāla* in Hebrew is TunJAr *ṭṛīfa* "unkosher food" (D. Cohen 1:1964:67, fn 1, 1981:98), Sp *trife* (Cantera Burgos 1954), *trefe* "thin, lean, weak, false, consumptive" (1386; *DCECH*) < He *ṭrefah*. An Old Moroccan Muslim Arabic reflex of He *ṭrefah* is *ẓarīfa* (Touat 15th century, cited by Vajda 1962:810; see also Steiger 1932:151 and Corriente 1977:40, fn 40 on Ar *ṭ* > *ẓ*) ~ TunMAr (Sers) *ṭarīfa* (Saada 1982:32). Crews gives JSp *trefán*, *trifá* (1954–55:309), which suggests that variants of the word with *imāla* were regionally embedded in Judeo-Spanish. This is further evidence of a stage of relexified Judeo-Arabic among some Jews. MorJSp *terefá* (Benoliel 1952:275) and IstJSp *trefá* (Wagner 1914, #173), without Arabic *imāla*, are probably later loans from written Hebrew after the Jews had ceased to be primarily speakers of Judeo-Arabic. For a Judeo-Arabic example of *imāla*, see TunJAr *kāšīr* "kosher" < He *kašer* (D. Cohen 1:1964:67, fn 1), which has no parallels in Judeo-Spanish. See also Lad *alamimes* cited earlier in this chapter.

A pressing desideratum of Judeo-Spanish and Iberian "Hebrew" linguistics is to determine where and when Arabized pronunciation norms of "Hebrew" were replaced by newer Ibero-Romance pronunciation norms. For example, initial clusters in Balkan Judeo-Spanish Hebraisms are often dismantled by the insertion of a schwa or unrounded mid vowel, for example, *tefillá* "prayer," but *trefá*; in Moroccan Judeo-Spanish, all clusters are dismantled, see MorJSp *terefá* cited earlier. I suggest two different chronologies of borrowing and sources for these two Balkan Judeo-Spanish Hebraisms: *trefá* could come from BalY *treyf* since there is no *imāla* (see above; in which case the question arises of whether the Iberian Jewish emigrés to the Balkans initially practiced Jewish dietary laws). I suppose that SalJSp *tefillá* was already known in Spain. Had Yiddish been the source of He *tfillah*, the Sephardim would have retained the initial cluster of Y *tfile*. On the break in the pronunciation norms of Hebrew before and after 1492, see discussion earlier in this chapter.

The devoicing of He *'ayin* > *x*, mainly in syllable-final position, is attested in some words, for example, JSp *(be)maxlamata* "more or less" (literally "up down'), *bemaxlata* "in limbo," but also *mal(u)mata, malamata* "more or less" (Bunis 1993:317) < He *bə-* "in" and *ma'alah matah* "up and down." The earliest Balkan example of the pronunciation of *x* for *'ayin* is from the Judeo-Spanish-speaking Jewish converts to Islam known as the *Dönmeh* from 18th-century Saloniki (ibid.:34). Under the impact of voiced *l*, *x* also became *ġ* in this word optionally in Saloniki Judeo-Spanish (Nehama 1977, Bunis 1993:316). *Malamata* in the meaning more or less is also attested in North African Judeo-Spanish. Otherwise, I would be tempted to posit Balkan Slavic as the source, e.g., Bg *gore-dolu* "more or less," literally "above below." Since the "Hebrew" phrase is not attested, to the best of my knowledge, in non-Sephardic recensions of Hebrew in any meaning, the expression could translate an Iberian pattern of discourse, but I am unable to suggest either an Arabic or a Spanish model. Sar, BgJSp *dearrib abašu* is also encountered (Marcus 1965:129, fn 26). In the Oran Judeo-Arabic name *Benisrah*, the final *h* might exemplify the devoicing of *'ayin* if the etymon is He *yizra'* "he will sow," though an alternative etymon is He *yizraḥ* "he will shine" (Eisenbeth 1936:98).

The change of ʿ > ḥ, not always in the environment of a voiceless consonant also characterizes Morrocan Muslim Arabic, for example, *ʿagūza* "old woman" > *ḥagūza* "hideous old female spirit; name for New Year and the following day"; *sáḥtsar* "thyme" ~ stAr *zaʿtar* (Westermarck 2:1926:161 and fn 3; see also Corriente 1977:56).

In contemporary Balkan Judeo-Spanish, except for a closed corpus of Hebraisms where syllable-final *ʿayin* is pronounced /x/, the letter has no phonetic reality; the latter pronunciation may be a more recent norm native to Judeo-Spanish speakers, possibily due to Romaniote or Ashkenazic influence (see later discussion in chapter 5 and discussion of Ar *al-ʿanṣara*/Sp *alhanzara* earlier in chapter 2).

Whenever an Arabized pronunciation (or unique meaning) of a Hebraism is found both in North African and Balkan Judeo-Spanish, it is clear that the word was acquired in Spain. For example, He *ḥɛvrah* "society" > Mor (Fès), AlgJAr *ḥabra* (Leslau 1945a:73, M. Cohen 1912:500, respectively), though in "literary" Hebrew (i.e., in the reading of monolingual Old Hebrew texts), ɛ prevails in the first syllable. The Hebraism has both the forms *xa-* and *xe-* in Balkan Judeo-Spanish (Bunis 1993:202), where the word means variously traditional Jewish elementary school for males, society, partnership.

The lowering of *e* > *a* after *ḥ* in both Sephardic diasporas shows that the lowering rule existed in Spanish Arabic and Iberian "Hebrew." The Arabic cognate is *ḥ-b-r*, as, for example, in *ḥabr, ḥibr* "learned man, doctor (among the Jews), pontiff, bishop; joy, favor." In Arabic vowels are typically lowered after pharyngeal consonants.

Balkan languages that borrow the term from Judeo-Spanish have it solely with the syllable *xa-*, for example, Bg *xavra*, Ser *(h)ȁvra*, Tu *havra*, Albanian *avrë*, Rum *havră*—all of which mean only synagogue, which is not the customary meaning of the Hebraism in Judeo-Spanish (see also chapter 5 this volume). There are two possible explanations for the semantic discrepancy:

(a) The Hebrew word in the pronunciation *xa-* once denoted the synagogue in Judeo-Spanish, on the model of He *qahal* "(Jewish) community" > JSp *kal* "synagogue."

(b) He *ḥɛvrah* in the non-Jewish Balkan languages and JSp *kal* are both semantic innovations that were modeled on a third Jewish language. A possible model could be Gk *synagōgē*, which among Jews traditionally denoted the Jewish community, but in non-Jewish parlance came to mean the synagogue building itself (see earlier in this chapter; for further comparative data, see Wexler 1987b:206, 222–26).

See also the discussion of He *š* > *s* under Arabic influence vs. the retention of He *š* intact in contemporary Balkan Judeo-Spanish Hebraisms (mentioned earlier in this chapter). On changes in the pronunciation of post-vocalic ungeminated stops in Iberian "Hebrew" before and after 1492, see chapter 5 this volume. For further examples, see earlier discussions this chapter.

Arabic Grammatical Processes in Judeo-Spanish and Judeo-Arabic/Judeo-Spanish "Hebrew"

As late as the 15th century we can still find "Hebrew" and Judeo-Spanish texts written by Jews which reveal a strong Arabic grammatical imprint—

i.e., several centuries after many Iberian Jews had switched to Spanish. Six phenomena merit attention: the Arabic broken plural; the integration of Hebrew participles in a special periphrastic conjugation in Judeo-Spanish, which is intended to accommodate only Hebrew loans; the possible imitation of the Arabic agentive formation; word order in compound numerals; a single definite article in definite modified noun phrases; Arabic derived verb forms in Judeo-Spanish "Hebrew."

The Broken Plural in Judeo-Spanish "Hebrew" and Judeo-Arabic. In Arabic, the expression of plurality in a noun usually involves changes in the vowels and sometimes consonants of the singular stem. This phenomenon is known as the "broken plural." An Arabic example in a "Hebrew" text written in Tudela, Navarra in 1413 is He *šm'yš* /samayes ~ šamayeš/ "sextons of a synagogue" (Fernández y González 1886:17–18). Bunis interpreted the form as He *šammāš* "sexton of a synagogue" with Sp *-es* plural (1993a:18, which follows the suggestion of M. Weinreich 1:1973:153), but this leaves unexplained the diphthong (which is accounted for by the Arabic broken plural) and the loss of He *-š* in the root (on the Iberian Jewish pronunciation of He *š* as *s*, see earlier this chapter). The Hebrew term is also attested in Spanish Christian writings from the same locale without an Arabic broken plural to mark plurality, for example, *samases* Tudela 1363 (Kayserling 1861:208, Crews 1935:208; see also the *Cancionero de Baena* mid-15th century, discussed by Cantera Burgos 1967:93). There is also internal vocalic and occasionally consonantal change to mark plurality in Hebrew nouns, for example, *mɛlɛx* "king": *mlaxim* plural, but in Hebrew the morphophonemic alternation is always accompanied by the addition of a suffix. See also the discussion of *çedaquin*, cited earlier in this chapter.

An alternative analysis is to derive *šm'yš* /samayes ~ *šamayeš*/ < Ar *šammās* "priest, monk" (which has the plural *šamāmisa*; Freytag 1830). Note that the standard Arabic plural of the root differs from that of Judeo-Spanish "Hebrew." Lane glosses the word as "Christian leader who shaves the middle of his head, deacon," ultimately a borrowing from Christian Aramaic, attested in Arabic writings between the late 8th and early 13th centuries (1863–93). The fact that *šammās* is a Christian Arabic term leads me to prefer the Hebrew etymon.

Contemporary AlgJAr *šəmmåš*, *səmmåš* have unexpected sibilant reflexes, which suggests that they were derived recently < He *šammāš* with subsequent dissimilation of He *š-* in the second variant (M. Cohen 1912:391; see also Y *šames* from the same Hebrew root with dissimilation of the second *š*); future research should explore whether the dissimilatory phenomenon in Algiers Judeo-Arabic and Yiddish are independent phenomena or continue a colloquial Old Hebrew pronunciation.

Hebrew words in Judeo-Arabic often take an Arabic broken plural, for example, JAr *ḥuzzān* "preceptors, teachers" (Andalusia, 14th century; Idris 1974:188); the etymon would have to be He *ḥazzān*, which usually denotes the reader (or chanter) in the synagogue, but Idris (*op.cit.*) notes that the *ḥuzzān* also performed ritual slaughtering (see discussion of *lḥḥ'm* earlier in this chapter). The only potential Arabic etymon would be *xuzzān* "treasurers," which is disqualified on semantic grounds. It is interesting that these two "Hebraisms" that appear with an Arabic broken plural formation have surface cognates or phonetically similar roots in Arabic; might this fact have encouraged the scribes to apply the broken plural to the "Hebrew" terms? He *šammāš* and *ḥazzān* are both agentive formations; on this topic, see also discussion of JSp *kabar* later in this chapter. In addition, historical Judeo-Arabic writings from outside the peninsula attest to the fact that Hebrew loans were often pluralized in Judeo-Arabic by means of a native broken plural formation, for example, JAr *maḥazīr, sdādīr* "prayer books" (< He *maḥzor, siddur*, cited by Blau 1958:187) and Sp *çedaquin* cited earlier in this chapter.

Periphrastic Verbs with Hebrew Components in Judeo-Spanish. Hebrew verbal elements are sparsely used in Judeo-Spanish. There are two patterns of integration: the 3rd person singular past tense form is conjugated like a native verb (for example, *darsar* "preach" < He *daraš* "he preached"), or the Hebrew present participle, indeclinable in Judeo-Spanish, is combined with the Judeo-Spanish auxiliary "be," which is declined for person, number, tense, and aspect; the latter, periphrastic conjugation is the most productive pattern.

Contemporary Judeo-Spanish selects as a rule the Hebrew masculine singular participle for use in the periphrastic conjugation; in this respect, Judeo-Spanish resembles the patterns of integration of Hebrew in Yiddish and of Arabic verbal elements in the Islamic languages (i.e., languages spoken by a predominantly Muslim population; Wexler 1974). In Iberian Judeo-Spanish, and in some, usually early Balkan Judeo-Spanish writings (which Bunis calls "Rabbinical"), the Hebrew participle is also inflected for number, for example, JSp /somos mexuyavim/ "we are obliged" (Valladolid 1432) < He *məḥuyav* "obligated" plus *-im* plural suffix (for late 16th-century Balkan Judeo-Spanish examples, see Bunis 1993a:29). Bunis also notes a rare instance of a plural participle in the contemporary Turkish Judeo-Spanish expression *no son mecarefim laminyan* "do not constitute a quorum" (ibid.:324), but this may be an instance where the Hebrew participle *məcarfim* "are adding" functions as a substantive (as in Hebrew), and hence, agrees with the auxiliary in number.

The preference for the Hebrew masculine singular participle makes sense from the point of view of bilingual theory, since it is the simplest form morphologically and the part of the verbal system closest to a noun; nouns are more amenable to cross-linguistic borrowing than verbs, and bilingual transfer tends to eschew morphophonemic complexities. A further impetus for not declining the participle in an Islamic target language might be the fact that Arabic verbal nouns, which are not marked for number, are also candidates for insertion into the periphrastic conjugation.

In the Iberian Judeo-Spanish/"Hebrew" text of 1432 from Valladolid, I suspect that Arabic grammar may be the reason for the declinability of the Hebrew participle for number, since complements of "be" in Arabic must agree with the copula in number and gender (gender may also have been marked in Old Judeo-Spanish Hebrew, but I have no examples of feminine participles). The more modern rule of an indeclinable masculine singular participle might have been prompted, in turn, by Spanish, where compound verb forms exist, consisting of the copula and an uninflected gerund, for example, *estoy trabajando* "I am working," *estamos trabajando* "we are working." A further factor influencing the contemporary Judeo-Spanish (and Yiddish) pattern may be the volume of Hebraisms accepted by the Jewish target language; perhaps an inordinately large number of Hebrew verbal elements also favors a simpler pattern of integration.

The Agentive Formation in Judeo-Spanish and Judeo-Spanish "Hebrew." In Judeo-Spanish "Hebrew" and Judeo-Spanish, the Hebrew root *q-b-r* "bury; grave" is the basis for an agentive noun, for example, BalJSp *qabar* "gravedigger" (Karo 1568:13a, cited by Bunis 1993:25) < JSp"He" *qabbār*, which represents the Old Hebrew derived agentive nominal pattern $C_1C_2C_3\bar{a}C_3$. Pre-1492 examples include JSp"He" *hqb'r* /haqab(b)ar/ "the gravedigger" (Mahon, Balearic Islands, early 14th century, cited by *IHE* 322; see also Neuman 2:1942:172), Cat"He" *qbrym* /qab(b)arim/ (in the writings of Šlomo ben Adret 1235–1310, Barcelona; I.Epstein 1925:155, fn 66). The innovative "He" *qab(b)ār* surfaces both in Castile and Catalunya. In Spanish Christian texts the word appears in the form Arag *caparins* Zaragoza 1390 (with a double plural—He *-im* plus Sp *-s*) and *cabarim* Zaragoza 1391 (Blasco Martínez 1990:280, 282), and with the accreted Arabic article, for example, Lat *acabarim* (1371; ibid.:31, fn 33).

No agentive noun **qabbār* exists in Arabic from this root, even though Arabic has the same agentive template. For gravedigger, Arabic uses another root altogether in the masculine singular present participial form, for example, Marrakech MAr *ḥāfir* (Westermarck 2:1926:459—who gives the geography of the term). The form *qabbār* that we find in Judeo-Spanish and Judeo-Spanish "Hebrew" is unattested in Old Palestinian Hebrew. It is also not found in non-Arabic recensions of "Hebrew," where the root may be used with a Hebrew agentive suffix, for example, Y("He") *kabren* < "He" *qavran* (with agentive OHe *-an*). I assume that either Iberian Arabic-speaking Jews applied their native derivational rules to "Hebrew" or Judeo-Spanish and/or Judeo-Arabic speakers generalized the Old Semitic Hebrew agentive template—sometime after the 11th century.

Word Order in Compound Numerals in Judeo-Spanish "Hebrew." In IbHe *(b)' "x šanim* "(in) twenty-one years" (mid 14th century, Toledo; *IHE* 139), the form *' "x* consists of the letters *'(alef)* and *k(af) ~x(af)* that in Hebrew have the numerical values of one and twenty, respectively. The order of the components imitates Ar *waḥad u'išrīn*, literally "one-and-twenty" rather than He *'ɛsrim və'ɛxad*, literally "twenty-and-one," which has a parallel in Spanish. Given the late date of the example, I assume the writer spoke Judeo-Spanish, but there is no certainty of this.

Determination in Modified Noun Phrases in Judeo-Spanish "Hebrew." A Turkish Judeo-Spanish text from the early 20th century has the Hebrew phrase *qabar hagadol* "the head gravedigger" (literally "gravedigger the big"; see Bunis 1993a, under *kabar*). Old Semitic Hebrew requires the article *ha-* on both the adjective and the noun in definite noun phrases, for example, *haqabar hagadol*. The use of one article in modified noun phrases, the age of which I cannot determine, needs to be studied systematically. It is characteristic of a wide variety of colloquial Arabic dialects, including Spanish Arabic, for example, Sp *Guadalquivir* river name < SpAr *wād al-kibīr* "the large wadi" (~ ClAr *al-wādī al-kabīr*; Corriente 1977:125, fn 213). De Alcalá 1505 gives SpAr *Guid alquibir*. An early Arabic example comes from the Quran, *ṣirāṭ al-mustaqīm* "the straight path" (c.700; Hopkins 1984:182). For discussion of this phenomenon in other Arabic dialects, see ibid. and Borg 1989.

The expression *qabar hagadol* may also be due to the influence of the definite "construct" phrase in Old Hebrew and Arabic, where the determiner is limited to the second noun, for example, He *bet hasefɛr* "the school" (literally "house [of] the book"). The construct construction is found in Mozarabic, for example, *fonte loš paštoreš* "the fountain of the shepherds" (Galmés de Fuentes 1983:114) without *de* (date unspecified, but from between the 12th and 14th centuries). Nowadays, with Arabic no longer spoken by the Sephardic Jews, the construct form has undergone a weakening in Judeo-Spanish "Hebraisms," for example, SalJSp *exa (d')akóδeš* "the holy ark" (literally "ark of the holiness") < He *hexal haqodeš* (Crews 1962:95), with the insertion of JSp *d* "of".

Derived Verb Forms in Judeo-Spanish "Hebrew." Verbs common to Arabic and "Hebrew" are often used in different derived forms; under Arabic influence, the Arabic derived form may be used in Iberian Judeo-Spanish "Hebrew" in place of the expected Old Hebrew verb pattern. For example, in the "Hebrew" passages embedded in the Valladolid *Taqqanot* of 1432 He *ḥ-r-m* "excommunicate, forbid" is used both in the *hif'il* derived conjugation (according to Old Hebrew grammatical practice) and in the *pi'el* derived conjugation (according to Arabic grammatical practice), for example, Arabized "He" *mḥwrm* /məxuram/ "excommunicated" (lines 679, 947 of text #16 in Minervini 1:1992) ~ Ar *ḥarrama* while elsewhere the scribe uses OHe *mwḥrm* /muxram/ "excommunicated" (line 507) and *mḥrymym* /maxrimim/ "excommunicating" (line 822). Earlier editors, Fernández y González 1886 and Baer 1/2:1936, corrected instances of the first form according to Old Semitic Hebrew grammar, but I think we have here a case of Arabization of non-Semitic "Hebrew." Even though the bulk of the document is in Judeo-Spanish and not in Judeo-Arabic, I have to assume either that the scribe's native language was actually Judeo-Arabic (possibly in a relexified form) or that monolingual Judeo-Spanish speakers inherited the Arabized "Hebrew" forms from an earlier period.

For a discussion of a possible Arabic impact on the Judeo-Spanish text known as the *Proverbios morales* written by Santob de Carrión (Šem Tov ben Yicxak Ardutiel) between 1355 and 1360, specifically in the preference for parataxis over hypotaxis and the use of pleonastic pronouns, see Alarcos Llorach 1951:309 and González Llubera 1940, 1947. On Arabic syntactic influences in Medieval Spanish, see Galmés de Fuentes 1955–56, 1981. It would be particularly instructive to examine Jewish translations from Judeo-Arabic to (Judeo-)Spanish, for example, the *Estoria de los bodos* c.1460 (cited by A. Alonso 1969:93), and to compare this translation literature with later North African Judeo-Arabic paraphrases and translations of Judeo-Spanish and Ladino texts (Corré 1971:7–8).

The Copying of Arabic Patterns of Discourse in Judeo-Spanish and Judeo-Spanish "Hebrew"

Iberian Judeo-Spanish and "Hebrew" expressions have been calqued on Arabic patterns of discourse; the few examples that I cite here are illustrative, not exhaustive.

For example, Sp"He" *mwqdmyn* /muqademin/ "administrative officers of the Jewish community" (Valladolid *Taqqanot* 1432; Loeb 1886:211) < Ar *muqaddimīn* from the root "proceed, go forward" also appears in translation form in both Spanish and Judeo-Spanish as *adelantado* (in the latter from Castile, Navarra, and Aragón; see van Wijk 1951, Wexler 1988:56–57). The Arabism has a number of meanings in Arabic, for example, stAr *muqaddam* "watchman," MorAr "grave watcher" (Meged and Goldberg 1986:90; see also chapter 2 this volume). The "Hebrew" of Catalunya, on the other hand, has *nɛ'ɛmanim* (literally "faithful ones") in this meaning, while another "Hebraism," *berurim*, surfaces in Aragón (Baer 1:1961:118, 217, 430–31). The form *berur(im)* is unusual since this is the inanimate noun "clarifications"; one would have expected He *borer* "arbitrator." Another example of an inanimate noun serving as an animate noun in Iberian "Hebrew" was *bet din* "court" > Ib"He" "judge in a rabbinical court" (see further discussion this chapter). Moreno Koch has noted that in the Valladolid text of 1432, He *ša'ar* "gate" has assumed the additional meaning of chapter under the influence of Ar *bāb* "gate; chapter" (1978:69, fn 27).

In a "Hebrew" text of 1102, possibly from Puente Castro, He *mədinah* "state" appears with the meaning city, on the model of cognate Ar *madīna* (*IEH* 18); conversely, the etymon might be JAram *mədinah* "large city" (a meaning also found in Western Yiddish); see also the discussion earlier in this chapter of Ar *madīna* in the compound *ṣāḥib al-madīna*.

Mor, BalJSp *blanko* "white" > "coal" in order to avoid the use of *karbon* "bad omen"; the model for this semantic shift is the Arabic word "white" (for Algerian data, both Jewish and Muslim, see Marçais 1906b:433 and fn 1, M. Cohen 1912:399, M. L. Wagner 1920a:549, 1931:231–32 and M. Weinreich 1:1973:156). I find no parallel development with Christian Sp *blanco*. Similarly, BalJSp *abašaδa* "cold (illness)" from the root "descend" is modeled on Ar *n-z-l* that expresses both meanings (Crews 1957:224–25, Wexler 1988:53). Arabic *n-z-l* could have been the source not only of JSp *abašaδa* but also of the cognate "He" *nazɛlɛt* < *n-z-l* "flow down, drip" (which is not attested in Old Hebrew). The semantic expansion of JSp *abašaδa* may have taken place in Spain, to judge from Montañes Sp *bajera* "diarrhea" (García-Lomas 1922; see also Crews ms). Another semantically close "Hebrew" word whose meaning may also have been expanded by contact with Arabic is *mata* "down" in JSp *ma(x)lamata* "more or less," literally "up down" (see earlier discussion of this term in this chapter).

SalJSp *papeleras* "sheets of paper covered with drawings and magical formulas which are placed on a person's cheeks in order to cure mumps" < *papel* "paper"; these formulas could even be written on the Sabbath when all work was proscribed (Molho 1950:121, Nehama 1977). The word is probably unrelated to Sp *papeleras* "paper case, writing desk," which is attested only since the early 18th century (*DCECH*). Hence, I suggest, tentatively, that the Judeo-Spanish word may be a unique Jewish calque of the Arabic root *'-m-l*, as in Ar *'amila* "be efficacious (medication)," *ma'āmila* "medical prescription," *'omla* "(paper-)money, cash" (Dozy 2:1881). Another possible model for the semantic shift from "paper" > "magical drawings" might be Ar *waraq* "sheet of paper; clot of blood." On the use of JSp *pulgar, purgar* "porge meat" modeled on Ar *n-q-y*, see earlier discussion this chapter.

The Portuguese playwright Gil Vicente (c.1465–c.1536) recorded the widespread exclamation *por vida de semaforá* "by the life of God" in a play written in 1518, which may be a merger of Arabic and "Hebrew" patterns of discourse. Maler derived the expression < He *šem haməforaš*, literally "the ineffable name," an epithet for God (1966), but the use of the term "by the life of" is reminiscent of Arabic exclamations, for example, *biḥayāt allah* "by the life of God."

Arabic patterns of discourse may influence Judeo-Spanish and Iberian "Hebrew" by means of linking the latter with Arabisms which are similar in form and/or meaning but not cognates. This topic deserves a comprehensive study. For example, He *cafuf* "crowded" was used in the meaning of row by row on the model of similar-sounding Ar *ṣaff* "row" (Wieder 1946:103–105, citing the writings of Avraham ben Moše ben Maymon, the Egyptian-born son of Maimonides, 1186–1237). In cognate sets, He *c* ~ Ar *ṣ*, *ḍ* or *ẟ*, for example, He *clav* ~ Ar *ṣalīb* "cross," He *cad* "side" ~ Ar *ḍidda* "against," He *cel* ~ Ar *ẟill* "shadow." In this instance, the proper cognate of He *cafuf* is Ar *ḍaffa* "crowd" (see earlier this chapter).

Another example of linkage on formal and semantic grounds might be (colloquial) JSp *talamo* that denotes a platform on which the bride and bridegroom are seated during the wedding ceremony ~ (learnèd) Sp *tálamo* "bridal bed, bridal chamber; thalamus." In an earlier discussion, I suggested that JSp *talamo* may have acquired the notion of sitting from (J)Cat *tàlem* "receptacle for carrying a holy image in a procession." Both JSp *talamo* and Cat *tàlem* < Gk *θalamos* "bridal chamber" (1988:32–35, with additional forms and derived meanings, and earlier this chapter). Given the absence of a significant Catalan component in Judeo-Spanish, I now would propose, alternatively, that the meaning of platform in JSp *talamo* might have resulted from a blend with Sp *tarima* "bench, dias, platform" (1607), itself < Ar *ṭārima* "cabin, wooden house" (the *DCECH* reconstructs penultimate stress in Spanish Arabic rather than standard Arabic initial stress). The existence of MorJAr *ṭalamōn* (Chetrit 1980:136) raises the possibility that the merger with *ṭārima* took place earlier in Judeo-Arabic, rather than in Judeo-Spanish.

The process of recalibrating Spanish terms on Arabic patterns of discourse continues in Moroccan Judeo-Spanish (for example, MorJSp *reinado* "belongings, property," discussed by Armistead and Silverman 1982:72).

The Common (")Hebrew(") and (")Judeo-Aramaic(") Corpus of Judeo-Arabic and Judeo-Spanish

Very little colloquial Old Semitic Hebrew and Judeo-Aramaic lexicon is preserved in the Judaized languages created in the first diasporas in southern Europe, Asia Minor, and North Africa. Such substratal elements can often be recognized by their form and meaning and by their presence in a variety of Jewish languages that have had little or no contact with one another. In addition to common inheritance from Old Semitic Hebrew and Judeo-Aramaic, a common corpus from the latter in two or more Jewish languages can also point to drift between the languages in contact—i.e., in the form of diffusion of genuine Old Semitic Hebrew or Judeo-Aramaic elements inherited in one Jewish language to a language which did not originally inherit this corpus, or of non-Semitic "Hebrew" and "Judeo-Aramaic" elements from one Jewish language to another. The presence of a shared corpus of Hebraisms (of any source) with common innovative meanings in both Judeo-Spanish and Iberian and North African Judeo-Arabic dialects suggests contact between the speech communities. Given the Arabic pronunciation norms of Judeo-Spanish

"Hebrew" (see earlier this chapter), and a corpus of (")Hebraisms(") shared by Judeo-Spanish and non-North African Judeo-Arabic, for example, in Yemen or Iraq, it stands to reason that Judeo-Arabic is the source of the common corpus. In general, the Hebraisms are not found in Yiddish or other European Jewish languages, at least, not with the same meanings.

The following Hebraisms are shared by Judeo-Spanish and Judeo-Arabic; in the present discussion, I make no attempt to distinguish between Semitic and non-Semitic Hebrew and Judeo-Aramaic components:

SalJSp *tevila* "ritual immersion, pool for ritual immersion" (Bunis 1993), Mor (Sefrou) JAr *ṭabila, ʿamal ṭəbiluc* "make a ritual immersion" (Stillman 1989:106; see also Udovitch and Valensi 1984:34, 50 [for Jerba Tunisian Judeo-Arabic] and Assaf 1940:271) < He *ṭvilah, ṭvilut* "immersion" (and Ar *ʿamal* "do"). In Judeo-Arabic, the term does not usually denote the pool itself, for which another Hebraism is used, for example, MorJAr *makoui* "pool for ritual immersion" (Shinar 1982:103) < He *miqveh*. In older forms of Judeo-Arabic, He *ṭ-v-l* is used in an Arabized form, for example, Palestinian JAr *maṭbal* (c.1034; Goitein 2:1971:552, fn 31), though the Hebrew root has no Arabic cognate. IrJAr He *ṭvila* is the word ordinarily used by the common folk, while *miqve* is used by rabbis (Ben-Ya'akov 1985). The use of He *miqveh* was probably motivated by considerations of Judaization and was favored since it alone appears in old written Hebrew. Bar-Ašer discusses the isoglosses of *ṭbila* and *məqvi* in North African Judeo-Arabic in 1993:178.

He *məʿarah* "cave" > "cemetery" in North African and Balkan Judeo-Spanish (Benoliel 1926:510, 1928:220, Stillman 1989:105, and Crews 1960:87, respectively), though the usual meaning in Balkan Judeo-Spanish is now "cave" (the meaning cemetery and Crews 1960 were not cited by Bunis 1993). It is noteworthy that in Moroccan Judeo-Spanish the Hebraism only denotes a Jewish cemetery (see also Yemenite Judeo-Arabic evidence in Goitein 1931:365) whereas when the term is used in Moroccan Judeo-Arabic, it denotes a cemetery in general (Leslau 1945a:74, for example, in Fès). The practice of burying in caves is not attested in the Balkans, thus the Balkan Judeo-Spanish usage must have been inherited from Spain. According to the geographical data given by Bar-Ašer (1993:180–81), *məʿarah* predominates in western North Africa, for example, in Morocco and western Algeria vs. He *bet haxaim* (a euphemism meaning house of life) in Tunisia and eastern Algeria (including Algiers). This is not the first time that we note the uniqueness of Moroccan Judeo-Arabic; see also MorJAr *sxīna* "Sabbath food" < JAr "hot" (discussed earlier in this chapter).

JSp *ekdés* "donation to a pious activity" ~ JAr *heqdeš* "communal-property" (Alexandria, Egypt c.1300; Goitein 3:1978:433, fn 168) ~ JAr *aqdas* "dedicate to a holy purpose" (ibid.:99) < He *q-d-š* "be holy" (Arabic has the root in the latter meaning, but not in this particular form). Y("He") *hekdeš* means hospital. In some dialects of Berber, the borrowed cognate Arabic root has other meanings, for example, Kabyle Ber *aqəddaš* "a boy who carries a market basket," *əqdəš* "serve"; Shleuch Ber *aqəddaš* "magician" (Vycichl 1972:244).

AlgJAr *mǝṭṭå* "funeral" (M. Cohen 1912:399), TunJAr *miṭa* (D. Cohen 1:1964:52); Mor (Tet, Lar) JSp *mitta* "bed, bier" (Benoliel 1926:230; M. Alvar 1971:230) < He *miṭṭah* "bed"; see also JSp *noze amitá* "corpse bearer" (Zaragoza late 14th century; Blasco Martínez 1990:30).

MorJSp *mizva* "funeral" (plural *mizvós*, with the Hebrew plural suffix; Benoliel 1926:230), BalJSp *mizva(s)* (plural) "coffin" (Bunis 1993, with the Judeo-Spanish plural suffix) < He *micvah* "commandment, good deed" (the latter meanings are also attested in Old Hebrew, Judeo-Spanish, and in AlgJAr *mǝṣva* "meritorious activity," see M. Cohen 1912:401). Goitein gives a Hebrew expression in an Arabic text, *met micvah* "forsaken corpse," whose burial is incumbent on the community (Alexandria, Egypt late 11th century; 5:1988:548, fn 159), which might be the basis of the meanings coffin, funeral. Morag also cited this Hebraism in Baghdad Judeo-Arabic in the meaning of funeral bier (1993:10). Another unique meaning is conjugal relations in Saloniki Judeo-Spanish (Karo 1568:113b, cited by Bunis 1993a:27).

On BalJSp, MorJAr(He) *maʿalah matah* "more or less," see the discussion early in this chapter; on the innovative meaning of *avel* "mourning" < He "mourner," see chapter 5 this volume. For a comparison of Sephardic and non-Sephardic Hebraisms, see Corré n.d.; on the distribution of Hebraisms in Judeo-Arabic, see Bar-Ašer 1989.

The Impact of Berber on Iberian (Judeo-)Arabic and (Judeo-)Spanish

Identifying Iberian Berber influences in Sephardic folk culture and language is complicated by the fact that Spanish Jews settled in Berber-speaking areas of North Africa after 1391, where they could have acquired Berber influences for the first time. Historians have pointed out (Glick 1979:180), that the Arabization of the Berbers was slower in the domains of culture and religion than in language. The same staggered Arabization seems to have been characteristic of the Spanish Jews—many of whom were also ultimately of North African Berber origin; the near total absence of Berber language among the Iberian Jews contrasts with the significant body of Berber folk customs practiced by the group (on Berber terms in 12th-century Iberian Judeo-Arabic literature, see earlier this chapter). Moreover, the Berber profile of the Spanish Jews probably varied in intensity through time and space. As Glick notes, Berber influence in Spanish Muslim society increased in the late 10th century as a result of the growing military and political power of the Berbers (ibid.:182–83; for example, the imitation of Berber styles of dress). By about the early 13th century, Berber power was again on the wane in Spain (ibid.:184).

There are three obvious indices of a Berber substratum in Iberian languages: Berber loans, Berber phonological features in one or more of the Jewish languages, and the accretion of the Arabic definite article to Ibero-Romance Arabisms.

(a) There is one example where Moroccan Judeo-Spanish uses a Berber term without the Berber prefixed feminine article *ta-*, in contrast to Spanish, for example, MorJSp *garnina* "golden thistle" (Benoliel 1928:192) ~ Sp *tagarnina*, SpAr *takarnīna* (on the Berber origin of the term, see M. Cohen 1912:426, Schuchardt 1918:26, M. L. Wagner 1931:242, Steiger 1932:207, fn 1). The absence of *ta-* suggests knowledge of Berber grammar on the part of Jews, though given the volume of Berber forms with *ta-* in North African Arabic, it would not be unusual if Moroccan Arabic, and Spanish speakers could recognize the meaning of *ta-* and delete it. Algerian Muslim Arabic has *gernīn* (Ben Sedira 1910). M. Cohen conjectured that Spanish did not acquire Ber *tagarnina* until the late 14th century (it is not listed in the Arabic lexicon of Martí 13th century). The problem with this example is that we cannot be sure that the Berberism was used by Jews in Spain and whether the *ta-* was dropped in Morocco under the impact of coterritorial Muslim Arabic.

A unique Berber element in North African Judeo-Arabic is TunJAr *ṭaḥṛami(y)ūt* "ruse, spite" (D. Cohen 2:1975:181), AlgJAr *taḥramīt* (M. Cohen 1912:281, fn 1), Mor (Tet, Lar) JSp *tahramía* "perfidy" (Benoliel 1952:273, Alvar 1971:273)—with the Arabic suffix *-ía* as in JSp *ḥakitía* "Moroccan Judeo-Spanish," *jennía* "fury, exasperation, impatience" < Ar *jinn* "spirit" (ibid.:209). In coterritorial Muslim Arabic, the Berberized Arabic word is only found in Morocco, where the Berberized template *ta-. . .-t* is also found occasionally (Marçais 1902:97, Tedjini 1923 [under *taḥramīt*], Kjamilev 1968:75). In Algeria and Tunisia it is apparently only the Jews who have this word. Future studies are needed to determine whether some dialects of North African Judeo-Arabic are systematically richer in Berberisms than the coterritorial Muslim dialects. Zavadovskij gives statistics for the percentage of Berber words in North African Muslim Arabic dialects: 10–15 percent Berber components in the Moroccan Arabic lexicon, 8–9 percent in Algerian and Tunisian Arabic, and only 2–3 percent in Libyan Arabic (1962:66).

A unique Berber term in Algiers Judeo-Arabic may be *j̈aj̈a* "married aunt" < Ber *jaja* "grandmother" (Schuchardt 1918:48), which is apparently unattested in Muslim Arabic (Ben Sedira 1910 gives AlgMAr *jemma el-kbira* for "grandmother"). Ultimately, the Berberism is from Romance, see for example, Sard *aja* (Schuchardt 1918:46).

(b) On possible Berber phonological features in Spanish Arabisms, see the alternation of *ṭ* ~ *ḍ* as in Ber *erreṭal* ~ *erreḍal*, discussed in chapter 5 this volume. A Berber impact might be responsable for SpAr *mōt* "death," *bēt* "room," *zēt* "oil" having feminine instead of the expected masculine gender, because Berber nouns ending in -V̄*t* are feminine (though Molan 1978:269–70 perfers to ascribe this development to Ibero-Romance influence). See also discussion in Corriente 1977:216, and on the possible Berber impact on Sp *seseo, ceceo*, see Baldinger 1972:88, fn 73.

(c) A distinctive property of Spanish Arabisms is the frequent accretion of the Arabic definite article *al-* (and variant forms). Steiger noted that use of the article with Catalan Arabisms is much smaller (1932:377–83), and almost absent altogether in Arabisms borrowed by other Romance languages. He concluded that since *al-*

was also found with many Arabisms in Berber, the presence of *al-* in Spanish Arabisms might be attributed to the speech habits of Arabized Berbers in Spain (for a list of Arabisms common to Spanish and Berber, see ibid.:381–82 and Baldinger 1972:70–72, fn 49 for references). A number of scholars have expressed support for Steiger's Berber substratal theory (Lüdtke 1968, Mattoso Camara 1972:173, fn 9).

Vycichl convincingly motivates the claim that the accreted *al-* with Spanish Arabisms is an instance of Berber influence (1957:139–41). Berber had prefixed definite articles in the forms *a-* masculine singular and *ta-* feminine singular. These morphemes had become obsolete at the time of the Arab invasion of North Africa, to judge from the fact that Arab writers often cite Berber toponyms both with and without the article. Yet articles must have still been recognized by native Berber speakers who were prompted to "copy" Berber grammatical patterns onto the recently borrowed Arabisms. For details, see later in the chapter discussion of the possibility that the article was acquired by speakers in the process of "relexification."

Arabic words in Berber often were borrowed together with the Arabic definite article, for example, Ber *lbit* "room" < Ar *al-bēt* "the room," though there are also cases where Arabisms appear in Berber with the Berber definite article, for example, Ber *taḥanut* "store" < Ar *ḥānūt*; rarely, Berber Arabisms have both Berber and Arabic articles, for example, Ber *talbabt* "small gate" < Ar *al-bāb* "the gate." Vycichl also notes that Berber words borrowed by North African Arabic often have the Berber article or are considered to be definite, and thus, are unable to take an Arabic definite article, for example, Ber *atay* "(the) tea" > Moroccan Arabic as such and not as **el-atay* "the tea" (though *atay* in Algerian Arabic can take the Arabic definite article) or MorAr *xizzu* "carrot" (Abu-Talib and Fox 1966) discussed earlier in this chapter. See also Zavadovskij 1962:107 and Kjamilev 1965:508, 1968:87. In Mauretanian Arabic of the 11th century, the Berber substratum seems to have caused the disappearance of the category of definiteness altogether (Thomason and Elgibali 1986:329–30).

Berber also has *a-* in Latinisms acquired via Arabic, for example, Lat *temo* "staff, rod, pole" > MorAr *temmun* "haystack" > Ber *atemmu* (*DCECH*, under *almiar*). The accreted Arabic article in African loans also points to a Berber carrier (Wexler 1980:536). Also Arabisms in Moroccan French have an accreted *l-* "the" (see examples in Tabouret-Keller 1969:42).

Had Spanish Christians borrowed Arabic words directly from Arabic speakers or texts, there would have been no need to accept the definite article as well. The presence of large numbers of Arabisms in Spanish with the accreted Arabic (but almost never the Berber) definite article suggests that Arabized Berbers in the Iberian Peninsula must have borrowed Arabisms with the accreted Arabic definite article into their Romance speech. It is from the later that Christians acquired the bulk of their Arabic corpus.

The geographical distribution of *al-* in Ibero-Romance can be seen from Ar *sāqiyya* "water wheel," which becomes Sp *acequia* (1140), Pt *acéquia* but Cat *sèquia* "irrigation ditch, canal, drainage." Older forms of Spanish also had the variant *cequia* (1154) without the article, still common in Aragón and Murcia especially, for example, Arag *cicoleta* "very small drainage," Murcian *cequeta* (*DCECH*). Doublet forms, with and without *al-*, are not so rare in Spanish, see also Sp *alcanería* "artichoke" (1599) vs. *canaría*

(1423) < MorAr *qannāriyya*. In the Romance speech of Muslims, the accreted *al-* can lose its determiner function altogether as in the case of Berber Arabisms and some Arabic Berberisms. In a Muslim aljamiado text of the 16th century the *al-* accreted to an Arabism lacks the determiner function, hence, the Spanish definite article is still required, for example, *los almalakes* "the angels" (Labib 1967:71, fn 52); Moše ben Ezra writes *'lrqyby* /alraqībī/, literally "the guard" after Sp *sw* /su/ "his," which suggests *al-* was not identified as the determiner (Cantera Burgos 1953), since the article and possessive pronoun cannot appear together in the same noun phrase in most dialects of Arabic. For a further example, SpAr *al-mawlānā* "(the) our Lord," see chapter 5 this volume.

Other scholars have advanced alternative explanations to account for the use of the agglutinated Arabic definite article with most Spanish Arabisms. Grossmann theorized that the distribution of *al-* in Spanish Arabisms was a function of the knowledge of Arabic, which decreased as the Reconquista progressed or was due to the fact that Arabisms were borrowed in the construct form, i.e., after the definite article, in a construction consisting of {noun plus *al-* plus noun}, expressing, *inter alia*, the notion of possession (1968:144). Later *al-* might have been retained as a sign of the Arabic origin of a word. Steiger himself also suggested, a few years after expressing his Berber hypothesis in 1932, that the presence of *al-* pointed to a borrowing from written Arabic, while its absence pointed to a colloquial Arabic source (1948–49). Others have proposed that *al-* is an index of the relative chronology of the borrowings, for example, early Arabic loans in Spanish tend to lack *al-* while later loans, after the mid-10th century, have it. Statistical studies reveal that 31.6 percent of the Arabisms that entered Spanish between 711 and the mid-11th century lacked *al-*, while from the mid-11th to the early 13th centuries, only 16.3 percent of the Arabisms lacked an accreted *al-* (Neuvonen 1941:81–82, cited also by Grossmann 1968:145). I wonder whether *al-* reflects the increasing Berberization that came after the Almohade invasion.

Neuvonen's characterization is acceptable for the most part, but there are problems, since sometimes the variant with *al-* proves to be younger than the variant without the article, for example, OSp *almadrueña*, Sp *almadreña*, "wooden clog, overshoe" is attested more recently than *madr(u)eña* c.1400 (used in the mountains of Castile and León; *DCECH*). See also the example of Sp *canaría* ~ *alcanería* "artichoke" cited earlier. This shows that for internal Spanish reasons Ar *al-* might have been added to Spanish Arabisms after the initial borrowing of the Arabisms without *al-*. Neuvonen's characterization of Spanish Arabisms finds a parallel in Berber Arabisms, where the distribution of *al-* also appears to be a function of the chronology of the borrowing: older Arabisms in Berber lack the accreted Arabic article, while newer loans have it, for example, after the banu Hilal invasion in the mid-11th century (Basset 1906:439–40, Schuchardt 1908:352).

In accepting the definite article, both Judeo-Spanish and Spanish occasionally reject the morphophonemic alternations that characterize the source language, i.e., in Arabic *-l-* assimilates to the initial dental or alveopalatal consonant of the nominal or adjectival root, thus resulting in a geminated dental or alveopalatal consonant. I cannot be sure of the status of the morphophonemic alternation in Old (Judeo-)Spanish examples, since the Jewish spellings may imitate the orthographic norms of Arabic, which are not required to mark assimilation and gemination. Only contemporary Judeo-Spanish examples, and sometimes Latin spellings in Christian texts, reveal whether the Arabic definite article was assimilated to the following consonant or not according to Arabic phonotactics. See, for example, JSp *'lrb* early 12th century (Ashtor 1964:65), JSp *'yl rb* (in the Valladolid *Taqqanot* of 1432) vs. SpLat *arrab* "the rabbi" (Calatayud 1229; Wexler 1988:62). A Hebrew tombstone from 14th-century Toledo has *'ln'qwh* /alnaqawa/ (the *IHE* 107), but the name appears with assimilation to *'n-* at Tlemcen, Algeria in 1442, and a Christian text from Toledo has *Anacahwa* (Baer 1/2:1936:246). Conversely, contemporary JSp *alsafran* shows that the Arabic assimilation rule could be abandoned altogether. Moreover, as in Old Spanish (including Mozarabic) texts, the accreted definite article is often perceived as part of the root, for example, SalJSp *la alfinete* "the pin" < Ar *al-xilāl* "the pin" (Steiger 1932:178).

A further complication is that once an Arabism has entered Spanish with *al-*, the latter may be subject to transformations under the impact of Spanish grammar. For example, *al-* may occasionally be reinterpreted as the similar-sounding Spanish masculine singular definite article, *el*, for example, *El Marín*, a locale near Salamanca < Ar *al-mar'īn* (Llorente Maldonado de Guevara 1963–64:102; see also Solà-Solé 1968a). See also Rhodes JSp *nuera* ~ *elmuera, ermuera* "daughter-in-law" with *el-* attached to a feminine Spanish word and *n* > *m* in prefixed forms (Penny 1993:138 and fn 7). There is also a tendency to remove *l* even if it belongs, historically, to the Romance root, for example, OSp *el aurel* (Cáceres 1525; Armistead and Silverman 1981:475) vs. stSp *laurel* "laurel." See also Mor (Alcaz) JSp *allaurel* (Alvar 1966, lexicon).

Mozarabic Arabisms almost always have *al-*. Solà-Solé says that Catalan lost *al-* with Arabisms because of the change of *al-* > *el-*, resulting in homophony with the Catalan masculine definite article (1968a:281, 284; see also Baldinger 1972:72). I am not altogether convinced by this argument, since the same process should then also have taken place in Spanish, and it rarely did. There is some evidence for deagglutination of the article in Ibero-Romance, for example, Arag *(l)o* > zero as in *obispo* > *bispo* "bishop" (Alvar and Bosch 1968, lexicon). Conversely, Romance words which begin with *a-* may occasionally attract an *-l-* in Spanish, for example, Sp *almorejo* "Setaria verticillata" < **amorejo* (1810), *almendra* "almond" and *almeja* "mussel"; according to the *DCECH*, this phenomenon is particularly common in Andalusian Spanish. See also Lat *mina* > Sp *mena* > *amena* (< *al-*) ~ *almena* (c.1270) "battlement" (*DCECH*).

Errors of interpretation also abound in Spanish Arabic, where *al-* might be deleted in Spanish words beginning with *al-* even though the latter was part of the root and the word itself was not of Arabic origin, for example, SpAr *barğariyya* "inn" < Sp *alberguería* (< Germanic) (Corriente 1977:85; for etymological details, see the *DCECH*).

There is no doubt that the accretion of *al-* in Judeo-Spanish developed on Iberian soil, since accreted *al-* is found in both Balkan and Moroccan Judeo-Spanish; in Moroccan Judeo-Spanish Arabisms acquired from coterritorial Moroccan Judeo-Arabic would be expected to have the article in its Moroccan form, i.e., *el-, l-, le-* (Schuchardt 1908: 352–53, Martínez Ruiz 1960:109). The assimilated Moroccan definite article is occasionally found in Moroccan Judeo-Spanish, with words of various components, for example, *er-rebbi* "the rabbi" < Hebrew and *en-ninyo* "the boy" < Spanish (Benoliel 1926:225).

As in Spanish, errors in reinterpretation can be found in Judeo-Spanish as well. It is common to find an inserted lateral in "Hebraisms," for example, He *'amidah* "prayer recited while standing" (< "standing") > BgJSp *a(l)midá* (Moskona ms; Nehama 1977 also cites the two variants for Saloniki Judeo-Spanish), BalJSp *alxaroset* "mixture of chopped apples, almonds, nuts, dried raisins, dates, cinnamon, and wine, eaten at the Passover feast as a reminder of the clay used by the Jews in Egypt in making bricks" (Bunis 1993a:228). It is significant that in Iberian sources *al-* could also be attached to Hebraisms, for example, León *albedyn* "Jewish judge" (Sahagun 1255; Steiger 1956–57; see also Baer 1934:231, 1:1961:87, Wexler 1988:61–63 and earlier in this chapter), JSp *Alcohen* name < He *kohen* "priest" (Teruel second half 15th century; Díaz Esteban 1975:108, fn 34); see also *arrab* "the rabbi" earlier. Similarly, "Hebraisms" used in Judeo-Arabic may acquire an accreted Arabic definite article perhaps with the function retained, for example, SpJAr *bet alkneset* "(the) synagogue," *altora* "(the) Torah," *alnedunya* "(the) dowry" 11th and 12th centuries in the writings of Maimonides (Blau 1958:190, fn 40; see also Sp *atora* masculine ~ *la tora* "Torah," Toledo 1488; Baer 1:1929:478 and Wexler 1988:62, fn 310).

In Judeo-Spanish, too, *al-* can be affixed to Romance words, for example, Mor (Alcaz) JSp *allaurel* "laurel" (see the Spanish treatment in this word earlier), *assiprés* "cyprus" (Martínez Ruiz 1960:109), Mac (Bit) JSp *alkansyon* "song," *aličuǵe* "lettuce" (Luria 1930:452) vs. Croatian JSp *lečuga* (S. Romano 1933) and Sp *canción, lechuga*. See also examples in Subak 1906:144 and Crews 1960:85. ModSp *ciprés* (attested since 1380) also surfaces with *a-* (< *al-* through assimilation to *s*) in OSp *aciprés* (14th through 17th centuries), but the *DCECH* takes the view that *a-* in this word results from a merger with *arcipreste* "archpriest" (why would these two words ever become merged?). OSp *onso* > ModSp *oso* "bear" vs. JSp *lonso* (with the accretion of the definite article; see also M. L. Wagner 1914:50, Crews 1935:199–200, M. Weinreich 3:1973:128). I wonder whether the Latin term was not originally used by Arabic speakers in Andalusia, and was thus regarded as an Arabism by the Jews when they switched to Spanish. See also JSp *el dyo* "God" < **addyo(?)* discussed later in chapter 5.

There are no obvious generalizations that can be made about the distribution of the Arabic definite article in Spanish and Judeo-Spanish. Both languages occasionally lack the definite article, but differ on the particular corpus of Arabisms so affected. On the one hand, Judeo-Spanish often lacks the article while Spanish tends to have it, see Sp *altramuz* (1328), and Laguna *atramoz* (1555; *DCECH*) vs. SalJSp *tramús*, *(al)tramuz*, Ist *attramús*, Rhodes *tarmuzes* (plural; Galante 1902:453), MorJSp *atarmúz* "lupine." See also Pt *tremoço*, Cat *tramús* < Ar *turmūs* (< Gk *θérmos*).

There are instances where Judeo-Spanish has *al-* with Arabisms while Spanish lacks the article or has it in an assimilated form, for example, JSp *alcofas* "round wickerwork coracles" (ibn Pakuda 1569:70b, cited by Bunis 1993a:22) vs. Sp *cofa* "frail two-handled basket, large basket" < Ar *(al-)quffa*, though there is a rare example with *al-* (in the first meaning) from the Spanish of Córdoba, c.1590 (*DCECH*). See JSp *alguža* "needle" vs. Sp *aguja* < Lat *acucūla*. BalJSp *a(l)safrán* (Crews 1961:30), MorJSp *asafrán* (Benoliel 1927:573) ~ OSp *(a)çafran*, ModSp *azafrán* "saffron" < Ar *(az-)za'farān*. Conceivably, in the Balkan Judeo-Spanish variant with *al-*, the latter may be a recent intrusion, and not an indication that the Jews were ignorant of the Arabic morphophonemic alternations in the article.

It is interesting that in Morocco, Judeo-Spanish Arabisms that appear to have come from Iberian Arabic retain their article intact, though coterritorial Moroccan Arabic could have provided a precedent for deletion, or at least for formal adjustment to the Moroccan Arabic article. Compare Sp *laca* "lacquer" (13th century), *lácar* < Ar *lakk* vs. MorJSp *allákar* (Benoliel 1926:225), which looks like a hybrid form with *-ll-* from Moroccan Arabic and *al-* from Spanish Arabic; MorJSp *alkuzza* [zz] vs. MorAr *kuza* "little jug" (ibid.: 232) vs. Sp *alcuza* 1253 (Crews ms notes that SalJSp *alkuza* denotes a jug for oil, while Sp *alcuza* is used for wine) with the geminated *z* of MorJSp *alkuzza* pointing to Moroccan Arabic influence. Sometimes *al-* is optionally dropped in Moroccan Judeo-Spanish with semantic implications, for example, MorJSp *alcamonía* "pastry of rhomboid shape consisting of linseed and honey" vs. *cománia* "snacks for a trip" < Ar *kammūniyya* (Benoliel 1927:569, 1928:50) ~ Sp *alcamonia, alco-* "seeds used in condiments such as anise, cumin, etc." (Steiger 1932:206, 356). M. L. Wagner had derived JSp *comanía* < Tu *kumanya* < Gk *kobania* < It *compagna* (1914, glossary, 1931:240), but MorJSp *cománia* points to an Iberian origin for the Judeo-Spanish Arabism. The two forms of the Arabism in Moroccan Judeo-Spanish suggest two different chronologies of the borrowings.

The last example illustrates a difficulty in my plan to identify Arabisms shared by Judeo-Spanish in the two Sephardic diasporas as Iberian in origin. Here, we see that an Arabism common to Moroccan and Balkan Judeo-Spanish may have been borrowed by the two dialects independently. There is also a problem when Turkish can, in theory, provide an Arabism which is identical in form and meaning to Iberian Arabic, for example, BalJSp *tabut* "coffin" < SpAr *tābūt* or < Tu *tâbût* vs. Sp *ataúd* (see also Wexler 1977b:185). The same problem affects the reconstruction of the origin of Sephardic customs. For example, the practice of women painting their faces with *ḥinnā'* "antimony" is found both among Sephardic women in Turkey until recently, and in Spain and North Africa (Yuhas 1989:204); the practice might be either of Iberian or Turkish Muslim origin.

In conclusion, the existence of *al-* with Hebraisms and Romanisms in Judeo-Spanish suggests that the accretion with these components occurred while the Jews were still predominantly speakers of Judeo-Arabic or possibly even (Judeo-)Berber.

Before I leave the topic of the agglutinated Arabic definite article in (Judeo-) Spanish, it is appropriate to consider parallel cases of agglutination of articles (and other parts of speech) in other speech communities. Creole language studies suggest a plausible origin for the agglutinated Ar *al-* with Spanish Arabisms (examples also exist in Portuguese and Catalan, but are less numerous in the latter where the Arabisms appear without the article).

The agglutination of the French definite articles that is found in a number of French Creoles is probably calqued on Bantu noun class prefixes. The African slaves relexified their native languages to French, all the time preserving their native grammatical and phonological systems. For details, see Taylor 1961, Manessy 1983, Baker 1984, Baker and Corne 1987, Ndayiragije 1989, Hazaël-Massieux 1993:115 and Lefebvre 1993:255–56.

On the basis of the experiences of the Creole languages that have a French lexicon, I wonder if the agglutinated Arabic definite article that appears with many Spanish words did not also come about in the process of relexifying Arabic (and Berber) to Spanish vocabulary. The process of relexification would have been common to Arabs and Jews who were exposed to Spanish. Later on, when a full language shift to Spanish had been carried out (acquiring Spanish grammatical and phonological norms, following the acquisition of Spanish vocabulary), a sizeable residue of Arabisms with the accreted Arabic definite article could have been introduced into the speech of monolingual Spaniards. To the best of my knowledge, no Hispanist has proposed that the agglutinated *al-* in Spanish Arabisms is the result of prior relexification.

Evidence from Religion and Folk Culture

Our knowledge of Iberian Jewish cultural and religious practices comes from three sources:

(a) Christian, mainly Inquisition, literature of the 15th and 16th centuries provides detailed descriptions of Jewish customs allegedly practiced by Marranos and Jews; occasionally, Christian observers also describe in varying detail Jewish practices that they observed in the diasporas beginning with the 16th century. The Iberian Christian literature is especially valuable since by admonishing the faithful against practicing certain customs, we learn which practices were unknown to the Christians; these practices were presumably unique to the Jews and/or Muslims.

(b) Rabbinical literature from Spain, North Africa, and the Balkans sheds light on the attitudes of rabbinical authorities to current folk practices. The earliest of these sources date from the 14th century.

(c) Since the late 19th century, ethnographers have been providing detailed descriptions of Jewish customs.

As in the case of linguistic examples, I can also reconstruct the outlines of Iberian Jewish culture prior to 1492 by establishing which folk practices were practiced in the two Sephardic diasporas, or in one of the diaporas and in Spain. It is unlikely that customs shared by Balkan and North African Sephardic Jews would be independent innovations in the two diasporas. A comparison of Jewish folkways and religious practices with those of the coterritorial non-Jews in North Africa and Spain suggests that the Berbers and the Arabs were the major suppliers of Sephardic Jewish practices. There are also some unique customs with circumscribed geographical areals among the Sephardic and North

African Jews whose origins require clarification, for example, the Jews of Jerba, the island off southern Tunisia, pronounce a *qidduš* (a benediction) on the eve of Passover and read some prophetic passages at certain Sabbaths (the latter custom is also shared with Jewish communities in Yemen and Tafilalt, Morocco). These practices may antedate the standardization of Jewish ritual practices in North Africa (Udovitch and Valensi 1984:8); hence, they could have spread with the Jews from the Near East to North Africa after the 8th century, but too late to reach Spain. Establishing the relative chronology of North African customs should be a pressing desideratum on the Sephardic ethnographic research agenda.

Some Jewish customs adopted from the Muslims may actually be of Jewish origin. For example, Ptaxja of Regensburg (late 12th century) states that the "Babylonian" (Iraqi) Jews prayed barefoot, under the impact of the Muslims (M. Kister 1989:364). The Jews apparently had earlier given up this practice once the Muslims adopted it, and the practice came to be regarded as "Muslim" (ibid.:367).

The relative chronology of some Iberian Jewish customs can be reconstructed by examining how Iberian emigrés to North Africa, beginning with 1391, reacted to indigenous Jewish customs. Yicxak ben Šešet Perfet (Barcelona, 1326–1408), who arrived in Algeria in 1391, wrote: "in this land most [Jews] act according to the rules of the Muslims" (cited by I. Epstein 1930:58, fn 11) and noted that Arabic was used in the synagogue (ibid.:fn 14). Unlike the North African Jews who practiced monogamy, the Spanish Jews were polygamous, especially when the wife was sterile (ibid.:88). Perfet's contemporary, Šim'on ben Cemax Duran (Mallorca 1361—Algeria 1444), also observed that Iberian Jewish (presumably Catalan) customs differed from those of the North African Jews (ibid.:36–40).

The significance of these late 14th-and early 15th-century statements is that Iberian and North African Jewish practices differed in a number of details. This means that either the Spanish Jews had become Christianized (i.e., de-Muslimized), or that the Iberian Jewish refugees to North Africa in 1391 preserved the early wave of North African Berbero-Arab customs (from 711) which the North African Jews had given up between the 8th and 14th centuries; the indigenous North African Jews may have acquired new practices that came in the wake of the banu Hilal invasions in the 12th century. For example, Duran says the North African Jews were lax about growing sidelocks, and that they wore a slender strip of hair down the side (ibid.:38 and fn 16; on Judeo-Spanish terms for the sidelock, see chapter 5 this volume). This would imply that the Spanish Jews, at least those from the northeast of the peninsula or from Mallorca, had sidelocks. On the other hand, the illuminations from Iberia give no indication of this practice (Wexler 1993c:168–69). While the Iberian Jews may have considered themselves more observant than their North African coreligionists, a French Jewish observor, Moše of Coucy, writing about a century and a half earlier in 1235, warned that Iberian Jews were lax in their Jewish observances (Freehof 1962:215). The Catalonian Yona ben Avraham Girondi (c.1200– 1263) noted laxity in the observance of the phylacteries, the use of the house amulet (He *məzuzah*), and the growing of beards, and criticized the habit of eating with Christians and having sexual relations with female non-Jewish slaves (Baer 1:1961:250).

North African Sephardic practices, which differ from those of the coterritorial Muslims, may be of Iberian origin, for example, whereas Sephardic Jews now name a child after a living relative, this is expressly forbidden in Moroccan Muslim society, except with the name Muḥammad (Westermarck 2:1926:404).

Following in random order, I list a number of Sephardic practices that were practiced with some certainty in Spain and which appear to be of Berber, Arab, or Ashkenazic origin (in the later case, often before 1492):

(a) The requirement that a male cover his head during prayer apparently first arose in Muslim Spain. Maimonides was in favor of this practice. But a late 13th-century Castilian Jewish illumination shows the Jews in a building (synagogue?) with uncovered heads (Zirlin 1986–88:66, figure #21). In the synagogue, the Jews removed their shoes both in Spain and Algeria (I. Epstein 1930:75).

(b) Moroccan Jews curently have a custom whereby guests at a wedding are expected to pay a tip to the musicians (Malka 1946: 58–59). This is reminiscent of an Ashkenazic practice in the Slavic lands, known in Yiddish as *šabaš* (denoting the tip given to musicians at a wedding only by those guests who participate in the dancing). The Yiddish term itself is of Iranian origin, but the custom itself is also attested among Slavs, as far west as Polabian territory in north-western Germany (Wexler 1993c:108–10). It is unclear to me if the Moroccan custom was acquired from the coterritorial Berbers and/or

Arabs, or is an example of Ashkenazic influence on North African Jews (chapter 5 this volume).

(c) In Morocco, the Jews throw out water from the home of the deceased to prevent the angel of death from spreading poisoned drops of water (Zafrani 1983:103). The Moroccan custom was first cited by Addison 1676:221. It must be of Iberian origin, since it is mentioned in an Inquisition testimony from León (Jiménez Lozano 1984:365; Levine Melammed 1991). A similar custom is attested among the Ashkenazic Jews; if there is a link, the practice might have been introduced to the Spanish Jews by Ashkenazic rabbis in the early 14th century.

Marranos were also accused of performing the ritual washing of a corpse, a practice also noted among Iberian Muslims (Cantera Montenegro 1985:82; Levine Melammed 1991). The joint Jewish-Muslim practice of washing the corpse apparently even spread to Christians (Imamuddin 1981:216–17). Antonio de Guevara, the bishop of Mondoñedo, described Christian practices in his unpublished "Constituciones sinodales" which he attributed to Jews (and Muslims):

> Some people who do not feel well with the [Christian] faith, at the time that a man is expiring and dying, wash the entire body, thinking that they are washing away the sins; and furthermore, they take off the beard, which they later keep to make spells; and since this is a Jewish, and even Muslim rite, we excommunicate all those people who from now on practice this. . . (1541, reprinted in Costes 1925:59).

He then inveighed against allegedly Muslim superstitious practices. Redondo, however, raises the possibility that the ritual washing that the bishop attacked was originally a Christian custom, which had been given up around the 12th century (1976:436, fn 69). Obsolete Christian and Muslims customs could be kept by the Jews as "Jewish" (chapter 5 this volume).

A number of Jewish funeral practices find reflection in the coterritorial Muslim communities: Both groups tended to construct their cemeteries out of town, while Christians built their cemeteries near the church (de Miguel Rodríguez 1989:133, describing a manuscript from 1502). According to Roselló Bordoy, the Muslim cemetery of San Nicolá in Murcia, in use between the 11th through 13th centuries, was atypical in that it was situated inside the city walls

(1989:158–60). Sometimes Jews and Muslims buried their dead at home. The rabbis opposed this practice since the obligatory mourning period of seven days could not be held separately from the grave (Ashtor 2:1966:255). Both Jews and Muslims often shipped the bodies some distances for burial. The rabbis also objected to the burying of personal effects with the body (ibid.:257).

(d) The practice of *kapparah*, the Hebrew term for the expiatory slaughtering of a cock or hen during Yom Kippur and the New Year, was not consistently practiced in Spain before 1492. In the responsa literature from Spain, opinions were divided on the usefulness of the practice. The Castilian Jews opposed it, for example, Yosef Karo objected to it on the grounds that it had been condemned by the Catalan rabbis Moše ben Naxman (or Nahmanides, Girona, 1194–Acre, Palestine, c.1270) and Šlomo ben Avraham ben Adret (Barcelona, c.1235–1320; Zimmels 1958:51, 248, 267). Adret recognized that Ashkenazic Jews in Germany followed the practice (I regard it as probably of Slavic origin, Wexler 1993c:171–72). Ben Naxman called it "idolworshipping" and Karo labeled it stupid (Schauss 1938:166). In Medieval France and Germany, the practice of *kapparah* was conducted at home, but in parts of Spain where it existed it was moved to the synagogue (Freehof 1962:225); this sounds like an attempt to Judaize the practice.

In North Africa, the custom is presently ubiquituous. For Morocco, see Zafrani 1983:278–79, for Tunisia, see D. Cohen 1:1964:78–79, and for Algiers, see M. Cohen 1912:397. The practice was first mentioned for Morocco by Addison 1676:182–83.

A significant difference between the ceremony of *kapparah* in Sephardic and Ashkenazic communities is that among the former, the fowl is slaughtered on a variety of occasions other than the Yom Kippur/New Year period, for example, before the feast of Jethro, for the purpose of providing a cure for an illness, and on the tombs of rabbis during a pilgrimage to the graves of the latter (the Muslims have the same practice on this occasion). This raises the possibility that the origins of the Ashkenazic and Sephardic *kapparah* practices differ, though the requirement of practicing the ritual during the two most solemn holidays of the Jewish calendar, which is common to Sephardim and Ashkenazim, could be due to Ashkenazic influences on the Sephardim, during a period of Judaization. The result is that the current North African practice of slaughtering the expiatory fowl may be a composite of Ashkenazic and Sephardic practices. Adret succeeded in extirpating the practices of slaughtering a cock on the occasion of a boy's birth, and of hanging the cock with its head and feathers cut off at the entrance of the house; his objection indicates that the Catalan Jews followed this practice at the time (Zimmels 1952:145). However, these customs have never been fully extirpated. For example, in Tlemcen, Algeria in 1950, if two deaths took place in the same year, or month, the second body had to be washed after slaughtering a cock on the threshhold of the deceased's house and rubbing the blood on the doorpost and lintle; subsequently, the cock was eaten by the deceased's family and neighbors (Zafrani 1983:107).

Abbou suggests that the *kapparah* practice in North Africa is probably of Berber origin (1953:364 and fn 1) and D. Cohen notes that the practice was possibly a revaluation of a pagan ceremony earlier denounced by the rabbis (1:1964:80). If Abbou is right, then the custom could have been initially brought from North Africa to Spain, and (re)introduced to North Africa after 1391. Alternatively, if it became extinct in Spain, it could have been re-acquired by Sephardic Jews in North Africa after 1391.

There may be a possible vestige of *kapparah* among Spanish Christians, if we may judge from the statement of Jiménez Lozano (1984:364), citing an informant in the region of El Bierzo, in the province of León, that the death of fowls "corre a cargo de hombres," i.e., takes the place of men by means of expiation.

(e) In 16th-century Tunis, fish was considered useful to combat evil spirits (Turki 1989:62–63); Scheftelowitz also noted that Arabs put the figure of a fish at the store entrance for good luck and sent greeting cards on 1 April with the sign of the fish (1911:347). Muslims also bury a fish in the construction of a new home (Turki 1989:62 and fn 5). Andalusian Muslim refugees to North Africa also recognized the fish symbol (ibid.:63), but it is not clear to me if they brought the custom from Spain or acquired it for the first time in North Africa.

In Jerba, southern Tunisia, the local Berbers had the custom that on the seventh day of a marriage, the groom buys a quantity of attractive fish, which he places in the middle of the courtyard of the house; the bride and groom then circle the fish seven times (seven is a magical number in many North African and European societies), then eat it with couscous. The fish is a symbol of richness and fecundity in other areas of Tunisia and North Africa. Related fish customs are also attested among the Muslims in Rabat and Fès, Morocco, and in Tunis and Sfax, Tunisia. Today in Jerba the fish custom is only practiced at Ḥumt Suq, an area with a venerable Jewish community; despite the availability of fish on the island, Jerba Muslims do not appear to consume much fish (Ben Tanfous 1987:506).

A variation on the custom of jumping over the fish among Muslims at Fès was depicted by Leo Africanus in the 16th century; here, as a sign of good luck, a fish was thrown at the feet of the wife (Africanus 1632:326; see also Scheftelowitz 1911:377, D. Cohen 1:1964:45, fn 1). According to Zachariae, the first description of the practice of jumping over the fish comes from a Muslim wedding in approximately 1563 (1906:291).

Among the Balkan Sephardim, the bride jumps a couple of times over a dish full of fish which is a symbol of fertility (idem. 1906: 291–94, 1908:434—specifically referring to the practice in Sarajevo in 1891 and in Turkey in 1897; Yuhas 1989:206, fn 54 cites a source in Atias 1955:44). In Saloniki the seventh day after the wedding was called JSp *dia del peškado* "the day of the fish" (Molho 1950:39–43).

The performance of the fish custom following the wedding in both the Balkans and North Africa shows that the practice must have existed in Spain itself and may be of Berber origin. The belief in the fish as protection against the devil apparently spread from Egypt to the Jews in the 3rd century A.D., and is mentioned in the Talmud (Scheftelowitz 1911:345). The problem is that the fish was also a symbol of fertility in the Bible; hence, the status of the fish among the North African Jews may be derived ultimately from the Bible (ibid.:376). However, there is no mention of this specific fish custom connected with the wedding in any Old Palestinian Jewish source.

The fish jumping custom has now disappeared totally among Moroccan Muslims (Ben-Ami 1974:93). This fact could guarantee its retention among the coterritorial Jews.

(f) In parts of North Africa, it was the practice at a wedding for the bride and groom to dress in the clothing of the opposite sex (on the disguising of the Jewish groom as a woman in south Morocco, see ibid.:28; on the practice among the Jews in 12th-century Egypt, see Abrahams 1896:193). This custom is also found among some Moroccan Muslims (Westermarck 1914:105). Espadas Burgos mentions the custom in a novel about Jewish converts to Catholicism written by Francisco Delicado in 1528 (1975:544, fn 19). The purpose of dressing in the clothing of the opposite sex was to protect the bridal couple against demons. Maimonides opposed the practice in Egypt on the grounds that it was of non-Jewish origin (Bergmann 1927:161, H. Lewy 1931:23), which suggests that he was familiar with the custom from his native Spain.

(g) Marrano women in Castile in 1590 were said to throw their nail clippings into the fire (Levine Melammed 1992:162, 168). Addison also noted the custom among the Moroccan Jews of burning or burying nail clippings in preparation for the sabbath. He also described the strict order required for the cutting of the fingernails—beginning with the left hand (1676:128–29). Contemporary descendants of the Marranos in the southwest United States trim the nails of the feet and hands on Saturdays, as well as the nails of the deceased (Hernández 1992:424, 436).

(h) Spanish Marranos in Castile in 1590 were described as holding their feet together with their hands folded during prayer and touching their eyes a few times during prayer (Levine Melammed 1992:165–66). Judaizers from Molina, Aragón at the end of the Middle Ages described a certain Pedro Bernal who was accused of praying in the Jewish manner—i.e., on his knees, and bowing down on the floor (Cantera Montenegro 1985:72). For a similar report about a Portuguese Judaizer in 1594, see C. Roth 1931:16–17. These reports sound very reminiscent of the Muslim manner of prayer. Note Sánchez Albornoz's claim that some Jews prayed in Muslim fashion (2:1956: 286; see also earlier discussion in chapter 2 this volume). Maimonides had eliminated prostration in prayer because of its importance to Christianity, but his son, Avraham ben Maymon, reintroduced the practice in Egypt (Wieder 1946:75–77, Goitein 1954:708). On prostration, see also chapter 5 this volume.

(i) Arab Jews from Morocco to Yemen, including Moroccan Sephardim, believe that a newborn child is in danger of being harmed, and that the mother gives birth to a spirit infant, which could take the place of the real infant if the latter is not properly attended. The Jews in a wide area have terms for this belief, for example, MorJSp *avoltado* "turned" or JAr *mgelleb* "changed" ~ YemJAr *mibaddal* "exchanged" (Ben-Ami 1993:259, 266, fn 26).

(j) Ben-Ami recounts the Moroccan Jewish practice of cutting the groom's pubic hairs prior to the wedding ceremony, even though the shaving of the hair of the pubic area and armpits was forbidden by Jewish religious law (1974:60 and fn 258). The custom is currently widespread among some Jews of the Sūs and the Atlas mountains of Morocco; Ben-Ami also notes that Berbers in Amizmiz, Morocco perform this custom—and he regards the latter as the source of the Jewish practice (ibid.:90). The ceremony was also practiced by Turkish Jews, but I lack details on the geography and chronology.

(k) The use of the six-pointed star (or "star of David") was commonly used by both Iberian Muslims and Jews—but not by Christians. It appears in an Arabic book written by Iberian Muslims (López-Baralt 1980:61) and in an Arabic book containing a syncretistic description of Islam and Christianity composed in Granada in the 16th century (Cabanelas 1981:351). Arabic books used the star for magical purposes (Martínez Ruiz 1985:227). On the decorative function of the star in Iberian Islam, see Zozaya 1992; the star is popular in North Africa as an amulet (Doutté 1909:157), where it is commonly drawn on paper along with Quranic inscriptions as a charm against the evil eye (Westermarck 1:1926:465, 475).

The six-pointed star was not originally a Jewish symbol (D. Romano 1988:135), though it was called in Arabic by Muslims and Jews alike as *xātem sulaymān*, literally "the seal of Solomon" (Doutté 1909:156 thinks the Muslims borrowed the symbol from the Jews). The pre-Christian West Slavic and Germanic six-pointed star first denoted the Jewish people (as opposed to a magical symbol) in Moravia, Bohemia, and Austria in the 18th century (Wexler 1993c: 122–24 and Oegema 1994). A Hebrew inscription from Toledo from 1180 found at the site of the synagogue, now known as the Santa Maria la Blanca, contains the six-pointed star (*IHE* 333). The star also appears on a coin from a Jewish tomb in Toledo (López Álvarez 1979: 122) and on an illuminated Hebrew manuscript housed at the Biblioteca Nacional in Lisbon (Ms.Il.72, folio 448 verso), prepared in Spain c.1300, which also displays the arms of the united Kingdom of Castile and León.

In Saloniki we have an example of a star with the Hebrew letters *mgndwd* (standing for He *magen david*, "the shield of David") distributed at each outer point; the star was written on two pages of white paper called in Judeo-Spanish *papeleras*. See the discussion of this term earlier in this chapter.

(l) In the Iberian Peninsula, Jews and Muslims shared a number of formulaic expressions, some of which were disapproved by the rabbis. See further discussion on syncretistic religious expression earlier in chapter 2. Yona (Abu l-Walid Marwan) ibn Janaḥ (Córdoba?, late 10th century through mid-11th century) opened his Hebrew grammar with a formula of clearly Quranic inspiration (see Busi 1986:179 on the profundity of Judeo-Arab symbiosis in 11th-century Spain). A Sephardic wedding contract (known in Hebrew as *ktubbah*) began with the phrase "in the name of the Lord, the ever lasting God," which Šim'on ben Cemax Duran (Mallorca 1361–Algeria 1444) objected to on the grounds that this was an imitation of Arab practice (Zimmels 1958:179). The Jewish practice of burying papers with the name of God and Hebrew liturgical writings in a *gnizah* (literally "storeroom") of a synagogue building finds a parallel in Muslim communities (Narváez 1981:154 and fn 47).

(m) Jews and Muslims venerate common saints in Morocco (of both Jewish and Muslim origin; see Lévi 1900, Basset 1901, Voinot 1948). The shrine of the ibn 'Ašur family in Tunis (of Andalusian origin) was venerated jointly by Jews, Muslims, and Christians (El Aziz Ben Achour 1983:21). It would be interesting to know if the custom of venerating the graves of famous clergymen was practiced by the Jews in Spain.

Additional Sephardic customs of Ashkenazic, Romaniote, and later North African Berber and Arab origin, discussed in the context of Judaization, are presented in chapter 5. See in particular the glass-breaking act during the wedding ceremony. On the Iberian Sephardic naming ceremony, see also chapter 5.

5

The Processes of Judaization

The institutionalization of Islam and Christianity in the Iberian Peninsula and North Africa eventually brought a halt to organized Jewish proselytizing activities and led to the increasing segregation of the Jews from non-Jewish society (especially in the Christian realms, which by the mid-11th century constituted the overwhelming majority of the peninsula). The cessation of conversion activities meant that the Iberian Jews in the Muslim-controlled areas were no longer likely to be receptive to innovative practices coming from the Berbero-Arab or Christian populations. By the 11th century, the main candidates for conversion to Judaism would have been the slave population, mainly of non-Iberian extraction. The growing segregation of the Jews within Iberian society also meant that the Jews experienced greater difficulty in defining themselves as part and parcel of the indigenous communities. In such an environment, it is not surprising to find Jewish scholars and rabbis cultivating unique practices for the Jewish religion and culture. I call the process of cultivating a heightened Jewish profile by the term Judaization. On the use of the term in the scholarly literature and in the Ashkenazic communities, see Wexler 1993c, chapter 7.

It is natural that whenever the Sephardic Jews conceived of themselves as more and more distinct from the indigenous Christian population, they would become attracted to the idea that Sephardic culture was the direct heir to Old Palestinian Jewish culture, and that the Jews were the descendants of Old Palestinian Jews.

The segregation that characterized life in the Christian north was initiated not just by the Christian rulers. Unwillingness to assimilate with the Christian society propelled many Jews themselves to seek insulation from non-Jewish society. Rabbi Ašer ben Yexiel opposed sexual intercourse between Jews and Christians, since many children were being born of non-Jewish maid servants (Zimmels 1958:257); Šlemo ibn Verga, the Seville-born(?) author of the famous history entitled *Ševet yehuda*, considered intercourse with Christians as one of the major causes for the expulsion in 1492 (1550:258). The Christians, in an effort to control contacts between Jews and non-Jews and to restrict the spread of syncretistic religious expression, passed laws prohibiting the Jews from reading anti-Jewish literature and requiring them to observe the Jewish Sabbath and their own holidays (see the *Fuero real* of 1255, discussed by Baer 1/2:1936:34–39, 45–47 and Glick 1979:340, fn 14).

Weinryb characterized the process of Judaization (found in all "Jewish" communities at different periods in history) as follows:

> Contradictions between actual practice and the religious prescriptions which were grounded in the Talmud developed early in Europe. The adopted deviant use was, however, made acceptable by a fictitious means which helped maintain the unbroken continuity of tradition—making Jewish life appear to be a continuation of that of earlier times. In this way tradition remained unaffected (Weinryb 1974:968).

While Halper insisted on the unbroken transmission of a written Hebrew tradition in the diasporas, he did recognize that the unavailability of a body of native speakers of the language encouraged Judaization (he did not use this word) in the form of imitating Biblical Hebrew style:

> The continuity of the Hebrew language as a literary medium. . .is unbroken. . .[post-biblical Hebrew literature] is the product of men, who. . .did not speak Hebrew as their mother-tongue. . . They were thus denied that freedom of expression which is essential to the creative genius, and *were compelled to fit their work to the [biblical] frame* (1921:6–7, italics supplied).

The broken tradition in the transmission of Hebrew and Judeo-Aramaic writings also finds a parallel in Jewish customs and proverbs. For example, original talmudic and biblical proverbs have been replaced by colloquial Jewish or non-Jewish paraphrases, for example, Yemenite Hebrew has the proverb *siman labanim bat* "an early announcement of a son is a daughter" (literally "a sign of sons is a daughter") which contrasts with the original Talmudic He *bat txila siman yafe labanim*, literally "a daughter first is a good sign of boys." The Yemenite Hebrew expression appears to be a translation of YemAr *bašārat al-walad bīnayyāh* (Goitein 1934:40; see also earlier in chapter 2 this volume).

Future research is needed to determine which biblical and talmudic customs that had originally never been practiced in the diasporas came into vogue in the Middle Ages. For instance, it is conceivable that Jews might have abandoned the ban on eating pig meat expressed in Old Palestinian Jewish writings in parts of Europe where the coterritorial or contiguous non-Jews lacked the ban (see the discussion of Slavic Europe in Wexler 1993c:175–77). For example, in North Africa, the Judaized Berbers might have given up the prohibition on pig meat, following the practice of those Berbers who ate wild boar (Lewicki 1966:33, 35); on the other hand, the ancient Libyans, the ancestors of the Berbers, like the ancient Egyptians, did refrain from consuming the meat of the pig. If the North African Jews are largely of Berber descent, then it is quite conceivable that the Jews ate the meat of the pig until Muslim religious law was established, calling a halt to the consumption of this meat among the Berbers and Arabs both; the decision of the Jews to reinstate the prohibition, while stimuated by Islam, finds an Old Palestinian Jewish precedent.

The relative chronology of the Judaization process is not always easy to reconstruct, though, clearly, it is predicated on the availability of Old Palestinian literature. Hence, the first instance of Judaization could not have taken place before the late 7th century in North Africa, the earliest date that Near Eastern and Arabian Jews might have brought Old Palestinian Jewish literature to North Africa; this body of writing could have reached Spain shortly thereafter during the Muslim invasion of the peninsula in 711. The latest date of the implantation of this literature would be approximately 1000. After this date, the Berber invasions of Spain would have made communication between Islamic Spain and the East more difficult as Muslim al-Andalus was drawn firmly into the North African orbit (Glick 1979:49). The heightened intolerance of Islamic Spain in the 12th and 13th centuries would also have been conducive to increased Judaization and might explain Yehuda ha-Levi's (c.1070–1141) anti-proselyte stance.

Despite the availability of Old Palestinian Jewish literature, Judaization was not consistently practiced in Spain; for example, Judaization was apparently not in full swing in Muslim Spain at the time of Maimonides (1138–1204), to judge from the latter's opposition to a number of proscriptions explicitly recorded in the Talmud, for example, he opposed the Egyptian custom of the bride dressing up like a man and the groom dressing up like a girl—the purpose of which was to protect the pair against demons (H. Lewy 1931:23–24 and earlier in chapter 4). The Talmud (Šabbat 67b) mentions the habit of giving a female name to a male and vice versa, yet Maimonides' objection suggests that either he was unfamiliar with this custom in his native Spain or chose to disregard it. In general, before the 15th century, Sephardic Judaization did not usually involve seeking Jewish "precedents" in Old Palestinian literature (the Bible, the Talmud). The practice of Judaization would have been blocked whenever the inroads of assimilation and the total absence of an influx of a new "Judaized" or Jewish population from abroad reduced the level of Jewish scholarship, for example, in 14th-century Spain.

It is useful to distinguish between the occasional Judaization of non-Jewish terms (see the many examples I give of Muslim Arab terms later in this chapter) and the process of seeking Old Palestinian Jewish precedents in the Bible and Talmud—with or without Hebraization of Jewish religious terminology.

In some cases, the Judaization of a non-Jewish folk custom appears to be extremely superficial and secondary; this would suggest that the attempt to Judaize the custom in question may have been fairly recent. For instance, in southern Tunisia, Jewish wedding customs are identical to those of the Muslims. Both groups rely on an "anonymous construct, a tradition that everybody accepts, enacts, and transmits" rather than on the orthodox practices of either community (Valensi 1989:83). To quote Valensi further:

> The aspects of the marriage celebration considered most fundamental by the participants actually derive from local custom—from a vernacular tradition broadly shared by Jews and Muslims. Within this vernacular tradition the place of orthodoxy is, in the end, limited and reduced for both Muslims and Jews (ibid.:67).

The Jewish woman finds a reference to religion in the wedding ceremony in the fact that the fiancé's mother tears away a sleeve of the bride's robe during the celebration known as the "night of the raised daughter" (the second evening before the wedding ceremony). This act is intended to symbolize the destruction of the Temple in Jerusalem and the loss of the land (the Temple theme in the wedding ceremony is discussed further in this chapter). Orthodox Judaism does not require this motif, but it is widespread in the ceremonial of Jewish weddings. In

Jerba, this act has another—pre-Judaized—intepretation: the tearing refers to the piercing of the hymen, over which the fiancé's mother has charge (ibid.:76, 82). Twelve days following the wedding, sex is prohibited since the rupture of the hymen makes the wife impure. She then has to go to the ritual bath before further sex is permitted; the Muslims have no such prohibition (ibid.:80; on this ceremony, known in Judeo-Spanish as *tornaboda*, see later in this chapter). The cultural symbiosis between the southern Tunisian Jews and Muslims is so pervasive that it is impossible to trace when local customs were invented and by whom. In the collective construct of the wedding customs neither the Jews nor the Muslims are, strictly speaking, "orthodox"; they are orthodox only vis-à-vis the local norms. For some North African Jews, local customs took precedence over the rulings of Jewish law, for example, the Talmud or *Šulxan arux* (ibid.:83 and Udovitch and Valensi 1984:18; for a Yiddish parallel, see Wexler 1993c:158).

Cultivating a unique "Jewish" profile could be accomplished in several ways: by eliminating Berber, Arab, and Spanish Christian practices that could not be successfully Judaized, by retaining Berber, Arab, and Spanish Christian practices that had become obsolete in the host communities, by espousing Ashkenazic, Romaniote, and new Arab and Berber folklore and religious practices, often together with a new Hebrew nomenclature, by applying Jewish meanings to Spanish words and by recalibrating Muslim Arabic terms to denote Jewish customs and artifacts. A number of other examples of Judaization were already mentioned in the preceding chapters.

The Elimination of Berber and Arab Practices

Berber, Arab, and Christian customs practiced by the Jews were recommended for elimination, whenever it was obvious to the practitioners of Judaization that the practices were patently not of Jewish origin, or when Old Palestinian Jewish precedents in the Bible and Talmud that were needed to justify their continuance could not be provided.

There is also some evidence that the rabbis recommended abandoning a number of Jewish customs that aroused the hostility of the surrounding non-Jewish majority, for example, customs which the Christians regarded as "magic"; this is a sign that the customs were unfamiliar to the latter, and, hence, probably of Berbero-Arab origin. The fear of cultivating in public a different profile from the Christians may have induced the Jews to abandon practices such as prostration in the synagogue (Neuman 2:1942:111, Goitein 1954:708; see also examples in the Responsa writings of Šlomo ben Adret of Barcelona); however, in Egypt, in a Muslim environment, Avraham ben Moše ben Maymon (1186–1237) reintroduced the practice or prostration (chapter 4 this volume). For similar reasons, some of the purification ceremonies mentioned in the Talmud and practiced by Muslims were dropped in Christian Spain (see details in Zimmels 1958:227–28 and chapters 2 and 4 this volume).

In the North African Sephardic diaspora, a number of Iberian Jewish customs were recommended for dropping due to similarity with coterritorial Muslim practices. The English observer, Lancelot Addison, noted in 1676 that Moroccan Jewish children were segregated from the Muslim children because

> there is so great likeness between many of their own and the Moresco customs, that a child may be easily induced to a promiscuous imbibing of either (80).

Algerian Jews now avoid eating mutton because this meat was endowed with a ritual function in the Muslim sacrifice of *ʿīd al-kabīr* (Bahloul 1989:90).

Rabbi Ašer ben Yexiel (Köln c.1250–Toledo 1327) opposed the use of a Muslim prayer rug in the synagogue of Toledo (Finkel 1990). The very mention of his objection shows that the practice must have been widespread. Indeed, an extant Toledo prayer rug from the 14th century even depicts the *kaʿba* at Mekka. Despite the rabbi's protests, the practice was clearly not discontinued; in the Balkan diaspora the Sephardic Jews continued to use prayer rugs with Islamic motifs in the mid-16th century. V. B. Mann has studied an example dated 1609, which depicts lamps near the ark, together with names of God, and a *miḥrāb* (niche in the mosque, indicating the direction of prayer) scene; the motif was inspired by a Quranic verse (ms a, b). Egyptian Jews also used Muslim prayer rugs in the synagogue, and here, too, the rabbis objected to their use (for example, the writings of David ben Zimra, 1479–1573).

The Retention of Obsolete Berber and Arab Practices and their Nomenclature

Non-Jewish practices that were abandoned by the Muslims and Christians, or not known in Christian-dominated areas of the peninsula, could in principle be retained by the Jews as distinctly "Jewish" even without the artificial attachment of an Old Palestinian Jewish pedigree. In the Christian north, where Berbero-Arab practices were less likely to be shared by the non-Jewish population, the Jews could, paradoxically, redefine many Berber and Arab practices as "Jewish," even if they were not yet obsolete among the Berbers and Arabs. This would explain the remarkable longevity of Berbero-Arab customs among the Sephardim, even up to our own days. The maintenance of Berbero-Arab practices—despite the lack of contact with a vibrant Iberian Berber culture since at least the 12th century—is expressed in a number of domains, including art and architecture. For example, in the Christian regions that had long been liberated from Muslim control, the Jews continued to cultivate Islamic patterns of architecture in the construction of their synagogues (see those in Córdoba and Toledo). Dodds suggests that the Jews were attracted to Muslim styles of architecture, since they were distinct from those of the conquering Christians who persecuted them after the Christianization of the Muslim areas (1992:122). Perhaps, but there is the further factor that Muslim architectural styles were attractive to the Jews in Christian Spain as a means of strengthening a separate "Jewish" profile; for the same reason, Jews in various parts of Europe in the late 19th and early 20th century cultivated pseudo-Moorish or Oriental styles in synagogue architecture. For details, see Wexler 1993c:240.

Significantly, the El Tránsito synagogue in Toledo has a bilingual inscription in Hebrew and Arabic (Rosen-Ayalon 1986:275, Dodds 1992:114, Scheindlin 1992:43, fn 11) and the Córdoba synagogue has an Arabic inscription (*IHE* 333–35, Cantera Burgos 1973:185, López Álvarez 1992). Córdoba fell under Christian control in 1235, yet the synagogue in question was built in 1314–15; Toledo became Christian as early as 1085, yet the Islamic-style El Tránsito synagogue was constructed in the 14th century. Wischnitzer implies that the presence of the Arabic inscription in the Toledo synagogue was due to a Muslim craftsman (1964:40), but Dodds believes it is simply a sign that the Jews regarded Muslim architecture as their own. The use of Arabic in synagogues is not so unique, since the Christians also used Arabic inscriptions in Christian religious buildings (Dodds 1992:123–24) as well as on Christian religious artifacts such as coffins, reliquaries, and textiles (Dodds and Walker 1992:xxii, Herrero Carretero 1992, Holod 1992:200, Partearroyo 1992a, b, c).

However, functionally, the use of Arabic inscriptions differed among Jews and Christians. Among the former they were an expression of their native culture, while among the Christians, they appear primarily on Muslim artifacts and buildings that were transformed for Christian use; only rarely were Arabic inscriptions spontaneously utilized by Christians.

The Berbero-Arab patrimony of the Iberian Jews had opposite impacts on the Christian and Jewish communities. For the Christians, the Berbero-Arab culture of the Jews could have contributed to increased Christian calls for segregation of the Jews as a population with alien, "un-Christian" practices. For the Jews, this patrimony was crucial to them as a means of strengthening their unique Jewish profile—in opposition to the surrounding Christian practices. In other words, the search for a unique Jewish cultural and religious profile in the Christian lands required the preservation of the "Jewish" Berbero-Arab customs brought north when Arabic-speaking Jews migrated in large numbers to the Christian regions to escape the intolerant Muslim societies in the 11th and 12th centuries. The Berbero-Arab patrimony of the Iberian Jews was especially important given the rapid acculturation of large segments of the Jewish population to Christian norms during the two very different processes of full and partial language shift from Judeo-Arabic to Spanish.

In addition to seeking out biblical and talmudic pedigrees, the Judaization processes of the Iberian Jews also involved Hebraization. The resumption of the Hebrew language tradition, which was so important to Judaization was, curiously, accompanied by the rise of a separate women's section in the synagogue building in the 12th and 13th centuries. (For further detail, see the discussion of the women's role in the synagogue service earlier in chapter 2.) The significance of the chronological overlap needs to be explored.

The Hebraization of Jewish religious terminology is not a prerequisite to the linguistic Judaization of a non-Jewish language (Wexler 1981b:119–24, 1993a:346 and chapter 4 this volume), but it is a prerequisite for widespread Judaization of cultural and religious practices (see also chapter 4). In fact, the gradual expansion of the Old Hebrew (and Old Judeo-Aramaic) vocabulary in Judeo-Spanish, and many other Jewish languages, can be plotted through time (see also earlier in chapter 2). On the acceptance of Biblical Hebrew terms from a non-Jewish language, see the discussion of BibHe *hexal* earlier in chapter 4; on generating new Hebraisms on the model of Biblical Hebrew, see the discussion of JSp *kabar* earlier in chapter 4, and further details in chapter 5 (the latter also on the expression "Sabbath food"); on the replacement of Arabisms by Hebrew words of similar form that have pejorative meanings and on the Judaization of the Sephardic name-giving ceremony known as *fada(s), tahdīθ*, etc., see further details this chapter. On the Hebraization of Arabic proper names, see earlier chapter 3 this volume; on the replacement of non-Hebrew toponyms by a Hebraism, see the discussion of He *sfarad* also in chapter 3. On onomastic differentiation of Iberian Jews, Muslims, and Christians, see chapter 4.

The Espousal of Ashkenazic, Provençal, Romaniote, and New Berber and Arab Practices

Judaization implied receptivity to Old Palestinian Jewish precedents and Hebrew and Judeo-Aramaic terminology, as well as to "Jewish" practices from the Ashkenazic and Provençal Jews who settled in Spain in the 1300s and from the indigenous Jews among whom the Sephardic emigrés settled in North Africa after 1391 and in the Balkans after 1492. In the Balkans, and to a lesser extent in North Africa at a later period, the process of Ashkenazicizing Sephardic culture accelerated—though not to the point where the Berbero-Arab roots of the latter were fully obliterated or abandoned. The reason for the survival power of Old Berbero-Arab customs, even after contact with Ashkenazic Jews, is that the acceptance of "Jewish" practices from Ashkenazic and other Jews raised the danger that the Sephardic Jews would become indistinguishable from other coterritorial and contiguous Jewish groups (Wasserstein 1992: 177–78). Hence, the Sephardic Jews steadfastly cultivated unique Berbero-Arab customs and retained the use of "Spanish": either the "Judeo-Spanish," which was actually relexified Judeo-Arabic (i.e., Judeo-Arabic grammar and phonology with a predominantly Spanish vocabulary) or a slightly Judaized variant of Christian Spanish. Eventually, relexified Judeo-Arabic became extinct in the two Sephardic diasporas. In the Balkan diaspora, in the absence of Christian Spanish speakers, a more "Christian" Spanish, as well as Iberian Christian folkways, could be adopted and cultivated without compromising the desire of the Sephardim for a separate ethnocultural and linguistic profile. On the cultivation of non-Judaized Iraqi Arabic by Iraqi Jewish immigrants to southeast Asia, beginning with the 18th century, see Wexler 1983b; on the de-Christianization of Iberian folkways, see, for example, Armistead and Silverman 1982:127–48. Hence, the cultivation of Christian Spanish (and Portuguese) language norms among the Iberian Jews in North Africa, the Balkans, and Northern Europe should thus not, strictly speaking, be defined as a process of "de-Judaization" (as I inaccurately suggested in 1987a).

In the diasporas, the Sephardic Jews even managed to spread the use of Spanish among the coterritorial non-Iberian Jews. The Portuguese Jewish communities of Marrano extraction in northern Europe resisted "intermarriage" with Ashkenazic Jews as late as the eve of World War II. There were two main reasons for this practice: the desire to maintain a separate Jewish profile in a society where most of the Jews were not of Iberian origin, and the disbelief in the notion of a "single Jewish people."

The Iberian Jews first cultivated links with Ashkenazic rabbis who came to the Iberian Peninsula to teach and to study in the early 14th century (Zimmels 1958:11). For example, Ašer ben Yexiel (1250–1327/8) came to Barcelona after 1303 and accepted a position in Toledo in 1305; Yosef ben Šalom Aškenazi lived in Catalunya (probably Barcelona) in the early 14th century (Vajda 1956:135ff; see also Marmorstein 1927). While German Jews settled in Spain, there is no evidence that Iberian Jews studied in the north (Wexler 1993c:255). Aside from the emigration of Ashkenazim to Spain, the Spanish rabbis may also have become familiar with Ashkenazic practices from a distance, via religious literature, for example, Šlomo ben Adret knew that the German rabbis practiced *kapparah* (Schauss 1938:166 and discussion later this chapter). The Ashkenazic Jews appear to have brought with them religious practices that had either never been known or had since fallen into disuse in Spain. Curiously, many of the Ashkenazic practices brought to Spain were themselves "Judaized" Slavic customs, derived from the Sorbs and other Slavs who had converted to Judaism up to approximately the 12th century.

The Marranos who abandoned the peninsula in the 16th and 17th centuries, in some cases to join established Jewish communities abroad, had little or no knowledge of Jewish or newly Judaized religion and culture. For some, the interest in a new or renewed Jewish identity was strengthened by the anti-Jewish persecutions instigated by the Inquisition. I would even submit that the Berberized Sephardic Jews who left the Iberian Peninsula with the Spanish expulsion edict in 1492 were also largely divorced from Jewish traditions; had they remained in Spain, most of them would have eventually merged with the Christian majority. In the emigration, the Sephardic Jews largely depended on the non-Iberian Jewish communities among whom they settled—the Arabic- and Berber-speaking Jews in North Africa and the Greek-, Yiddish-, and Slavic-speaking Jews in the Ottoman Empire—for (re-)education in Judaism. This is why such an imposing array of Ashkenazic folk customs (mainly of Slavic origin!) surfaces among the North African Jews as early as the 17th century.

North African Jewish practices which appear to be of Ashkenazic origin include the following practices:

(a) *Tašlix*, the ceremony of symbolically throwing one's sins into a body of flowing water during the New Year and Day of Atonement, though not necessarily the name, was cited by Addison 1676:188; there is no mention of this ceremony in Yosef Karo's *Šulxan arux* 1565 (Zimmels 1958:51 and discussed later this chapter). The custom is currently practiced in Jerba, southern Tunisia (Udovitch and Valensi 1984:72).

(b) Plucking the grass at the grave site and casting it behind one's back (ibid.:221). However, Levine Melammed cites the practice in an inquisition protocol of 1520–23 from Toledo (1991:164).

(c) Breaking a glass at the wedding in commemoration of the destructions of the Temple in Jerusalem (Valensi 1984:48) and having men who wait on the bridegroom break earthen pots as a sign of good luck (ibid.:51; this looks like the German custom known as *Polterabend*, for details, see Wexler 1993c:164–65).

The breaking of a glass at the wedding is unknown among Muslims, though the latter do throw an egg at the wedding to encourage an easy childbirth (Addison 1676:52, Westermarck 2:1926:371). Ben-Ami sketches the geography of the glass-breaking ceremony in Morroco (either empty or full of milk; 1974:48ff; see also Malka 1946:70 and Zafrani 1983:87), and M. Cohen cites the custom among Arab Jews in Algiers (1912:507, fn 27); for Morocco, Ben-Ami also mentions non-Jewish interpretations of the glass-breaking ceremony which do not appear to have been received from the Ashkenazim, for example, in addition to the Ashkenazic interpretation that the act symbolized the two destructions of the Temple (1974:48), the ceremony was also useful for annulling magic directed against the newly weds and for making them less timid (ibid.:61), and was a sign of the groom's sadness at leaving his parents (ibid.:63). These interpretations are unknown in Ashkenazic sources. The variety of symbolism points to a practice of great antiquity, over which the recent Ashkenazic reference to the Temple in Jerusalem was superimposed. The notion of the two destructions of the Temple was added by Medieval Ashkenazic rabbis in order to supplant the originally pre-Christian Germano-Slavic belief that smashing a glass on the northern side of the building would deter the devil, who was expected to come from the north, in order to obstruct the joy of the newly weds. Even among the Sephardim in Saloniki during the first half of the century, Molho notes that the glass was not intended just to symbolize the Temple, but also to mark the fragility of life (1950:28). De Modena mentioned the glass ceremony among the Italian Jews in the late 17th century (he does not specify if they were Ashkenazic or not), but makes no mention of the Temple; instead, the glass smashing symbolized, in his view, death in the midst of joy (1683:117; see also Leibovici 1986:238).

Future research should try to plot the diffusion and chronology of Ashkenazic practices in Spain, North Africa, and the Balkans. For example, it is unclear whether Ashkenazic customs came to Libya from the Italian Ashkenazim or from Ashkenazicized Italians (either indigenous or Iberian in origin). Descriptions of late 19th-century Libya relate that in Jebel Nefūsa the Jews broke an egg at the wedding ceremony, rather than a glass, to commemorate the destructions of the Temple, while Jews in Tripoli performed the ceremony of the glass breaking (Goldberg 1990:65–66). It is interesting to observe the subsequent diffusion of Ashkenazic customs from Tripoli into the Libyan countryside. In the 20th-century wedding ceremony conducted at Tripoli, the bridegroom throws a pail of water on the street and smashes it before the arrival of the bride, in memory of the Temple; despite the presumed austere tone of the event, the women in attendance emit shouts of joy (Lewy 1930:248). In Ashkenazic practice, the guests also shout "good luck" to the couple after the breaking of the glass. In Libya, both Jewish and Muslim brides throw an egg on the outer and inner walls of the bedroom, as protection against the evil eye. See the wedding practices of the southern Tunisian Jews, described earlier in this chapter.

(d) Ashkenazic customs practiced by the Iberian Sephardim may have been abandoned, only to be resumed in the Sephardic diasporas. For instance, *kapparah*, the expiatory ceremony of slaughtering a cock or hen, is practiced currently in Saloniki (Molho 1950:296), but it is *not* likely that it continues, without interruption, the earlier Iberian custom, which had been given up in large parts of Spain (chapter 4 this volume).

(e) Another custom, known to contemporary Tunisian Jews, that is reminiscent of an Ashkenazic practice, is the throwing of water behind the back of a traveler at the moment of his departure to symbolize good luck, especially when money or jewels are placed in the water (D. Cohen 1:1964:102). This practice is also attested among the Muslims; among some Ashkenazic Jews, the money given to a traveler is expected to be returned to the donor upon the safe return of the traveler. The component of "throwing behind one's back" is reminiscent of Sorbian pre-Christian practice (Wexler 1993c:174–75). For example, in Saloniki, the Jews threw stones behind their back at the grave site (Molho 1950:187). Of course, not all instances of "throwing" that are currently practiced by North African Jews need be of Ashkenazic-Sorbian origin. For example, in Ġardaia, Algeria, the Jews had a unique custom of throwing a mixture of gold powder or silver with "earth from Palestine" during a funeral cortège (Shinar 1982:106); there was also an analogous custom from the city of Algiers, where just before the burial of a male, the rabbi throws a handful of gold coins as far as possible from the tomb in order to distract the devil from the deceased (ibid.:fn 135).

(f) Judeo-Spanish lexical borrowings from Yiddish include SalJSp *yarseat* (< Y *yorcayt*; Nehama 1977) "anniversary of the death of a close relative or famous scholar." The Yiddishism has also been borrowed by Judeo-Italian and Judeo-Persian as well (M. L. Wagner 1950:101), a fact which emphasizes the broad geographical parameters of Ashkenazicization. The custom of commemorating a death also appears to be relatively recent among the Sephardim, to judge from the variety of terms that can denote it, for example, *yešiva, petira, midraš, zexira, limud* (S. Romano 1933, Molho ms) and *naxala* < He *yəšivah* "sitting," *ptirah* "death," *midraš* "study," *zxirah* "remembrance," *limud* "studying," and *naḥalah* "inheritance" and JSp *meldado* "(been) read" (< Greek, see earlier in chapter 4), *anyos* "years" and SalJSp *nočada* "night of prayer in memory of a dead friend" (Kosover 1954:780). Despite the use of the Yiddishism, the performance of the act differs somewhat from the Ashkenazic *yorcayt*, which requires only the lighting of a candle at home (on the non-Jewish elements of this Ashkenazic Jewish custom, see Wexler 1993c:120–22).

Benardete describes the practice of *meldado*, which is observed at sunset in the presence of ten males over the age of 13: the table is covered, candles are burned, and Hebrew liturgical books are read—hence, the name *meldado* (1963:134).

Among the Jewish descendants of the Portuguese Marranos in Holland and England, the ceremony is known as *meldadura* (literally, "reading [of Hebrew books]") "commemoration on the anniversary of a person's death; donation to the synagogue on such an occasion." These meanings of *meldadura* are not shared by all Portuguese Marrano speech communities, for example, in Bordeaux the term denoted the reading of the Law on the first night of Pentecost or the reading of one or several verses of the Bible the night of a circumcision (see references in Wexler 1982:95). There is no mention of the custom or any of these concepts in Yosef Karo's *Šulxan arux* (1565; see Zimmels 1958:51, 187). Differences in meaning can help us reconstruct the place(s) and time(s) of Ashkenazicization.

In Judeo-Arabic dialects, there is also quite a variety of terms for the commemoration of a relative's death. The Old Eastern Judeo-Arabic term is *tarḥīm*, borowed from Muslim and Christian Arabic; for an example from Ramla, Palestine from 1039, see Blau 1984:164, and for an Egyptian Karaite Arabic attestation and "new" *raḥamanut* (based on the Arabic root) in 17th-century Egyptian "Hebrew," see J.Mann 1972: 256, fn 1. In contrast, see TunJAr *qandīl*, literally "oil lamp," lit to symbolize the soul of the defunct right after death. The candle remains at the home of the deceased for an entire year, whereupon it is transferred to the synagogue to be burned every Friday before sundown, as long as there is a relative alive; the lamps of rabbis and venerated men are always lit (D. Cohen 1:1964:46). Would the use of the candle imply Ashkenazic influence?

BalJSp *benaxas* "comfortably" (Bunis 1993a:128) is < "He" *bənaxat*, literally "in comfort," but the final *-s* suggests a Yiddish pronunciation (see Y *naxes* "comfort"). I doubt that this word is a left-over from Iberian Hebrew pronunciation norms, which often observed the Old Hebrew spirantization rule in the pronunciation of Hebrew words, whereby postvocalic, non-geminated OHe *b, d, g, p, t, k* > homorganic fricatives. This rule is not found now in either the Balkan or the North African Sephardic diaspora. This is important evidence of a break in the transmission of a Hebrew pronunciation norm; the loss of the spirantization rule may have been due to Romaniote practice (it is observed partly in Yiddish Hebraisms and in the Ashkenazic pronunciation of monolingual Hebrew texts).

For example, He *'blwt* "mourning" was spelled in a Mexican Spanish text from 1649 as *avelus, -z* "mourning rites" (Wexler 1982: 66–67) but in contemporary Balkan and North African Judeo-Spanish, it is pronounced as *avelut/aveluδ* or *abelut* (Molho 1950:189, Bunis 1993a:86 and Benoliel 1927:566, respectively). See also TunJAr *äbīl* "mourning" (with *imāla*; D. Cohen 1:1964, index) ~ SalJSp *avel* < He *'avel* "mourner" (vs. *'evɛl* "mourning"). AlgJAr *labe^{i}l* "mourning" < He "mourner" with the agglutinated Arabic definite article (M. Cohen 1912:498–99, fn 27).

The radical change in the pronunciation of the *'ayin* before and after 1492 also suggests a Romaniote or Ashkenazic impact on the pronunciation norms of the Sephardic emigrés; in North Africa, the *'ayin* has come to be pronounced in the Arabic manner. For details, see earlier in chapter 4 and Wexler 1982:65–66.

Future research is needed to determine whether the espousal of Balkan cultural and linguistic features by the Sephardim was precipitated exclusively by contact with the indigenous Balkan Jews or also resulted from significant interaction with Balkan non-Jews. A possible example of the latter is BalJSp *los mižores de mozotros,* a euphemism for the devil, literally "those who are better than us"—a proverb common to a number of Balkan non-Jewish peoples (see Theodoridis 1990–93).

In addition to Ashkenazic scholars in Spain, Provençal Jewish scholars also had an impact on Sephardic Jewry, for example, Avraham ben Yarxi went from Provence to Toledo in 1204 (Freehof 1962:223). Future research will need to determine whether the uniqueness of Aragonese, Navarran, and Catalan Jewish practices and terminology, as opposed to Castile, was due to a Provençal Jewish impact on the north Iberian Jews. See the inner-Ibero-Romance isogloss involving Hebraisms mentioned earlier in chapter 4.

An interesting example of probable Romaniote influence on the Balkan Jews is the naming of children by the holiday on which they were born (Molho 1950:70). See, for example, JSp *xanuka* < "Hannukah" used as a male name in Izmir and as a surname in Saloniki (Bunis 1993a:224), *(y)intó*, a personal name and a surname in Saloniki < JSp, JSp"He" *yom ṭov* "holiday," literally "good day" (ibid.:240; Yiddish also has a different pronunciation of He *yom ṭov* in the meaning of holiday and as a male name). See also JSp *pesaxa* a feminine name and a surname in Istanbul < *pεsaḥ* "Passover" (ibid.:382); Molho 1950:75 considers the corresponding male name *pesax* "Sephardic." The name was totally unknown in Spain. The practice of naming a male child by the holiday on which he was born has a parallel in coterritorial Turkish society; among Turkic groups, the earliest examples are actually from Khazar "Hebrew" of the 10th century (Wexler 1987b:74–77 discusses Khazar names derived < He *pεsaḥ* "Passover," *ḥanukkah* "Hannukah," and the geography of the practice). For contemporary Saloniki examples, see the practice of naming a male child born on Purim—*Mordexay*, in the month of Nisan—*Nisim*, on Hannukah—*Matityahu*, on Shavuot—*Moše*, from the 10th of Av up to the end of the month—*Menaxem*.

The success of the Ashkenazicization and Arabization of diaspora Sephardic culture can be ascribed to three factors:

(a) The Sephardic Jews felt a need to find some Jewish content—not only for ideological, but also for commercial reasons. The Iberian "Jewish" emigrés, like the Marranos who emigrated from Spain and Portugal in the following century, often decided to join the Jewish communities abroad for reasons of expediency. The Ottoman Turkish authorities would probably not have welcomed the emigrés and allowed them freedom of commercial activity had they identified themselves as members of a Christian sect.

(b) Iberian Jewry was very fragmented in its practices (and Hebrew terminology) and Ashkenazicization promised to impart a more or less standard norm to the diaspora communities. For example, *šmiṭat ksafim* "release of loans in the sabbatical year" (based on a passage in Deuteronomy 15:1ff), was not practiced by the Sephardim except in Aragón, thanks to the efforts of Šlomo ben Adret; Ašer ben Yexiel had tried unsuccessfully to revive the practice in Castile (Neuman 1:1942:218–19, Zimmels 1958:214, Eidelberg 1962:56, fn 103). The Iberian Jews also differed in their mourning customs. For example, in Catalunya mourners were accustomed to going to the synagogue only on Saturday, whereas in Zaragoza (Aragón), they went daily (Freehof 1962:223).

The isoglosses dividing the use of "Hebraisms" within Spain do not just separate usage in Islamic and Christian areas, but also separate Ibero-Romance areas (chapter 4 this volume). See also Navarran "He" *yom hakippurim* (Tudela 1363, in a text from 1413; Fernández y González 1886:17) vs. Castilian "He" *kippur*. While Zimmels was not sufficiently precise about the linguistic differences within the Ibero-Romance areas, he does cite differences in Jewish legal practice within the Ibero-Romance domain (1958:47), for example, Aragón and Valencia used the code of Maimonides (Córdoba, 1138–1204), while Catalunya used that of Moše ben Naxman (also known as Nahmanides, Girona 1194–c.1270), Šlomo ben Avraham ben Adret (Barcelona, c. 1235–1310), Aharon ben Yosef ha-Levi (Barcelona, 1235–1300), and Nisim ben Re'uven Girondi (Aragón c.1310–c.1375), and Castile followed Ya'akov ben Ašer ben Yexiel (Köln, c.1270–1340). The age of such isoglosses that divide the Judeo-Ibero-Romance-speaking territory needs to be ascertained; I suspect that many may be older than the full and partial language shifts from Judeo-Arabic to Spanish that began in the 11th century.

Iberian Jews also differed radically in their linguistic preferences—even after the abandonment of Judeo-Arabic; some Jews spoke Spanish while others spoke relexified Judeo-Arabic (Judeo-Arabic with a predominantly Spanish lexicon). Future research should try to find a correlation between linguistic and cultural differences.

(c) Jewish religious practice was generally lax in Spain. For example, the wearing of the phylacteries or *tfillin*, the affixing of the house amulet known as the *məzuzah*, and the visitation of the ritual bath (*miqveh*) in Catalunya were three practices said to be poorly observed (Zimmels 1958:255 and D. Romano 1988:134). The laxity of observance overlaps with the language shift from Judeo-Arabic to Spanish. In fact, according to Spiegel, Sephardic culture (in "Hebrew" and Arabic) was already in decline when the Jews switched from Judeo-Arabic to Spanish (1952:3). The *məzuzah* had magical purposes in 20th-century Saloniki, for example, if a child did not come out of the womb, psalms should be recited in front of the *məzuzah*, with best results when performed by the husband (Molho 1950:58; on the use of the amulet in Ashkenazic circles, see Wexler 1993c:167–68).

Old Hebrew terms were cultivated by the Iberian Jews in place of non-Hebrew terminology, though often both sets of terminology continued to coexist to some extent. The adoption of Hebrew terms did not necessarily mean that the latter were used in the same meanings they enjoyed in Old Palestinian sources. BibHe *ḥuppah* denoted a tent, covering, seat, room of the bride and groom, or booth where the bride and bridegroom sat for the seven days of the wedding celebration; the meaning of wedding canopy, now standard in Modern "Hebrew" and Ashkenazic (Yiddish) "Hebrew," is first attested in the "Hebrew" writings of Raš"i (Champagne 1028/40–1104) and Yehuda (Abu l-Ḥasan) ben Šmuel ha-Levi (Tudela c.1070–1141). In contrast, in the Judeo-Spanish of Alcazarquivir, Morocco, the Hebraism denoted the seven days after the wedding (Benoliel 1926:227, Martínez Ruiz 1963:112) and in Saloniki Judeo-Spanish the eight days of the wedding celebrations (Nehama 1977). The Ashkenazic meaning of the Hebraism surfaces as AlgJAr *ẹ̆lḥůppå*, with the Arabic definite article (M. Cohen 1912:509, fn 35).

Another example of an innovative meaning associated with a Judeo-Spanish Hebraism is *xuva* "duty, obligation" (< He *xovah*), which in Sephardic parlance has come to mean the set of religious rituals in the first night of Passover and Shavuot or the symbolic dishes eaten during those rituals (Bunis 1993a:203). JSp"He" *el arbáveesrim*, BosJSp"He" *arbåveezrim* "(twenty-four parts of the) Bible" < He *'arbaʽ vəʽɛsrim* "twenty-four" (Subak 1906:168, Bunis 1993a) is unique and apparently not attested in other Jewish languages. The literal meaning of He *'arbaʽ vəʽɛsrim* is "four and twenty," following Arabic word order; this phenomenon was noted earlier in chapter 4. Normative Hebrew has *ʽɛsrim və'arbaʽ*, literally "twenty and four." See also the discussion of BibHe *hexal* earlier in chapter 4.

There are several distinctive features which give away the relative recency of most Hebrew and Judeo-Aramaic components in a Jewish language:

(a) Recent Hebrew and Judeo-Aramaic components preserve the form and meaning of the source etyma better than older borrowings that have become part of the colloquial Judeo-Spanish lexicon. Judeo-Spanish has a considerably higher percentage of borrowings from written Old Hebrew and Judeo-Aramaic texts (called by some scholars "whole Hebrew") than from spoken Old Hebrew sources (known as "merged Hebrew"; see the discussion in Bunis 1993a, especially 63). A problem for the future is to compare the ratio of "whole" to "merged" Hebrew and Judeo-Aramaic in Judeo-Spanish with that in other Jewish languages, especially Yiddish.

(b) Post-1492 Judeo-Spanish contains far more Hebraisms than pre-1492 texts. Bunis does not make clear when approximately the increase of Hebraization began in the Balkans, but he does suggest that many Hebraisms found in 19th and 20th-century Judeo-Spanish can be found in late 16th-century Judeo-Spanish texts from Saloniki. A detailed collection and analysis of pre-1492 Hebraisms is urgently needed.

(c) There are wide differences in the Hebrew (and Judeo-Aramaic) corpus of Judeo-Spanish and those of other Jewish languages (see the comparative data in Corré n.d.), which proves that no Jewish language was likely to have inherited a significant corpus either from old colloquial Hebrew and Judeo-Aramaic, or from a Jewish language that was in contact with the latter. The tiny corpus of possible Old Hebrew and Judeo-Aramaic loans is due to the fact that the early diaspora Jews lacked both a spoken and written Hebrew tradition, and were not unanimously receptive to Palestinian Judaism. Most Hebraisms in the Jewish languages are later independent borrowings from written Old Hebrew literature.

(d) Contemporary Judeo-Spanish now uses Hebraisms, whose meanings are expressed by other Hebraisms in Ladino Bible translations, for example, BalJSp *yovel* "jubilee, the fiftieth year, the year following the succession of seven Sabbatical years; (ironically) never; a long time" (Bunis 1993a). BibHe *yovel* (Exodus 19:13) was replaced by *el šofar* (< He *šofar* "ram's horn") in the Istanbul Ladino translation of 1547, which suggests that He *yovel* may not have been in use among 16th-century Sephardim.

(e) Hebrew doublets in a Jewish language are an indication of multiple borrowing. For example, TunJAr *ṛāb* "rabbi-saint cult" seems to be a relatively recent Hebraism intended to Judaize an originally non-Jewish custom (though the innovative meaning of the Hebraism gives away the non-Jewish origins of the practice) vs. TunJAr *rəbbī* "religious teacher, rabbi" (D. Cohen 1:1964; see also chapter 4 this volume). Sometimes recent Judaization involves the replacement of an older Arabized Hebraism, for example, AlgJAr (old) *mä'bi* ~ (new) *məqvi* "ritual bath," respectively. AlgJAr uses *'ọrlå* for "foreskin" (said to be preferred by rabbis) ~ colloquial AlgJAr *brīt*. Given the differences between the Arabic of the Jews and Muslims, there would actually be little point in borrowing He *'orlah* or *brit*, except to Judaize the ceremony (also practiced by Muslims). Sometimes, the new Hebraism is only intended to express Jewish, but not general connotations, for example, AlgJAr *mnūṛå* "big chandelier in the synagogue" (M. Cohen 1912:391) < He *mənorah* does not displace AlgJAr *mnǎṛå* "Arab lamp" (in turn < Aramaic).

The fact that Muslims in Tunisia call Jewish holidays after the name of the food consumed on the occasion might appear to be a sign that Muslims were very well versed with Jewish practice. This might be the case with the names of one or two major holidays—but not with all holidays. Hence, I suspect the Muslims got the names from the Jews, before the Jews underwent Judaization and started calling the holidays by Hebrew names. Examples are Tun (Jerba) JAr *ʿid et-tmar* "New Year," literally, "festival of fruit," *ʿid ed-djaj* "Yom Kippur," literally "festival of poultry," *ʿid el-ftira* "Passover," literally "festival of unleavened bread" (Udovitch and Valensi 1984:63, who claim that the Jews were also very familiar with Muslim religious festivals). The latter term is found in other Arabic-speaking communities, for example, MorAr *l-ftira* "Passover" (Attal 1963:425; see also Schreiner 1886:263, fn 9 and Goitein 1931:359 for examples from Ṣanʿā' Yemenite Judeo-Arabic). It is significant that (Judeo-)Arabic holiday terms often vary from region to region, see also Yem(J)Ar *ʿīd an-nuδūr* "Passover" (Newby 1988:144, fn 103, literally "feast of the vows"; see also Heller 1927) < He *nedεr* "vow."

Finally, Hebrew may provide a gauge for choosing the form of an expression in a Jewish language, for example, AlgJAr *wuḷḷå el-ʿazīz* "almighty God" is more common among the Jews while the Muslims use *wuḷḷåh el-ʿaḏīm* (M. Cohen 1912:398), perhaps because Ar *ʿazīz* has a Hebrew cognate. See also lexical bifurcation involving Spanish-Hebrew-Arabic terminology cited later in this chapter.

The status and chronology of Judaization in one Jewish language can help us determine the status and chronology of Judaization in another language. For example, Y *xale* as the name of a festive bread is a relatively recent Hebraism (< He *ḥallah*) intended to replace the similar-sounding name of a Germanic pre-Christian goddess (Wexler 1993c:115–18 and chapter 2 this volume); the original Biblical Hebrew meaning is preserved by MorJSp *xalla* and BalJSp *xala* "small portion of unbaked dough given as a tithe," which is not a bread term (Benoliel 1928:201 and Bunis 1993a, respectively; see also earlier in chapter 2). Of course, I still cannot determine the relative chronology of this Sephardic borrowing from Biblical Hebrew. JAram *yoma' ṭabba'* (literally "the good day") in Judeo-Spanish denotes a banquet at which rabbis convene, on the occasion of a happy family event (Molho ms) or the two first and last days of Passover or Sukkot whereas cognate Y"He" *yontef* denotes a Jewish holiday and *xoylemoed* is the expression for the intermediate days of lesser sanctity between the first and last days of Passover and Sukkot (< He *ḥol hamoʿed*). Contrast also JSp *kabar* vs. Y *kabren* "gravedigger" < He *q-b-r*, discussed earlier in chapter 4. On the other hand, there is a small common Old Hebrew corpus in many Jewish languages, for example, Y *reb(e)* ~ JSp *ribi, rubi* "rabbi, teacher." Yiddish uses He *-im* plural with Hebrew masculine nouns that take the Hebrew plural marker *-ot* in native old written Hebrew; some of the Yiddish Hebraisms with *-im* have parallels in a number of other non-contiguous and non-coterritorial Jewish languages. Examples are Y *taleysim* ~ YemJAr *ṭəlītīm* ~ *ṭəlītōt* "male prayer shawls" (Goitein 1931:365 for the Yemenite data and Wexler 1990a for Yiddish and comparative Jewish language data). See also the discussion of JSp *ribi* and TunJAr *ṛāb* earlier in chapter 4 and He *ṭaman et haḥammin* "he hid the Sabbath food" also in chapter 4.

A common corpus of Hebraisms need not always be due to inheritance of old colloquial Hebrew material. In one Jewish language, a Hebraism may be inherited from Old Hebrew, but in another, it may be a more recent borrowing in periods of intensified Judaization from Old Hebrew or a borrowing from another Jewish language (where it might have been inherited from colloquial Old Palestinian Hebrew). On the use of Hebraisms in place of, or alongside of Arabic cognates, see He *daraš* "sermonize"/Ar *darasa* "to study," and the folk etymology that interpreted the Judeo-Spanish Grecism *meldar* "read (Hebrew) books" as a derivative of He *limud* "study" (noted earlier in chapter 4); see also the addition of a Jewish meaning to a neutral or Muslim Arabic term, examples of which are presented later in this chapter.

An old common Hebrew terminology, as small as it may be, nevertheless suggests that some Jewish languages did manage to retain elements of old colloquial Palestinian Hebrew (and Judeo-Aramaic), and passed them on from generation to generation through an unbroken chain of Jewish language shift—i.e., from Old Palestinian Hebrew > Judeo-Aramaic > Judeo-Greek > Judeo-Latin > Yiddish, etc. It is presently unclear whether all Jewish languages possess an Old Palestinian Hebrew substratum. These data are valuable evidence that some Palestinian Jews must have participated in the formation of Jewish diaspora communities. The geography of the putative substratal Hebraisms may tell us in which diasporas a significant Palestinian Jewish population may have taken root.

The Judeo-Aramaic component in Jewish languages also has its own geographical parameters. Significantly, Judeo-Arabic dialects lack JAram *yoma' rabba'* "Yom Kippur," literally "the great day"; see instead native YemJAr (San'āʿ and vicinity, Central Yemen) *sabt as-subūt* "Yom Kippur," literally "the Sabbath of Sabbaths" (Goitein 1931:359). The presence of He *yom kippur* in a Judeo-Arabic dialect looks like a later borrowing from written (non-indigenous) Hebrew, for example, YemJAr *kpūr* (ibid.:362; Piamenta 1990–91 gives the form *kffūr*, where the ungrammatical *pp* is replaced by *ff*). The Judeo-Aramaism is found in Judeo-Greek, Latin, and Yiddish (see data in Wexler 1987b:19). This suggests that a Judeo-Aramaic tradition might have been inherited by Greek, Latin, and some European Jewish diasporas, but not by the Arabic- and hence, Spanish-speaking Jews. See also the discussion earlier of JAram *yoma' ṭabba'*, used in Judeo-Spanish.

The Recalibration of Christian Terms and Practices

Judeo-Spanish and Judeo-Arabic have a few Spanish terms that had Christian meanings and associations in the donor language that have acquired new Jewish meanings and associations in the two target languages. This category comprises fewer examples than the category of recalibrated Muslim terms and expressions used in Judeo-Arabic and/or Judeo-Spanish. Quite a number of the examples cited later are limited to North African Judeo-Spanish, which suggests a post-1492 borrowing. A pressing desideratum of Iberian Jewish studies is to establish the relative chronology of all the Christian examples.

There are four explanations for the relative paucity of Christian examples: Iberian Jewish culture was less receptive to Christian than to Muslim influences in Spain; the exposure to Spanish Christian culture was shorter in duration than to Iberian Muslim culture; the process of eliminating Christian imagery and of Hebraizing terminology in Sephardic folklore was so successful that few examples remain (Armistead and Silverman 1982:127–48); the Judaization of Christian terms took place passively, i.e., *by default* and not by active planning, due to the obsolescence of a term or particular form in the Spanish speech of Christians.

The common Judeo-Spanish term for "God," *el dyo*, usually with the definite article, continues the oblique cases of Lat *deus* and is a good example of "Judaization by default." In contrast, Christian Sp *Dios* continues the nominative/vocative case form of Lat *deus*. In other

Romance speech communities, the form without *s* also became the norm, for example, It *dio*. The variant *deus* eventually prevailed in Spanish Christian circles, probably under the impact of *deus* in Latin ecclesiastical texts. Once *Dios* became identified as exclusively "Christian," then the variant *(el) dyo*—no longer used in Spanish—was free to be marked as "exclusively Jewish." The use of the definite article might have been patterned on Ar *al-*, following Arabic practice, for example, *ar-rab*, literally "the master," SpAr *al-mawlānā* "our Lord," literally "the-lord-our" (where *al-* has been accreted to *mawlānā* in violation of Classical Arabic grammatical norms; Corriente 1977:123). The use of the definite article with the name of the deity might also find a precedent in He *haɛlohim*, literally "the God" (Wexler 1982:74; on *dio* in Christian literature, see Combet 1966).

The "Christian" variant *dyos*, often alongside *el dyo*, is also attested among Iberian Jews and conversos (Foulché-Delbosc 1894a:197, 1894b: 69–70, González Llubera 1935:xxiv, Alarcos Llorach 1951:274, Caro Baroja 1:1978:100, 229, Gutwirth 1992:104, Mackay 1992:234, fn 9, Minervini 1:1992:393). The retention by Jews of *dyos* might have been prompted by familiarity of the Jews with un-Judaized Christian texts. Outside the peninsula, a variant with *-s* (*-z*) still appears in Judeo-Spanish, for example, EJSp *dyozes* "gods" (Bunis 1985:48) and *el dyez* "God" in romances from Macedonia, Bulgaria, and Turkey (Marcus 1965:40 and fn 20); both *Dios* and *el Dio* are attested in early 17th-century Marrano Spanish literature printed in Amsterdam (for example, the former appears in the text while the latter is in the preface of Cohen de Lara 1633).

The notion of "Judaization by default" is not restricted to the Iberian Jewish experience. Contemporary Iraqi Judeo-Arabic was itself created by default, since this dialect actually continues the general Baghdadi urban dialect, which was also spoken by the Muslims and Christians until the 14th century, when the Muslims acquired Bedouin Arabic (Blanc 1964:166ff; for references to other case studies, see Wexler 1981a:107, fn 12). Thus, the claim by Bunis 1991:9 and Busse 1991a:6 that Judeo-Spanish results from a conscious effort on the part of the Jews to maintain a separate linguistic profile in the peninsula needs qualification.

The Spanish-speaking Jews may have acquired Romance elements from the Ibero-Romance dialects spoken by Mozarabs that became obsolete in Christian areas of the country; no religious functions were expressed by these terms, but the use of Mozarabic Romance terms could have contributed a unique Jewish profile to the Spanish speech of the Jews in areas of the peninsula where Mozarabic was not spoken. Mozarabic examples show that some Jews indeed learned Spanish from Arabized speakers of Romance.

For example, Malkiel noted that Lat *-antia* and *-entia* survived in Spanish, as *-ança, -ença*, only up to 1300, but survived until the early 15th century in the writings of Jews, for example, Lad *enemigança* "enmity" (Arragel 1422–33, cited by Malkiel 1945:82). This term was also used in the Spanish writings of Muslims (ibid.:84). Aljamiado texts written by Muslims have a few examples of *-ança* up through the late 16th century, even with an Arabic root, for example, *(a)xaricança* "status of an associate" < Ar *šarīk* "associate" (Dozy and Engelmann 1869:355; Steiger 1932:198 cites OSp *ašaraka*, ModSp *ajaraka* "bond, ties, connection" [1585]). Malkiel interpreted these parallels as a sign of the provincial character of Judeo-Spanish, which was unreceptive to the centripetal tendencies of the language of the church and the royal administration (1945:83).

The Mozarabic features of Iberian and post-Iberian Judeo-Spanish need to be examined systematically. It is significant that Judeo-Spanish shares some unique Romance lexicon with the Mozarabic written by Muslims, for example, Moz *averdacer* "validate, make genuine" ~ SalJSp *averdaδear* "confirm, control, find to be correct" vs. Sp *validar* "validate," Moz *sufrencia* "suffering, sufferance" ~ SalJSp *sufriénsa* (see earlier) vs. Sp *sufrimiento* (Galmés de Fuentes 1981:434). Iberian Judeo-Arabic also shares Mozarabic patterns of integrating Romance loans, for example, Toledo Moz *arsdiāqn, aržδiāqn, arždiākns*, Huesca Moz *arkdyākna* (1183), *arsyāqni* (1202), *arδyaqni* (1230), and SpJAr *'rsdy'qny* /arsdiakani/ "archdeacon" vs. OSp *arcediagno* (1154; *DCECH*), Sp *arcediano, archidiácono* (Bosch Vilá 1954:193, fn 18). See also discussion of JSp *mwerte de šapetanya* earlier in chapter 4.

There are few Judeo-Spanish terms of Romance origin that expressed no specific Christian functions in Spanish, but which acquired Jewish connotations in Judeo-Spanish.

Compare SalJSp *alvorada* "ceremony of sending the bride's dowry to the bridegroom; evaluation of the dowry" with Sp *alborada, alvorada* "dawn," which have no ritual connotations (Molho 1950:22), or JSp *lumbradžias* "Gentile women who light the fire in Jewish homes on the Sabbath, when all work is proscribed" vs. Sp *lumbre* "fire" (Bunis 1985:45). AlgJAr *ximinīs* denotes a cracker that is similar to the unleavened bread eaten on Passover, but thicker and with bigger holes (M. Cohen 1912:439). If the term comes from OSp *Ximenes*, a personal name, then the object in question could be a Spanish Christian baking practice taken over by the Jews. For other examples, see Cooper 1993:105, 107, 115–16, 119, 137–38, 198. For a discussion of Christian practices among contemporary Moroccan Jews, see de Larrea Palacín 1954:131, but the relative chronology of these practices is unclear.

On the possible replacement of Arabisms with Jewish meanings by Hispanisms, see the discussion of JAr *ṭārima*/(J)Sp *tálamo* and JSp *korača* (earlier in chapter 4).

There are also examples of Christian religious terms which acquired Jewish meanings in Judeo-Spanish.

TunJAr *bilāḍa* "night preceding the circumcision of a new born child" < Sp *velada* (D. Cohen 1:1964:22), corresponding to SalJSp *viola* (Molho 1950:80 must be derived from coterritorial Judeo-Spanish. The Tunisian Muslims also have a ceremony on the night before the circumcision that is intended to protect the child against evil spirits (D. Cohen 1:1964:22; see the birth ceremony and the spirit infant mentioned earlier in chapter 4). The use of Spanish terms suggests an original Christian custom, with possible reinforcement from North African Muslim culture. MorJSp *tornaboda* "ritual bath taken by the bride after the wedding" and Mor (Fès) JAr *tsọrnabôda* "holiday on the occasion of the first time that the wife goes out after her wedding" (Vajda 1948:321) < Sp *tornaboda* "celebration of the day after the wedding" (literally "the return of the bride"; Brunot 1936:31, M. Alonso 1958, #3989). This Moroccan Jewish custom, required since the bride is regarded as impure after having lost her virginity (Ben-Ami 1974:67 and fn 282), appears to be of Spanish Christian origin. The bride spends the period of "impurity" with her parents, then goes home to the groom. Among Muslims in Fès, the girl performs the ceremony on the sixth day after her wedding (Westermarck 1914:277, Ben-Ami 1974:69, fn 286).

Mor (Lar) JSp *saeta* "funeral dirge" may have been promoted by the Christian associations of AndSp *saeta* "processional song" (Alvar 1958:31). The etymon seems to be Ar *ṣayyit(a)* "gifted with a sonorous voice"; Alvar believes the term is post-1492 in Moroccan Judeo-Spanish (ibid.:34 and *idem*. 1960:20).

An unusual type of Christian influence in Judeo-Spanish involves the re-borrowing by the Jews of a Christianized Hebraism with new pejorative meanings.

For example, BgJSp *xaburá* "disorder, chaos" (Bunis 1993) < He *ḥavurah* "group, association," SalJSp *xavra* "society, Jewish religious elementary school; disorderly meeting" < He *ḥεvrah* "society" (Nehama 1977). The pejorative meaning probably did not develop within Judeo-Spanish, but rather in Bg *xavra* "synagogue; confused, deafening chatter" (< JSp *xavra*). There are similar pejorative meanings in Rum *havră* and Gk *xavra, xaũra* (Wexler 1987b:225). On the Balkan non-Jewish use of this root for synagogue, for example, Bg *xavra*, etc., see chapter 4 this volume. For a Yiddish parallel, see Y *šaxermaxer* "wheeler and dealer" < He *saḥar* "(to) trade" plus G *Macher* "wheeler and dealer" where the change of He *s* > Y *š* points to a German Christian creation, using a Hebraism, for example, G *Schachermacher*, since initial s is ungrammatical in German (ibid.:181, fn 157). Initial *s* is grammatical in Yiddish.

In Iberian Spanish Christian texts Jewish holidays are often designated by Spanish terms. Most likely this nomenclature is of Jewish invention, since some of the terms also appear in Romance texts in Hebrew characters penned by Jews; it is unlikely that Christians would have been familiar with the names of minor Jewish holidays. See also the discussion of Arabic names for Jewish holidays earlier in this chapter.

An example is JSp *p'šqw'h dy p'n qwṭ'sw* /pascua de pan cotaço/ "Passover" (literally, "feast of unleavened bread") (Zaragoza 1488; Luis Lacave 1975:23). The use of Sp *pascua* "feast" (see *pascua de navidad* "Christmas," *pascua [de resurrección, florida]* "Easter") is typical of 15th-century Inquisition literature, for example, Sp *pascua del pan çençeño* "Passover," *pascua de cinquesma* "Shavuot," *pascua de las cabañuelas* "Sukkot," *pascua de las candeillas* "Hannukah," *pascua del cuerno* "New Year" (Ciudad Real 1483: Beinart 1:1974:58; Liebman 1971:115 cites the variant *fiesta de las candellilas* from a Mexican inquisition document of 1639). On the possible Greek origin of the last expression, see Wexler 1987b:135–36. The Inquisition protocols also have Hebrew names with *pascua*, for example, *pascua de hanuca* "Hannukah," *pascua de roxiaxania* "New Year" (Ciudad Real 1484; Beinart 1:1974:575). Marranos also coined holiday names without *pascua*, for example, *el dia mayor* "Yom Kippur," literally "the great day" (Castillo de Garcimuñoz late 15th century: Moreno Koch 1977:367; see also discussion earlier in this chapter; for Marrano examples in the emigration, see Wexler 1982:78–83, 89).

I have the impression that there are few examples of "Hebrew" words that have been calqued on Spanish patterns of discourse. This fact would suggest that Iberian Judeo-Spanish was not receptive to new "Hebrew" borrowings after the shift from Judeo-Arabic. I can only cite one instance where a Judeo-Spanish Arabism may have acquired an Ibero-Romance meaning, for example, JSp *xazino* "sick" (< Ar *ḥazīn* "sad"), if this parallels Sp *doliente*, SCat *dolent* "sick" vs. the Aragonese cognate that means sad (Huarte Morton 1951:329, 334). But the semantic recalibration may have taken place in OSp *hacino* c.1400, which had a variety of meanings such as sad, afflicted, poor, miserable and cheap—though not sick (Steiger 1932:340).

Contemporary Moroccan Judeo-Spanish speakers show a tendency not to Judaize Spanish and Arabic terms that have pronounced Christian and Muslim connotations, respectively. The result is that other, usually non-Spanish, terms are used in Judeo-Spanish alongside the Spanish and Arabic terms to denote parallel Jewish and non-Jewish practices or artifacts; often, but not always, Hebraisms are employed to mark Jewish, Hispanisms to mark Christian, and Arabisms to mark Muslim connotations. This process can be called "lexical bifurcation" and is attested in a number of Jewish and Christian languages. For Yiddish examples, see Wexler 1987b:130–32. The chronology of these terms needs to be established.

Sephardic examples (from Benoliel 1926–52) are MorJSp *rezar* "pray (Christians)" (< Sp *rezar* "pray [in general])" ~ *sallear* "pray (Muslims)" (< MorMAr *ṣeḷḷa* "pray [in general])" ~ *dizer tefilla* "pray (Jews)" (< JSp *dizer* ~ Sp *decir* "say" plus He *tfillah* "prayer"); MorJSp *misa* "Christian prayer" (< Sp *misa* "mass") ~ *la sla* "Muslim prayer" (< MorAr *ṣlā* "prayer") ~ *la tefilla* "Jewish prayer" (<He *tfillah* "prayer"); MorJSp *el bawtismo* "Christian baptism" (< Sp *baptismo*) ~ *la thara* "Muslim circumcision" (< MorAr *ṭhaṛa*) ~ *la serkusyon* "Jewish circumcision" (also expressed by He *brit* ~ Sp *circumcisión*; on haplology, see also JSp *esnoga* < Lat *synagōga* in chapter 4 this volume); MorJSp *kasamyento* "Christian wedding" (< Sp *casamiento*) ~ *èers* "Muslim wedding" (< MorAr *ʿers)* ~ *boda* "Jewish wedding" (~ Sp *boda* "wedding"); MorJSp *simenteryo, se-* "Christian cemetery" (< Sp *cementerio* "cemetery") ~ *los emqabar* "Muslim cemetery" (< MorAr *mqabeṛ* "graves") ~ *la meàará* "Jewish cemetery" (< He *məʿarah* "cave"; see also later in this chapter). The use of Spanish terms to denote circumcision and the wedding suggests that the Judaization process in Morocco may have been relatively recent. Bifurcation can also involve native Spanish vocabulary, see MorJSp *ninyo* "Jewish boy," *kistyanito* "Christian boy," and *morito* "Muslim boy," with the diminutive suffix *-ito*, discussed later in this chapter. The citation of some Hebrew, Judeo-Spanish, and Arabic terms with the Judeo-Spanish definite article is reminiscent of the massive Arabic corpus in (Judeo-)Spanish (discussed in chapter 4 this volume).

The Recalibration of Muslim Arabic Terms and Names in Iberian Judeo-Arabic and (Judeo-)Spanish

The Judaization of Muslim Arabic terms denoting aspects of Muslim religion and culture comprises two chronologically distinct phenomena:

(a) Arabisms with or without original Muslim connotations acquired Jewish meanings; these are used in Iberian Jewish and Christian writings both.

(b) Arabisms were replaced by similar-sounding Hebrew words which had pejorative meanings. To the best of my knowledge, this category is found only in Jewish writings, both in Spain and in other Arabic-speaking countries.

The first phenomenon is a reflection of the common religious patterns of Muslims and Jews that could have resulted from the close ties obtaining between the two groups either in North Africa and/or Spain. Derision of Islamic concepts (the second phenomenon) would be expected whenever the agenda of Jewish religious leaders included heightening the differences between the two religions, as, for example, in periods of Judaization—when most Jews were living in a state of general separation from Muslims. The apparent absence of derogatory terms for Christians in either Iberian Judeo-Spanish or Judeo-Arabic needs further exploration.

Before examining specific examples, it will be useful to consider the origins of Judaized Muslim terminology and the significance of the fact that the Christians used these terms to denote both Jewish and Muslim practices and artifacts (even though not all were actually shared by the two groups). Two explanations suggest themselves:

(a) Though Jews spoke Arabic, it is still surprising to find them giving Jewish meanings to Muslim Arabic terminology rather than taking ready-made terms from Hebrew and Judeo-Aramaic. The only explanation is that the bulk of the Iberian Jewish communities comprised recent proselytes.

(b) The Christians perceived similarities between Jews and Muslims in language, culture, geographical, or ethnic origin and sometimes even in the political aspirations of the two groups. For example, the Christians believed that Iberian Jews assisted the Arabs in the conquest of Iberian towns in 711 in order to gain alleviation from Christian discriminatory acts during the Visigothic period. Alternatively, the Christians might have applied Muslim terms to Jews as a convenient means of designating all non-Christian minorities. The creation of ethnically coded vocabulary (for example, a Romance word for a Christian cemetery vs. an Arabic word for a Muslim or Jewish cemetery) would also have suited a militant church policy of separating Christians from non-Christians. In a similar vein, the Valladolid Ordinances of 1412 passed by Juan II required Muslims and Jews to grow beards and long hair, in order to differentiate them from the clean-shaven Christian population (Horovitz 1994:133–34). Further research is needed to determine whether the Christians acquired "Jewish" terminology in Arabic from the Arabs.

I am inclined to credit Jews and Judaizers with the creation of Judaized Muslim terms, many of which were used by Christians in Spanish as well. To suggest that the Christians took the initiative in applying Muslim terminology to the Jews is tantamount to saying that the Catholic majority was largely ignorant of unique Jewish practices; this is an unconvincing claim. Confusion over the defining features of

Jews and Muslims was characteristic of French writings in the early 1600s (Michel 1989:167 and fn 49); given the near-total absence of Jews and Muslims in that country at the time, it would not be surprising if unfamiliarity with minority groups led to their "consolidation" in the eyes of the majority population. In Spain, however, the significant population of Jews and Judaizers living among the Christians, as well as the large Muslim populations which had been gradually coming under Christian jurisdiction since the late 11th century, guarantees that many Christians would have been aware of the differences between the two minority groups. For further details, see also the mutual religious and cultural influences among the three groups and the detailed knowledge of Jewish practices documented in the Christian literature of the 15th and 16th centuries that I discussed earlier in chapter 2. Moreover, Biblical Hebrew was studied by small circles of Spanish intellectuals (A. Alonso 1969: 210–26) and abundant Hebrew terms are found in the Inquisition proceedings.

Arabic-speaking Christians might even have given some Arabic vocabulary new Muslim and Jewish connotations that did not exist in Arabic itself. For example, Ar *al-ḥakīm* "doctor" > Sp *alfaquín* (in variant spellings) "Muslim doctor" 1275–76, possibly revalued semantically by confusion with the near-homonym, Sp *alfaquí*, meaning "Muslim learnèd man, priest" < Ar *al-faqīh* (Steiger 1932:112, 259, 336). Ar *al-ḥakīm* was also a common Jewish family name (Wexler 1977b:179). In the *Libro conplido de las estrellas*, a Spanish translation made by Yehuda ben Moše ha-Kohen in Toledo in 1254 of an original Arabic text known as *Kitāb al-bāriʿ*, all people who appear with the title *alfaquim* are Jews (Hilty 1955:8, fn 2 and Solà-Solé 1965). See also the name *Yuçaf alfaqui* borne by a Jew in a Spanish text from Seville 1253 (Baer 1/2:1936:50).

The fact that there are Judaized Arabisms in Spanish Jewish texts which are not attested among the Christians makes it more likely that the Jews were the initiators of this category of terms. Yehuda ben Šlomo al-Ḥarizi (c.1170–c.1230), a Spanish Hebrew poet and translator, was one of the first Arab Jews to give Arabic words Jewish meanings.

Examples from his *Mīzān al-'amal* are Ar *rasūl allāh*, an epithet for Muḥammad (literally "the messenger of God") > Moses, *ʿOmr* name of a caliph (633–44) > rabbi Akiva, *ʿĀiša* a wife of Muḥammad > the Prophetess Deborah, *al-qur'ān* "the Quran" > "religion" (Gottstein 1952:210, 216 and fn 27). Other Jewish writers share some of this corpus, but not necessarily with the same meanings. For example, David ben Avraham al-Fasi (a Moroccan Karaite grammarian of the 10th century, born in Fès) used Ar *al-qur'ān* to designate the Hebrew Bible (Hiršberg 1:1965:114). Avraham ben Moše ben Maymon (1186–1237), the Egyptian-born son of Maimonides, also has examples in his writings, but the corpus and meanings are not always identical to those of al-Ḥarizi, for example, Ar *as-sayyid* "chief, lord" > Moses, *al-kitāb* "a sacred book" > "Torah," (see also discussion of Ar *muṣḥaf* later in this chapter), *al-qur'ān* "the Quran" > "Bible," *ar-rasūl* "the messenger," i.e., Muḥammad > Abraham (Blau 1958:194; see also the examples in the writings of the Egyptian Jew, Sa'adya Gaon, al-Fayyūm, Egypt, 882–942, discussed by Hiršberg 1:1965:113–15, 144 and J. Mann 1:1972:655, fn 191). For other examples, see Blau 1978:129.

The lumping together of Jews and Muslims also had some impact on Spanish derivational morphology. For example, in 15th-century Spanish there are diminutive forms of *judío* "Jew" and *moro* "Muslim" formed with *-ezno* (productive with names of animals and pejorative elsewhere) but not of *cristiano* "Christian," for example, Sp *judezno* "Jewish boy" and *morezno* "Muslim boy" (Malkiel 1958, 1992:16). A Moroccan Judeo-Spanish parallel is the use of *ninyo* for "Jewish boy" vs. the use of *-ito* for diminutive non-Jews, as in *kistyanito* "Christian boy" and *morito* "Muslim boy" (Benoliel 1926:510; see also earlier in this chapter).

The use of Arabic terminology cannot prove beyond doubt that the Iberian Jews were of Arab origin, but it is, nonetheless, suggestive. In Balkan languages, the Sephardic Jews are often designated by Turkish loans. For example, Tu *bula* "aunt" is used in Serbo-Croatian and Bulgarian in the meaning of a Turkish woman; in addition, Serbo-Croatian has the meaning teacher, though the derivative *bulica* denotes a Jewess (on this suffix, see JSp *rebissa* discussed earlier in chapter 2); Gk *boúla* also denotes a Jewish woman. Might not the facts of Serbo-Croatian and Greek suggest that in these societies Jews were identified as carriers of Turkish culture, emigrés from Turkey and/or Turkish speakers? In Balkan Judeo-Spanish the Turkism simply means madame (the data are given in M. L. Wagner 1909:499). On the other hand, contemporary SalJSp *los moros* designates Jewish fishermen expelled from Sicily in 1493 who took refuge in Saloniki and whose descendants continued to work in this profession up to the early 20th century (Nehama 1977); the choice of epithet suggests these Jews may have been speakers of Arabic, but not necessarily that the Saloniki Sephardim regarded this group to be of "Muslim" origin. For further details, see also the discussion of Sp *moros* "Berbero-Arabs" discussed earlier in chapter 3.

Below are Arabic terms (almost all with Muslim religious connotations) that were used by, or attributed to, Jews (both Arabic- and Spanish-speaking) to denote Jewish practices or artifacts (for Yiddish parallels, see Wexler 1993c):

(a) The first Christian characterization of a rabbi speaking Spanish has the Muslim exclamation, *hamihala*, which MacDonald (1964:36) derived from Ar *al-ḥamdu lillahi* "praise to God" (*Acto de los reyes magos*, 12th century); an alternative etymon would be Ar *ḥāmi allah* "the protector Allah" (Keightley 1964:190; MacDonald also cites Ar *ḥāmī allah* "my protector is Allah" as a possible etymon). Hence, Spiegel's claim that there are no examples of stereotyped Jewish speech in Christian literature before the expulsion needs some revision (1952:119).

(b) Sp *aljama* "Jewish community" (1212), "Muslim community" (1219) with penultimate stress. Corriente has suggested that Sp *aljama* results from a cross of Ar *al-jamáʿa* "the community" (feminine gender) and *al-jámiʿ* "the mosque" (masculine gender), both derived from the root *j-m-ʿ* "gather," and the accreted Arabic definite article; he reasoned that if the first Arabism alone were the etymon, then the expected Spanish form would have been **aljamá* (1977, paragraph 1.2.3 and 1984:10). I can offer additional data in support of this proposal: Minervini cites the example of JSp *gmh* /jama/ "Jewish community" without the letter *ʿayin* and with masculine gender in a text from Aragón or Castile dated 1354 (1:1992, #10, line 5), while Colin notes that MorAr *jāmiʿ* "mosque" can be feminine gender, following Berber practice (1930b:112; for further discussion, see Wexler 1988:41–42).

(c) Sp *almocáver, macaber* "Jewish and Muslim cemetery" (Solà-Solé 1968b[1983]:176–78, Kontzi 1:1974:214, Caro Baroja 1:1978:65); see also *al-Muqaybara*, Muslim section of Huesca (late 13th century; Naval Más 1980:88). The etymon is Ar *q-b-r* "bury," for example, MorMAr *mqābar*, literally "graves," but MorJAr *'borāt* (where ' < *q*) does not use the prefix *m-* indicating place. No lexical bifurcation attends the use of Sp"Lat" *fossarium*, which can denote the cemeteries of all three groups (for the term together with *saracenorum*, "cemetery of the Muslims" Huesca 1274, see Torres Balbás 1957:190). The Arabism also appears in Portuguese Latin 1137–39 with reference only to Jews. The restriction to Jews is not surprising, since by then there were few Muslims left in Portugal. Santa Rosa de Viterbo suggested that Pt *almocávar* "Muslim cemetery" vs. Pt *almocóvar* "Jewish cemetery" (1798–99). In Barcelos, north of Porto, *almocóvar* is still known in the meaning Jewish cemetery (Pires de Lima 1940:93; Wexler 1988:42–43).

On the use of the Hebrew root *q-b-r* "bury; grave" and the Arabic broken plural, see earlier in chapter 4.

(d) SalJSp *almosama* "the Saturday before the day of the wedding celebration" (Molho 1950:18, Leibovici 1986:234), which in the Balkans has been interpreted as He *alamot šamah*, literally "girls there." The word may be < Ar *mawsam* "harvest time, fair, time of meeting of pilgrims in Mekka" with Ar *al-*; see also OMorJAr *måsåm* "religious holiday" (Mainz 1949:80, line 5). Leibovici (1986:234) notes that the term is limited to Saloniki and corresponds to TuJSp *šabbat de besamano*, MorJAr *sebt l-islam*, and MorJAr, MorJSp *saftar(r)ay* (Benoliel 1952:267–68, who derives the latter < MorJSpHe *sabbat haftarah* "the Saturday of the parting," with sibilant confusion, and He *šabbat* "Saturday" abbreviated to *s*; mainly women say *saftar(r)ay* by analogy with Arabic and in ignorance of the real meaning). The plethora of terms suggests the practice may have developed independently in a variety of locales.

(e) Pt *beraka* "Jewish blessing on the oldest person participating in a festivity" (Freire 1939-44, de Morais Silva 1948) < Ar *baraka* "blessing." An alternative, but less convincing, etymon is cognate He *braxah*, which also surfaces—in the spelling *baraha* "blessing"—in a Portuguese poem by Luís Enriques (15th or 16th century; Benoliel 1926:211—with the spelling *beraha*; see also Mendes dos Remédios 1927: 243).

(f) Sp *fada(s), hadas* "secular naming ceremony for boys and (less frequently) girls shortly after birth," *fadar* "perform the naming ceremony" (Inquisition protocols, Ciudad Real 1483–85, in Beinart 1:1974:73, 85; see other examples in *idem.* 1965:222, 299; 1:1974:75, 77, 85, 88, 239, 241, 300–301, 303, 308, 449, 456, 458; 2:1977:10; for contemporaneous documentation from Cuenca, see García-Arenal 1978:56–59, and from Toledo, see León Tello 1979:270). The terms *fadaš, faδaš, fadar* also appear in 15th-century Muslim Spanish texts (Longás Bartibas 1915, Harvey 1960:71, Gallego y Burín and Gámir Sandoval 1968:34, and Kontzi 1:1974:268, 2:470, 667, 673).

Among Jews, a religious name (either from Old Semitic Hebrew or non-Semitic "Hebrew") was bestowed on a baby boy on the eighth day after birth when the circumcision ceremony was performed. The Arabism is found in both the Balkan and the North African Sephardic diasporas in various forms, for example, SalJsp *fada(s)* and *fadamyento* (Molho 1950:80, Nehama 1977; for Bosnia, see Baruch 1930:146, fn 9, for Croatia, see S. Romano 1933, and for Morocco, see Benoliel 1928:188). In the Balkans and Morocco the ceremony is performed exclusively for a girl, since circumcision is the appropriate venue for giving a baby boy his Hebrew name. Iberian Marranos practiced the naming ceremony, but not necessarily circumcision (on the latter practice, see earlier in chapter 2). The Western Ashkenazic Jews have a parallel naming custom known in Yiddish as *holekrāš* that is performed either for girls only or for both sexes, depending on the locale, and that has its roots in pre-Christian Germanic society (Wexler 1993c:119–20).

Scholars have long suggested deriving OSp *fada(s), hadas* from a Romance root, either < Lat *fata* "fairy" (Kayserling 1898:267, Longás Bartibas 1915:256–61, 313, and Bramon 1989:37—who assumes that pagans believed that fairies protected the new-born child) or < Sp *hado* "fate" < Lat *fatum* (Beinart 1981:279–80—though with hesitation). In my opinion, the fact that the custom was practiced only by Muslims and Jews tips the scale in favor of Ar *ḥadaθ* "event, novelty" as the etymon, which is appropriate both semantically and formally, since Ar and He *ḥ, h, x* > *f* in a number of Ibero-Romance target languages and ClAr *θ* surfaces as *s* in a number of Arabic dialects (Steiger 1932:121–25, 218ff, 248ff, 267ff, Wexler 1977b:175ff and earlier in chapter 4). In theory, the term could also be derived from cognate He *ḥadaš*, which would also have yielded *fadas* in a Romance target language. In Christian parlance, the final *s* was apparently interpreted as the plural marker and deleted to produce *fada*—a rare form actually found in Judeo-Spanish as well, to denote the naming ceremony for a girl (S. Romano 1933). The Judeo-Spanish deletion of *-s* suggests ignorance of the etymon and reinterpretation of *-s* as the Spanish plural suffix—but not necessarily the belief in the role of fairies in protecting the infant.

Ar *ḥ-d-θ* used, in different forms, in the meanings new, event, fame, has led to the semantic recalibration of Sp *nuevas* (Labib 1967:67, fn 22). In a Romance aljamiado text, *fada*—without *-s*—denotes baptism (Sánchez Álvarez 1981:393, unless this word, like ModSp *hada*, actually continues Lat *fata* "fairy").

However, since this term is limited to Spain and Morocco, it may be that we deal here with an African Latinism or early Ibero-Romanism; then I would have cause to favor the Latin and Spanish etyma proposed earlier. This raises the intriguing possibility that the Arabs might have acquired the naming custom along with the name from pagan or Christian North Africans and that Ar *ḥadaθ* is not the ultimate etymon.

SpAr *ḥ-d-θ* is not used by contemporary Moroccan Muslims to designate the naming ceremony; instead the latter call the ceremony *l-gézra ḍe t-tˁesmîya* "the slaughter of the name-giving" (Westermarck 2:1926:389). However, Moroccan Arabic-speaking Jews have a cognate name for the ceremony; they originally called it *taḥdīd* "aversion of evil," but the name was subsequently changed to *taḥdīθ* "recitation of a story," from the same root as *ḥadaθ* (Malka 1946:25–26, specifically for baby boys). *Taḥdīd* and *taḥdīθ* each designate different aspects of the ceremony: during the event, the guests spend the night with the mother for a period of a week, reading psalms and pronouncing exorcisms against evil spirits to protect the infant. Zafrani notes that the exorcizing procedure requires the use of a sword directed against the evil spirit Lilith, which could be inspired by Ar *ḥadīd* "iron," a word that is derived from the same root as *taḥdīd* (1986:172). Zafrani suggests that the practice of women telling stories at the nocturnal watch is what led to the change of the name from *taḥdīd* > *taḥdīθ* (*idem.* 1983:54). Elsewhere in North Africa, the ceremony has different names, for example, TunJAr *šābâˁ* "ceremony of naming a *girl* on the seventh day after her birth" < the Arabic root for seven (D. Cohen 1:1964).

The contemporary Moroccan Jewish terminology might appear to lend some support to my derivation of *fadas* < Ar *ḥ-d-θ*; deriving *fadas* < Ar *taḥdīd* would be unconvincing since Ar *d* regularly > Sp *d* and only in a few words > *t* (Steiger 1932:133–35). *Taḥdīθ* showns that both Morocco and Spain used a common root, though in different forms. The problem is that Moroccan Jewish testimony suggests that *taḥdīd* is older than *taḥdīθ*. A solution might be to assume that the earliest term in North Africa was, in fact, *taḥdīθ* or *ḥadaθ*; *taḥdīd* apparently never existed in Spain either because it arose too late to reach the peninsula, or it was, by chance, not recorded there. If I accept the charge of the Moroccan Jews, I would have to assume that the Muslims once had *taḥdīd* as well. Following this reasoning, the decision of the Jews to change the name from *taḥdīd* > *taḥdīθ* might have been part of the attempt to Judaize the custom—by emphasizing the "recitation" from the Hebrew Bible over the (non-Jewish) "exorcizing." The Jewish contribution to the custom, known both to Moroccan Berbers and Arabs, is the recitation from the Bible (Zafrani 1983:51). The insertion of Bible reading is often intended to "Judaize" an originally non-Jewish magical rite (see earlier in this chapter). In this case, MorJAr *taḥdīθ* "telling a story" would have to be regarded as considerably later than (*J)Ar/JSp *ḥadaθ/fadas* "new (name)" and independent of the latter.

A clue to the relative recency of *taḥdīθ* among the Moroccan Jews may be the fact that coterritorial Judeo-Spanish-speaking refugees from the peninsula never adjusted the word *fadas* to the Judeo-Arabic form of the root. Phonological "Arabization" of Judeo-Spanish Arabisms is common in Moroccan Judeo-Spanish, for example, Sp *alforza*, OSp *alfoza* (on epenthetic *r* in Spanish Arabisms, see Steiger 1932:253, fn 1) "hem of a garment" (1438) ~ MorJSp *alforsa* but also *alxozza* (Benoliel 1927:570), all < Ar *al-ḥuzza*; the retention of *al-* in the second Judeo-Spanish variant suggests that the term was brought from Spain but phonologically adjusted, optionally, to Moroccan (Judeo-)Arabic, i.e., JSp *f* was replaced in Morocco by *x* (< Ar *ḥ*)—a sort of retrograde sound shift (on the latter, see U. Weinreich 1958) and the gemination of /z/ was restored. The failure to drop the accreted Arabic definite article (in any case ~ MorAr *el-*) and to assume the canonic shape of Moroccan Arabic—see current *teḥžīž* with sibilant confusion—shows that Arabization did not assume *morphological* parameters. The adjustment of Morrocan Judeo-Spanish Arabisms to resemble the form of their surface cognates in coterritorial Moroccan (Judeo-)Arabic needs a close study; on the piecemeal nature of the "Moroccanization" of Judeo-Spanish, see Martínez Ruiz 1982:243. A fascinating topic that calls for immediate study is the possibility that the Judaization of pre-Islamic Berber customs may have been prompted, at least in part, by attempts at "Islamization" in the majority society.

One final observation: there may be additional grounds for assuming that the earliest form is *taḥdīθ*, since in Berber Arabisms and native words voiceless dental stops became voiced, for example, *erreṭal* ~ *erreḍal* "money, measure of weight" < Ar *ar-raṭl* (with the definite article preserved—see Schuchardt 1908:353 and earlier in chapter 4); both variants surface in Ibero-Romance, for example, OPt *arredell* ~ *arretel*, but this could be due to a Romance phonological development such as I described earlier in chapter 4 (ibid.:354, fn 4, Steiger 1932:156). In this case, Ar *taḥdīd* would have originally been a Berberized form of *taḥdīθ* (there is no **taḥdīδ* in Arabic). For Arabic speakers, the variant *taḥdīd* would have been homophonous with the native Arabic word meaning "aversion of evil."

(g) Sp *Marrano* "Jewish or Muslim convert to Christianity, who retains elements of his former religious practices clandestinely." See the etymology advanced for this word earlier in chapter 2.

(h) Ar *muṣḥaf* denotes a sacred book in the Arabic of Muslims, Christians, and Jews alike. Ar *muṣḥaf* "book, Quran" surfaces in Ottoman Turkish texts of the second half of the 16th century, but in a Christian source from 1553 *musaf* means the Book of Moses (Stachowski 1977). In a Christian Mozarabic text from 1049 the word meant Christian book and together with the numeral four, denoted the four Gospels (Abu-Haidar 1987:227–28). While the meaning Book of Moses was recorded in a Christian source, it could reflect Jewish usage—perhaps Judeo-Spanish. In a Judeo-Arabic Genizah manuscript from the 12th or early 13th century (of unknown geographical provenience) *muṣḥaf* denotes the Hebrew Bible (Goitein 1954:713). The term is not found in Muslim North African dialects but AlgJAr *məṣḥ̄āf* denotes a book in general (M. Cohen 1912:304; see also Mor [Sefrou] JAr *meṣḥaf* "book" ~ MorMAr *kitāb* in Stillman 1989:105). Conversely, the latter root is attested in

Andalusian Arabic (de Alcalá 1505, cited by Corriente 1977:92, 128) in the meanings of book or Quran, but not in contemporary Algiers Judeo-Arabic; either this is because *kitāb* "book" became obsolete in Algiers or Moroccan (Sefrou) Judeo-Arabic (a unique development among Arabic dialects in general), or because Iberian Judeo-Arabic differed (in this and presumably other ways) from Iberian Muslim Arabic.

In Algiers Judeo-Arabic *məṣḥăf* has final stress, which is unusual for this dialect (M. Cohen 1912:304, 481; 165), but typical of Spanish Arabic (Corriente 1977:128), and Moroccan Muslim Arabic (Zavadovskij 1962:56–57). This type of stress is also characteristic of Arabic dialects where Berber influence is particularly strong, for example, in urban Morocco. Tunisian Judeo-Arabic has the unique *moqšīyä* "entire Old Testament" (D. Cohen 1:1964:166, 173) < (?) stAr *q-š-'* "to peel."

(i) *Aladma, alalma* "rabbinical excommunication" is attested in Aragonese, Navarran, Catalan, Valencian, and occasionaly Castilian Christian texts from between the 13th and 15th centuries (Wexler 1988:25–26). Ekblom (1942–43) and Malkiel (1946) suggested Gk *anaθēma* via Lat *anathema* as the etymon, but both scholars noted phonological problems with this etymology. Ekblom called attention to the difficulty of deriving *-dm-* < Lat *-them-*, for which there are apparently no precedents from Latin to Spanish, and to the non-existence of *n* ~ *l*-confusion in the intervocalic position (1942–43:335–36). Ekblom appealed to Cat *sanate me* > Sp *sanadme*, but Catalan is irrelevant for us. Malkiel also noted that medial clusters of the type *-dm-*, *-tm-* are unattested in Spanish (1946:138).

A phonologically less problematic etymon might be provided from Arabic. Possible roots, all of which are semantically plausible, include, for example, *'-d-m* "total absence, loss" (*'adam*), *'-δ-m* "blame" (*'aδīma*), *'-δ̣-m* "portentous event, frightful (crime), grievous (affair)" (for example, *'aδ̣īma*) or *'-l-m* "mark" (*'alāma*) plus *al-* "the." Steiger notes that medial Ar *δ* > Sp *d* or occasionally *z*, while non-final *d, ḍ* usually > *d* (1932:160–65, 171–72).

(j) Sp *açuna* "Jewish, Muslim religious law" (1282; D. Romano 1953:74, fn 6; see also *idem.*:1979:348, fn 3 and Régné 1978, glossary under *azuna*; Glick 1979:171 cites *suna* for Jewish and Muslim law in the Charter of Denia of Jaime I); an example with the Arabic definite article is Sp"Lat" *azunam iudeorum* "law of the Jews" 1270 (Burns 1973:228, and fn 28). The etymon is Ar *sunna* "Muslim religious law." Glick has suggested that the Christian application of this Muslim religious term to the Jews reflected both the strong Arabization of the Jews in the 13th century, as well as Jaime I's confusion (*sic*!) about the two ethnic minorities (ibid.).

The Arabism is, however, used in Karaite (Halyč, Ukraine) in the form *sunet* "circumcision" (Zajączkowski 1961:196), following the practice of other Turkic or Balkan languages, for example, Tu *sünnet* and Ser *sunet* "Muslim religious law; circumcision." I have not encountered Ar *sunna* in Spanish Jewish texts in the meaning of circumcision. In the same semantic field, note IstJSp *almodrása* "circumcision knife" (Marcus 1965:110). This form looks like an Arabism, though I cannot propose a plausible Arabic etymon other than *darasa* "beat (grain), remove the quilting," which is not fully satisfactory on semantic grounds.

(k) A Brazilian inquisitional source from 17th-century Bahia cites Pt *cádi* (< Ar *qāḍī* "judge") as a person learnèd in the Jewish religion (Novinsky 1972:133).

Examples of Muslim Arabic terms with Jewish connotations used in Jewish languages spoken in Muslim territories include Tun (Jerba) JAr *ziyara* "pilgrimage to the tomb of a marabout, often venerated by both Muslims and Jews" (Udovitch and Valensi 1984:178—see also discussion of TunJAr *ṛāb* "rabbi-saint cult" cited earlier in chapter 4 and in this chapter); CrKar *šaraat* "Jewish religious law" < Ar *šarī'a* "Muslim religious law" (see also the two meanings of JAr *šarī'a* mentioned by Hiršberg 1:1965:113, 144), *x"èlel'*, *x"èljal* "kosher" < Ar *ḥalāl* "Muslim ritually permitted meat" (Wexler 1983a:40), CrKar *xag* "pilgrimage to Jerusalem," *xogeg* "pilgrim to Jerusalem" (14th century; Bacher 1882) have the forms of He *ḥag* "holiday"; and *ḥogeg* "holiday maker" with the meanings of cognate Ar *ḥajj* "pilgrimage to Mekka," *ḥājj* "pilgrim to Mekka."

I know of one example where Christians may have adopted a Hebraism to refer both to Jews and Muslims, for example, He *taqqanah* "protocol" > Arag *tacana* ~ *tecana* "Jewish rule, constitution; tributes paid by Jews and Muslims to Jaime I" (1279ff), Pr *tacana* "tax paid on meat slaughtered by Jewish butchers" (1452; Wexler 1988:72 and fns 376, 378).

Occasionally, Arabic terms with no Muslim ritual connotations acquire a Jewish ritual connotation in the speech of the Jews:

(a) The Judeo-Arabic root for "porge the meat of ritually impure elements in order to make it kosher" is *n-q-y*, which in Arabic means simply to clean, with no reference to food. JSp *purgar, pulgar*, with the Jewish meaning, may be calqued on Arabic, since Sp *purgar* "purge, clean" at best can be used with grain, foods that can be peeled or blossoms (in Aragonese and Catalan or the Asturias), but not with meat (ibid.:91–92). See also the Judeo-Arabic surname *Anqawa* discussed earlier in chapter 4. In some Judeo-Arabic dialects, there is an attempt to express the act of porging the meat by an Arabized Hebraism, for example, IrJAr *(i)mnaqer* < "He" *n-q-r*; according to Ben Ya'akov, Iraqi Jewish men prefer this term while women prefer the original Arabism *n-q-y* (1985:136). In some Yiddish dialects, an original Judeo-Romance or Judeo-Slavic verb was also replaced by "He" *n-q-r*, for example, Y *menakern, menaker zayn* (Wexler 1987b:183).

(b) Bunis derives SarJSp *ulúfya* "sidelocks (worn by religious Jewish males)" < Tu *zülüf*, by assuming that in the position after the plural definite article, *z-* became interpreted as part of the preceding plural article *las/laz* and, hence, was removed (1985:47). Left unexplained is the suffix *-ya*. Since the word is also attested in Arabic as *sālifa*, plural *sawālif*, I would not rule out a Spanish Arabic source (though no such form has yet been cited in that dialect or in Moroccan Judeo-Spanish); subsequently the Arabism could have been restructured along the lines of the Turkish surface cognate in Balkan Judeo-Spanish. JSp *-ya* might be related to the Ibero-Romance suffix *-ia* that we encounter in MorJSp *ḥakitía* "Moroccan Judeo-Spanish." Subak's derivation of BosJSp *čulúfyas* < Ser *čelo* "forehead" vs. IstJSp *(u)rúfyas* < Tu *örmek* "to plait, braid, mat" (1906:141) is unconvincing, but interference from Ser *čelo* is conceivable.

Crews 1957:239 notes other names for the sidelocks, for example, BalJSp *pea* (with derivatives given by Bunis 1993a—including *pealino* "religious Ashkenazic Jew"—a hint that the practice of wearing sidelocks was not native to the Sephardim) < He *pe'ah*, MorJSp *melenas* (Benoliel 1928:221) ~ Sp *melena* "long, loose hair; mane." For further details, see the discussion of Spanish terms with unique Jewish meanings earlier in this chapter. The plethora of terms suggests that the custom might have been acquired relatively late (on Judaization, see chapter 4 and earlier in this chapter).

(c) BosJSp *las xadras* "month before Passover when women prepare house," etc. See the discussion earlier in chapter 4.

(d) On IbJSp *adafina, adefina*, MorJAr *sxīna*, Alg, TunJAr *tfīna* "Sabbath food prepared on Friday," see earlier in chapter 4.

(e) BalJSp *talega* ~ *taleka* "bag for phylacteries and prayer shawl" < Ar *ta'līqa*, see earlier discussion in chapter 4. A synonymous Latinism is Mac (Kastoria) JSp *korača, koračina*, IstJSp *koračika* < Lat *coriacea*. The latter appears to have circulated in Andalusian Mozarabic; the Castilian cognate is *cuero* "leather, skin" (Wexler 1988:45 and earlier in this chapter).

Jewish writers in Arabic often ridiculed Muslim terms and names by replacing them by similar-sounding Hebrew words that have pejorative meanings; while there are examples of this phenomenon from North Africa and Near Eastern countries, I know of no examples from Spain.

For example, Ar *al-qur'ān* "the Quran" > Yem"He" *qalon* "shame," Ar *imām* "imam" > YemHe *mum* "blemish," Ar *masjid* "mosque" > Yem"He" *masgef* "torture, afflict, mortify"; in one case a Hebrew term, *tfillah* "prayer" was replaced by He *tiflut* "abomination," which acquired the meaning of non-Jewish house of worship (Goitein 1931:365; for Yiddish parallels, Wexler 1991:39–40). Ar *ar-rasūl* "the messenger" (an epithet for Muḥammad) is converted into Mor, AlgJAr *lpasūl, lbašūl*, literally "the null and void, abrogated" (Bar-Ašer 1991:45); this example is also found in the Hebrew of Karaites in Trakai, Lithuania in the 16th century, for example, *mḥmyṭ hapasul*—vocalization is unclear < He *ḥ-m-ṭ* ("faint?") plus "the null and void" for "Muḥammad the messenger of God" (for another example in the Hebrew writings of the Karaite Yafat or Abu [ibn] 'Ali Ḥasan ibn 'Ali al-Lawi al-Baṣri, who moved from Baṣra to Jerusalem in the second half of the 10th century, see ibid.:46 and earlier in chapter 2).

Jews loosely translate into "Hebrew" Muslim Arab proverbs that cast aspersions on the sincerity of Jewish converts to Islam; the Jewish version is generally critical of Muslims (who do not necessarily convert to Judaism). The "recalibration" reflects an atmosphere of segregation and turning inward of the Jewish communities, i.e., a time when proselytism was less feasible. These parallels need to be systematically collected and dated.

An example is MorMAr *la-tceq b-lihūdī ída slem ala yebqa arba'īn 'ām* "do not believe in a Jew even if he became a Muslim forty years ago" > MorJAr"He" *lo emuna [sic!] bagoy afilu baqever arba'im šana* "don't believe a Muslim even if he has been dead for forty years" (Stillman 1975:13).

6

Findings and Challenges

Here I will summarize the innovative findings of the book and outline research challenges for the future.

(1) The Sephardic Jews are largely descended from a mixed population consisting of a majority of proselytes of Near Eastern, Arabian, and North African origin and a small community of ethnic Palestinian Jews (and their mixed descendants). The minor Palestinian Jewish component served as the catalyst for conversion acts in Arabia, the Near East (especially Iraq) and Roman North Africa.

I advanced this claim primarily on the basis of linguistic and ethnographic evidence, supported by historical documentation of conversion to Judaism. To the best of my knowledge, no one has presented the heterogeneous data for conversion to Judaism in a systematic and comprehensive manner nor suggested that Jewish linguistic and ethnographic data could provide valuable clues to the ethnic origins of the Jews.

(2) One of the immediate consequences of my theory is the recognition that the so-called Judaized versions of non-Jewish languages that were created in the Jewish diasporas as early as the 6th century B.C., but which proliferated in the first millennium of the present era in Asia, Africa, and Europe, were, in fact, created by "Jewish proselytes" and not "Jews."

(3) Conversion played a major role in the creation of all Jewish diaspora communities after the destruction of Judea at the hands of the Romans in the late 1st century A.D. Conversion (to and from Judaism) led to the creation of syncretistic religious expression, consisting, variously, of Jewish, Christian, Muslim, and pagan traditions; syncretistic religious practices, in turn, encouraged proselytism in all directions.

A dramatic illustration of the rise of syncretistic religious expression in the Iberian Peninsula is the phenomenon of the Marranos—Jews (and Muslims) who, for the most part voluntarily, and in some periods of history, involuntarily, converted to Catholicism between the late 14th and late 15th centuries in Spain and Portugal. (By the same token, Christians also espoused syncretistic religions that led many to convert to Islam and Judaism, but they are not labeled "Marranos," even though conversion to Islam was sometimes forced upon them.)

The evidence presented of syncretistic religious expression and reciprocal influences between Christians, Jews, and Muslims supports the claim made by scholars such as Rivkin 1957, Netanyahu 1966, and M. A. Cohen 1992 that at the time of their conversion, most Sephardic Marranos were not, *sensu strictu*, practicing Jews; in the late 15th and 16th centuries, Christian persecution of the Sephardic Marrano population led to a heightened clandestine espousal and (re-)creation of selected "Jewish" practices. In the emigration, some of these Marranos and their descendants openly joined Jewish communities.

(4) The ethnic origins of the converts to Judaism who contributed to the Sephardic community are to be sought among Arabs in the Near East and the Arabian Peninsula (also Ḥimyarites?), among Berbers, Arabs, and, more marginally, other peoples (for example, Punic speakers?) in North Africa, and partly among the indigenous peoples of Spain. The significant Berber impact on Sephardic folklore and religious practice (though with a lesser impact on language) leads me to suspect that the North African Berbers played the most significant role in the ethnogenesis of the Sephardic Jews.

When Spanish Jews emigrated to North Africa in increasing numbers after 1391 they often noted differences between their religious practices and those of the indigenous Berber and Arab Jews. Theoretically, the differences between Iberian and North African Jewish culture and religious practices could mean either that the Iberian Jews had become heavily Christianized after approximately 500 years under Christian hegemony, with ever diminishing contact with their fellow Berbers and Arabs, or that they actually preserved much of their original Berbero-Arab patrimony in an earlier form than the North African Jews who never formed colonies in the Iberian Peninsula. The linguistic and ethnographic facts incline me to prefer the second interpretation. Hence, the Iberian Sephardic Jews are very likely to be one of the best living repositories of early Berbero-Arabic folklore and religious practices.

(5) Contrary to the universal view that placed the homeland of the Sephardim in Spain, I proposed that Sephardic Jewish culture was initially conceived in North Africa when Romance, Arabic, and Berber proselytes to Judaism fused with a tiny Palestinian Jewish population in the late 7th century. The theory of an African homeland is supported by the use of the Biblical Hebrew placename *sfarad* for Spain, which I am inclined to regard as a similar sounding substitute for the Gothic word for "black" (following Bruckus 1942), and by the application of the term in 13th-century Jewish literature to North Africa, as well as the Iberian Peninsula. It is historically inaccurate to apply the term to the indigenous Iberian Jewish community of European non-Jewish and Palestinian Jewish origin that existed in the peninsula between the Roman period and the Muslim invasion in 711 and that may have been absorbed by the North African Jewish majority after 711. The widespread habit today of labeling all non-Ashkenazic Jews as "Sephardic" is a particularly regrettable development.

I have proposed for the first time in the scholarly literature that Judeo-Arabic and Judeo-Spanish both preserve evidence of North African Latin elements. The mixing of Romance, Berber, and Arab Jews took place several times between 711 and 1492 and resulted in retrograde changes in the dominant language of the Sephardic Jews:

(a) Romance-speaking Iberian Jews who went to North Africa to escape discrimination during Visigothic rule in Spain merged with indigenous North African Latin- and Berber-speaking Jews. This newly enlarged Romance-speaking Jewry could have fused with Arabic-speaking Jews emigrating from the Near East and Arabia in the late 7th century.

(b) In Spain after 711, the North African Jews, their numbers possibly swelled after absorbing a residual Romance-speaking Jewish population, quickly made Arabic the dominant language of the community. With the gradual return of Christian hegemony to much of the peninsula beginning with the 11th century, more and more Iberian Jews became speakers of Romance.

(c) After the nation-wide pogroms in Spain in 1391, sizeable numbers of Sephardic Jews, speaking Arabic and/or Ibero-Romance, began to migrate to North Africa. These Iberian returnees to Africa were augmented by a much larger number of refugees who were expelled in 1492, most of whom were speakers of Romance. Abroad the Iberian Jews maintained Judeo-Spanish for several centuries in North Africa, though not without attrition in certain locales in favor of Judeo-Arabic, until the early 20th century when standard Spanish, Arabic, and French definitively replaced Judeo-Spanish in Morocco. The emigrés who settled in the Balkans appear to have been primarily speakers of Judeo-Spanish, whose loyalty to that language weakened substantially only in the present century.

(6) The strong proselyte component in the North African and Iberian Jewries in the Roman period explains why Old Palestinian Jews early abandoned the use of spoken Hebrew and Judeo-Aramaic outside of Palestine. There is barely evidence of Hebrew or Judeo-Aramaic on Iberian stone inscriptions, and no evidence of texts (either original or copied) until the 10th century. Proselytes to Judaism would have found little merit in learning Semitic languages such as Old Hebrew and Judeo-Aramaic, especially since they constituted the overwhelming majority within the Jewish communities. Quite likely, most Jewish emigrés to Spain were themselves not speakers or writers of Hebrew and Judeo-Aramaic.

The status of Hebrew and Judeo-Aramaic led me to conclude that the Sephardic Jews could not have had substantial access to an Old Palestinian Jewish culture or gene pool, as some scholars have suggested (for example, Battenberg 1990:45, who, at the same time, denies the Ashkenazic Jews such access). The diluted Judaism of the North African and Iberian diasporas and the absence of a Hebrew and Judeo-Aramaic literature (composed by native and non-native speakers both) explain why we find a plethora of non-Hebrew terms denoting aspects of the Jewish religion and culture (some of the concepts acquired alternative or exclusive Hebrew terms only during later periods of Judaization—on the latter, see section 12 later in this chapter).

(7) The North African and Iberian Jews could not have received any of the original Old Palestinian Jewish literature (the Bible and Talmud) or a written Hebrew- or Judeo-Aramaic-language tradition

until the arrival of Near Eastern and Arabian Jews, beginning with the late 7th century, but there is no actual evidence of this literature in North Africa or Spain until the 10th century, when contacts between Spanish and North African Jews and the Iraqi Jewish religious academies are first documented. After the 10th or 11th century, the Sephardic Jews became independent in matters of Jewish scholarship and no longer relied on the Iraqi and North African schools for religious training.

I do not think it an exaggeration to say that the migration of Iraqi (and other Near Eastern) Jews to North Africa and Europe in the 7th and 8th centuries was the single most important factor in the preservation of a diaspora Jewish entity, since it provided access to Hebrew and Judeo-Aramaic literature that was essential to the process of Judaization that preserved a great many Jewish communities from disappearance.

(8) The linguistic evidence suggested that Jews did not leave North Africa for Spain in large numbers with the Almohade and Almoravide invaders in the 11th and 12th centuries. Jews came mainly in one early wave to Spain in the 8th and 9th centuries, though North African Arabs and Berbers came to Spain repeatedly between the 8th and 12th centuries. I have proposed reconstructing the waves of linguistic diffusion from North Africa and Spain as well as Old Iberian Judeo-Arabic and Judeo-Spanish linguistic and ethnographic patterns on the basis of features shared by Iberian Jews and at least one Sephardic diaspora—either in the Balkans or in North Africa.

(9) A major research goal should be to determine the nature of the Arabic spoken by the Iberian Jews. The written documentation is not always useful due to the pressures of standardization which conceal spoken reality. Blau claims that Spanish Judeo-Arabic contains few uniquely Spanish features, but otherwise resembles North African Judeo-Arabic closely (1992:7). This claim is not altogether convincing—at least not for some forms of colloquial North African Judeo-Arabic, which differ from coterritorial Muslim Arabic, for example, Algiers Judeo-Arabic. There are two explanations that might account for the unique features of Algiers Judeo-Arabic:

(a) Algiers Judeo-Arabic was brought there from Spain and thus continues Iberian Judeo-Arabic, which, in turn, is a continuation of a still earlier form of North African Arabic. M. Cohen believes the Spanish Jews arrived in Algeria in 1391 as speakers of Spanish (1912:6), though he also assumes that Iberian Jews who migrated to Turkey in 1492 may have spoken Arabic as a second language (ibid.:2). Cohen's first claim is not altogether convincing, since contemporary Algiers Judeo-Arabic has a number of features that align it with Spanish Arabic rather than with coterritorial Muslim speech. For example, Algiers Judeo-Arabic has the rare feature of merging *t* and $\theta > t$ ~ AlgMAr *c* (ibid.:21) and *k* and *q* into a glottal stop (ibid.:26; this feature also appears in the Medieval Moroccan Judeo-Arabic manuscript studied by Mainz 1949:55); Algiers Muslims preserve *q*. The evaluation of Algiers Judeo-Arabic data is complicated by the fact that in other parts of Algeria, for example, in Tlemcen, the Jews preserve historical *q*, which the local Muslims pronounce as a glottal stop (M. Cohen 1912:43); Tunisian Judeo-Arabic also has *q* (D. Cohen 2:1974: 31–32). Another distinctive feature of Algiers Judeo-Arabic is the retention of *p* in loans from Romance, Turkish, and Hebrew and in the ritual reading of the Hebrew Bible ~ MAr *b* in Romance and Turkish loans. In grammar, Algiers Judeo-Arabic makes no gender distinction in the 2nd singular and 3rd plural perfect and imperfect verb forms (it uses the masculine forms exclusively; M. Cohen 1912:182). This feature is also found in Spanish Arabic in the 2nd person singular forms (Corriente 1977:100).

The presence of Spanish Arabisms in Algiers Judeo-Arabic does support M. Cohen's claim, by showing that some Iberian Jews may have already become fluent in Spanish before reaching Algeria (M. Cohen 1912:481). For example, see AlgJAr *flīr* "pin," plural *flā̊ịər* < Sp *alfiler* < Ar *al-xilāl* (vs. BalJSp *alfinete*). It is unlikely that *flīr* could have been acquired in North Africa, since the Muslims there have native *məssāk* for pin. While Cohen does not comment on doublet forms of Ar *d-f-n* "hide," I proposed that *dfīna* "Sabbath food" was brought from Spain, while *tfīnä* "funeral" was acquired regionally (ibid.:495–96). Algiers Judeo-Arabic, like Iberian Arabic, also has the raising of *a* > *ä* (*imāla*), which is weak in Muslim Arabic (ibid.:104).

The old urban Arabic dialects spoken in North Africa were leveled out after the banu Hilal and Maʿqil Bedouin invasions in the 11th and 12th centuries (Stillman 1989:103, 110, fn 24). Iberian

Judeo-Arabic that was transported back to Africa, such as possibly contemporary Algiers Judeo-Arabic, may represent the original North African urban speech. On the antiquity of Spanish Arabic and the Arabization of Berber language and culture, see E. Wagner 1966:267–68, 276.

(b) On the other hand, Algiers Judeo-Arabic might be a survival of the original urban Arabic speech in North Africa prior to the Bedouin invasions of the 10th and 11th centuries that was never exported to Spain; the Bedouin invasions that led to the Bedouinization of urban speech among the Muslims may have bypassed the Jews (an analogous situation took place in Iraq in the 14th century, whereby Jews and Christians continued to speak old urban Baghdadi Arabic; see Blanc's description of Baghdadi Judeo-Arabic, 1964:166ff and Wexler 1981b:105–106).

The systematic study of the unique features of North African Judeo-Arabic is a pressing desideratum. Kaye, in a discussion of verbs for "see" in Arabic dialects, points out that it is primarily Jews who preserve OAr *ra'ā*, replaced by the early 14th century among Muslims by the root *šūf* (1986:212ff). But, where Kaye attributes the "archaicity" of North African Judeo-Arabic to segregation from Muslim society (ibid.:213), I would prefer to explore the possibilities that the Jews preserved Old North African Arabic best either by resisting subsequent Beduinization or by preserving Old Iberian Arabic upon their return to North Africa after 1391.

Algiers Judeo-Arabic, and possibly other North African Judeo-Arabic dialects, may prove to be extremely valuable, largely untapped, sources for reconstructing colloquial Iberian Judeo-Arabic. The unique Arabic component in Judeo-Spanish, in all its temporal and spatial variants, is also an indispensable source of data for reconstructing both Iberian Judeo- and Muslim Arabic. To the best of my knowledge, no one has proposed utilizing these Jewish sources for the recovery of Iberian Arabic.

Judeo-Spanish may also be in a position to shed some light on the origin of colloquial Judeo-Arabic. Most Arabists assume that each dialect of Judeo-Arabic is a development *in situ*, i.e., the origins of Judeo-Arabic should be sought in the coterritorial or contiguous non-Jewish Arabic dialects; hence, it is unnecessary to reconstruct a Common Judeo-Arabic in the Arabian Peninsula, parallel to Common Arabic (Stillman 1989:99). Indeed, the existence of lexical isoglosses linking most of the Judeo-Arabic dialects, such as *ṣlā* "synagogue" < "prayer" in Moroccan, Tunisian, Libyan, Iraqi, and Yemenite Judeo-Arabic, or *adefina* "Sabbath food" < "secret, buried object" in Iberian and North African (except Moroccan) Judeo-Arabic are too few in number to support the hypothesis of a Common Judeo-Arabic.

Even if Arabian and Near Eastern Jews spoke a Judaized form of Arabic at the time of their migration to North Africa, the accretion of a larger non-Jewish, mainly Berber, population to the Jewish communities would inevitably have led to radical changes in the dialect basis of North African Judeo-Arabic. Thus, the latter now looks mainly like the result of multiple processes of linguistic Judaization *in situ*.

(10) A thorny question is the relationship of Judeo-Spanish to a reconstructed Judeo-Latin. I can conceive of three relationships:

(a) All Judeo-Romance languages are descended from Judeo-Latin. This is the view of Blondheim 1925 and M. Weinreich 1956. Most proponents of Judeo-Latin assume that all forms of Latin spoken by Jews (for example, in Rome, North Africa, and the Balkans) were Judaized.

(b) Some Judeo-Romance languages (for example, Catalan, Italian, and Provençal) may be descended from Judeo-Latin; the others developed at a later date in the individual Romance territories when Jews settled there or when they acquired the local languages, for example, Judeo-Spanish from Spanish, Judeo-French from French (Wexler 1989a).

(c) Not all Jews in the Roman Empire spoke Judeo-Latin, for example, it may have been spoken in Rome, but not in the Balkan Peninsula, to judge from the fact that Yiddish, which I believe developed when Balkan Jews settled in the mixed Germano-Sorbian lands at the latest by the 10th century, may preserve a small unique Romance component that is not found in the Judeo-Romance languages themselves; conversely, elements common to a number of Judeo-Romance languages are missing in Yiddish (Wexler 1992).

Obviously, the claim that Judeo-Spanish came into existence only in the 11th century makes it impossible to maintain that Judeo-Spanish was a descendant of Judeo-Latin.

(11) The absence of a Judeo-Greek substratum in Judeo-Arabic or Judeo-Spanish suggests that the ethnic make-up of the Jewish population of pre-Islamic Spain—which might have preserved a more substantial Old Palestinian Jewish component, and certainly also included a Greek component—differed from that of the Berbero-Arab Jews who entered the peninsula after 711.

(12) Periodically, the growing overlap in religion and culture between the Spanish Jews and non-Jews (especially Berbers and Arabs) or the physical separation of most Jews from the coterritorial non-Jews could have propelled many Jews to create a more uniquely Jewish profile; I have called this process "Judaization." Intensive acts of Judaization involve the following heterogeneous processes:

(a) Berber, Arab, and Christian practices were eliminated, except for those practices that had become obsolete in the original non-Jewish donor communities. Obsolescence allowed the Jews to define non-Jewish practices as "Jewish."

(b) Old Palestinian Jewish precedents for current practices and beliefs were sought in the Bible and the Talmud, and Hebrew (Semitic and non-Semitic) and Judeo-Aramaic terminology was cultivated to denote Jewish religious practices and artifacts—of heterogeneous origins.

(c) Jewish meanings were given to Spanish vocabulary (some of which originally denoted Christian practices), and more especially, to Arabic vocabulary (often with Muslim associations).

(d) Non-Sephardic "Jewish" practices could supplement the search for Old Palestinian Jewish precedents. Hence, the Sephardic Jews were receptive to Ashkenazic Jewish influences (which were largely of Slavic pre-Christian origin) beginning with the early 14th century in Spain and continuing in both the North African and Balkan diasporas, as well as to Romaniote (Judeo-Greek) influences in the Balkans, and to new Arab and Berber Jewish folklore and religious practices in North Africa. The role of Provençal Jews in the development of Sephardic culture requires further study.

More research is needed to determine the extent to which Judaization was stimulated by the institutionalization of Christianity and Islam in Spain and North Africa by the 11th century and whether the rising interest in cultivating a tradition of original "Hebrew" letters was inspired by the rise of Classical Arabic and Medieval

"Latin" as the languages of Islam and Christianity, respectively. On a new religious group's need for a separate liturgical language, see Bulliet 1979b:35.

(13) Had the bulk of the Jews remained in Muslim areas, their Berbero-Arabic cultural patrimony, without some form of Judaization, might well have proven inadequate to permit the Jews to maintain a separate Jewish profile. In Christian regions, the desire for a unique Jewish cultural and religious profile gave a powerful impetus to the preservation of many "Jewish" customs of Berber and Arab provenience—even those for which Old Palestinian Jewish precedents in the Bible and Talmud could not be readily supplied; the retention of non-Judaized Berbero-Arab customs in Christian Spain posed no dilemma for the Jews since these customs were, for the most part, unknown to the coterritorial Christians. Outside Spain, the need to cultivate Berbero-Arab customs continued—this time as a means of maintaining a separate Sephardic profile in proximity to non-Iberian Jews.

Judeo-Spanish is mainly unique vis-à-vis Spanish in its non-Castilian components. This shows that the majority Spanish component was essentially never Judaized. The reason for this is that Spanish was not spoken by the majority of the Iberian Jews until shortly before their expulsion in 1492. In the two Sephardic diasporas, there was little need to cultivate a separate Judeo-Spanish norm, since the latter was not spoken in the same environment as Spanish (except for the northwest corner of Morocco, parts of which were occupied by the Spanish beginning with 1860).

(14) The Sephardic Jews were originally Arabic and Berber speakers; their language loyalty gradually began to change in favor of Spanish in the 11th century as more and more Jews migrated to the Christian-dominated areas in the north of the peninsula. Nevertheless, in the domain of culture and religious practice, the Sephardic Jews maintained a great many elements of their Berbero-Arab patrimony. Hence, the claims voiced by many Sephardic Jews and non-Sephardic observers alike that the former are "quintessentially Hispanic" is ill-conceived. The Christian Spanish contribution to Sephardic culture is minimal, late and superficial.

(15) There are several facts that support my hypothesis that the language shift from Judeo-Arabic to Spanish may have been, at least for some Jews, partial, i.e., it took the form of relexification of Judeo-Arabic

to Spanish vocabulary rather than a complete replacement of Judeo-Arabic by Spanish.

(a) The persistence of Arabic phonological and morphological features in the "Hebraisms" and some Arabisms of late Iberian Judeo-Spanish, for example, the pronunciation of Ar and He *x*, *ḥ* as *x* (as in JSp *alkoxolarse* "apply antimony to one's face," 1568). Future research will have to examine closely the few extant Iberian Judeo-Spanish texts for more evidence of a "hidden Arabic syntactic and phonological standard" in the language. The retention of Arabic phonological norms in Arabisms (and even some Romanisms) is in keeping with the hypothesis that Judeo-Arabic was relexified to Spanish.

(b) The low percentage of Arabisms in Judeo-Spanish is also a clue to a partial language shift. When Spanish vocabulary was accepted, the latter's Arabisms were largely filtered out, even if they were an integral part of the Spanish lexicon. Furthermore, even in the Ibero-Romance component, Judeo-Spanish has a much smaller Castilian corpus than Spanish itself. For example, for "water jug" Spanish has *tinaja* and *jarro* ~ JSp *tinaža*, for "spell" Spanish has *hechizo, ensalmo* ~ JSp *fečizo*, for "belly" Spanish has *vientre, barriga, panza, tripas* ~ JSp *vyentre, tripa*, for "hunt, chase, pursue" Spanish has *cazar, perseguir* ~ JSp *perseġ(w)ir*. These examples are tentative, since the Iberian Judeo-Spanish literature is extremely limited and the lexicon of the early diaspora texts has yet to be studied systematically.

An impoverished lexicon is found in other cases of relexification. For instance, when Yiddish, a West Slavic language of Sorbian origin, relexified to High German vocabulary, many basic German words appear never to have been accepted, for example, Y *loyfn* ~ G *laufen, rennen* "run," Y *re(y)dn* ~ G *reden, sprechen* "speak." The so-called Creole languages, spoken by millions in Africa, Asia, and the Americas primarily, are largely instances of relexification from an indigenous language to a European language; here, too, the European lexicon of the creole language (< English, French, Spanish, etc.) is smaller than that of the European lexifier language itself. For discussion, see Horvath and Wexler ms.

(c) There were several distinctive types of Ibero-Romance used by the Jews that need to be carefully delineated. The first use of

Spanish by Iberian Jews was in the pre-Islamic period and probably did not survive the Islamic invasion of 711, except possibly very marginally in the extreme northeast corner of the peninsula; there are no extant remains.

The second use of Spanish involved Mozarabic (Arabized Romance) in Andalusia, for which we have attestation from the 11th and 12th centuries. In the Muslim-dominated areas, Mozarabic was spoken by many Jews, Muslims, and Christians. Mozarabic was carried to the Christian areas of the peninsula beginning with the 11th century, to judge from possible Mozarabic elements in (Judeo-)Spanish, but eventually the Jews shifted to standard (Christian) Spanish (which gradually became slightly Judaized) either directly or via an intermediary stage of relexified Judeo-Arabic (i.e., Arabic with an overwhelmingly Spanish lexicon). I suspect that both relexified Judeo-Arabic and Spanish were transported to the two Sephardic diasporas between 1391 and 1492.

Since (Judeo-)Arabic speakers were extremely numerous and formed compact groups within Spanish Christian society, they could conceivably become "semi-speakers" of Spanish who learned non-native variants of the language from each other rather than from native speakers of the language. For further deatil, see the Mozarabic features I discussed earlier in chapter 5. Later this "semi-Spanish" or relexified Judeo-Arabic could have become progressively Hispanized, or in fact replaced by standard Spanish altogether as the knowledge of Arabic became restricted to smaller and smaller circles. This meant that for several generations, depending on the locale, the Jews and the Muslims would have spoken either a language that consisted of Arabic syntax and phonology plus a Spanish lexicon, or standard Spanish—along with Arabic.

Relexification required that all Judeo-Arabic vocabulary be replaced by genuine Spanish vocabulary (i.e., to the exclusion of most Spanish Arabisms). Only Arabized "Hebraisms" were kept, along with some Romanisms that were in use in Judeo-Arabic (or Mozarabic). This would explain why the number of Arabisms in Judeo-Spanish, as well as in the Spanish spoken by the Muslims and Muslim converts to Christianity, is strikingly low compared with that of most forms of Spanish. Andalusian Spanish has a particularly impoverished Arabic lexicon (see Garulo Muñoz 1983, based on the findings of the Andalusian dialect atlas compiled by Alvar et al. 1961–73). Most of the Arabisms in Andalusian Spanish today are not of local origin; they were imported into the area by speakers of Castilian and Catalan who repopulated Andalusia in the 13th century (Garulo Muñoz 1983).

A better understanding of the nature of the language shift will come from a study of how Judeo-Arabic texts were translated by Jews into Ibero-Romance; an example, is Sadik ben Yosef Formón's vernacular Judeo-Spanish rendition of Baḥya ibn Pakuda's *Sefer xovat halvavot bela'az* (Saloniki 1569). This research remains to be carried out.

I assume that by the 14th century at the latest, a growing body of Jews had switched from relexified Judeo-Arabic (that had the appearance of Spanish) to standard Spanish. A parallel situation existed in Germany up to the 18th century where Yiddish coexisted for several centuries with German as the languages of the Jews. As Yiddish became obsolescent in the mid-18th century, the standard German spoken and written by the German Jews underwent a slight Judaization (Wexler 1981a). Sephardic Spanish, Judaized to varying degrees depending on speaker and locale, was carried to the diasporas and prevailed over relexified Judeo-Arabic (assuming that the latter was carried to the diasporas after 1492; Bunis describes the "Hispanicization" of Judeo-Spanish in 16th-century Ottoman Turkey, 1993a:23, 1993b:537–40). Not all genres of Sephardic Spanish followed standard Spanish norms to the same extent; proverbs tended to be freer of foreign influences than colloquial Judeo-Spanish (for Moroccan examples, see Bénichou 1944:365–68); similarly, Balkan Judeo-Spanish proverbs seem to be less innovative in the use of Turkishisms than colloquial Judeo-Spanish, for example, *saka* "water carrier" < Tu *saka* (ultimately from Arabic) appears in proverbs vs. colloquial JSp *sakadži* with the accreted Turkish agentive suffix, which is not used with this root in Turkish itself (the example is discussed by Crews 1935:271 and Bunis 1991:24).

Relexified Judeo-Arabic lost its raison d'être in Spain since Spanish had high prestige in the peninsula. In the Sephardic diasporas a non- or lightly Judaized Spanish was sufficient to insulate the Sephardic Jews from the indigenous Jewish and non-Jewish cultures of the Balkans and North Africa. Given the fact that

Spaniards in the 16th century praised the "purity" of the Spanish spoken by the Ottoman and Maghrib Jews (for example, de Illescas 1578), we must assume that at least some of the Spanish Jews abroad had already replaced relexified Judeo-Arabic with standard Spanish by the 16th century. It would be interesting to know if the choice of language (Spanish or relexified Judeo-Arabic) was matched by religious preferences, with Marranos who practiced a syncretistic religion preferring Spanish and practicing Jews preferring relexified Judeo-Arabic. Another interesting question that awaits study is whether relexified Iberian Judeo-Arabic was spoken more in some areas (for example, in Andalusia) than in others. On the need to explore relexification in the history of all the Jewish languages, see Wexler 1993a:353.

(16) In the traditional view, the Iberian Jews are said to have utilized six variants of three languages: two forms of Judeo-Romance, two forms of Judeo-Arabic, and two forms of Hebrew and Judeo-Aramaic (I count these two unspoken languages as one; see Wasserstein 1991). I do not subscribe to this characterization of Sephardic linguistic behavior. I believe rather that the number of variants was seven, and I disagree with the traditional membership in each group:

The traditional characterization of the Sephardic linguistic baggage:
Judeo-Romance:
—spoken/written
—"translation" of the Hebrew Bible (Ladino)
Judeo-Arabic:
—spoken/written
—"translation" of the Hebrew Bible (*Šarḥ*)
Hebrew/Judeo-Aramaic:
—old native literature (Bible, Talmud)
—original writings ("Hebrew")

My proposed correction to the characterization of the Sephardic linguistic baggage:
Judeo-Romance:
—spoken/written
—original "Medieval Hebrew" writings (relexified to "Hebrew")
Judeo-Arabic:
—spoken/written

—original "Medieval Hebrew" writings (relexified to "Hebrew")
—"Medieval Judeo-Spanish" (relexified to Judeo-Spanish)
Hebrew/Judeo-Aramaic:
—old native literature (Bible, Talmud)
—"translations" of the Bible and Talmud (relexified to Spanish and Arabic, see Ladino and the *Šarḥ*)

I want to make four points about my proposed characterization:

(a) I disagree with the traditional view that posits the "translations" of Old Palestinian Hebrew and Judeo-Aramaic literature, so-called Ladino and the *Šarḥ*, as variants of Judeo-Spanish and Judeo-Arabic, respectively. In my view, these two unspoken "translation" languages are both variants of Old Semitic Hebrew and Judeo-Aramaic that have an unusual Judeo-Spanish or Judeo-Arabic lexicon, respectively—i.e., Ladino and the *Šarḥ* are genetically related.

(b) I regard the original "Medieval Hebrew" (and "Judeo-Aramaic") literature penned by native speakers of Judeo-Spanish and Judeo-Arabic as variants of the scribes' spoken languages, since original "Hebrew" and "Judeo-Aramaic" employed the grammar of Judeo-Spanish and Judeo-Arabic, respectively. The traditional terms "Medieval Hebrew" and "Medieval Judeo-Aramaic" are misleading, since Iberian "Hebrew" and "Judeo-Aramaic" are in no sense "continuations" or "later stages" of Old Palestinian Semitic Hebrew and Judeo-Aramaic. (In my opinion, "Medieval Latin" is also a non-Latin grammar with a Latin vocabulary; see Wright 1982 and Horvath and Wexler 1994.)

(c) In the traditional view, Judeo-Spanish and Judeo-Arabic coexist through the history of the Sephardic presence in Spain. In my view, they are largely consecutive: Judeo-Spanish (?) > Judeo-Arabic > Judeo-Spanish, broadly overlapping for the first time in the last stage.

(d) Séphiha has proposed that Ladino developed in the 12th and 13th centuries, though colloquial Judeo-Spanish did not come into being until the 1600s in the diasporas (1975:198 and n.d.:86–87); nowhere did Séphiha motivate this claim. For some time I was of the opinion that a prerequisite for the existence of a calque language of translation, such as Ladino, was the existence of a colloquial

Judaized language (Wexler 1981b:106). While this may be true for most Jewish speech communities, it might not have been the case in the Iberian Peninsula, if Ladino developed on the model of the Judeo-Arabic calque language, the *Šarḥ*, prior to the full language shift from Judeo-Arabic to Spanish and the eventual partial Judaization of the latter. Hence, Séphiha's proposal now seems reasonable to me, in principle.

(17) I would like to end with a brief comparison of Sephardic and Ashkenazic evolution—in ethnic make-up, language, culture, and religion. Some of the points to be cited still require further investigation.

(a) Ashkenazic Jewish culture was created by cyclical mergers of Slavo-Turkic stock with the assimilated descendants of Mediterranean Jews; the first such ethnic merger took place in the Balkan Peninsula after the 6th century when the ancestors of the Southern Slavs encountered Judaized Turkic Avars and Mediterranean Jews; in the 8th century, the conditions for this merger were duplicated in the Ponto-Caspian steppelands when Turkic Khazars and some Eastern Slavs converted to Judaism. These mergers were repeated for the last time in the mixed Germano-Slavic lands of present-day Germany after the 9th and 10th centuries. Sorbs converting to Judaism would have greatly increased the Slavic element in the Ashkenazic community from the 9th and 12th centuries. I do not subscribe to the standard view that the Ashkenazic Jews were created from the merger of French and Italian Jewish communities in the southwest (and marginally southeast) German lands between the 9th and 10th centuries (Wexler 1991, 1992, 1993c).

Just as Sephardic Jewry became largely identified with a territory in which it was not originally conceived, so, too, can the Ashkenazic Jews of northern Europe trace their roots to the Balkans though the German and neighboring West and East Slavic lands became their primary domiciles.

(b) Both the Sephardic and Ashkenazic Jews absorbed a small coterritorial Jewish group of different language and culture. Curiously, in both contexts, the latter have been generally regarded as the source of the Ashkenazic and Sephardic Jewish communities. I believe these assumptions have to be rejected.

For example, the southwest German lands were settled between the 10th and 15th centuries by French Jews (the latter were definitively expelled from the Kingdom of France in 1394). While the French Jewish immigrants had an important impact on Ashkenazic religious culture, they did not conceive it; in fact, they were ultimately absorbed by the Slavo-Turkic Jews, by then Yiddish-speaking, when the latter began to move into the southwestern German lands. Hence, the French Jews did not participate in the formation of Yiddish and Judeo-French is unlikely to be the source of the few unique Romanisms in Yiddish. Yiddish was a Judaized dialect of Sorbian that had acquired—through relexification—a majority High German vocabulary by the 12th century at the latest in the eastern bilingual Germano-Sorbian lands.

The Sephardic Jews may have absorbed a small indigenous Iberian Jewish population primarily in northeastern Spain, if the latter indeed survived through to 711. The Visigothic Jews who inhabited Spain before the Muslim invasion were probably Romance-speaking, though Greek and possibly also Gothic, were also spoken. This population was too small to appreciably influence the masses of Sephardic Jews coming from North Africa.

(c) In terms of their linguistic histories, the Sephardic and Ashkenazic Jews also appear to share similar experiences. It is difficult to reconstruct the linguistic behavior of the Ashkenazic Jews and Judaizers in the Balkans, but a variety of evidence suggests that they could have spoken Greek, Romance, and/or Slavic. After emigrating northward to the Germano-Sorbian lands they apparently joined the Sorbian speech community. At different times between the 9th and 12th centuries, the Sorbian Jews committed a partial language shift to High German lexicon, which resulted in the formation of what is known now as Yiddish (Wexler 1991 and 1993c). Yiddish should be defined as a language having a Slavic grammar and phonology with a superimposed High German vocabulary (approximately 75 percent of the standard Yiddish lexicon today is of German origin); hence, Yiddish is a form of Sorbian, i.e., Slavic. Most of the Sorbs made a complete shift to High German and assimilated to German culture in the Middle Ages; today the Sorbs number at most some 70,000 speakers, bilingual in German and Sorbian.

While the nature of the shift from Arabic to Spanish among the Iberian Jews still needs further study, I have already given some support for the hypothesis that the Arabic-speaking Jews also carried out a partial language shift from Judeo-Arabic to Spanish vocabulary.

In the case of the Ashkenazic Jews, there was little opportunity for the Jews to acquire native German norms, even if they had cared to, since the area they inhabited was at first predominantly Sorbian-speaking. Since the full switch to German was tantamount to accepting the religion of the Germans—Christianity, the Sorbian Jews carried out a partial language shift from Judeo-Sorbian to High German, which resulted in the language known as Yiddish (Judeo-Sorbian with a predominantly High German lexicon). In Spain some of the Arabic-speaking Jews in the north of the peninsula could have been in contact with Romance speakers who could provide a native model of Castilian, though most Arabic-speaking Jews either learned Spanish imperfectly, or produced a relexified form of Judeo-Arabic with a rich Spanish vocabulary. It is important to note that both the Ashkenazim and the Sephardim developed in the shadow of major national struggles between two coterritorial non-Jewish groups: the Germans vs. the Sorbs on the one hand, the Arabs vs. the Spanish on the other.

(d) Both the Ashkenazim and Sephardim resulted from the fusion of more than one non-Jewish group with a handful of descendants of Palestinian emigrés to Europe and Africa. The Ashkenazic Jews very quickly lost contact with native Slavs; by the 14th century, most of the Slavic population in the German lands was heavily Germanized in religion, culture, and language and the Ashkenazic Slavic-speaking Jews in the German lands had all become speakers of Yiddish by the time of their eastward migrations into Poland that began in the 13th century. There was no significant conversion of Poles to Judaism. The Slavic-speaking Jews in the monolingual Eastern Slavic lands also became submerged in the masses of Jews migrating eastward from the German lands—speakers of Yiddish, i.e., relexified Judeo-Sorbian, at the latest by the late 17th century.

In contrast to the Ashkenazim, the creation of the Iberian Sephardim did not lead to the extinction of the Arab and Berber Jews who contributed to the creation of the Sephardim. The large

Berber and Arab Jewish populations of North Africa, whose ancestors did not participate in the formation of the Sephardic Jews either in North Africa or in Spain, have retained their native cultures to this day. In this regard, the ethnically diverse Sephardic and Ashkenazic Jews form a sharp contrast to the Berber and Arabic Jews whose origins were relatively more monolithic.

(e) The Sephardic and Ashkenazic Jews share one non-Jewish ethnic component: the Slavs. Most of the Iberian Slavs came as slaves from areas of Europe where Slavic conversion to Ashkenazic Judaism has been attested or postulated, for example, in the Sorbian lands and the Balkans. There is no way to determine whether Slavic slaves acquired by Iberian Jews were first Judaized in their lands of origin or in the Iberian Peninsula (I am reminded of the case of African slaves, many of whom spoke creolized forms of English in addition to African languages, prior to their arrival in the New World).

(f) One hypothesis that has loomed large in discussions of the origins of the Sephardim and Ashkenazim is the possibility that the two groups were originally an identical Palestinian population that grew apart as a result of the differential impact of coterritorial non-Jewish populations and later Palestinian vs. Babylonian (Iraqi) cultural influences—with the latter having the greatest impact on the Iberian Jews. The differential Iraqi and Palestinian (and possibly also Yemenite) Jewish impact is often called upon to explain the rise of distinct pronunciation patterns of written Hebrew among the Sephardic and Ashkenazic Jews (Zimmels 1958:5, 82).

Some scholars have also thought that the differences between the Ashkenazic and Sephardic forms of Judaism may have derived from different origins within Palestine, for example, according to the tradition of the Spanish Jews, their ancestors came from southern Palestine and were descended from the Jerusalem nobility while the Ashkenazic Jews came from the north of Palestine (Zimmels 1958:3, Schwarzfuchs 1961:198). I do not know of any evidence in support of this hypothesis.

While the differential impact of Iraqi and Palestinian forms of Judaism could conceivably account for some of the differences dividing Ashkenazim and Sephardim, I suggest that the major reason for the historical differences between the two groups is the different proselyte populations that merged with the tiny Palestinian

Jewish nuclei in North Africa and Spain on the one hand, and in the Balkans and northern Europe on the other.

Bibliography

Abbreviations

AA—Al-Andalus.

AAAIS—Al-Andalus. The art of Islamic Spain. J. D. Dodds (ed.). New York 1992.

AAALV—Africanisms in Afro-American language varieties. S. S. Mufwene (ed.) (with the assistance of N. Condon). Athens, GA and London 1993.

AAJRP—American Academy for Jewish Research. Proceedings.

AIUO—Annali. Istituto Universitario Orientale di Napoli.

AJA—American Jewish archives.

AmS—The American Sephardi.

AnA—Antiquités africaines.

AS—Die Architektur der Synagoge. H.-P. Schwarz (ed.). Stuttgart 1988.

BHS—Bulletin of Hispanic studies.

BRAE—Boletín de la Real Academia española.

BRAH—Boletín de la Real Academia de la Historia.

CEA—Cuadernos de estudios africanos.

CIETC—Congreso Internacional "Encuentro de las tres Culturas" 1–3. Toledo 1983–88.

Circa—Circa 1492. Proceedings of the Jerusalem Colloquium: Litterae judaeorum in terra hispanica. I. Benabu (ed.). Jerusalem 1992.

CJMCMS—Convivencia. Jews, Muslims, and Christians in Medieval Spain. V. B. Mann, T. F. Glick, and J. D. Dodds (eds.). New York 1992.

CJMSM—Communautés juives des marges sahariennes du Maghreb. M. Abitbol (ed.). Jerusalem 1982.

CSIC—Consejo superior de investigaciones científicas. Madrid.

DCECH—Diccionario crítico etimológico castellano e hispánico 1–5. J. Corominas and J. A. Pascual (eds.). Madrid 1980–83.

EB—Encyclopédie berbère. La Calade, Aix-en-Provence. 1984ff.

EHCSA—Estudios en homenaje a Don Claudio Sánchez Albornoz en sus 90 años 2. Buenos Aires 1983.

EJ—Encyclopaedia judaica. Berlin 1–10, 1928–34; Jerusalem 1–16, 1971.

EO—Etudes d'orientalisme dediées à la mémoire de Lévi-Provençal 1–2. Paris 1962.

FO—Folia orientalia.

FRCS—Folklore Research Center Studies. Jerusalem.

HJ—Hispania judaica 1–3. J. M. Solà-Solé, S. G. Armistead, and J. H. Silverman (eds.). Barcelona [n.d.].

HMV—Homenaje a Millás-Vallicrosa 1–2. Barcelona 1954–56.

HR—Hispanic review.

IHE—Las inscripciones hebraicas de España. F. Cantera Burgos and J. M. Millás-Vallicrosa. Madrid 1956.

IJSL—International journal of the sociology of language.

JA—Journal asiatique.

JAACB—Jews among Arabs. Contacts and boundaries. M. R. Cohen and A. L. Udovich (eds.). Princeton 1989.

JAOS—Journal of the American Oriental Society.

JCSSI—Jews and conversos. Studies in society and the Inquisition. Y. Kaplan (ed.). Jerusalem 1985.

JESHO—Journal of the economic and social history of the Orient.

JJS—Journal of Jewish studies.

JQR—Jewish quarterly review.

JRS—Journal of Roman studies.

JSAI—Jerusalem studies in Arabic and Islam.

JSS—Journal of Semitic studies.

LC—La corónica.

MAGW—Mitteilungen der Anthropologischen Gesellschaft in Wien.

MEAH—Miscelanea de estudios árabes y hebraicos.

MedLR— Mediterranean language review.

MGWJ—Monatsschrift für Geschichte und Wissenschaft des Judenthums.

MHR—Mediterranean historical review.

MI—Les morisques et l'Inquisition. B. Vincent (ed.). Paris 1990.

MIAA—Mélanges d'islamologie. Volume dédié à la mémoire de Armand Abel. P. Salmon (ed.). Leiden 1974; 2 Brussels 1976.

NHSS—New horizons in Sephardic studies. Y. K. Stillman and G. K. Zucker (eds.). Albany 1993.

NR—Neue Romania 11. W. Busse (ed.). Berlin 1991.

NRFH—Nueva revista de filología hispánica.

OS—Orientalische Studien. Theodor Nöldeke zum siebzigsten Geburtstag 1-2. C. Bezold (ed.). Giessen 1906.

RDTP—Revista de dialectología y tradiciones populares.

REI—Revue des études islamiques.

REJ—Revue des études juives.

RFE—Revista de filología española.

RFH—Revista de filología hispánica.

RH—Revue hispanique.

RHM—Revue d'histoire maghrébine.

ROMM—Revue de l'Occident musulman et de la Méditerranée.

RP—Romance philology.

SEHAAN—Studies and essays in honor of Abraham A. Neuman. M. Ben-Horin, B. D. Weinryb, and S. Zeitlin (eds.). Leiden and Philadelphia 1962.

SI—Studia islamica.

SLOMHBD—Studia linguistica et orientalia memoriae Haim Blanc dedicata. P. Wexler, A. Borg, and S. Somekh (eds.). (*Mediterranean language and culture monograph series* 6.) Wiesbaden 1989.

SRRK—Die Sprachen im Römischen Reich der Kaiserzeit. G. Neumann and J. Untermann (eds.). Köln and Bonn 1980.

SSS—Słownik starożytności słowiańskich 1ff. Wrocław, Warsaw, and Kraków 1961ff.

SWBJV—Salo W. Baron Jubilee volume 2. Jerusalem 1974.

VKR—Volkstum und Kulturen der Romanen.

VR—Vox romanica.

WZKM—Wiener Zeitschrift für die Kunde des Morgenlandes.

ZDMG—Zeitschrift der Deutschen Morgenländischen Gesellschaft.

ZRP—Zeitschrift für romanische Philologie.

Abbou, I. S. (1953). *Musulmans andalous et judéo-espagnols.* Casablanca.

Abitbol, M. (1982). Juifs maghrebins et commerce transsaharien au Moyen-Age. *CJMSM*, 229–51.

Abrahams, I. (1896). *Jewish life in the Middle Ages.* London; New York and Philadelphia 1958, 2nd edition.

Abu-Haider, J. (1987). A document of cultural symbiosis: Arabic Ms.1623 of the Escorial Library. *Journal of the Royal Asiatic Society*, 223–35.

Abu-Talib, M. and T. R. Fox (1966). *A dictionary of Moroccan Arabic: Arabic-English.* R. S. Harrell (ed.). Washington.

Addison, L. (1676). *The present state of the Jews: wherein is contained an excellent account of their customs, secular and religious.* London.
Adler, E. N. (1904). The Inquisition in Peru. *Publications of the American Jewish Historical Society* 12:5–37.
Africanus, L. (1632). *Africae descriptio...* Leiden; reprinted as *The history and description of Africa.* London 1896.
Agnadé, J. (1986). Some remarks about sectarian movements in al-Andalus. *SI* 64:53–77.
Ahroni, R. (1986). *Yemenite Jewry. Origins, culture, and literature.* Bloomington.
Alarcos Llorach, E. (1951). La lengua de los "Proverbios morales" de Don Sem Tob. *RFE* 35:249–309.
Alcalá, P. de (1505). *Arte para ligeramente saber la lengua aráviga.* New York 1928, Osnabrück 1971.
Alonso, A. (1969). *De la pronunciación medieval a la moderna en español* 2; R. Lapesa (ed.). Madrid.
Alonso, M. (1958). *Enciclopedia del idioma.* Madrid.
Althaus, H. P. (1965). Wortgeographie und sprachsoziologische Studien zum jiddischen Lehnwortschatz im Deutschen (am Beispiel *Kazzow* 'Fleischer'). *Zeitschrift für deutsche Sprache* 21:20–41.
Alvar, M. (1958). Judeo-esp. *saeta* 'endecha'. *Cercetări de linguistică* 3:31–34.
———(1960). Cantos de muerte sefardíes. *Revista do livro* (Rio de Janeiro) 20:19–31.
———(1966). *Poesía tradicional de los judíos españoles.* Mexico.
———(1971). *Cantos de boda judeo-españoles.* Madrid.
———and J. Bosch (1968). Interpretación de un texto oscense en aljamía hebrea. *Miscelánea ofrecida al Ilmo Sr. D. José Maria Lacavra y de Miguel*, 11–22. Zaragoza.
———et al. (eds.) (1961–73). *Atlas lingüístico y etnográfico de Andalucía.* Granada.
Anahory-Librowicz, O. (1993). Expressive modes in the Judeo-Spanish wedding song. *NHSS*, 285–96.
Andrea da Cunha e Freitas, E. da (1954). Tradições judio-portuguesas: novos subsídios. *Douro-Litoral* 6th series 1–2:145–49.
Andree, R. (1881). *Zur Volkskunde der Juden.* Bielefeld and Leipzig.
Ángel de Bunes Ibarra, M. (1989). *La imagen de los musulmanes y del norte de África en la España de los siglos XVI y XVII. Los caracteres de una hostilidad.* Madrid.

Anqawa, A. (1871). *Kerem xemar* 2. Leghorn.

Armistead, S. G. and J. T. Monroe (1983). *Albas, mammas*, and code-switching in the *Kharjas*. A reply to Keith Whinnom. *LC* 11:174–207.

Armistead, S. G. and J. H. Silverman (1981). El antiguo cancionero sefardí: citas de romances en himnarios hebreos (siglos XVI–XIX). *NRFH* 30:453–512.

———(1982). *En torno al romancero sefardí*. Madrid.

———(1990). A Judeo-Spanish prayer. *LC* 19(1):22–31.

Arragel, M. de (1422–33). *La Biblia de la Casa de Alba;* edited by A. Paz y Mélia 1–2. Madrid 1920–22.

Ashtor, E. (1960–66). *Korot hayehudim besfarad hamuslimit* 1–2. Jerusalem.

———(1964). Documentos españoles de la Genizah. *Sefarad* 24:41–80.

———(1972). Un mouvement migratoire au haut Moyen Age. Migrations de l'Irak vers les pays méditerranéens. *Annales. Economies. Sociétés. Civilisations* 27:185–214.

Aškoli, A.Z. (1936). Mekorot leocar hamilim haivri. *Lešonenu* 7:283–90.

Assaf, S. (1939–40). Avadim vesaxar avadim bime habenaim (al pi mekorot ivri'im). *Cion* 4:91–125; 5:271–80; reprinted in his *Beohale ya'akov*, 223–56. Jerusalem 1943.

Atias, M. (1955). *Romansero sfaradi*. Jerusalem.

Attal, R. (1963). Le Juif dans le proverbe arabe du Maghreb. *REJ* 122:419–30.

———(1973). *Les Juifs d'Afrique du Nord: bibliographie*. Jerusalem.

Auerbach, E. (1907). Die jüdische Rassenfrage. *Archiv für Rassen- und Gesellschaftsbiologie* 4(3):332–61.

Avalle Arce, J. B. (1946). Sobre Juan Alfonso de Baena. *RFH* 8:141–47.

Avisur, Y. (1993). Yesodot arameim kdumim ba'aravit hayehudit šel irak. *Massorot* 7:1–24.

Ayuso Marazuela, T. (1944). Un apócrifo español del siglo sexto de probable origen judeo-cristiano. *Sefarad* 4:3–29.

Bacher, W. (1882). Additions et rectifications. *REJ* 6:159.

Bachrach, B. S. (1973). A reassessment of Visigothic Jewish policy, 589–711. *American historical review* 78:11–34.

Baer, F. (1929–36). *Die Juden im christlichen Spanien* 1–1/2. Berlin.

———(1934). Review of González Palencia. *Tarbic* 5:228–36.

———[Y.] (1961–66). *A history of the Jews in Christian Spain* 1–2. Philadelphia.

Bahloul, J. (1989). From a Muslim banquet to a Jewish seder: foodways and ethnicity among North African Jews. *JAACB*, 85–95.

Baker, P. (1984). The significance of agglutinated French articles in the Creole languages of the Indian Ocean and elsewhere. *York papers in linguistics* 11:19–29.

———and C. Corne (1987). Histoire sociale et créolisation à la Réunion et à Maurice. *Langues en contact, langues de contact et emprunt*. R. Fournier (ed.). Special issue of *Revue Québécoise de linguistique théorique et appliquée* 6(2):71–87.

Baldinger, K. (1972). *La formación de los dominios lingüísticos en la península ibérica*. Madrid, 2nd edition.

Banitt, M. (1985). *Rashi. Interpreter of the biblical letter.* Tel-Aviv.

Bar-Ašer, M. (1989). Bxinot bexeker hamarkiv haivri bearvit hayehudit haxadaša bamizrax uvama'arav. *Massorot* 3–4:147–69.

———(1991). Al kama xiduše lašon bamarkiv haivri bearavit hayehudit bama'arav (uvamizrax). *Massorot* 5–6:35–49.

———(1993). Hamarkiv haivri ba'aravit šel yehude aldžeria (kehilot tlemsen ve'en timušent). *Xekre ever vearav mugašim lihošua blaw.* X. Ben-Šamai (ed.). 135–91. Tel-Aviv and Jerusalem.

Barceló Perelló, M. (1985). Un topònim berber més: *Manqur, Mankur* > *Mancor, Manacor. Butlletí de la Societat Arqueològica Lul.liana* (Palma de Mallorca) 41 (no. 839):35–36.

Baron, S. W. (1952–80). *A social and religious history of the Jews* 1–17. Philadelphia.

———(1962). Medieval nationalism and Jewish serfdom. *SEEHAN*, 17–48.

Baruch, K. (1923). La lingwa de los sefaradim. *El mundo sefaradí* 1:20–25.

———(1930). El judeo-español de Bosnia. *RFE* 17:113–54.

Basset, R. (1901). *Nédromah et les Traras*. Paris.

———(1906). Les mots arabes passés en berbère. *OS*, 1:439–53.

Bates, M. L. (1992). The Islamic coinage of Spain. *AAAIS*, 384–91.

Battenberg, F. (1990). *Das europäische Zeitalter der Juden* 1. *Von den Anfängen bis 1650*. Darmstadt.

Becker, C. H. (1906). Die Kanzel im Kultus des alten Islam. *OS*, 1:331–51.

Becker, D. (1984). *Ha"risāla" šel yehuda ben kurayš. Mahadura bikortit.* Tel-Aviv.

Beinart, H. (1965). *Anusim bedin hainkvizicya*. Jerusalem.

———(ed.) (1974–81). *Records of the trials of the Spanish Inquisition in Ciudad Real* 1–3. Jerusalem.

———(1980). *Trujillo. A Jewish community in Extremadura on the eve of the Expulsion from Spain.* Jerusalem.

———(1987). Introdución. In J. Luis Lacave (ed.), *Sefarad, Sefarad. La España judía*, 9–12. Barcelona and Madrid.

Beit-Arié, M. (1981). *Hebrew codicology.* Jerusalem.

Ben-Ami, I. (1974). Le mariage traditionel chez les Juifs marocains. *FRCS* 4:9–103; reprinted in his *Yahadut maroko. Prakim bexeker tarbutam.* Jerusalem 1976.

———(1993). Customs of pregnance and childbirth among Sephardic and Oriental Jews. *NHSS*, 253–67.

Benardete, M. J. (1963). *Hispanismo de los sefardíes levantinos*. Madrid.

Bencherifa, M. (ed.) (1971). *Amthāl al-ʿawām fī l-andalus*. Rabat.

Bénichou, P. (1944). Romances judeo-españoles de Marruecos. *RFH* 6:314–81.

———(1968). *Romancero judeo-español de Marreucos*. Madrid.

Ben Moše, J. (early 13th century). *Or zarua*. Žytomyr 1862; reprinted in Kupfer and Lewicki 1956:202–62.

Benoliel, J. (1926–52). Dialecto judeo-hispano-marroquí o hakitía. *BRAE* 13 (1926), 209–33, 342–63, 507–38; 14 (1927), 137–68, 196–234, 357–73, 566–80; 15 (1928), 47–61, 188–233; 32 (1952), 255–89; reprinted Madrid 1977.

Ben Sedira, B. K. (1910). *Dictionnaire français-arabe de la langue parlée en Algérie*. Algiers.

Ben Tanfous, A. (1987). Alimentation à Jerba. *EB* 4:502–507.

Ben-Ya'akov, A. (1985). *Ivrit vearamit bilšon yehude bavel*. Jerusalem.

Ben-Zvi, I. (1961). *The exiled and the redeemed.* Philadelphia.

Bergmann, J. (1927). Zur Geschichte religiöser Bräuche. *MGWJ* 71:161–71.

Besso, H. V. (1981). Los sefardíes: españoles sin patria y su lengua. *NRFH* 30:648–65.

Bickermann, E. (1928). Adiabene. *EJ* 1:columns 860–63.

Biella, J. C. (1982). *Dictionary of Old South Arabic. Sabaean dialect*. Chico, CA.

Birnbaum, S. A. (1954–71). *The Hebrew scripts* 2 (1954–57). London; 1 (1971). Leiden.

Blanc, H. (1964). *Communal dialects in Baghdad.* Cambridge, MA.

———(1969). The fronting of Semitic *g* and the *qāl-gāl* dialect split in Arabic. *Proceedings of the International Conference on Semitic Studies*, 1–37. Jerusalem.

Blasco Martínez, A. (1988). *La judería de Zaragoza en el siglo XIV.* Zaragoza.

———(1990). Instituciones sociorreligiosas judías de Zaragoza (siglos XIV–XV). Sinagogas, cofradías, hospitales. *Sefarad* 50:3–46, 265–88.

Blau, Y. (1958). Al hayesodot haivri'im betekstim arvi'im-yehudi'im mime habenaim. *Lešonenu* 22:183–96.

———(1959). The status of Arabic as used by Jews in the Middle Ages. *JJS* 10:15–23; reprinted in his 1988.

———(1962). Al ma'amadan šel haivrit veha'aravit ben yehudim dovre aravit bameot harišonot šel haislam. *Lešonenu* 26:281–84.

———(1964). Al kavim makbilim umafridim axadim ba'aravit-hayehudit uva'aravit-hanocrit. *Tarbic* 33:131–39.

———(1965). *The emergence and linguistic background of Judaeo-Arabic.* Oxford; Jerusalem 1981, 2nd edition.

———(1978). Medieval Judeo-Arabic. In *Jewish languages: theme and variation*. H. H. Paper (ed.), 121–31. Cambridge, MA; reprinted in his 1988.

———(1984). Halašon ha'aravit šebemixtave hagniza. *Tarbic* 53:154–66.

———(1988). *Studies in Middle Arabic and its Judaeo-Arabic variety.* Jerusalem.

———(1992). The Spanish offshoot of medieval Judeo-Arabic. *Circa*, 3–10.

Blázquez, J. M. (1969). Relaciones entre Hispania y los Semitas en la antiguedad. *Beiträge zur alten Geschichte und deren Nachleben. Festschrift für Franz Altheim zum 6.10.1968.* R. Stiehl and H. E. Stier (eds.), 1:42–75. Berlin.

Bleiberg, G. (1979). *Diccionario de historia de España* 1–3. Madrid.

Blondheim, D. S. (1925). *Les parlers judéo-romans et la Vetus latina*. Paris.

Bohec, Y. le (1981a). Inscriptions juives et judaïsantes de l'Afrique romaine. *AnA* 17:165–207.

———(1981b). Juifs et judaïsants dans l'Afrique romaine. Remarques onomastiques. *AnA* 17:209–29.

———(1991). *Religiones en la España antigua*. Madrid.

Bonfante, G. (1949). Tracce del calendario ebràico in Sardegna? *Word* 5:171–75.

Borg, A. (1989). Some Maltese toponyms in historical and comparative perspective. *SLOMHBD*, 62–85.

Borrow, G. (1869). *The Bible in Spain*. London.

Bosch Vilá, J. (1954). Escrituras oscenses en aljamía hebraicoárabe. *HMV* 1:183–214.

———(1976). Pour une étude historico-sociologique sur les berbères d' "Al-Andalus." *MIAA* 2:53–69.

———(1988). Al-Andalus (Les Berbères en Andalus). *EB* 5:641–47.

Boughanmi, M., et al. (1979). Recherches sur les Moriscos-Andalous au Maghreb (bilan et perspectives). *RHM* 13–14:21–26.

Bramon, D. (1989). El rito de las fadas, pervivencia de la ceremonia pre-islámica de la " 'Aqiqa." *Actas del III Simpósio Internacional de Estudios Moriscos. Las practicas musulmanas de los moriscos andaluces* (1492–1609), . . . Zaghouan (Tunisia).

Brockelmann, C. (1905). Haplologische Silbenellipse im Semitischen. *ZDMG* 59:629–33.

———(1908). *Grundriss der vergleichenden Grammatik der semitischen Sprachen* 1. Berlin.

Brooten, B. J. (1982). *Women leaders in the ancient synagogue; inscriptional evidence and background issues.* Chico, CA.

Brown, R. (1968). Christianity and local culture in late Roman Africa. *JRS* 58:85–95.

Bruckus, Y. (1942). Sfarad un corfes. *Yidn in frankrayx. Študyes un materialn*. E. Tcherikover (ed.), 9–15. New York.

Brunot, L. (1936). Notes sur le parler arabe des Juifs de Fès. *Hespéris* 22:1–32.

Brunschvig, R. (1954). L'argumentation d'un théologien musulman du Xe siècle contre le judaïsme. *HMV* 1:225–41.

Bulliet, R. W. (1979a). Conversion to Islam and the emergence of a Muslim society in Iran. *Conversion to Islam*. N. Levtzion (ed.), 30–51. New York and London.

———(1979b). *Conversion to Islam in the medieval period. An essay in quantitative history.* Cambridge, MA and London.

Bunardžić, R. (1980). *Menore iz Čelareva*. Belgrade.

Bunis, D. M. (1981). *Sephardic studies. A research bibliography incorporating Judezmo language, literature and folklore, and historical background*. New York and London.

———(1985). Plural formation in Modern Eastern Judezmo. *Judeo-Romance languages*. I. Benabu and J. Sermoneta (eds.), 41–67. Jerusalem.

———(1991). Una introducción a la lengua de los sefardíes a traves de refranes en ǰudezmo. *NR*, 7–36.

———(1992). Lešon hayehudim hasfaradim—skira historit. *Morešet sfarad*. H. Beinart (ed.), 694–713. Jerusalem.

———(1993a). *A lexicon of the Hebrew and Aramaic elements in Modern Judezmo.* Jerusalem.

———(1993b). Le *ǰudezmo*: autres cadres, autre rôles. *La société juive à travers l'histoire* 4:532–55, 715–16. Paris.

Burns, R. I. (1973). *Islam under the Crusaders.* Princeton.

Busi, G. (1986). Materiali per una storia della filologia e dell'esegesi ebraica. Abū-'l-Walīd Marwān ibn Ǧanāḥ. *AIUO.* 46:167–95.

Busse, W. (1991a). Vorwort. *NR*, 3–6.

———(1991b). Zur Problematik des Judenspanischen. *NR*, 37–84.

Cabanelas, D. (1981). Intento de supervivencia en el ocaso de una cultura: los libros plúmbeos de Granada. *NRFH* 30:334–58.

———[Cabanelas Rodríguez] (1992). The Alhambra: an introduction. *AAAIS*, 127–33.

Cabezudo Astrain, J. (1956). Noticias y documentos sobre moriscos aragones. *MEAH* 5:105–17.

Cagigas, I. de las (1946a). Los estudios beréberes en relación con España. *CEA* 1:117–21.

———(1946b). Tres cartas públicas de comanda. *Sefarad* 6:73–93.

———(1947). *Los Mozárabes* 1. Madrid.

Camós Cabruja, L. (1946). Esclavos orientales en Barcelona en el s. XIV. *Sefarad* 6:128–29.

Camps, G. (1982). Reflexions sur l'origine des juifs des régions nord-sahariennes. *CJMSM*, 57–67.

Canard, M. (ed.) (1958). *Vie de l'Ustadh Jaudhar.* Algiers.

Cantera Burgos, F. (1953). Unas palabras más sobre la nueva jarǰa de Mošé ibn 'Ezra. *Sefarad* 13:360–61.

———(1954). Carne trifa. *Sefarad* 14:126–27.

———(1957). *La canción mozárabe*. Santander.

———(1967). El Cancionero de Baena: judíos y conversos en él. *Sefarad* 27:71–111.

———(1973). *Sinagogas de Toledo, Segovia y Córdoba*. Madrid.

Cantera Montenegro, E. (1985). Solemnidades, ritos y costumbres de los judaizantes de Molina de Aragón a fines de la Edad Media. *CIETC* 2:59–88.

Cantineau, J. (1960). *Cours de phonétique arabe*. Paris.

Cardaillac, L. (1977). *Morisques et chrétiens. Un affrontement polémique*. (1492–1640). Paris.

——— and J.-P. Dedieu (1990). Introduction à l'histoire des morisques. *MI*, 11–28.

Caro Baroja, J. (1978). *Los Judíos en la España moderna y contemporánea* 1–3. Madrid.

Carpenter, D. E. (1986). *Alfonso X and the Jews: an edition of and commentary on Siete Partidas 7:24 "De los judíos."* Berkeley, Los Angeles, and London.

Carrasco, R. and A. González (1984). Le problème morisque dans les îles de la Méditerranée. *RHM* 35–36:39–70.

Carrete Parrondo, C. (1978). Fraternization between Jews and Christians in Spain before 1492. *AmS* 9:15–21.

———(1991). Nostalgia for the past (and for the future?) among the Castilian Judeoconversos. *MHR* 6:25–43.

Castro, A. (1914). Disputa entre en cristiano y un judío. *RFE* 1:173–80.

———(1984). *España en su historia. Cristianos, moros y judíos*. Barcelona, 3rd edition.

Catalán Pidal, D. (ed.) (1975). *Crónica del Moro Rasis*. Madrid.

Chaker, S. (1989). Arabisation. *EB* 5:834–43.

Cheyne, A. G. (1969). *The Arabic language: its role in history*. Minneapolis.

Chouraqui, A. N. (1968). *Between East and West. A history of the Jews of North Africa*. Philadelphia.

Cirac Estopañán, S. (1965). *Registros de los documentos del Santo Oficio de Cuenca y Sigüenza*. Cuenca and Barcelona.

Clemen, C. (1931). *Religionsgeschichte Europas* 2. Heidelberg.

Cohen, D. (1964–75). *Le parler arabe des juifs de Tunis* 1–2. The Hague and Paris.

———(1970). Les deux parlers arabes de Tunis: notes de phonologie comparée. In his *Etudes de linguistique sémitique et arabe*, 150–71. The Hague and Paris.

———(1971). Review of Galand-Pernet and Zafrani. *REI* 39:411–14.

———(1981). Remarques historiques et sociolinguistiques sur les parlers arabes des Juifs maghrébins. *IJSL* 30:91–105.

Cohen, H. J. (1970). The economic background and the secular occupations of Muslim jurisprudents and traditionalists in the classical period of Islam (until the middle of the eleventh century). *JESHO* 13:16–61.

Cohen, M. (1912). *Le parler arabe des juifs d'Alger.* Paris.

Cohen, M. A. (1992). The Sephardic phenomenon: a reappraisal. *AJA* 44:1–79.

Cohen de Lara, D. (1633). *Maimonides. Da lei divina. Traducção hespanhola de David Cohen de Lara novamente impresa e com uma introducção de M. B. Amzalak.* Lisbon 1925.

Colin, G. S. (1927). Etymologies maġribines II. *Hespéris* 7:85–102.

———(1930a). Etymologies maġribines III. *Hespéris* 10:125–27.

———(1930b). Notes de dialectologie arabe. *Hespéris* 10:91–120.

———(1931). Un document nouveau sur l'arabe dialectal d'Occident au XIIe siècle. *Hespéris* 12:1–32.

———(1970). Emprunts grecs et turcs dans le dialecte arabe de Malte. *Mélanges Marcel Cohen.* D. Cohen (ed.), 229–31. The Hague and Paris.

Combet, L. (1966). Lexicographie judéo-espagnole: *dío* ou *dió, judío* et *judió. Bulletin Hispanique* 68:323–27.

Cooper, J. (1993). *Eat and be satisfied. A social history of Jewish food.* Northvale, NJ and London.

Corcos, D. (1972). Les Juifs du Maroc et leurs mellahs. *Zakor le Abraham. Mélanges Abraham Elmaleh*, xiv–lxxviii. Jerusalem.

Coromines, J. (1972). Sobre els noms de lloc d'origen bereber. *Studia hispanica in honorem R. Lapesa* 1:207–18. Madrid.

———, with the collaboration of J. Gulsoy and M. Cahner (1980ff). *Diccionari etimològic i complementari de la llengua catalana* 1ff. Barcelona.

Corré, A. D. (1971). *The daughter of my people. Arabic and Hebrew paraphrases of Jeremiah 8.13–9.23.* Leiden.

———(1991). Milim šeulot basefer šay lamora. *Mexkarim betarbutam šel yehude cfon-afrika.* Y. Ben-Ami (ed.), 41–46. Jerusalem.

———[n.d.] A comparative Sephardic lexicon. *HJ* 3:39–59.

Corriente, F. (1969). A survey of spirantization in Semitic and Arabic phonetics. *JQR* 60:147–71.

———(1977). *A grammatical sketch of the Spanish Arabic dialect bundle.* Madrid.

———(1984). Nuevas apostillas de lexicografía hispanoárabe. *Sharq al-Andalus* 1:7–14.

———(1989). South Arabian features in Andalusī Arabic. *SLOMHBD*, 94–103.

———with the assistance of H. Bouzineb [ms.] *Recopilación de refranes andalusíes de Alonso del Castillo.*

Corso, R. (1935). La diffusione geografica di una costumanza nuziale nell'Africa e il suo significato. *Annali del R. Istituto Orientale di Napoli* 1:14–36.

Costa Fontes, M. da (1990–93). Four Portuguese crypto-Jewish prayers and their 'Inquisitorial' counterparts. *MedLR* 6–7:67–104.

———(1991). Orações criptojudias na tradição oral portuguesa. *Hispania* 74:511–18.

Costes, R. (1925). *Antonio de Guevara. Sa vie.* Bordeaux and Paris (= *Bibliothèque de l'école des hautes études hispaniques* 10, part 1.)

Courtois, Ch. (1945). Grégoire VII et l'Afrique du Nord. Remarques sur les communautés chrétiennes d'Afrique au XIe siècle. *Revue historique* 195:97–122, 193–226.

Crews, C. (1935). *Recherches sur le judéo-espagnol dans les pays balkaniques.* Paris.

———(1953). Review of Schmid. *VR* 13:206–209.

———(1954–55). Some Arabic and Hebrew words in oriental Judaeo-Spanish. *VR* 14:296–309.

———(1957–61). Miscellanea hispano-judaica. *VR* 16:224–45; 20:13–38.

———(1960). Extracts from the Meam Loez (Genesis) with a translation and a glossary. *Proceedings of the Leeds Philosophical and Literary Society* 9, part 2, 13–106.

———(1962). The vulgar pronunciation of Hebrew in the Judeo-Spanish of Salonica. *JJS* 13:83–95.

———[ms.] Unpublished Judeo-Spanish dictionary. Housed at the CSIC.

Díaz Esteban, F. (1975). Un documento hebreo inédito de Teruel. *Anuario de filología* 1:95–108.

Díaz-Mas, P. (1986). *Los sefardíes, historia, lengua y cultura*. Barcelona.

Didier, H. (1981). Le biconfessionalisme en Espagne: esquisse d'un itinéraire historique (Ier–XVIIe s.). *Islamochristiana* 7:79–126.

Dodds, J.D. (1992). Mudejar tradition and the synagogues of Medieval Spain: cultural identity and cultural hegemony. *CJMCMS*, 113–31.

——— and D. Walker (1992). Introduction. *AAAIS*, xix–xxiii.

Doutté, E. (1909). *Magie et religion dans l'Afrique du Nord*. Algiers.

Dozy, R. P. A. (1881). *Supplément aux dictionnaires arabes* 1–2. Leiden; Beirut 1968, 2nd edition.

——— and W. H. Engelmann (1869). *Glossaire des mots espagnols et portugais dérivés de l'arabe*. Leiden; Amsterdam 1965, 2nd edition.

Dubler, C. E. (1942). Über Berbersiedlungen auf der iberischen Halbinsel. *Sache, Ort und Worte. Jakob Jud zum sechzigsten Geburtstag*, 182–96. (= *Romanica helvetica* 20). Geneva, Zurich, and Erlenbach.

———(1943). *Über das Wirtschaftsleben auf der iberischen Halbinsel vom XI. zum XIII. Jahrhundert*. Geneva, Erlenbach, and Zurich.

Efron, J. M. (1994). *Defenders of the race. Jewish doctors and race science in fin-de-siècle Europe*. New Haven and London.

Eidelberg, S. (1962). *Jewish life in Austria in the XVth century. As reflected in the legal writings of Rabbi Israel Isserlein and his contemporaries*. Philadelphia.

Eisenbeth, M. (1936). *Les juifs d'Afrique du Nord, démographie et onomastique*. Algiers.

Ekblom, R. (1942–43). El origen de esp. *aladma*. *Studia neophilologica* 15:334–36.

Elazar, S. (1966). Narodna medicina sefardskih Jevreja u Bosni. *Spomenica. 400 godina od dolaska Jevreja u Bosnu i Hercegovinu*, 155–66. Sarajevo.

El Aziz Ben Achour, M. (1983). L'Itinéraire d'une famille tunisienne d'origine andalouse: les ibn ʻAshûr (XVIIe–XXe ss). *Etudes sur les morisques andalous*. S.-M. Zbiss et al. (eds.), 15–33. Tunis.

Eppenstein, S. (1900–1901). Ishak ibn Baroun et ses comparaisons de l'hébreu avec l'arabe. *REJ* 41:233–49, 42:76–102.

Epstein, I. (1925). *The "Responsa" of Rabbi Solomon ben Adreth of Barcelona (1235–1310) as a source of the history of Spain*. London. Reprinted (with Epstein 1930) New York 1968.

———(1930). *The Responsa of Rabbi Simon b. Zemaḥ Duran as a source of the history of the Jews in North Africa*. London. Reprinted (with Epstein 1925) New York 1968.

Epstein, Y. N. (1950). Tirgum aravi šel mišnayot. *Sefer hayovel lixvod aleksander marks limleat lo šiv'im šana*, 23–48. New York.

Espadas Burgos, M. (1975). Aspectos sociorreligiosos de la alimentación española. *Hispania* 131:537–65.

Esteban Ibáñez, P. (1961). Supervivencia de voces latinas en el dialecto beréber del Rif. *Orbis* 10:447–55.

Faur, J. (1990). Four classes of conversos: a typological study. *REJ* 149:113–24.

———(1992). *In the shadow of history. Jews and conversos at the dawn of modernity.* Albany.

Felipe, H. de (1990). Leyendas árabes sobre el origen de los beréberes. *Al-Qanṭara* 11:379–96.

Fernández y González, F. (1886). Ordenamiento formado por los procurados de las aljamas hebreas, pertenecientes al territorio de los Estados de Castilla, en la Asamblea celebrada en Valladolid el año 1432. Apéndice. *BRAH* 8:15–21.

Fernández Nieva, J. (1990). L'Inquisition de Llerena. *MI*, 258–75.

Finkel, A. Y. (1990). *The Responsa anthology.* Northvale, NJ and London.

Fitz, J. (1972). *Les Syriens à Intercisa.* Brussels.

Foulché-Delbosc, R. (1894a). Le testament d'un Juif d'Alba de Tormes en 1410. *RH* 1:197–99.

———(1894b). Une poésie inédite de Rodrigo Cota. *RH* 1:69–72.

Fraenkel, S. (1886). *Die aramäische Lehnwörter im Arabischen.* Leiden; Hildesheim 1962, 2nd edition.

Freehof, S. B. (1962). Home rituals and the Spanish synagogues. *SEHAAN*, 215–27.

Freire, L. (1939–44). *Grande e novíssimo dicionário da língua portugesa* 1–5. Rio de Janeiro.

Frey, J. B. (1975). *Corpus inscriptionum iudaicarum* 1–2. New York; originally Città del Vaticano 1936–52.

Freytag, G. W. (1830). *Lexicon arabico-latinum* 1. Halle.

Fück, J. (1955). *'Arabiya. Recherches sur l'histoire de la langue et du style arabe.* Paris.

Gaden, H. (1909). *Essai de grammaire de la langue baguirmienne.* Paris.

Gais, N. E. (1970). Aperçu sur la population musulmane de Majorque au XIVe siècle. *Revue d'histoire et de civilisation du Maghreb* 9:19–30.

Galand-Pernet, P. and H. Zafrani (1970). *Une version berbère de la Haggadah de Pesah. Texte de Tinrhir du Todrha (Maroc)* 1–2. Paris.

Galante, A. (1902). Proverbes judéo-espagnols. *RH* 9:440–54.

Gallego y Burín, A. and A. Gámir Sandoval (1968). *Los moriscos del Reino de Granada según el Sínodo de Guadix de 1554.* Granada.

Galmés de Fuentes, Á. (1955–56). Influencias sintácticas y estilísticas del árabe en la prosa medieval castellana. *BRAE* 35:213–75, 415–51; 36:65–131, 255–307.

———(1977). El dialecto mozárabe de Toledo. *AA* 42:183–206; 249–99.

———(1981). Lengua y estilo en la literatura aljamiado-morisca. *NRFH* 30:420–40.

———(1983). *Dialectología mozárabe*. Madrid.

Gampel, B. R. (1992). Jews, Christians, and Muslims in Medieval Iberia. *CJMCMS*, 11–37.

Garbell, I. (1954). The pronunciation of Hebrew in medieval Spain. *HMV* 1:647–96.

García-Arenal, M. (1978). *Inquisición y moriscos. Los procesos del Tribunal de Cuenca*. Madrid.

———(1987). Les bildiyyīn de Fès, un groupe de néo-musulmans d'origine juive. *SI* 66:113–43.

García de Diego, V. (1921). Review of W. von Wartburg, *Zur Benennung des Schafes in den romanischen Sprachen*. . . Berlin 1918. *RFE* 8:407–12.

García Gomez, E. (1977). Prólogo. In Corriente 1977: ix–xvi.

García-Lomas, G. A. (1922). *Estudio del dialecto popular montañes: fonética, etimologías y glosario de voces*. San Sabastian; revised Santander 1949.

Garrad, K. (1960). La Inquisición y los moriscos granadinos (1526–1580). *MEAH* 9(1):55–73.

Garulo Muñoz, T. (1983). Aragonesismos de origen árabe en Andalucía. *Archivo de filología aragonesa* 30–31:143–71.

Gerson-Kiwi, E. (1981). Die Musik der jüdischen Volksstämme. *Begegnungen mit dem Judentum*. B. Rübenach (ed.), 155–66. Berlin.

Gil, M. (1974). The Rādhānite merchants and the land of Rādhān. *JESHO* 17:299–328.

———(1984). The origin of the Jews of Yathrib. *JSAI* 4:203–24.

Gilbert, G. G. (ed. and translator) (1980). *Pidgin and Creole languages. Selected essays by Hugo Schuchardt*. Cambridge.

Ginio, A. M. (1993). Self-perception and images of the Judeo-Conversos in fifteenth-century Spain and Portugal. *Tel-Aviver Jahrbuch für deutsche Geschichte* 22:127–52.

Gitlitz, D. (1990–93). The book called Alboraique. *MedLR* 6–7:121–43.

Glick, T. F. (1978). The ethnic systems of premodern Spain. *Comparative studies in sociology* 1:157–71.

———(1979). *Islamic and Christian Spain in the early Middle Ages*. Princeton.

Godbey, A. H. (1930). *The lost tribes, a myth. Suggestions towards rewriting Hebrew history.* Durham, SC.
Goitein, S. D. (1931). Hayesodot haivri'im bisfat hadibur šel yehude teman. *Lešonenu* 3:356–80; reprinted in his *Hatemanim—historya, sidre xevra, xaye haruax*, 269–87. Jerusalem 1983.
———(1934). *Jemenica. Sprichwörter und Redensarten aus Zentral-Jemen.* Leipzig; Leiden 1970, 2nd edition.
———(1954). New documents from the Cairo geniza. *HMV* 1:707–20.
———(1960). The language of Al-Gadès: the main characteristics of an Arabic dialect spoken in Lower Yemen. *Le muséon* 73:351–94.
———(1961). Anbol—bima šel bet-kneset. *Erec yisrael* 6:162–67.
———(1962). Slaves and slavegirls in the Cairo Geniza records. *Arabica* 9:1–20.
———(1967–88). *A Mediterranean society* 1–5. Berkeley, Los Angeles, and London.
———(1969). The Jews of Yemen. *Religion in the Middle East.* A. J. Arberry (ed.) 1:226–35. Cambridge.
———(1974). Judaeo-Arabic letters from Spain (early twelfth century). *Orientalia hispanica. Sive studia F. M. Pareja octogenario dicata.* J. M. Barral (ed.), 1:331–50. Leiden.
Golb, N. (1965). The topography of the Jews of medieval Egypt. *Journal of Near Eastern studies* 24:251–70.
——— and O. Pritsak (1982). *Khazarian Hebrew documents of the tenth century.* Ithaca and London.
Goldberg, H. E. (1972). The social context of North African Jewish patronyms. *FRCS* 3:245–57.
———(1983). Language and culture of the Jews of Tripolitania: a preliminary view. *MedLR* 1:85–102.
———(1990). *Jewish life in Muslim Libya. Rivals and relatives.* Chicago and London.
González Llubera, I. (1929). Notas sobre la literatura hispano-judaica. *Bulletin of Spanish studies* 6:4–9.
———(ed.) (1935). *Coplas de Yoçef: A medieval Spanish poem in Hebrew characters.* Cambridge.
———(1940). The text and language of Santob de Carrión's Proverbios morales. *HR* 8:113–24.
———(1947). *Santob de Carrión: Proverbios morales.* Cambridge.
González Palencia, A. (1926–30). *Los Mozárabes de Toledo en los siglos XII y XIII* 1–4. Madrid.

González Raymond, A. (1989). Les esclaves maures et l'Inquisition dans les îles espagnoles de la Méditerranée (1550–1700). *RHM* 53-54: 101-22.

Gonzalo Maeso, D. (1960). *Manual de historia de la literatura hebrea*. Madrid.

Gottheil, R. J. H. (1907). An eleventh-century document concerning a Cairo synagogue. *JQR* 19:467-539.

Gottstein, M. (1952). Midarxe hatirgum vehametargemim bime habenaim. *Tarbic* 23:210–16.

Granda, G. de (1988). Datos antroponímicos sobre negros esclavos musulmanes en Nueva Granada. In his *Lingüística e historia. Temas afro-hispánicas*, 105–15. Valladolid.

Granja, F. de la (1969–70). Fiestas cristianas en al-Andalus. *AA* 34:1-53; 35:119-42.

Grayzel, S. (1933). *The Church and the Jews in the XIIIth century.* Philadelphia; revised, New York 1966, 2nd edition.

Greenfield, J. C. (1974). *rtyn mgwš*? *Joshua Finkel Festschrift*. S. B. Hoenig and L. D. Stitskin (eds.), 63–69. New York.

Greenleaf, R. E. (1969). *The Mexican Inquisition of the sixteenth century.* Albuquerque, NM.

Griffin, D. A. (1958–60). Los mozarabismos del "Vocabulista" atribuido a Ramón Martí. *AA* 23:251-337; 25:92-154.

Grossmann, M. (1968). Observaciones sobre los arabismos con la aglutinación del artículo árabe *al-*. *Revue roumaine de linguistique* 13:143-45.

Guershon, I. (1993). Tétouan. Une communauté hispanique parmi les Judéo-Espagnols du Moyen-Orient. *Los muestros* 13:19-20.

Guevara, A. de (1541). Constituciones sinodales. Ms 3/13282, Biblioteca Nacional, Madrid.

Guggenheim-Grünberg, F. (1954). The horse dealers' language of the Swiss Jews in Endingen and Lengnau. *The field of Yiddish*. U. Weinreich (ed.), 48-62. New York.

Guichard, P. (1985). Les Mozarabes de Valence et d'Al-Andalus entre l'histoire et le mythe. *ROMM* 40:17-27.

Gutmann, J. (1929). Babylonien in nachbiblischer Zeit. *EJ* 3:columns 890-905.

Gutwirth, E. (1980). Fragmentos de siddurim españoles de la Genizah. *Sefarad* 40:389–401.

———(1985a). Elementos étnicos e históricos en las relaciones judeo-conversas en Segovia. *JCSSI*, 83–102.

———(1985b). On the background to Cota's Epitalamio burlesco. *Romanische Forschungen* 97:1–14.

———(1986). On the hispanicity of Sephardi Jewry. *REJ* 145:347–57.

———(1988). Religión, historia y las Biblias romanceadas. *Revista catalana de teología* 13:115–34.

———(1989a). A medieval Spanish translation of Avot: Genizah fragments. *AIUO* 49:289–300.

———(1989b). Hispano-Jewish attitudes to the Moors in the fifteenth century. *Sefarad* 49:237–62.

———(1992). A medieval manuscript of gnomic verse in Judeo-Spanish aljamía. *Circa*, 98–108.

Haedo, D. de (1612). *Topografía e historia general de Árgel*. Valladolid; reprinted Madrid 1:1927.

Ha-Lapíd, o facho (1927–58). Porto.

Haliczer, S. (1990). *Inquisition and society in the kingdom of Valencia, 1478–1834*. Berkeley, Los Angeles, and London.

Halm, H. (1989). Al-Andalus und Gothica Sors. *Der Islam* 66:252–63.

Halper, B. (1921). *Post-Biblical Hebrew literature. An anthology.* Philadelphia.

Hamet, I. (1928). *Les Juifs du Nord de l'Afrique. (Noms et prénoms)*. Paris.

Handler, A. (1974). *The Zirids of Granada*. Coral Gables, FL.

Harnack, A. (1903). *History of dogma* 5. Boston.

Harvey, L. P. (1960). *Amaḥo, dešamaḥo, maḥo, amaḥar. . .*: A family of words common to the Spanish of the Jews and Moriscos. *BHS* 37:69–74.

———(1964). Crypto-Islam in sixteenth-century Spain. *Primer Congreso de Estudios Árabes e Islámicos, Córdoba 1962. Actas*, 163–78. Madrid.

———(1981). Leyenda morisca de Ibrahim. *NRFH* 30:1–20.

Haxen, U. (1980). A Hebrew *muwaššaḥa* and its "bilingual" *ḫarǧa*. *Sefarad* 40:65–75.

Hazaël-Massieux, G. (1993). The African filter in the genesis of Guadeloupean Creole: at the confluence of genetics and typology. *AAALV*, 109–22.

Heath, J. and M. Bar-Asher (1982). A Judeo-Arabic dialect of Tafilalt (southeastern Morocco). *Zeitschrift für arabische Linguistik* 9:32–78.

Hefele, C. J. von (1907). *Histoire des conciles* 1. Paris; Hildesheim and New York 1973.

Hegyi, O. (1978). Observaciones sobre el léxico árabe en los textos aljamiados. *AA* 43:303–21.

Heller, B. (1927). Yoûscha' Al-Akbar et les Juifs de Kheybar dans le roman d'Antar. *REJ* 84:113–37.

Hernández, F. (1992). The secret Jews of the Southwest. *AJA* 44:411–54.

Herrero Carretero, C. (1992). [Notes to the pillow cover of María de Almenar.] *AAAIS*, 322–23.

Hilty, G. (1955). El *Libro conplido en los iudizios de las estrellas*. *AA* 20:1–74.

Hinojosa Montalvo, J. (1978). Sinagogas valencianas (1383–1492). *Sefarad* 38:293–307.

Hiršberg, H. Z. [Hirschberg] (1963). The problem of the Judaized Berbers. *Journal of African history* 4:313–39.

———(1965). *Toldot hayehudim beafrika hacfonit* 1–2. Jerusalem; translated as *A history of the Jews in North Africa* 1–2. Leiden 1974–82.

———(1975). Al haktuvot hayehudiot hexadašot šenitgalu beteman. *Tarbic* 44:151–58.

Hitchcock, R. (1981). ¿Quiénes fueron los verdaderos mozárabes? Una contribución a la historia del mozarabismo. *NRFH* 30:574–85.

Hitti, P. K. (1951). *History of the Arabs from the earliest times to the present*. New York, 5th edition.

Hoenerbach, W. (1965). *Spanisch-islamische Urkunden aus der Zeit der Nasriden und Moriscos*. Bonn.

Holod, R. (1992). [Notes to the Pamplona casket.] *AAAIS*, 198–201.

Hopkins, S. (1984). *Studies in the grammar of early Arabic*. Oxford.

Horovitz, E. (1994). Al mašmauyot hazakan bikhilot yisrael. *Peamim* 59:124–48.

Horvath, J. and P. Wexler (1994). Unspoken languages and the issue of genetic classification: the case of Hebrew. *Linguistics* 32(2): 241–69.

———[ms.] Relexification in creole and non-creole languages: prolegomena to a research program.

Huarte Morton, F. (1951). Un vocabulario castellano del siglo XV. *RFE* 35:310–40.

Hunwick, J. O. (1985). Al-Maghîlî and the Jews of Tuwât: the demise of a community. *SI* 61:155–83.

Ibn Buklariš (c.1106). *Al-musta'īnī*.

Ibn Pakuda, B. (1569). *Sefer xovat halvavot bela'az*. Saloniki. (Judeo-Spanish translation from Judeo-Arabic by S. ben Yosef Formón.)

Ibn Verga, Š. (1550). *Ševet yehuda*. Edirne; reprinted and edited by M. Wiener, Hannover 1856.

Ibn Xaldun, 'Abd-ar-Raḥman [ibn Khaldun] (14th century). *Histoire des Berbères et des dynasties musulmanes de l'Afrique septentrionale* 1–2. Baron de Slane (ed.). Algiers 1852.

Ibn Xordadhbeh, Abu l-Qasim 'Obaydallah ibn 'Abdallah [ibn Khordadh-beh] (10th century). *Kitāb al-masālik wa'l-mamālik*. M. J. de Goeje (ed.), 6. Leiden 1889.

Idelsohn, A. Z. (1913). Die gegenwärtige Aussprache des Hebräischen bei Juden und Samaritanern. *MGWJ* 57:527–45.

———(1923). *Gesänge der orientalischen Sefardim* 4. Jerusalem, Berlin, and Warsaw.

Idris, H. R. (1962). *La Berbérie orientale sous les Zīrīdes. Xe–XIIe siècles* 1–2. Paris.

———(1974). Les tributaires en occident musulman médiéval d'après le "Mi'yār" d'al Wanšarīšī. *MIAA* 1:172–96.

Illescas, G. de (1578). *Historia pontifical y catholica*. . . . Burgos.

Imamuddin, S. M. (1981). *Muslim Spain 711–1492 A.D. A sociological study*. Leiden.

Jiménez Lozano, J. (1984). Supervivencia de cultemas islamo-hebraicos en la sociedad española o el fracaso histórico de la Inquisición. *Inquisición española y mentalidad inquisitorial*. A. Alcalá et al. (eds.), 353–70. Barcelona.

Johnson, P. (1987). *A history of the Jews*. New York.

Kahane, H. and R. (1964). Christian and un-Christian etymologies. *Harvard theological review* 57:23–38.

Kampffmeyer, G. (1899). Materialien zum Studium der arabischen Beduinendialekte Innerafrikas. *Mitteilungen des Seminars für orientalische Sprachen* 2/2:143–221.

———(1900). Beiträge zur Dialektologie des Arabischen 3. Südarabisches. *ZDMG* 54:621–60.

Kaplan, Y. (1985). The travels of Portuguese Jews from Amsterdam to the "Lands of idolatry" (1644–1724). *JCSSI*, 197–224.

———(1992). The Jewish profile of the Spanish-Portuguese community of London during the seventeenth century. *Judaism* 41:229–40.

Karo, J. (1565). *Šulxan arux*. Venice.

———(1568). *Šulxan hapanim, livro lyamado en ladino meza de el alma.* Saloniki. (Anonymous Judeo-Spanish translation.)

Kassis, H. E. (1990). Muslim revival in the fifth/eleventh century. *Der Islam* 67:78–110.

Katz, I. J. (1973). The "myth" of the Sephardic legacy from Spain. *Proceedings of the 5th World Congress of Jewish Studies (1969)* 4:237–43. Jerusalem.

Katz, K. (1968). Jewish tradition in art. In K. Katz, P. P. Kahane and M. Broshi (eds.), *From the beginning. Archaeology and art in the Israel Museum, Jerusalem*, 148–215. New York.

Katz, M. (1950). *Sefer igeret rabi yehuda ibn kureyš*. Tel-Aviv.

Katz, S. (1937). *The Jews in the Visigothic and Frankish kingdoms of Spain and Gaul*. Cambridge, MA; New York 1970.

Kaye, A. S. (1986). The verb 'see' in Arabic dialects. *The Fergusonian Impact. In Honor of Charles A. Ferguson on the occasion of his 65th birthday.* J. A. Fishman et al. (eds.), 1:211–21. Berlin, New York, and Amsterdam.

Kayserling, M. (1861). *Die Juden in Navarra, den Baskenländern und den Balearen*. Berlin.

———(1898). Notes sur l'histoire de l'Inquisition et des judaïsants d'Espagne. *REJ* 37:266–73.

Kedar, B. Z. (1973). Toponymic surnames as evidence of origin: some medieval views. *Viator* 4:123–29.

Kedourie, E. (1979). *The Jewish world. History and culture of the Jewish people*. New York.

Keightley, R. G. (1964). Spanish studies. *The year's work in modern language studies* 26:189–246.

Kister, M. (1989). Appendix. *JSAI* 12:354–71.

Kister, M. J. (1989). "Do not assimilate yourselves. . ." *Lā tashabbahū*." *JSAI* 12:321–53.

——— and M. Kister (1979). Al yehude arav—hearot. *Tarbic* 48:231–43.

Kjamilev, S. X. (1965). O nekotoryx morfologičeskix osobennostjax sovremennogo marokkanskogo dialekta. *Semitskie jazyki* 2/2:500–512. Moscow.

———(1968). *Marokkanskij dialekt arabskogo jazyka*. Moscow.

Kohring, H. (1991). Judenspanisch in hebräischer Schrift. *NR*, 95–170.

Kontzi, R. (1974). *Aljamiadotexte* 1-2. Wiesbaden.

———(1985). Observaciones acerca del fragmento 41.1 de la Biblioteca de la Junta.—Allah: *guāldahu/ bīlehi. Homenaje a Álvaro Galmés de Fuentes* 2:529–45. Oviedo and Madrid.

Kosover, M. (1954). Ashkenazim and Sephardim in Palestine. (A study in intercommunal relations.) *HMV* 1:753–88.

Kraabel, A. T. (1979). The Diaspora synagogue: archaeological and epigraphic evidence since Sukenik. *Aufstieg und Niedergang der römischen Welt*. W. Haase (ed.), 2, 19/1:477–510. Berlin and New York.

Kraemer, J. L. (1991). Spanish ladies from the Cairo Genizah. *MHR* 6:237–67.

Krauss, S. (1922). *Synagogale Altertümer*. Berlin and Vienna.

———[Kroys, Š.] (1932). Hašemot aškenaz usfarad. *Tarbic* 3:423–35.

———(1935). Die hebräischen Benennungen der modernen Völker. *Jewish studies in memory of George A. Kohut*. S. Baron and A. Marx (eds.), 379–412. New York.

Krautheimer, R. (1927). *Mittelalterliche Synagogen*. Berlin.

Krüger, R. (1968). *Die Kunst der Synagoge. Eine Einführung in die Probleme von Kunst und Kult des Judentums*. Leipzig.

Kuli, J. (1730ff). *Meam loez* 1. Istanbul. (Posthumous volumes, as well as volumes continued by other authors, appeared throughout the 18th and 19th centuries; a Latin transliteration of the first volume appeared in Granada 1964.)

Kunchev, I. (1977). A basket of lyrical Judeo-Spanish songs from Sofia. *Annual of the Social, Cultural, and Educational Association of the Jews in the People's Republic of Bulgaria* 12:147–69.

———[Kənčev] (1979). Za edna ispano-evrejska (špan'olska) zaemka v smoljanskija (srednorodopski) govor. *Bəlgarski ezik* 29(1):66–67.

Künzl, H. (1988a). Der Synagogenbau im Mittelalter. *AS*, 61–87, 424.

———(1988b). Europäischer Synagogenbau vom 16. bis zum 18. Jahrhundert. *AS*, 89–114, 425.

Kupfer, F. and T. Lewicki (1956). *Źródła hebrajskie do dziejów słowian i niektórych innych ludów środkowej i wschodniej Europy*. Wrocław and Warsaw.

Labib, G. (1967). Spanische Lautentwicklung und arabisch-islamischer Geist in einem Aljamiado-Manuskript des 16. Jahrhunderts. *VR* 26:37–109.

Lagarta, A. and M. García Arenal (1981). Algunos fragmentos aljamiados del proceso inquisitorial contra Yuçe de la Vaçía, alfaquí de la Villa de Molina (1495). *NRFH* 30:127–42.

Landberg, Comte de (1906). *Etudes sur les dialectes de l'arabe méridionale* 1. Leiden.

Lane, E. W. (1863–93). *An Arabic-English lexicon* 1–8. London; Beirut 1968, 2nd edition.

Laoust, E. (1921). Noms et cérémonies des feux de joie chez les Berbères du haut et de l'anti-Atlas. *Hespéris* 1:253–316.

Lapesa, R. (1965). *Historia de la lengua española*. Madrid, 6th edition.

Laredo, A. I. (1944). "Sefarad" en la literatura hebraica. *Sefarad* 4: 349–58.

———(1954). *Beréberes y hebreos en Marruecos: sus origenes según las leyendas, tradiciones y fuentes hebraicas antiguas*. Madrid.

———(1978). *Les noms des Juifs du Maroc. Essai d'onomastique judéo-marocaine*. Madrid.

Larrea Palacín, A. de (1954). *Cancionero judío del norte de Marruecos* 3. Madrid.

Lasker, J. (1990). Proselyte Judaism, Christianity, and Islam in the thought of Judah Halevi. *JQR* 81:75–91.

Lazar, M. (1972). *The Sephardic tradition*. New York.

Lea, H. C. (1906). *The history of the Inquisition* 1. New York.

Lebedev, V. V. (1977). *Pozdnij srednearabskij jazyk*. Moscow.

Lefebvre, C. (1993). The role of relexification and syntactic reanalysis in Haitian creole: methodological aspects of a research program. *AAALV*, 254–79.

Leibovici, S. (1986). Noces séfarades. Quelques rites. *REJ* 145:227–41.

Lenormant, F. (1882). La catacombe juive de Venosa. *REJ* 6:200–207.

León Tello, P. (1979). *Judíos de Toledo* 1. Madrid.

Leroy, B. (1985). *Une famille sépharade à travers les siècles: Les Menir (XIIe–XXe siècles)*. Paris.

Lešem, X. (1972). *'vn—'yvn. Sinay* 423–24:57–78.

Leslau, W. (1945a). Hebrew elements in the Judaeo-Arabic dialect of Fez. *JQR* 36:61–78.

———(1945b). Yidiš-arabiše dialektn. *YIVO-bleter* 26:58–78.

———(1957). *Coutumes et croyances des Falachas (Juifs d'Abyssinie)*. Paris.

———(1979). *Etymological dictionary of Gurage (Ethiopic)* 3. Wiesbaden.

Lévi, I. (1900). Notes et extraits divers. *REJ* 41:300.

Lévi-Provençal, E. (1950–67). *Histoire de l'Espagne musulmane* 1–3. Paris and Leiden.

Levine Melammed, R. (1991). Some death and mourning customs of Castilian *conversos*. *Exilio y diáspora*, A. Mirsky, et al. (eds.), 157–67. Jerusalem.

———(1992). Women in (post-1492) Spanish crypto-Jewish society. *Judaism* 41:156–68.

Levtzion, N. (1982). The Jews of Sijilmasa and the Saharan trade. *CJMSM*, 253–63.

Levy, R. (1942). El castellano < <joroba> > y el judeofrancés < <haldrobe> >. *Anales del Instituto de Lingüística (Universidad Nacional de Cuyo, Mendoza)* 2:155–59.

———(1960). *Contributions à la lexicographie française selon d'anciens textes d'origine juive.* Syracuse.

Lewicki, T. (1951–52). Une langue romane oubliée de l'Afrique du Nord. Observations d'un arabisant. *Rocznik orientalistyczny* 17:415–80.

———(1958). Źródła arabskie i hebrajskie do dziejów Słowian w okresie wczesnego średniowiecza. *Studia źródłoznawcze* 3:61–100.

———(1964a). Handel niewolnikami słowianskimi w krajach arabskich. *SSS* 3:190–92.

———(1964b). Hiszpania. Słowianie w Hiszpanii. *SSS* 3:217–18.

———(1966). Survivances chez les Berbères médiévaux d'ère musulman de cultes anciens et de croyances païennes. *FO* 8:1–40.

———(1967). Prophètes antimusulmans chez les Berbères médiévaux. *Boletín de la Asociación Española de Orientalistas* 3:143–49.

———(1969). *Źródła arabskie do dziejów słowiańszczyzny* 2/1. Wrocław, Warsaw, and Kraków.

———(1974). Les noms propres berbères employés chez les Nafūsa médiévaux (VIIIe–XVIe siècle). *FO* 15:7–21.

Lewis, B. (1984). *The Jews of Islam.* Princeton.

Lewy, H. (1930). Zum Dämonenglauben. *Archiv für Religionswissenschaft* 28:241–52.

———(1931). Kleine Beiträge zu Bibel und Volkskunde. *MGWJ* 75:19–29.

Lida de Malkiel, M. R. (1962). Review of F. J. E. Raby, *The Oxford book of medieval Latin verse*, Oxford 1959. *RP* 16:96–102.

Liebman, S. B. (1964). *A guide to Jewish references in the Mexican colonial era 1521–1821.* Philadelphia.

———(1971). *Los judíos en México y América Central (fe, llamas e Inquisición).* Mexico.

———(1974). *The Inquisitors and the Jews in the New World: summaries of processes, 1500–1810 and bibliographical guide.* Coral Gables, FL.

Lifshitz, B. (1967). *Donateurs et fondateurs dans les synagogues juives.* Paris.

Lincoln, J. N. (1945). Aljamiado texts: legal and religious. *HR* 13:102–24.
Livshits, G., R. R. Sokal and E. Kobyliansky (1991). Genetic affinities of Jewish populations. *American journal of human genetics* 49: 131–46.
Llorente Maldonado de Guevara, A. (1963–64). La toponomia árabe, mozárabe y morisca de la provincia de Salamanca. *MEAH* 12–13(1): 89–112.
Loeb, I. (1884). Un convoi d'exilés d'Espagne à Marseille en 1492. *REJ* 9:66–76.
———(1885). Notes sur l'histoire des Juifs. *REJ* 10:232–50.
———(1886). Règlement des juifs de Castille en 1432. *REJ* 13:187–216.
———(1888). Les négociants juifs à Marseille au milieu du XIIIe siècle. *REJ* 16:73–83.
———(1889). Polémistes chrétiens et juifs en France et en Espagne. *REJ* 18:219–42.
Lokotsch, K. (1927). *Etymologisches Wörterbuch der europäischen (germanischen, romanischen und slavischen) Wörter orientalischen Ursprungs*. Heidelberg.
Longás Bartibas, P. (1915). *Vida religiosa de los moriscos*. Madrid; reprinted Granada 1990.
López Álvarez, A. M. (1979). Nuevas noticias sobre el cementerio judío de Toledo. *Sefarad* 39:120–22.
———(1992). Capital. *CJMCMS*, 215–16.
López Baralt, L. (1980). Chronique de la destruction d'un monde: la littérature aljamiado-morisque. *RHM* 17–18:43–73.
López Mata, T. (1951). Morería y judería. *BRAH* 129:335–84.
Loupias, B. (1965). La pratique secrète de l'Islam dans les évêchés de Cuenca et de Sigüenza aux XVIe et XVIIe siècles. *Hespéris Tamuda* 6:115–31.
Löwe, H. (1988). Die Apostasie des Pfalzdiakons Bodo (838) und das Judentum der Chasaren. Person und Gemeinschaft im Mittelalter. *Karl Schmid zum fünfundsechzigsten*. G. Althof et al. (eds.), 157–69. Sigmaringen.
Lowenthal, D. (1985). *The past is a foreign country*. Cambridge.
Lüdtke, H. (1968). El beréber y la lingüística románica. *XI Congreso Internacional de Lingüística y Filología Románicas. Actas* 2:467–71. Madrid.
Luis Lacave, J. (1970–71). Pleito judío por una herencia en aragonés y caracteres hebreos. *Sefarad* 30:325–37; 31:49–101.

———(1975). La carnicería de la aljama zaragozana a fines del s. XV. *Sefarad* 35:3–35.

———(1985). Nueva identificación de sinagogas en España. *JCSSI*, 9–20.

Lunski, X. (1924). Iserlins yidiš. *Yidiše filologye* 1:288–97.

Luria, M. A. (1930). *A study of the Monastir dialect of Judeo-Spanish based on oral material collected in Monastir, Yugo-Slavia*. New York; reprinted from *RH* 79 (1930), 323–583.

Macdonald, G. J. (1964). *Hamihala*. A hapax in the Auto de los Reyes Magos. *RP* 18:35–36.

Mackay, A. (1992). A lost generation: Francisco Delicado, Fernando del Pulgar and the conversas of Andalusia. *Circa*, 224–35.

Madariaga, S. de (1946). *Spain and the Jews*. London.

Maíllo Salgado, F. (1983). *Los arabismos del castellano en la baja edad media. (Consideraciones históricas y filológicas)*. Madrid.

Mainz, E. (1949). Quelques poésies judéo-arabes du manuscrit 411 de la Bibliothèque du Vatican. *JA* 237:51–83.

Maler, B. (1966). Duas notulas vicentinas. *Ibero-Romanskt 1966*. n.p.

Malka, E. (1946). *Essai d'ethnographie traditionelle des mellahs*. Rabat.

Malkiel, Y. (1945). *Development of the Latin suffixes -antia and -entia in the Romance languages, with special regard to Ibero-Romance. (University of California Papers in Linguistics* I.4.) Berkeley and Los Angeles.

———(1946). Antiguo judeo-aragonés *aladma, alalma* 'excomunión'. *RFH* 8:136–41.

———(1947). A Latin-Hebrew blend: Hispanic *desmazalado. HR* 15:272–301.

———(1948). Hispano-Arabic *marrano* and its Hispano-Latin homophone. *JAOS* 68:175–84.

———(1955). Review of M. L. Wagner 1953. *RP* 9:50–68.

———(1958). Old Spanish *judezno, morezno, pecadezno. Philological quarterly* 37:95–99.

———(1983). Las peripecias luso-españolas de la voz *synagoga*. *NRFH* 32:1–40.

———(1992). The designations of Jews in the Luso-Hispanic tradition. *Circa*, 11–35.

Manessy, G. (1983). Bantou et Créole: l'agglutination de l'article français. *Afrique et langage* 20:17–28.

Mann, J. (1916–19). The responsa of the Babylonian Geonim as a source of Jewish history. *JQR* 7 (1916–17):457–90, 8 (1917–18):339–66, 9 (1918–19):139–79.

———(1935). *Texts and studies in Jewish history and literature* 1–2. Philadelphia; New York 1972, 2nd edition.

Mann, V. B. [ms a.] Jewish-Muslim acculturation in the Ottoman Empire: the evidence of ceremonial art.

———[ms b.] Muslim prayer rugs in Ottoman synagogues: the evidence of extant works and the Responsa literature.

Marçais, W. (1902). *Le dialecte arabe parlé à Tlemcen, grammaire, textes et glossaire*. Paris.

———(1906a). Le dialecte arabe chez Ulâd Bṛahîm de Saïda (département d'Oran). *Mémoires de la Société de Linguistique de Paris* 14, fascicule 2, 97–164, 416–72, 481–500.

———(1906b). L'euphémisme et l'antiphrase dans les dialectes arabes d'Algérie. *OS*, 1:425–38.

———(1911). *Textes arabes de Tanger.* Paris.

———(1913). [xnqṭira—xlqṭira = xaraktēr.] *JA* 11th series 1:201–203.

Marcus, Š. (1965). *Hasafa hasfaradit-hayehudit.* Jerusalem.

Marcy, G. (1936). Le Dieu des Abâdites et les Barġwâṭa. *Hespéris* 22:33–56.

Mármol Carvajal, L. del (1573). *Descripción general de África* 1–2. Granada; Madrid 1953.

Marmorstein, A. (1927). David ben Jehuda Hasid. *MGWJ* 71:29–48.

Márquez Villaneuva, F. [n.d.] El problema de los conversos: cuatro puntos cardinales. *HJ* 1:51–75.

Martí, R. (13th century). *Vocabulista in arabico.* Florence 1871.

Martínez Ruiz, J. (1957). *F-, H*-aspirada y *h*-muda en el judeo-español de Alcazarquivir. *Tamuda* 5:150–61.

———(1960). Morfología del judeoespañol de Alcazarquivir. *Miscelánea filológica dedicada a Mons. A. Griera* 2:105–28. Barcelona.

———(1963). Textos judeo-españoles de Alcazarquivir (Marruecos) (1948–1951). *RDTP* 19:78–115.

———(1966). Arabismos en el judeo-español de Alcazarquivir (Marruecos) 1948–51. *RFE* 49:39–71.

———(1976). Latinidad norteafricana contingente a la hispánica. *Atti. XIV Congresso internazionale di linguistica e filologia romanza* 2: 51–60.

———(1980). Descendientes romances de "vervex" en el judeoespañol de Marruecos. *MEAH* 29(2):81–85.

———(1982). Lenguas en contacto: judeoespañol y árabe marroquí. Interferencias léxicas, fonéticas y sintácticas. *Actas del Cuarto Congreso International de Hispanistas.* E. de Bustos Tovar (ed.) 2:237–49. Salamanca.

———(1985). Ensalmos curativos del manuscrito árabe "Misceláneo de Salomon" de Ocaña (Toledo) en el marco juridico de convivencia de las tres culturas. *CIETC* 2:217–27.

Mattoso Camara, J., Jr. (1972). *The Portuguese language.* Chicago and London.

Meged, A. and H. E. Goldberg (1986). Rav sa'adya adati. Sipuro šel cadik vexavayato haxevratit bešule hare harif šebemaroko hasfaradit. *Mexkare yerušalaim befolklor yehudi* 9:89–103.

Melvinger, A. (1955). *Les premières incursions des Vikings en Occident d'après les sources arabes.* Uppsala.

Mendes dos Remédios, J. (1911). *Os Judeus em Amsterdam.* Coimbra.

———(1927). Os judeus portugueses através dalguns documentos literários. *Biblos* 3:237–63.

Menéndez Pidal, R. (1929). *Orígenes del español.* Madrid, 2nd edition.

Mercier, G. (1907). Le nom des plantes en dialecte chaouia de l'Aourès. *Actes du XIVe Congrès International des Orientalistes. Algiers 1905* 2:79–92 (section IV). Paris.

Metzger, T. and M. (1982). *Jewish life in the Middle Ages. Illuminated Hebrew manuscripts of the thirteenth to the sixteenth centuries.* Secaucus, NJ.

Meyerhof, M. (1940). *Un glossaire de matière médicale composé par Maïmonide.* (= *Mémoires présentés à l'Institut d'Egypte* 41). Cairo.

Mézan, S. (1925). *Les juifs espagnols en Bulgarie.* Sofia.

Michel, F. (1989). Les Morisques en France. *RHM* 55–56:147–69.

Migne, J.-P. [n.d.] *Patrologiae cursus completus. . . series latina prima.* 88. Turnhout.

Miguel Rodríguez, J. C. de (1989). *La communidad mudéjar de Madrid.* Madrid.

Millar, F. (1968). Local cultures in the Roman Empire: Libyan, Punic, and Latin in Roman Africa. *JRS* 58:126–34.

Millás Vallicrosa, J. M.ª and J. Busquets Mulet (1944). Albaranes mallorquines en aljamiado hebraicoárabe. *Sefarad* 4:275–86.

Minervini, L. (1992). *Testi giudeospagnoli medievali* 1–2. Naples.

Modena, L. de [de Modene] (1683). *Kerk-Zeeden ende gewoonten. Die huiden in gebruik zijn onder de Jooden.* Amsterdam.

Molan, P. D. (1978). Medieval Western Arabic: reconstructing elements of the dialects of al-Andalus, Sicily, and North Africa from the *laḥn al-ʿĀmmah* literature. Unpublished PhD, University of California, Berkeley.

Molho, M. (1950). *Usos y costumbres de los sefardíes de Salónica.* Madrid and Barcelona.

———[ms.] Dictionary of Judeo-Spanish. Housed at the CSIC.

Monceaux, P. (1902a). Les colonies juives dans l'Afrique romaine. *REJ* 44:1–28.

———(1902b). Païens judaïsants. Essai d'explication d'une inscription africaine. *Revue archéologique* series 3 40:208–27.

Monteil, Ch. (1951). Problèmes du Soudan Occidental: Juifs et Judaïsés. *Hespéris* 265–98.

Morag, Š. (1988). *Aramit bimsoret teman: lešon hatalmud habavli. Mevo torat hahege ucurat-hapoal.* Jerusalem.

———(1993). Preface to Bunis 1993, 9–11. Jerusalem.

Morais Silva, A. de (1948). *Grande dicionário da lingua portuguêsa.* Rio de Janeiro.

Moreno Koch, Y. (1977). La comunidad judaizante de Castillo de Garcimuñoz: 1489–1492. *Sefarad* 37:351–71.

———(1978). The Taqqanot of Valladolid of 1432. *AmS* 9:58–145.

Morley, S. G. (1947). A new Jewish-Spanish romancero. *RP* 1:1–9.

Morreale, M. (1961). El glosario de Rabí Mosé Arragel en la "Biblia de Alba." *BHS* 38:145–52.

———(1962). Review of R. Levy 1960. *RFE* 40:345–50.

Moskona, I. [ms.] Judeo-Spanish dictionary. Housed at the CSIC.

Mourant, A. E., A. C. Kopeć and K. Domaniewska-Sobczak (1978). *The genetics of the Jews.* Oxford.

Müller, W. W. (1973). Ergebnisse der Deutschen Jemen-Expedition 1970. *Archiv für Orientforschung* 24:150–61.

Münch, A. (1991). Die hebräisch-aramäische Sprachtradition der Sepharden in ihrem Verhältnis zum Spanischen in Sepharad I sowie zum djudeo-espanyol in Sepharad II und die Rolle des *ladino. NR*, 171–239.

Nahon, M. (1909). Les Israélites du Maroc. *Revue des études ethnographiques et sociologiques* 2 (no. 21–22):258–79.

Narváez, M. T. (1981). Mitificación de Andalucía como "Nueva Israel": el capítulo "Kaída del-Andaluzziyya" del manuscrito aljamiado la Tafçira del Mancebo de Arévalo. *NRFH* 30:143–167.

Naval Más, A. (1980). El arrabal de la judería oscense. *Sefarad* 40:77–97.

Ndayiragije, J. (1989). La source du déterminant agglutiné en créole haïtien. *Canadian journal of linguistics* 34:313–17.

Nehama, J., with the collaboration of J. Cantera (1977). *Dictionnaire du judéo-espagnol*. Madrid.

Nemoy, L. (1974). The attitude of the early Karaites towards Christianity. *SWBJV* 2:697–715.

Netanyahu, B. (1963). The Marranos according to the Hebrew sources of the 15th and early 16th centuries. *AAJRP* 31:81–164.

———(1966). *The Marranos of Spain. From the late 14th to the early 16th century*. New York.

———[n.d.] On the historical meaning of the Hebrew sources related to the Marranos. (A reply to critics.) *HJ* 1:79–102.

Neuman, A. A. (1942). *The Jews in Spain* 1–2. Philadelphia.

Neuvonen, E. K. (1941). *Los arabismos del español en el siglo XIII*. Helsinki.

Newby, G. D. (1971). Observations about an early Judaeo-Arabic. *JQR* n.s. 61:214–21.

———(1988). *A history of the Jews of Arabia. From ancient times to their eclipse under Islam*. Columbia, SC.

Niehoff-Panagiotidis, J. (1994). *Koine und Diglossie*. Wiesbaden.

Nirenberg, D. (1991). A female rabbi in fourteenth century Zaragoza? *Sefarad* 51:179–82.

Novinsky, A. (1972). *Cristãos novos na Bahia*. São Paulo.

Noy, D. (1993). *Jewish inscriptions of Western Europe* 1. *Italy (excluding the city of Rome), Spain, and Gaul*. Cambridge.

Oegema, G. S. (1994). Der Davidsschild als magisches Zeichen von der Antike bis zum Mittelalter. *Aschkenas* 4:13–32.

Olagüe, I. (1969). *Les Arabes n'ont jamais envahi l'Espagne*. Paris.

———(1974). *La revolución islámica en occidente*. Guadarrama.

Oliver-Asín, J. (1973). En torno a los orígenes de Castilla: su toponimia en relación con los árabes y los beréberes. *AA* 38:319–91.

Papo, E. ben Š. T. (1862). *Sefer damesek eliezer* 1. Belgrade.

Parks, R. (1992). "El leñador y los enanitos": a crypto-Jewish version of a Spanish folktale. *RP* 46:13–28.

Partearroyo, C. (1992a). [Notes to the chasuble.] *AAAIS*, 318–19.

———(1992b). [Notes to the textile fragment: the lion strangler.] *AAAIS*, 320.

———(1992c). [Notes to the veil of Hisham II.] *AAAIS*, 225–26.

Parzymies, A. (1979). Noms de personne en Algérie. *FO* 20:107–18.

Patai, R. and J. Patai-Wing (1989). *The myth of the Jewish race*. Detroit.
Peñarroja Torrejón, L. (1990). *El mozárabe de Valencia. Nuevas cuestiones de fonología mozárabe*. Madrid.
Penny, R. (1993). Dialect contact and social networks in Judeo-Spanish. *RP* 46:125–40.
Pérès, H. (1950). L'arabe dialectal en Espagne musulmane aux Xe et XIe siècles de notre ère. *Mélanges offerts à William Marçais*, 289–300. Paris.
———(1953). *La poésie andalouse en arabe classique au onzième siècle*. Paris.
———(1962). Les éléments ethniques de l'Espagne musulmane et arabe au 5e/11e siècle. *EO* 2:717–31.
Perlmann, M. (1948–49). Eleventh-century Andalusian authors on the Jews of Granada. *AAJRP* 18:269–90.
Piamenta, M. (1990–91). *Dictionary of post-Classical Yemeni Arabic* 1–2. Leiden, New York, and Copenhagen.
Pimienta, G. (1991). Espagnol et haketía à travers les chansons judéo-espagnoles du Maroc. *Yod* 33–34:133–39.
Pimienta, J. (1991). Une chronique en haketía. *Yod* 33–34:99–114.
Pires de Lima, J. A. (1940). *Mouros, Judeus e Negros na história de Portugal*. Porto.
Poliakov, L. (1961). *De Mahomet aux marranes*. Paris.
Popkin, R. H. (1992). Jewish Christians and Christian Jews. *Judaism* 41:248–67.
Praag, J. A. van (1940). Dos comedias sefarditas. *Neophilologus* 25: 12–24, 93–101.
Prevosti, A. (1951). Estudio tipológico de los restos humanos hallados en la necrópolis judaica de Montjuich (Barcelona). *Sefarad* 11:75–90.
Pritsak, O. (1981). *The origin of Rus' 1. Old Scandinavian sources other than the sagas*. Cambridge, MA.
R[abin], H. (1971). Dunash ben Labrat. *EJ* 6:columns 270–71.
Redondo, A. (1976). *Antonio de Guevara (1480?–1545) et l'Espagne de son temps*. Geneva.
Régné, J. (1978). *History of the Jews in Aragon. Regesta, and documents 1213–1327*. Jerusalem.
R[einach], T. (1882). Review of E. Renan, *Le judaïsme comme race et comme religion*, lecture of 27.1.1883. *REJ* 6:141–47.
Rivkin, E. (1957). The utilization of non-Jewish sources for the reconstruction of Jewish history. *JQR* 48:183–203.

———[n.d.] How Jewish were the New Christians? *HJ* 1:105–15.
Röllig, W. (1980). Das Punische im Römischen Reich. *SRRK*, 285–99.
Romano, D. (1953). El reparto del subsidio de 1282 entre las aljamas catalanas. *Sefarad* 13:73–86.
———(1956). Los hermanos Abenmenassé al servicio de Pedro el Grande de Aragón. *HMV* 2:243–92.
———(1976). Conversión de judíos al islam. (Corona de Aragón 1280 y 1284.) *Sefarad* 36:333–37.
———(1979). Aljama frente a judería, call y sus sinónimos. *Sefarad* 39:347–54.
———(1988). Arqueología judía en Cataluña. *CIETC* 3:131–36.
Romano, S. (1933). Dictionnaire judéo-espagnol parlé-français-allemand, avec une introduction sur la phonétique et sur la formation des mots dans le judéo-espagnol. Unpublished PhD, University of Zagreb. Housed at the CSIC.
Roselló Bordoy, G. (1989). Almacabras, ritos funerarios y organización social en Al-Andalus. *III Congreso de Arqueología medieval española* 1:153–68. Oviedo.
Rosen-Ayalon, M. (1986). Artistic interaction in late medieval Spain: synagogal decoration. *REI* 54:271–82.
Rosenthal, F. (1980). From the "unorthodox" Judaism of medieval Yemen. *Hommage à Georges Vajda. Etudes d'histoire et de pensée juives*. G. Nahon and G. Touati (eds.), 279–90. Louvain.
Rössler, O. (1962). Die lateinischen Reliktwörter im Berberischen und die Frage des Vokalsystems der afrikanischen Latinität. *Beiträge zur Namenforschung* 13:258–62.
Roth, C. (1931). The religion of the Marranos. *JQR* 22:1–35.
———(1932). *A history of the Marranos*. Philadelphia.
———(1948). The Judaeo-Latin inscription of Mérida. *Sefarad* 8:391–96.
———(1953). Jewish antecedents of Christian art. *Journal of the Warburg and Courtauld Institutes* 16:24–44.
Roth, N. (1976). The Jews and the Muslim conquest of Spain. *Jewish social studies* 38:145–58.
———(1983a). Jewish reactions to the ʿArabiyya and the renaissance of Hebrew in Spain. *JSS* 28:63–84.
———(1983b). Some aspects of Muslim-Jewish relations in Spain. *EHCSA* 179–214.
———(1986). New light on the Jews of Mozarabic Toledo. *AJS Review* 11:189–220.

Saada, L. (1982). Un type d'archive "Les chansons de Geste." *CJMSM*, 25–38.

Sachs, G. (1934). La formación de los gentilicios en español. *RFE* 21:393–99.

Sáenz-Badillos, A. and J. Targarona Borrás (1988). *Diccionario de autores judíos (Sefarad. Siglos X–XV)*. Córdoba.

Sala, M. (1976). Innovaciones del fonetismo judeoespañol. *RDTP* 32:537–49.

Salomon, H. P. (1973). Was there a Spanish translation of Sephardi prayers before 1552? *AmS* 6:79–90.

———(1976). The Captain, the *Abade* and 20th century 'Marranisms' in Portugal. *Arquivos do centro cultural português* 10:631–42.

Salvador, G. (1958–59). El habla de Cúllar-Baza. *RFE* 42:37–89.

Sánchez, M. (1990). Música sefardí: ¿Música castellana? Las tres culturas en la Corona de Castilla y los Sefardíes. *Actas de las Jornadas Sefardíes. . .y del Seminario de las Tres Culturas. . .*, 127–35. Salamanca.

Sánchez Albornoz, C. (1956). *España, un enigma histórico* 1–2. Buenos Aires.

Sánchez Álvarez, M. (1981). Simbiosis árabe-romance en el léxico de los textos aljamiados. *Actas de las Jornadas de Cultura Arabe e Islámica (1978)*, 389–93. Madrid.

Santa Rosa de Viterbo, J. de (1798–99). *Elucidário das palavras, termos e frazes que em Portugal antigamente se usaram e que hoje regularmente se ignoram* 1–2. Lisbon.

Saporta y Beja, E. [ms.] Judeo-Spanish dictionary. Housed at the CSIC.

Schacht, J. (1931). Review of González Palencia 1926–30. *Der Islam* 19:172–77.

Schauss, H. (1938). *The Jewish festivals. From their beginnings to our day.* New York; 1958, 8th edition.

Scheftelowitz, I. (1911). Das Fischsymbol im Judentum und Christentum. *Archiv für Religionswissenschaft* 14:1–53, 321–92.

Scheindlin, R. P. (1992). Hebrew poetry in Medieval Iberia. *CJMCMS*, 39–59.

Schmid, W. (1951). *Der Wortschatz des "Canconiero de Baena."* Berne.

Scholem, G. (1965). Some sources of Jewish-Arabic demonology. *JJS* 16:1–13.

Schreiner, M. (1886). Les juifs dans al-Beruni. *REJ* 12:258–66.

Schuchardt, H. (1908). Berberische Studien II. *WZKM* 22:351–84.

———(1909). Die lingua franca. *ZRP* 33:441–61.

———(1918). *Die romanischen Lehnwörter im Berberischen. (Akademie der Wissenschaften in Wien, Philosophisch-historische Klasse. Sitzungsberichte* 188, section 4.) Vienna.

Schwarzfuchs, S. (1961). Review of Zimmels 1958. *REJ* 119:197–98.

Schwarzwald, O. R. (1993a). Mixed translation pattern: the Ladino translation of Biblical and Mishnaic Hebrew verbs. *Target* 5:71–88.

———(1993b). Morphological aspects in the development of Judeo-Spanish. *Folia linguistica* 27:27–44.

Sed-Rajna, G. (1992). Hebrew illustrated manuscripts from the Iberian Peninsula. *CJMCMS*, 133–55.

Selke, A. S. (1986). *The Conversos of Majorca. Life and death in a crypto-Jewish community in XVII century Spain.* Jerusalem.

Séphiha, H. V. (1973). *Le ladino. Judéo-espagnol calque. Deutéronome. Versions de Constantinople (1547) et de Ferrare (1553). Edition, étude linguistique et lexique.* Paris.

———(1975). Evolution du ladino judéo-calque du XIIIe siècle à nos jours. *REJ* 134:198–201.

———[n.d.] Hispanité du ladino. *HJ* 3:85–100.

Septimus, B. (1982). *Hispano-Jewish culture in transition. The career and controversies of Ramah.* Cambridge, MA and London.

Seroussi, E. (1991). Between the eastern and western Mediterranean: Sephardic music after the Expulsion from Spain and Portugal. *MHR* 6:198–206.

Shinar, P. (1982). Reflexions sur la symbiose judéo-ibaḍite en Afrique du Nord. *CJMSM*, 81–114.

Šifman, I. Š. (1963). *Finikijskij jazyk.* Moscow.

Simon, M. (1946). Le judaïsme berbère en l'Afrique ancienne. *Revue d'histoire et de philosophie religieuses* 26:1–31, 105–45.

Simonet, F. J. (1888). *Glosario de voces ibéricas y latinas usadas entre los mozárabes.* Madrid; Amsterdam 1967.

Simonsohn, S. (1974). The Hebrew revival among early medieval European Jews. *SWBJV* 2:831–58.

Singerman, R. (1975). *The Jews of Spain and Portugal; a bibliography.* New York.

———(1993). *Spanish and Portuguese Jewry. A classified bibliography.* Westport, CT and London.

Sittl, K. (1882). *Die lokalen Verschiedenheiten der lateinischen Sprache mit besonderer Berücksichtigung des afrikanischen Lateins.* Erlangen; Hildesheim 1972, 2nd edition.

Slouschz, N. (1908). *Hébraeo-phéniciens et judéo-berbères*. Paris. (= *Archives marocaines* 14.)

Sobleman, H. and R. S. Harrell (1963). *A dictionary of Moroccan Arabic: English-Moroccan*. Washington.

Solà-Solé, J. M. (1965). El rabí y el alfaqui en la *Dança general de la muerte. RP* 18:272–83; reprinted in his 1983:145–62.

———(1968a). El artículo *al-* en los arabismos del iberorrománico. *RP* 21:275–85; reprinted in his 1983:71–85.

———(1968b). En torno a la *Dança general de la muerte. HR* 36: 303–27; reprinted in his 1983:163–89.

———(1983). *Sobre árabes, judíos y marranos y su impacto en la lengua y literatura española*. Barcelona.

——— and S. E. Rose (1976). Judíos y conversos en la poesía cortesana del siglo XV: el estilo poligloto de fray Diego de Valencia. *HR* 44:371–85; reprinted in Solà-Solé 1983:191–206.

Solin, H. (1980). Juden und Syrer im römischen Reich. *SRRK*, 301–30.

Spiegel, I. (1952). Old Judaeo-Spanish evidence of Old Spanish pronunciation. Unpublished PhD, University of Minnesota, Minneapolis.

Stachowski, S. (1977). *Studien über die arabischen Lehnwörter im Osmanisch-Türkischen* 2. Wrocław, Warsaw, Kraków, and Gdańsk.

Steiger, A. (1932). *Contribución a la fonética del hispano-árabe y de los arabismos en el ibero-románico y el siciliano*. Madrid.

———(1948–49). Aufmarschstrassen des morgenländischen Sprachgutes. *VR* 10:1–62.

———(1956–57). Aragonés antiguo *albedí*. *Archivo de filología aragonesa* 8–9:161–62.

Stern, M. S. (1948). Les vers finaux en espagnol dans les *muwaššaḥs* hispano-hébraïques. Une contribution à l'histoire des *muwaššaḥs* et à l'étude du vieux dialecte espagnol "mozarabe." *AA* 13:299–346; reprinted in English in his *Hispano-Arabic strophic poetry*. L. P. Harvey (ed.), Oxford 1974.

———(1949). The explanation of a difficult verse of Yehuda Halevi and the Spanish etymology of the name Ibn Baron. *JQR* 40:189–91.

Stillman, N. A. (1975). Comments in *Proceedings of the Seminar on Muslim-Jewish relations in North Africa (May 19, 1974, Princeton)*. New York.

———(1979a). Aspects of Jewish life in Islamic Spain. *Aspects of Jewish culture in the Middle Ages*. P. Szarmach (ed.), 65–84. Albany.

———(1979b). *The Jews in Arab lands: a history and source book.* Philadelphia.

———(1981). Some notes on the Judaeo-Arabic dialect of Sefrou (Morocco). *Studies in Judaism and Islam presented to Shelomo Dov Goitein*. S. Morag, et al. (eds), 231–52. Jerusalem.

———(1989). Contacts and boundaries in the domain of language: the case of Sefriwi Judeo-Arabic. *JAACB*, 97–111.

Strohmaier, G. (1979). 'Der Saalefluss, in dem die Bode fällt'—ein Romanismus im Reisebericht des Ibrāhīm ibn Yaʿqūb. *Philologus* 123:149–53.

Subak, J. (1906). Zum Judenspanischen. *ZRP* 30:129–85.

Swoboda, W. (1975). Völkermarkt. *SSS* 5:564–65.

Tabouret-Keller, A. (1969). La motivation des emprunts. Un exemple pris sur le vif de l'apparition d'un sabir. *La linguistique* 1969(1): 25–60.

Tavil, A. C. (1982). Meguraše sfarad bikhilat aram-cova (xalav) bamea hašeš-esre. *Morešet yehude sfarad vehamizrax. Mexkarim*. I. Ben-Ami (ed.), 97–107. Jerusalem.

Taylor, D. (1961). Some Dominican-Creole descendants of the French definite article. *Proceedings of the Conference on Creole Language Studies*. R. B. LePage (ed.), 85–90. London.

Tedjini, A. B. (1923). *Dictionnaire arabe-français. [Maroc]*. Paris.

Theodoridis, D. (1990–93). Der Euphemismus *los mižores de mozotros* im Judezmo und seine Parallelen in anderen Sprachen. *MedLR* 6-7:105–12.

Thomason, S. G. and A. Elgibali (1986). Before the Lingua franca. Pidginized Arabic in the eleventh century A.D. *Lingua* 68:317–49.

Thouvenot, R. (1943). Chrétiens et Juifs à Grenade au IVe siècle après J.-C. *Hespéris* 201–11.

Tobi, Y. (1982). The Siddur of Rabbi Shelomo ben Nathan of Sijilmasa. *CJMSM*, 407–25.

———(1993). Sride targum aravi latora kodem letafsir rav sa'adya gaon. *Massorot* 7:87–127.

Toledano, I. M. (1911). *Ner hama'arav*. Jerusalem.

Torreblanca, M. (1974). Estado actual del lleísmo y de la *h*- aspirada en el noroeste de la provincia de Toledo. *RDTP* 30:77–89.

———(1982). La *s* hispanolatina: el testimonio árabe. *RP* 35:447–63.

Torres Balbás, L. (1954). Mozarabías y juderías de las ciudades hispano-musulmanas. *AA* 19:172–97.

———(1957). Cementerios hispanomusulmanes. *AA* 22:131–91.

Tovar Llorente, A. (1946). Los estudios beréberes en relación con España. *CEA* 1:113–21.

Trebilco, P. R. (1991). *Jewish communities in Asia Minor.* Cambridge.

Treimer, K. (1922). *Slawische und baltische Studien. Beiträge zur slawisch-baltischen Sprach- und Altertumskunde.* Vienna and Leipzig.

Trend, J. B. (1959). The oldest Spanish poetry. *Hispanic studies in honour of I. González Llubera.* F. Pierce (ed.), 415–28. Oxford.

Tritton, A. S. (1958). The Old Testament in Muslim Spain. *Bulletin of the School of Oriental and African Studies* 21:392–95.

Turki, M. (1989). Les andalous-morisques en Tunisie à la recherche d'un univers mythique et religieux. *RHM* 55–56:59–74.

Udovitch, A. L. and L. Valensi (1984). *The last Arab Jews. The communities of Jerba, Tunisia.* Chur, London, Paris, and New York.

Vajda, G. (1948). Un recueil de textes historiques judéo-marocains. *Hespéris* 311–58.

———(1956). Un chapitre de l'histoire du conflit entre la Kabbale et la philosophie. La polémique anti-intellectualiste de Joseph ben Shalom Ashkenazi de Catalogne. *Archives d'histoire doctrinale et littérature du moyen âge,* 45–144.

———(1962). Un traité maghrébien "adversus Judaeos": *"Aḥkām ahl al-ḏimma"* du Šayḫ Muḥammad b. ʿAbd al-Karīm Al-Maġīlī. *EO* 2:805–13.

Valensi, L. (1989). Religious orthodoxy or local tradition: marriage celebration in southern Tunisia. *JAACB,* 65–84.

Vega, A. C. (1941). Una herejía judaizante de principios del siglo VIII en España. *Ciudad de Dios* 153:57–100.

Verber, E. (1983). [Separate notes to the facsimile edition.] *Sarajevska Hagada.* Belgrade and Sarajevo.

Verlinden, C. (1955–77). *L'Esclavage dans l'Europe médiévale* 1–2. Brugge and Ghent.

———(1958). Traite et esclavage dans la vallé de la Meuse. *Etudes sur l'histoire du pays mosan au moyen âge. Mélanges F. Rousseau,* 673–86. Brussels.

———(1967). Patarins ou bogomiles en esclavage. *Studi e materiali di storia delle religioni* 38(2):683–700.

———(1974a). A propos de la place des juifs dans l'économie de l'Europe occidentale aux IXe et Xe siècles. Agobard de Lyon et l'historiographie arabe. *Storiografia e storia. Studi in onore di Eugenio Dupré Theseider,* 21–37. Rome.

———(1974b). La traite des esclaves. Un grand commerce international au Xe siècle. *Etudes de civilisation médiéval (IXe–XIIe siècles). Mélanges offerts à Edmond-René Labande*, 721–30. Poitiers.
———(1977). Traite des esclaves et cols alpins au haut moyen-âge. *Erzeugung, Verkehr und Handel in der Geschichte der Alpenländer. Herbert-Hassinger Festschrift*, 377–87. Innsbruck.
———(1979). Sklavenhandel en economische ontwikkeling in Midden-, Oost- en Noord-Europa, gedurende de hoge middeleeuwen. *Mededelingen van de Koninklijke Academie voor Wetenschappen* 41.
———(1983). Les Radaniya et Verdun. A propos de la traite des esclaves slaves vers l'Espagne musulmane aux IXe et Xe siècles. *EHCSA* 2:105–32.
Viera, D. J. (1985). The treatment of the Jew and the Moor in the Catalan works of Francesc Eiximenis. *Revista canadiense de estudios hispánicos* 9:203–13.
Voinot, L. (1948). *Pèlerinages judéo-musulmans au Maroc*. Paris.
Vycichl, W. (1952a). Al-Andalus (sobre la historia de un nombre). *AA* 17:449–50.
———(1952b). Punischer Spracheinfluss im Berberischen. *Journal of Near Eastern studies* 11:198–204.
———(1957). L'article défini du berbère. *Mémorial André Basset (1895–1956)*, 139–46. Paris.
———(1972). Vier hebräische Lehnwörter im Berberischen. *AIUO* 32:242–44.
Wagenseil, J. Chr. (1699). *Belehrung der jüdisch-teutschen Red- und Schreibart*. Königsberg.
Wagner, E. (1966). Das Jemen als Vermittler äthiopischen Sprachgutes nach Nordwestafrika. *Die Sprache* 12:252–79.
Wagner, K. (1978). *Regesto de documentos del Archivo de Protocolos de Sevilla referentes a judíos y moros*. Seville.
Wagner, M. L. (1909). Los judíos de Levante. Kritischer Rückblick bis 1907. *Revue de dialectologie romane* 1:470–506.
———(1914). *Beiträge zur Kenntnis des Judenspanischen von Konstantinopel*. Vienna.
———(1920a). Judenspanisches-arabisches. *ZRP* 40:543–49; reprinted in his 1990.
———(1920b). Sardisch *kenábura* 'Freitag'. *ZRP* 40:619–21.
———(1931). Zum Judenspanischen von Marokko. *VKR* 4:221–45; reprinted in his 1990.

———(1934). Etimologías españolas y arábigo-hispánicas. *RFE* 21: 225–47.

———(1936a). Restos de latinidad en el Norte de África. *Biblioteca Geral da Universidade* 45–46. Coimbra.

———(1936b). Review of Crews 1935. *VKR* 9:167–71.

———(1950). Espigueo judeo-español. *RFE* 34:9–199; reprinted in his 1990.

———(1953). Etymologische Randbemerkungen zu neueren iberoromanischen Dialektarbeiten und Wörterbüchern. *ZRP* 69:347–91.

———(1956). Sard. *féstina*—berb. *ta-fesna*. *VR* 15(2):81–86.

———(1990). *Judenspanisch* 1-2. H. Kröll (ed.). Stuttgart.

Wasserstein, D. J. (1983). Slavica hispano-hebraica: a contribution to the linguistic history of the Iberian peninsula. *Sefarad* 43:87–98.

———(1985). *The rise and fall of the Party-kings: politics and society in Islamic Spain 1002–1086*. Princeton.

———(1987). An Arabic version of *Abot* 1:3 from Umayyad Spain. *Arabica* 34:370–74.

———(1991). The language situation in al-Andalus. Studies on the *Muwaššaḥ* and the *Kharja*. A. Jones and R. Hitchcock (eds.). Ithaca and Oxford, 1–15.

———(1992). Jews, Christians, and Muslims in Medieval Spain. *JJS* 43:175–87.

Wechter, P. (1964). *Ibn Barun's Arabic works on Hebrew grammar and lexicography*. Philadelphia.

Wehr, H. (1971). *A dictionary of modern written Arabic*. Wiesbaden.

Weil, G. E. (1968). Prolegomena to S. Frensdorff, *Die Massora magna* 1 (1876), i–xxxii. New York.

Weill, R. (1920). La cité de David. *REJ* 71:1–36.

Weinreich, M. (1956). The Jewish languages of Romance stock and their relation to earliest Yiddish. *RP* 9:403–28.

———[Vaynrayx] (1973). *Gešixte fun der yidišer šprax* 1–4. New York; a partial English translation appeared in Chicago 1980.

Weinreich, U. (1958). A retrograde sound shift in the guise of a survival. An aspect of Yiddish vowel development. *Miscelánea homenaje a André Martinet* 2:221–67. Tenerife.

Weinryb, B. D. (1962). The beginnings of East-European Jewry in legend and historiography. *SEHAAN*, 445–502.

———(1974). Reappraisals in Jewish history. *SWBJV*, 939–74.

Weiss, G. (1977). A testimony from the Cairo Geniza documents. *JQR* 68:99–103.

Weissenberg, S. (1909). Die Spaniolen: eine anthropometrische Skizze. *MAGW* 39:225–36.

———(1911). Die persischen Juden in anthropologischer Beziehung. *Zeitschrift für Demographie und Statistik der Juden* 7(1):1–6.

———(1913a). Die zentralasiatischen Juden in anthropologischer Beziehung. *MAGW* 43:257–69.

———(1913b). Zur Anthropologie der persischen Juden. *Zeitschrift für Ethnologie* 45:108–19.

Westermarck, E. (1914). *Marriage ceremonies in Morroco.* London.

———(1926). *Ritual and belief in Morocco* 1–2. London; New York 1968.

Wexler, P. (1974). The cartography of unspoken languages of culture and liturgy. Reflections on the diffusion of Arabic and Hebrew. *Orbis* 23:30–51.

———(1977a). *A historical phonology of the Belorussian language.* Heidelberg.

———(1977b). Ascertaining the position of Judezmo within Ibero-Romance. *VR* 36:162–95.

———(1978). The term 'Sabbath food': a challenge for Jewish interlinguistics. *JAOS* 98:461–65.

———(1980). Problems in monitoring the diffusion of Arabic into West and Central African languages. *ZDMG* 130:522–56.

———(1981a). Ashkenazic German (1760–1895). *IJSL* 30:119–30.

———(1981b). Jewish interlinguistics: facts and conceptual framework. *Language* 57:99–149.

———(1981c). Terms for 'synagogue' in Hebrew and Jewish languages. Explorations in historical Jewish interlinguistics. *REJ* 102:101–38.

———(1982). Marrano Ibero-Romance: classification and research tasks. *ZRP* 98:59–108.

———(1983a). Is Karaite a Jewish language? *MedLR* 1:27–54.

———(1983b). Notes on the Iraqi Judeo-Arabic of Eastern Asia. *JSS* 28:337–54.

———(1984). Zihui yesodot lešoni'im yehudi'im bisfat džudezmo. *Peamim* 18:38–52.

———(1985). Recovering the dialects and sociology of Judeo-Greek in non-Hellenic Europe. *Readings in the sociology of Jewish languages.* J. A. Fishman (ed.), 1:227–40. Leiden.

———(1987a). De-Judaicization and incipient re-Judaicization in 18th century Portuguese Ladino. *Iberoromania* 25:23–37.

———(1987b). *Explorations in Judeo-Slavic linguistics*. Leiden.

———(1988). *Three heirs to a Judeo-Latin legacy: Judeo-Ibero-Romance, Yiddish and Rotwelsch*. Wiesbaden.

———(1989a). *Judeo-Romance linguistics. A bibliography (Latin, Italo-, Gallo-, Ibero- and Rhaeto-Romance except Castilian)*. New York and London.

———(1989b). Review of Garulo Muñoz. *MedLR* 4–5:186–88.

———(1990a). The role of Yiddish in reconstructing and reviving old colloquial Hebrew. *Studies in Yiddish*. P. Wexler (ed.), 111–26. Tübingen.

———(1990b). *The schizoid nature of Modern Hebrew: a Slavic language in search of a Semitic past*. Wiesbaden.

———(1991). Yiddish—the fifteenth Slavic language. A study of partial language shift from Judeo-Sorbian to German. *IJSL* 91:1–150, 215–25.

———(1992). *The Balkan substratum of Yiddish. (A reassessment of the unique Romance and Greek components.)* Wiesbaden.

———(1993a). Jewish linguistics: 1981–1991–2001. *Historical linguistics 1991. Papers from the 10th International Conference on Historical Linguistics*. J. van Marle (ed.), 343–61. Amsterdam and Philadelphia.

———(1993b). Review of Díaz-Mas. *ZRP* 109:479–82.

———(1993c). *The Ashkenazic Jews: a Slavo-Turkic people in search of a Jewish identity*. Columbus, OH.

———(1993d). Uncovering the origins of the Judeo-Ibero-Romance languages. *NHSS*, 211–14.

———(1994a). Four new books in Judeo-Spanish and Judeo-Romance linguistics. *MedLR* 8:95–117.

———(1994b). Review of Bunis 1993a. *Peamim* 59:154–59.

———(1995). The Slavonic standard of Modern Hebrew. *Slavonic and East European Review* 73:201–25.

Wieder, N. (1946). Hašpaot islamiot al hapulxan hayehudi. *Melila* 2:37–120.

Wijk, H. K. A. van (1951). El calco árabe semántico en esp. "adelantado," port. "adiantado." *Neophilologus* 35:91.

Williams, J. J. (1930). *Hebrewisms in West Africa. From Nile to Niger with the Jews*. New York.

Wischnitzer, R. (1964). *The architecture of the European synagogue.* Philadelphia.

Wolf, M. (1977). Haomnam hevi r' binyamin mitudela milim mi"lšon kna'an." *Tarbic* 46:150–51.

Wright, R. (1982). *Late Latin and Early Romance in Spain and Carolingian France*. Liverpool.

———(1992). Early medieval Spanish, Latin, and Ladino. *Circa*, 36–45.

Yerushalmi, Y. H. (1971). *From Spanish court to Italian ghetto, Isaac Cardoso: a study in seventeenth-century Marranism and Jewish apologetics*. New York and London.

Yuhas, E. (1989). Hanisuin—xafacim uminhagim. *Yehude sfarad baimperya haot'omanit. Prakim betarbutam haxomrit*. E. Yuhas (ed.), 196–217. Jerusalem.

Zachariae, T. (1906). Ein jüdischer Hochzeitsbrauch. *WZKM* 20:291–301.

———(1908). Fischzauber. *WZKM* 22:431–36.

Zafrani, H. (1967). Les langues juives du Maroc. *ROMM* 4:175–88.

———(1968). Notes sur G. Vajda, *Inscriptions antiques du Maroc:* inscriptions hébraïques. *REJ* 127:125–26.

———(1983). *Mille ans de vie juive au Maroc. Histoire et culture, religion et magie*. Paris.

———(1986). Conscience historique et mémoire collective judéoberbères. *Massorot* 2:159–80.

Zajączkowski, A. (1961). Die arabischen und neupersischen Lehnwörter im Karaimischen. *FO* 3:177–212.

Zavadovskij, Ja. N. (1962). *Arabskie dialekty Magriba*. Moscow.

———(1979). *Tunisskij dialekt arabskogo jazyka*. Moscow.

Zayat, H. (1948). Al-'asma' wa'l-kunya wa'l-alqāb an-naṣrāniyya. *Almašriq* 42:1–21.

Zimmels, H. J. (1952). *Magicians, theologians, and doctors*. London.

———(1958). *Ashkenazim and Sephardim. Their relations, differences, and problems as reflected in the rabbinical responsa*. London.

Zirlin, Y. (1986–88). The Schocken Italian Haggadah of c.1400 and its origins. *Jewish art* 12–13:55–72.

Zozaya, J. (1992). [Notes to the jewelry elements.] *AAAIS*, 222–23.

Zunz, L. (1823). Ueber die in den hebräisch-jüdischen Schriften vorkommenden hispanischen Ortnamen. *Zeitschrift für die Wissenschaft des Judenthums* 1:114–76.

———(1837). *Die Namen der Juden*. Leipzig; revised in his *Gesammelte Schriften* 2:1–82. Berlin 1876; Hildesheim 1967.

Index of Names and Topics

Only language names and geographical locales that are not accompanied by examples are cited here. Arabic and Hebrew proper names (other than examples) involving patronymic or agnatic data are alphabetized by the first name. The Arabic definite article, *al-*, *ar-*, as well as *de,* ', and ' are disregarded in the alphabetical listings. All linguistic examples are listed in the Index of Segments, Words, and Phrases.

al-Andalus. *See* Andalusia
Andalusia, Arabic brought to North Africa from, 13–15, 193; Christians in, 127; dialects of Spanish in, 97, 240–41; Jews in, 27, 32, 70–71, 92–93, 241–42; Muslims in, 14, 16, 134, 185, 189, 193, 240. *See* also Córdoba; Elvira; Granada; Jaén; Lorca; Málaga; Murcia; Seville; Spain
Aphrodisias, 23–24. *See* also Asia Minor
Aquinas, Thomas, 96
Arabian Peninsula, 25, 29, 31, 118, 230, 235; Christian missionizing in the, 29. *See* also Jews; Madīna; Mekka; Persian(s); Taymā; Yemen
Arabic, 33, 40, 90, 101, 116, 126, 159, 213, 232, 237; as carrier of Latin, to Berber, 139, 175, to Spanish, 139; chronology of loans in Spanish, 176; Classical, 126, 142, 237; codification of by non-Arabs, 118; definite article in Spanish, 174–80; influence on Spanish syntax, 169; influenced by Ibero-Romance, 67; loss of the category of definiteness in Mauretanian dialects of, 175; major language of the Jews in Spain, 92; metathesis in Spanish loans from, 151–52; in Moroccan Judeo-Spanish, 156–57; paucity of in Judeo-Spanish, received indirectly through Spanish, 162; phonology, 101–102; relationship to Hebrew and Aramaic, 43, 113; Tunisian, 14; Turkish Arabisms in Judeo-Spanish, 16; unique elements in Judeo-Spanish, 156–63; use of by Christians in Spain, 67, 197–98; volume of in Spanish, 162, 176; waves of diffusion into North Africa and Spain, 13, 25; written language of Berbers in Spain and North Africa, 25. *See* also Aramaic; Christian; Hebrew; *imāla*; Judeo-Arabic; (Judeo-)Spanish; Spanish Arabic
Arabization, of Berbers, 19, 25, 106, 112, 173, 235, of Jews in Spain, 18, 91–93, 97–98, 224–25, of Latin, Spanish, 97, 144, of Sephardic diaspora culture and language, 169, 173, 206, 224. *See* also aljamiado literature; Berbers; Islamization; Judaization; Hebrew
Arabs, 5
Aragón, 67–68, 70, 72, 77, 90, 92, 95–96, 99, 128, 143, 149, 205–207. *See* also Calatayud; Huesca; Molina; Monzon; Spain; Teruel; Zaragoza
Aramaic, as a liturgical language of Christians, 119; loans in North African Arabic, 125–26; spoken in Kurdistan, 118, Malta and Europe 125; supplanted by Arabic in Iraq, 118. *See* also Judeo-Aramaic; Syriac
Arévalo, Mancebo de, 72. *See* also Marranos
Arians, 41. *See* also Visigothic Spain
Aristotle, Metaphysics of, 96
Armenians, denoted as "Philistines" by Balkan Sephardim, 36
Arragel, Moše, 30, 82, 122, 157, 214. *See* also *Biblia de Alba*
Arvellano, Fernando Rauniez de, 72. *See* also "Muslim Jew"
Ašer ben Yexiel, 48, 96, 124, 191, 196, 200, 206. *See* also Ashkenazic Jews, influence on Sephardic Jews
Ashkenaz I, II, 100. *See* also Ashkenazic Jews; *aškenaz*
Ashkenazic Jews (Ashkenazim), 3, 102, 200–206, 232, 246; ceremony of breaking a glass at the wedding, 201–202; comparison of with Sephardic Jews, 9, 244–47; definition of, 4–5, 56, 75; folk practices of, 183–85, 200; influence of on Sephardic Jews, 54–55, 63–64, 100, 102, 122, 124, 163, 165, 183–85, 189, 195, 199–206, 237; as a mix of Slavic and Turkic proselytes, 6–7, 102, 206, 244; naming customs of, 129, 133, 222; as a repository of Old Sorbian cultural and linguistic patterns, 6–7,

of the Muslims as descended from the Jews, 71; practice, of cleaning house on Saturday, 65, of *kapparah*, 185, of ritual washing of the corpse, 183, of whitewashing houses after Holy Week, 65; preoccupation with intermarriage between Jews and non-Jews, 21–22, 39, 44; religious propaganda to Jews in Spain, 96; Spanish, used by Balkan Jews, 155, 199, 241; use of Arabic inscriptions, 197–98. *See* also Inquisition protocols

Christianity 2, 24, 81, 106; Donatist sect of in North Africa, 39; heresies of in northern Spain, 41; relationship of to Judaism, 2; sects of in the Near East, Pakistan, Sinkiang province of China, southwest India, 119; weakness of in 8th-century Spain, 41. *See* also conversion to Judaism; institutionalization; Marranos

chuetas. *See* Marranos

church, designated by the word for mosque in Valencian Arabic, 142. *See* also Central and West African languages; synagogue

Church Council of, Carthage, 39, Elvira 41, 89, Tarragona 44. *See* also Decrees

cicit (fringe of male prayer garment), 22

circumcision, 51, 153, 225; among, Christians, 66, crypto-Jews and crypto-Muslims, 50, 70, 204, 222; as a requirement for conversion to Judaism in Morocco, 22. *See* also conversion to Judaism; crypto-Islam; crypto-Judaism; Sephardic Jews

Ciudad, Juan de, 50, 63. *See* also Marannos

Ciudad Real, 62, 68. *See* also Castile; Spain

Cohen de Lara, D., 213

Coimbra, 67. *See* also Portugal

"Constituciones sinodales," 183. *See* also de Guevara

conversion of, Christians to Islam in Spain, 49, 127, Jews to Christianity, 44–45, 111, 133, 229, Jews to Islam in Spain and North Africa, 46, 49, 67, 127, 145, Muslims to Christianity, 240. *See* also Álvaro; Jews; Sephardic Jews

conversion to Judaism, xvii, 21ff, 41, 45, 48–49, 89, 100–101, 105, 107, 109, 114, 116, 227, 229, 232, 247; in Adiabene, 21, 24, 28; of Africans, xv, 12, 45–46; of Balkan peoples, 23, 34; of Berbers, 28, 50, 127; Christian fears of, by Slavic slaves, 46; church opposition to, 44, 49; cyclical, 45, 64, 72; documentation of, 24; in Europe, xv, 33, 50; of Goths, Vandals, Visigoths, 23, 38; of Iberians, 13, 38, 218; impact of on Jewish racial purity, 12, 23; impediments to in Spain, 48, 85, 191; in Iraq, 23; in the Khazar Kingdom, 7, 21, 24, 28, 50; in North Africa, 12, 33, 36ff; of Slavo-Turks, 245; of Slavs, 6–7, 23, 38, 46, 200, 247; in Western Asia, xv, 23, 27–28; in the Western Sudan, 45; of women, 28, 51ff; in Yemen, 23–24, 28. *See* also Bodo the Frank; circumcision; Díaz Pimienta; "God-fearers"; Ḥasday Kreskas; Khazars; de Luna; Sephardic Jews, attitudes; Yehuda ben Šmuel ha-Levi

conversos. *See* Marranos

converts to Judaism participate in Jewish ritual, 48; persecution of in Calatayud, 49. *See* also Calatayud

Coplas de Yosef, 158

Coptic (Christianity, language), Copts, 24–25, 66, 81–82, 115, 125, 152

Córdoba, 32, 54, 70, 77, 84, 87, 94, 111, 116–17, 133, 142, 152, 189, 197, 207. *See* also Andalusia; Spain; synagogue; Umayyad reign

Corfu, 120. *See* also Greece

Cota, Rodrigo, 159

Creole languages, 179–80, 239, 247. *See* also relexification

Iraq, 23, 25, 31-32, 35, 37, 47, 75, 92, 108, 118, 125, 129-30, 172, 181, 199, 247. *See* also Baghdad; Başra; Jews; Kurdistan; Parthia; Pumbedita
Iraqi Jews, in Cairo, 27; use of non-Judaized Arabic in the diaspora by, 89
Iserlin, Yisrael, 161
Islam, 106; relationship of to Judaism, 2. *See* also institutionalization
Islamization, of Berbers, 39, of Christianity, 69, of Jews, 63, 67–68, 97, 224. *See* also Arabization; Judaization
Israel, 7–8, 155
Issawites ('Isawiyya), 35
Istanbul, Ladino Pentateuch (1547), 53, 95, 121–22, 209. *See* also Ferrara; Ladino; Turkey
Italian, 161. *See* also Judeo-Italian
Italy, 23, 32, 34, 43, 53, 82, 112, 202. *See* also Florence; Palermo; Rome; Sardinia; Sicily; Taranto; Venosa
Izmir, 47. *See* also Turkey

Jaén, 27, 84. *See* also Andalusia; Spain
Jaime I, 225. *See* also Charter of Denia
Játiva, 45, 48, 68. *See* also Valencia; Spain
Jebel Nefūsa, 202. *See* also Berbers; Libya
Jerba, 51, 181, 185–86, 194–95, 201. *See* also Tunisia
Jerusalem, 50, 125, 227; destruction of the Second Temple in, 2, 10, 35, 194, 201–202. *See* also Palestine; Theodotos
Jethro, feast of, 184
"Jewish Arabs" in south Tunisia, 38, 83. *See* also Tunisia
Jewish, customs, of praying barefoot, *qidduš*, 181, shared with North African Muslims, 184, 189, 194–95; geography, unique territorial units in, 76–77; holidays: Hannukah, 205–206, 216, New Year, 184, 201, 210, 216, Passover, 45, 62–63, 65, 123, 178, 181, 206, 208, 210–11, 216, 227, Pentecost (Shavuot), 204, 206, 208, 216, Purim, 64, 206, Sukkot (Tabernacles), 66, 211, 216, Tenth of Ab, 206, Yom Kippur (Day of Atonement), 184, 201, 206–207, 210, 212, 216; people, concept of, 2, 117, 200; ritual practice in North Africa, standardization of, 181. *See* also Sephardic Jews
Jewish languages, 140ff, 171–72, 229, 236, 239–44; in Africa and Asia, 140; common Hebrew and Judeo-Aramaic corpus in, 211–12; in contact with German and Russian, 151; developed by non-Jewish proselytes to Judaism, 10, 229; inherited colloquial Old Hebrew and Judeo-Aramaic elements, 209; parallels among, 27. *See* also Hebrew; Judeo-; Yiddish
Jews, in, Afghanistan, 4; Arabia, 26, 43, 118; Asia Minor, 6; Buxara, 34; the Caucasus, 31, 34; China, 3–4, 34; Cochin, 4, 34; Crimea, 31, 34; Cyrenaica, 35; Daghestan, 4; Egypt, 35–37; Ethiopia, 3, 29–30, 35–36; Europe, 3, 6, 34; India, 3–4, 89; Iran, 4, 34; Iraq, 4, 27, 31, 37, 43, 47, 89, 118, 181, 199, 233, 247; Kurdistan, 4; Libya, 4, 52, 127; North Africa, 6, 8, 12–13, 29, 34ff, 97, 242; Palestine, 43, 97, 247; southeast Asia, 89; Turkey, 4, 188, 242; Uzbekistan, 4; Yemen, 4, 29–32, 34, 36–37, 97; defined as "giants," 34; definition of, in the diaspora, 3; eliminate Berber and Arab practices, 128, 195-96; migrations of as reflected in Judeo-Spanish and Judeo-Arabic, 25ff, 135ff; preserve traditions about ancient settlement history, 34–35; undergo Arabization, Berberization, and Christianization, 18–19. *See* also Berbers; conversion to Judaism; diaspora; Sephardic Jews; Yemenite Jews

Judeo-Provençal, 143, 153. *See* also Provençal
Judeo-Spanish, 11, 15, 19, 27, 47, 83, 86, 91–92, 143, 153–54, 167; apparent absence of derogatory terms for Christians in, 218; Arabic imprint on, 154–73; Arabisms, compared with those in Spanish, 173–79, replaced by Hispanisms, 215; borrowing back of Christianized terms, 215; Castilianization of, 99, 163; chronology of Arabisms in Morrocan, 179; de-Arabized phonology of, 158; definite article in, 173–79; Greek elements in, 32–34, 149, 151–54; Hebraization of, 99; infinitive, 140–41, 146; language of proverbs, 123, 241; Latinisms and Grecisms, 105, 153; lexical bifurcation in, 216–17, 220; metathesis in Arabisms, 151–52, 157–58; "Moroccanization" of, 156–57, 224; native epithets (Ḥakitía, Jidyo, Judezmo, Judyo), 15, 86; not derived from Judeo-Latin, 154, 236; paucity of Arabisms in, 96, 162–63, 239–40; "Rabbinical", 167; recalibration of, Christian terms in, 212–17, Muslim Arabic terms and names in, 217–21, 226–28; regarded as "conservative" or "archaic," 88; replaced in Morocco and the Balkans, 232; Turkish Arabisms in, 156–57, 241. *See* also Arabization; Hebrew; relexification; Spanish
Judezmo, Judyo. *See* Judeo-Spanish
Juvenal, 140

Kairouan, 39, 66, 82, 128. *See* also Tunisia
kapparah (expiatory fowl) practiced by Berbers, Christians, Muslims, 184–85. *See* also Sephardic Jews
Karaites, 31, 35, 204, 220, 225, 227; attitude of toward Christianity, 35
Karo, Yosef, 59, 93, 125, 158, 168, 173, 184, 201, 204. *See* also *Šulxan arux*
kashrut, 68; neutral food category in, 61; prohibition against pork products, 61–62, 70, 160, 193
Kaufmann Haggadah, 54. *See* also illuminations
Khazars, 50, 111, 206, 244; kingdom of the, 7, 24, 31; possible migration of to Spain, 27, 31, 50; Yosef, king of the, 27, 31, 111. *See* also conversion to Judaism
Khwārizm, 31
Kiev, 31
Kitāb al-bāri', 219
Kitāb al-muwāzana bayn al-luġa al-'ibrāniyya wa'l-'arabiyya, 26. *See* also Yicxak ben Yosef ibn Barun
kna'an, as designation for blacks, Carthaginians, Slavs, 47. *See* also black Africans; conversion to Judaism; Slavs; Sorbian
Köln, 54, 124, 196, 207. *See* also Germany
Kurdistan, 118. *See* also Iran; Iraq; Jews; Syria; Turkey

La lozana andaluza, 159. *See* also Delicado
Ladino, xvii, 9, 82, 86, 93–95, 107, 113–14, 119ff, 153, 155–56, 209, 242ff; relationship of to, Old Hebrew, 113, 119ff, spoken Judeo-Spanish, 95. *See* also *Biblia de Alba*; Ferrara; Istanbul; Judeo-Spanish; relexification; *Šarḥ*
Las leyes de Moros, 158. *See* also aljamiado texts
Latin, xvi, 78–80, 91, 109–110, 121, 161, 212–13; elements in Berber, 139, 147; lexical bifurcation in Spanish, 221; North African loans in Iberian Judeo-Arabic and Ibero-Romance, 135–36, 223, 231; origin of "Medieval," xii, 118, 237–38, 243. *See* also (Judeo-)Arabic; Judeo-Latin; (Judeo-)Spanish
Lebanon, 39. *See* also Phoenician(s)
Leipzig *Maḥzor*, 124
León, 40, 77, 94, 134, 183, 188. *See* also El Bierzo; Spain; Toro

San Nicolá (Murcia), 183. *See* also Spain
Ṣan'ā', 28. *See* also Yemen
Santa María la Blanca synagogue. *See* synagogue; Toledo
"Santo Mordochay," 64
Sarajevo, 186; Haggadah, 45, 54. *See* also illuminations; Yugoslavia
Sardinia, Jewish linguistic influence in, 121, 150. *See* also Italy
Šarḥ, xvii, 9, 95, 119–122, 155–56, 242–44. *See* also Ladino; relexification; *Tafsīr*
Sefer hakabala, 36, 77. *See* also Avraham ben David ha-Levi ibn Da'ud
Sefer xovat halvavot bela'az, 241. *See* also Baḥya (Abu Isḥaq) ben Yosef ibn Pakuda
Segorbe, 63, 71. *See* also Spain; Valencia
Šem Tov ben Yicxak Ardutiel. *See* de Carrión
semi-Spanish, semi-speakers of Spanish, 83, 240. *See* also para-Romani
Sepharad I, II, III, 100, 102–103. *See* also Sephardic history; Sephardic Jews; *sfarad*
Sephardic history, depth and periodization of, 78–80, 89, 98–103. *See* also Sepharad; Sephardic Jews; *sfarad*
Sephardic Jews (Sephardim), anthropomorphic representations in the art of, 41–42, 70; Arabization of, 81, 97–98; attitudes of towards, Arabic, 95–96, intermarriage with Ashkenazim, 200, intermarriage with non-Sephardic North African Jews, 16–17; attraction of to Islam in Spain, 67–68; avoidance of Christian and Muslim practices, 187, 195–96; balladry and music of, relative age of, 88; believe in spirit infants, 187, 215; Berbero-Arab culture of, xvii, 13, 16, 65, 69, 85, 87, 100, 102, 105ff, 181, 185–89, 193, 195–202, 219–220, 231, 237–38; Bible illustrations among, 42; bride and groom dress in the clothing of the opposite sex among, 186–87, 193–94; bury in caves, 172; burn and bury nail clippings, 187; Christianization of Iberian folkways of, 101, 163, 181, 215; comparison of with non-Jews, 26, 180; contributions of to Hebrew letters in Spain, 91; cover the head during prayer, 182; pray barefoot, 181–82; cut the groom's pubic hairs, 187–88; de-Christianization of Iberian folkways of, 199–200; de-Muslimization of Iberian folkways of, 181; diaspora split between North Africa and the Eastern Mediterranean, 16, 180–81; documentation of, 11; had earlier contacts with Muslims than with Christians, 78, 87; early mention of in Spain, 11, 84–85; espouse Ashkenazic, Provençal, Romaniote and new Arab and Berber practices, 182ff, 199ff, 204; ethnic origins of, 3, 8, 10–11, 18, 28, 36ff, 81, 87; ethnographic and religious profile of, 15, 37, 180; expulsions of from the Iberian Peninsula, 8, 13–14, 16, 26, 54–55, 57, 60, 79, 82, 87, 98–100, 102–103, 128, 143, 145, 151, 180, 184, 192, 199–200, 232, 234, 238, 240; formulaic expressions of shared with Muslims, 188–89; fragmentation of, 206; funeral practices of shared with Muslims, 183–84; guests pay a tip to musicians at a wedding among, 182–83; "Hispanicity" of, 86ff, 238; impact of on Arab, Ashkenazic, and Balkan Jews, 12; integration of in North Africa, 83; intermarriage of with non-Jews, 23, 41, 46, 97, 110; *kapparah* (expiatory fowl) among, 184–85, 200, 202–203; as a label for all non-Ashkenazic Jews, 231; lax observance of *tfillin* (phylacteries)

Index of Segments, Words, and Phrases

Spoken Judaized languages are listed together with the cognate non-Judaized languages, except for Judeo-Aramaic, Judeo-Arabic, Judeo-Spanish, and Yiddish, which are listed separately. The listings for Hebrew and Judeo-Aramaic include both Semitic and non-Semitic examples. Portuguese and Spanish Ladino are listed together under Ladino. Schwa is treated as *e* for purposes of the alphabet, while ' and ' are listed at the end of the alphabet, in that order. Initial ' is written only in transliterations of some Hebrew and Arabic examples. Interdental *δ* and *θ* are treated as *dh* and *th*, respectively.

ḥīzzo 152; ibn ʻAknin 127; in 132; jaja 174; Janūnī 128; lbit 175; Mām(e)d, Mām(e)t 73; Nafūsī, o-, Ohayon, Ouhaïoun 128; š, šbényä 147; səfrāniyya, sənnār(iy)ya, sfannār 152; šqālya 147; ṭ, -t 174; tā 174–75; tagarnina 174; taḥanut 175; taḥdīd 224; talbabt 175; taqmižt 136; u- 128; v- 76; Verga(s) 128; x 112; zrūdga 152
Bulgarian: gore-dolu 164; papel'aška, pepel'aška 65; xavra 165, 215
Čaha: mäsgid 29
Catalan: al- 177; aladma, alalma 225; alborneç 61; alfàb(r)ega 151; Barcelona, c 132; cal(l) 55; dolent 216; el(-) 177; garbell 138; maldar 153; š 146; sanate me 225; sèquia 175; taleca 137; tàlem 153, 171; tramús 178
Coptic: haykal 115; pitarixon 152
Czech: veveřice 47
English: Cornwall 129; shul, synagogue, temple 143; Welsh 129
Eža: mäsgid 29
French: bon homme 56; l- 175
Fula: dabsala 141
Geez: tährat 30
German: Holle 68–69; Kauderwelsch 129; laufen 239; Litau 76; Macher 215; -n 52; Polterabend 201; reden, rennen 239; s-, Schachermacher 215; schwarz 76; sprechen 239; Welsch 129
Gogot: dəfun 30; mäsgid 29
Gothic: svard, swarts 76
Greek: Alexander 51; ắmbōn 115; anaθēma 153, 225; arxēgissa, arxisynagōgissa 53; asfaragos 146; augotáraxo 152; boúla 220; butárga, buttágra 152; ẽmboloi 115; isagōgē 144; -issa, Kalonimos 52; kandíli 139; kobania 179; leúkē 139; magos 33; mamma 137; mauros 76; megas 32; mēlōtē 139; -ōgē 144; pandokeíon 126; paragōgē 144; paraskevē 150; presbetérēssa 53; proseuxē 110, 140–41, 143–44; s 34, 147; stafinari, stafylínos 151; sxolē 142; synagōgē 55, 144, 165; θalamos 153, 171; θérmos 178; xalaktēras, xaraktēr(ion) 126; xaũra, xavra 215
Gurage: ḥaḍra 140
Gyeto: mäsgid 29
Harari: mäsgīd 29
Hausa: mā. . .-ci, masallāci 141
Hebrew: alamot šamah 221; -an 168; anbol 115; aškənaz 75–76; Avraham 130–31; b 204; -b 149; baḥucim 38, 61, 83; Barcelonah 132; bat txila siman yafe labanim 192; (bate) midraš 163; bə- 164; bənaxat 204; berur(im) 170; bet din 124, 170; bet hasefɛr 169; bet (ha)xaim 145, 172; (bet) knɛsɛt 142; bet tfillah 141; bəzzåyọn, bizayon, biz(z)ui 147; borer 170; braxah 222; brit 209, 217; (b)'"x šanim 168; c 132, 171; cad 171; cadiq 163; cafuf 171; cdyqym 163; cel 171; cicit 22; clav 171; d 204; daraš 146, 167, 211; g 204; ġ 164; gavɛn 125; ger 113–14; giyyer 114; goy 78; h 123, 131, 222; ḥ 123, 131, 222, 239; ha- 168; ḥadaš 222; haɛlohim 213; ḥag 226; ḥallah 68–69, 210; ḥam 160; ḥammin 160–61; ḥanukkah 206; (ha)qabar hagadol 168; ḥavurah 215; ḥaxam 150; ḥazzan 166–67; hclmydynh 163; ḥɛbra 165; ḥɛvrah 165, 215; hexal 115, 198, 208; hexal haqodeš 169; ḥ-m-ṭ 227; ḥogeg 226; ḥol hamoʻed 211; hqb'r 168; ḥ-r-m 169; ḥuppah 207; i šfanim 77-78; -im 160, 167-68, 211; k 101, 168, 204; kapparah 184-85, 200, 202; kašer 164; kippur 207; knafav 101; knaʻan(i) 47; kohen, kohɛnɛt 53; kuti 78; l 164; lamad 153; lašon 93, 146; limud 203, 211; lo emuna bagoy afilu baqever arbaʻim šana 228; lwvy' 75; ly 163; maccāh 123; magen david 188; maḥrimim 61; maḥzor 167; mar'ɛh 62; masgef 227;

Made in the USA
Monee, IL
11 October 2024

67737009R00187